Secrecy and Disclosure in Victorian Fiction

Why were the Victorians more fascinated with secrecy than people of other periods? What is the function of secrets in Victorian fiction and in the society depicted, how does it differ from that of other periods, and how did readers of Victorian fiction respond to the secrecy they encountered? These are some of the questions Leila May poses in her study of the dynamics of secrecy and disclosure in fiction from Queen Victoria's coronation to the century's end. May argues that the works of writers such as Charlotte Brontë, William Makepeace Thackeray, Mary Elizabeth Braddon, Edward Bulwer-Lytton, and Arthur Conan Doyle reflect a distinctly Victorian obsession with the veiling and unveiling of information. She argues that there are two opposing vectors in Victorian culture concerning secrecy and subjectivity, one presupposing a form of radical Cartesian selfhood always remaining a secret to other selves and another showing that nothing can be hidden from the trained eye. (May calls the relation between these clashing tendencies the "dialectics" of secrecy and disclosure.) May's theories of secrecy and disclosure are informed by the work of twentieth-century social scientists. She emphasizes Georg Simmel's thesis that sociality and subjectivity are impossible without secrecy and Erving Goffman's claim that sociality can be understood in terms of performativity, "the presentation of the self in everyday life," and his revelation that performance always involves disguise, hence secrecy. May's study offers convincing evidence that secrecy and duplicity, in contrast to the Victorian period's emphasis on honesty and earnestness, emerged in response to the social pressures of class, gender, monarchy, and empire, and were key factors in producing both the subjectivity and the sociality that we now recognize as Victorian.

Leila Silvana May is Professor of English at North Carolina State University, USA. She is also the author of *Disorderly Sisters: Sibling Relations and Sororal Resistance in Nineteenth-Century British Literature*.

Among the Victorians and Modernists
Series Editor
Dennis Denisoff, Professor of English, Ryerson University, Toronto

This series publishes monographs and essay collections on literature, art, and culture in the context of the diverse aesthetic, political, social, technological, and scientific innovations that arose among the Victorians and Modernists. Viable topics include, but are not limited to, artistic and cultural debates and movements; influential figures and communities; and agitations and developments regarding subjects such as animals, commodification, decadence, degeneracy, democracy, desire, ecology, gender, nationalism, the paranormal, performance, public art, sex, socialism, spiritualities, transnationalism, and the urban. Studies that address continuities between the Victorians and Modernists are welcome. Work on recent responses to the periods such as Neo-Victorian novels, graphic novels, and film will also be considered.

Secrecy and Disclosure in Victorian Fiction

Leila Silvana May

Taylor & Francis Group

LONDON AND NEW YORK

First published 2017
by Routledge
2 Park Square, Milton Park, Abingdon, Oxon OX14 4RN

and by Routledge
711 Third Avenue, New York, NY 10017

Routledge is an imprint of the Taylor & Francis Group, an informa business

© 2017 Leila Silvana May

The right of Leila Silvana May to be identified as author of this work has been asserted by her in accordance with sections 77 and 78 of the Copyright, Designs and Patents Act 1988.

All rights reserved. No part of this book may be reprinted or reproduced or utilised in any form or by any electronic, mechanical, or other means, now known or hereafter invented, including photocopying and recording, or in any information storage or retrieval system, without permission in writing from the publishers.

Trademark notice: Product or corporate names may be trademarks or registered trademarks, and are used only for identification and explanation without intent to infringe.

British Library Cataloguing in Publication Data
A catalogue record for this book is available from the British Library

Library of Congress Cataloging-in-Publication Data
A catalog record for this book has been requested

ISBN: 9781472484390 (hbk)
ISBN: 9781315607979 (ebk)

Typeset in Times New Roman
by Apex CoVantage, LLC

Contents

Acknowledgments vi
List of abbreviations viii

Introduction: The paradox of duplicity   1

1   Dialectics of secrecy and disclosure: Sociology and the narratology of secrecy   20

2   Lost in Labassecour: *Villette* and the privatization of secrecy   40

3   Selfishness and secrecy in the "howling wilderness": Thackeray's *Vanity Fair*   79

4   Madness and class conflicts: *Lady Audley*'s sensational secrets   109

5   Veiled secrets, veiled subjects: Scheherazade and the orientalizing of Victorian secrecy in Bulwer-Lytton's *Leila: or, The Siege of Granada*   142

6   The end of secrecy? *The Adventures of Sherlock Holmes*   179

    Afterword   210

Bibliography   220
Index   237

Acknowledgments

This project has been a part of my life for a very long time now and, as a result, many friends and colleagues have been subjected to the manuscript in various stages of its development. I owe a particular debt from early on to Antony Harrison, my friend, mentor, and department head who has shown unfailing faith in me despite the often tortuous process involved in bringing this book into being. My cherished colleagues and friends at NC State University – Barbara Baines, Sharon Setzer, Jon Thompson, and Mary Helen Thuente – have all read chapters and provided invaluable encouragement and critiques. Deborah Wyrick generously read the manuscript in its entirety and, as was the case with my first book, provided me with insights that led me to rethink and reframe portions of my argument. Richard Hardack, Christian Marouby, and Toni Wein have been not only the best of friends for half a lifetime but were also more than generous in their carefully considered readings of my work. One of my earliest inspirations while still in graduate school came from John Kucich's brilliant work, and I am more grateful than I can express that he took the time to read and comment on an early version of the *Villette* chapter as I was preparing to send it out in article form. From Barbara Phillips, Professor Emeritus at San Francisco State University, and Alan Kolata, chair of the University of Chicago's Department of Anthropology, I received much-needed validation that enabled me to feel less like an interloper as I ventured into the field of social sciences. I have had the immeasurable good fortune over the years to have around me so many people who have provided invaluable intellectual support, friendship, humor, and steadfast friendship in Berkeley and beyond: Elizabeth Abel, Frederick Crews, Leigh DeNeef, Elliot Engel, Jane Garrity, Karen Jacobs, Dorothy Kaufman, Carolyn Losee, Sharon Marcus, Maggie O'Shaughnessy, Francine Ostrem, Maria Pramaggiore, Edmund and Louise Reiss, Kirsten Shepherd-Barr, Rebecca Stern, Beverly Taylor, Tom Wallis, Cat Warren, and Alex Zwerdling. Thanks also to the College of Humanities and Social Sciences at NC State University for providing funding for research leaves and summer grants, as well as to my students for their persistent keenness and enthusiasm, and for always giving me something more to think about. I am indebted to my anonymous readers for the astute suggestions that aided me no end in my revisions. From my earliest contact with her, my editor Ann Donaghue has been nothing but responsive, smart, and resourceful. She is the editor that every author dreams of finding. Finally, it is no secret that my greatest source of intellectual inspiration and emotional sustenance has come from my beloved husband and sparring partner, Don Palmer, who has been with me through every step of this process, and whom I expect will be walking right beside me during many adventures and misadventures to come.

I would also like to acknowledge the permission granted by publishers to reuse parts of this book that have been previously published elsewhere. One section of chapter 2 was first published as "How Lucy Snowe Became an Amnesiac," in *Brontë Studies* 34.3 (November 2009): 220–33. Another portion of chapter 2 that expands on my argument against materialism in *Villette* appeared as "Lucy Snowe, A Material Girl? Phrenology, Surveillance and the Sociology of Interiority," in *Criticism* (Winter 2013): 43–68. An earlier version of a section of chapter 3 was published in "The Sociology of Thackeray's 'Howling Wilderness': Selfishness, Secrecy and Performance in *Vanity Fair*," *Modern Language Studies* 37.1 (Summer 2007): 18–41.

Abbreviations

BLUE   Arthur Conan Doyle. "The Adventure of the Blue Carbuncle." *The New Annotated Sherlock Holmes*. Volumes 1, 2, and 3. Edited with a foreword and notes by Leslie S. Klinger. Introduction by John le Carré. New York and London: W. W. Norton, 2005.

BOSC   Arthur Conan Doyle. "The Boscombe Valley Mystery." *The New Annotated Sherlock Holmes*. Volumes 1, 2, and 3. Edited with a foreword and notes by Leslie S. Klinger. Introduction by John le Carré. New York and London: W. W. Norton, 2005.

CARD   Arthur Conan Doyle. "The Adventure of the Cardboard Box." *The New Annotated Sherlock Holmes*. Volumes 1, 2, and 3. Edited with a foreword and notes by Leslie S. Klinger. Introduction by John le Carré. New York and London: W. W. Norton, 2005.

COPP   Arthur Conan Doyle. "The Adventure of the Copper Beeches." *The New Annotated Sherlock Holmes*. Volumes 1, 2, and 3. Edited with a foreword and notes by Leslie S. Klinger. Introduction by John le Carré. New York and London: W. W. Norton, 2005.

ELH   *English Literary History*

ENGI   Arthur Conan Doyle. "The Adventure of the Engineer's Thumb." *The New Annotated Sherlock Holmes*. Volumes 1, 2, and 3. Edited with a foreword and notes by Leslie S. Klinger. Introduction by John le Carré. New York and London: W. W. Norton, 2005.

FIVE   Arthur Conan Doyle. "The Five Orange Pips." *The New Annotated Sherlock Holmes*. Volumes 1, 2, and 3. Edited with a foreword and notes by Leslie S. Klinger. Introduction by John le Carré. New York and London: W. W. Norton, 2005.

GLOR   Arthur Conan Doyle. "The Adventure of the *Gloria Scott*." *The New Annotated Sherlock Holmes*. Volumes 1, 2, and 3. Edited with a foreword and notes by Leslie S. Klinger. Introduction by John le Carré. New York and London: W. W. Norton, 2005.

GRAN   Arthur Conan Doyle. "The Adventure of the Abbey Grange." *The New Annotated Sherlock Holmes*. Volumes 1, 2, and 3. Edited with a foreword and notes by Leslie S. Klinger. Introduction by John le Carré. New York and London: W. W. Norton, 2005.

Abbreviations ix

HOUN Arthur Conan Doyle. *The Hound of the Baskervilles. The New Annotated Sherlock Holmes*. Volumes 1, 2, and 3. Edited with a foreword and notes by Leslie S. Klinger. Introduction by John le Carré. New York and London: W. W. Norton, 2005.

MILV Arthur Conan Doyle. "The Adventure of Charles Augustus Milverton." *The New Annotated Sherlock Holmes*. Volumes 1, 2, and 3. Edited with a foreword and notes by Leslie S. Klinger. Introduction by John le Carré. New York and London: W. W. Norton, 2005.

MUSG Arthur Conan Doyle. "The Adventure of the Musgrave Ritual." *The New Annotated Sherlock Holmes*. Volumes 1, 2, and 3. Edited with a foreword and notes by Leslie S. Klinger. Introduction by John le Carré. New York and London: W. W. Norton, 2005.

REIG Arthur Conan Doyle. "The Adventure of the Reigate Puzzle." *The New Annotated Sherlock Holmes*. Volumes 1, 2, and 3. Edited with a foreword and notes by Leslie S. Klinger. Introduction by John le Carré. New York and London: W. W. Norton, 2005.

RESI Arthur Conan Doyle. "The Adventure of the Resident Patient." *The New Annotated Sherlock Holmes*. Volumes 1, 2, and 3. Edited with a foreword and notes by Leslie S. Klinger. Introduction by John le Carré. New York and London: W. W. Norton, 2005.

SCAN Arthur Conan Doyle. "A Scandal in Bohemia." *The New Annotated Sherlock Holmes*. Volumes 1, 2, and 3. Edited with a foreword and notes by Leslie S. Klinger. Introduction by John le Carré. New York and London: W. W. Norton, 2005.

SEL *Studies in English Literature*

SIGN Arthur Conan Doyle. *The Sign of the Four. The New Annotated Sherlock Holmes*. Volumes 1, 2, and 3. Edited with a foreword and notes by Leslie S. Klinger. Introduction by John le Carré. New York and London: W. W. Norton, 2005.

SILV Arthur Conan Doyle. "The Adventure of Silver Blaze." *The New Annotated Sherlock Holmes*. Volumes 1, 2, and 3. Edited with a foreword and notes by Leslie S. Klinger. Introduction by John le Carré. New York and London: W. W. Norton, 2005.

SPEC Arthur Conan Doyle. "The Adventure of the Speckled Band." *The New Annotated Sherlock Holmes*. Volumes 1, 2, and 3. Edited with a foreword and notes by Leslie S. Klinger. Introduction by John le Carré. New York and London: W. W. Norton, 2005.

STUD Arthur Conan Doyle. *A Study in Scarlet. The New Annotated Sherlock Holmes*. Volumes 1, 2, and 3. Edited with a foreword and notes by Leslie S. Klinger. Introduction by John le Carré. New York and London: W. W. Norton, 2005.

YELL Arthur Conan Doyle. "The Adventure of the Yellow Face." *The New Annotated Sherlock Holmes*. Volumes 1, 2, and 3. Edited with a foreword and notes by Leslie S. Klinger. Introduction by John le Carré. New York and London: W. W. Norton, 2005.

Introduction
The paradox of duplicity

> Three can keep a secret if two of them are dead.
> —Benjamin Franklin

Jean-Paul Sartre imagined a future day when secrecy would be obsolete and transparency absolute, both in social and private spheres.[1] His contemporary, the sociologist Erving Goffman, who admired many of Sartre's ideas,[2] would strongly disagree, saying that, far from describing a future socialist utopia, Sartre was describing impossible – or at least disastrous – private and social worlds. Goffman and his mentor, Georg Simmel, hold that certain forms of secrecy are requisite to functional human interaction and even to nonpathological subjectivity. Following the lead of these sociologists, I argue in this book that the study of secrecy in Victorian fiction is not merely a matter of plot construction and revelation (from the narrative point of view) or of concealment of shameful material (from the characters' point of view), but actually contributes – indeed is essential – to the formation of subjectivity itself. This indispensable aid given to the construction of the subject is itself not fictitious but mirrors the role of secrecy in the human life of the period. In both spheres, the fictional and social, secrecy mediates between competing needs for privacy, on the one hand, and sociality on the other – a conflict that perhaps subtends modern subjectivity in general, but that takes on particular and urgent forms in the Victorian period.

On the other hand, human sociality demands that, verbally and behaviorally, participants reveal to each other massive amounts of information about their goals and intentions, about their personalities, interests, histories, skills, and knowledge. Simmel and Goffman, recognizing such a necessity, argue at the same time that the efficacy and even the survival of the projects of these participants – indeed, the wellbeing and survival of the participants themselves – requires the skill of withholding large amounts of information at any given moment; it requires, in short, an ability to keep secrets. Here, the word "secret," used as a noun or an adjective, names information or objects hidden or protected by one or more individuals or groups who try to prevent the discovery of this information or these objects by others. "Secrecy" is defined as the action of withholding information from others who would enjoy or otherwise benefit from the discovery of the information or objects that are hidden, or it is the state achieved when such items are withheld. The motive of secrecy may be self-interest (survival, prosperity, fear, power, etc.), or the interests of others (information that could be damaging to friends or relatives), or social obligation (fidelity to agreements, contracts, or other obligations). There may also be cases in which the motivation is perverse (as one sometimes suspects in the case of the secrecy maintained by Brontë's Lucy Snowe). The word secret may be used metaphorically, as when one speaks of "the secrets of nature" or "the secrets of history." The necessity to keep secrets is tested by the perpetual curiosity and aggressive determination of others to reveal the information that an individual desires to keep secret. Individuals and groups, recognizing the urgent need for secrecy about themselves and their activities, as well as secrets about members of their familial, romantic, and work circles, often have recourse to lying, a militant strategic defense of secrets. This book is not primarily about lying, but the lie is a common natural extension of secrecy. By beginning with the role of lying in human interaction I hope to develop the idea of what I will call the "paradox of duplicity" in an instructive way. Every lie involves duplicity. Most secrets also necessitate duplicity because, as I have defined it, secrecy entails the attempt to prevent others from acquiring certain information. Usually such an attempt is duplicitous because one must feign that one is not making such an attempt. An exception can be noted in the case in which the holder of a secret confronts her inquisitor and announces a refusal to divulge the secret. There have been many cases, both in fiction and in the actual social world, when such a refusal – both direct and indirect – provokes punishment, including expulsion, violence, or death.

A notorious deduction that Immanuel Kant draws from his categorical imperative is that lying is always immoral – even if a lie to a murderer would save the life of an innocent victim[3] – for, according to Kant, the slightest act of deception subverts the very idea of a true human community. Each human being must be considered an end in itself. A truly human community would be what Kant calls "a realm of ends": "[I]f all human beings speak the truth, then among them a system of ends is possible; but if only one should lie, then his end is no longer in connection with the others."[4] Yet, when we turn to Kant's theory of human nature, we find him asserting, "The human being has from nature a propensity to dissemble."[5] It is not that we are born liars: rather, in the name of personal advancement, we must necessarily withhold information from others while attempting to penetrate their secrets. As I have acknowledged, a lie is not the same thing as a secret, but a lie is the armed prosthesis of a secret; in fact, lies always involve at least two secrets. First, a lie is a speech-act whose purpose is to make someone believe something that is not true; therefore, the truth must be suppressed if the lie is to succeed. Second, the fact that one is lying must also be suppressed, so there is both a formal secret and a material secret in every lie. Liars usually believe that it is to their advantage to perpetrate a falsehood as the truth.[6] They must keep secret the fact that they hope to benefit in some way from causing another person to accept a falsehood as the truth. Lying, then, is a way of keeping secrets, and is sometimes a way of penetrating the secrets of others.

Lying, while common, is not the only strategy for keeping secrets. An even more common technique of guarding secrets is to remain silent, though in a number of contexts remaining silent can be considered a variation of lying. Simmel says that the kind of privacy needed for the development of selfhood and sociation[7] requires secrets. Often, simply withholding information is adequate for achieving such an end, but outright lying is an "aggressive technique" for doing so. Nevertheless, writes Simmel, "The ethically negative value of the lie must not blind us to its sociologically quite positive significance for the formation of certain concrete relations" (316). Therefore, Simmel, a close student of Kant (Simmel wrote his doctoral dissertation on Kant and taught courses on Kant's philosophy at the University of Berlin) agrees with Kant's thesis concerning the naturalness of human dissimulation but, unlike Kant, he does not always prioritize honesty over dissimulation in this respect, recognizing that sociation would be impossible without both "virtues."

According to both Kant and Simmel, then, we are necessarily self-interested social psychologists: we must try to guess what others are thinking, and learn to protect ourselves against those plans of others that would be detrimental to us. Allen Wood, paraphrasing Kant's surprisingly pessimistic *Anthropologie*, says:

> It belongs to the basic constitution of the human creature and to the concept of his species to explore the thoughts of others, but to withhold one's own – a nice quality that does not fail to progress gradually from *dissimulation* to *deception* and finally to *lying*.[8]

Kant talks about "the secret falsity in even the closest friendship."[9] Wood, in his gloss of Kant, says: "If we let others know too much about us, they will not only come to despise us, but they will also use this knowledge to their advantage and our discredit. Therefore no human being in his right mind is candid" (269). If we place end to end Kant's two propositions (Lying is always immoral/No one in his right mind is candid), we confront what may be called the Paradox of Duplicity. Secrets are required for both advancement and survival, and secrecy naturally evolves into lying. If the concept of the lie is incompatible with the idea of a human world, and if we are all liars, how is a human world possible? What kind of a self could inhabit such a world?

This paradox, which in Kant's version seems to pit the nature of sociation and the nature of moral obligation against one another, has fascinated theologians, philosophers, social scientists, and novelists. In political science and social philosophy the issue can be stated as the conflict between the need for trust and transparency in social life and the need for secrecy and dissimulation in private life. The key problem is that of secrecy, of the veiling of information, of dissembling, lying, providing false or misleading information and disinformation as a means not only to profit and gain but to survive. And why are novelists so profoundly interested in these topics? Would it be too strong to say that all stories are about secrets and their revelation? The narrator of Thackeray's *Vanity Fair* observes, "if we are to be peering into everyone's private life, . . . why, what a howling wilderness and intolerable dwelling Vanity Fair would be!"[10] The irony here is manifest on a number of levels. In Thackeray's depiction, Vanity Fair (i.e., society) *is* a howling wilderness and an intolerable dwelling. Not only does the novel's anti-hero, Rebecca Sharp, pry into the business of her benefactors and her enemies but so does the narrator pry into Becky's business, as all novels pry into everyone's business. This is the business of novels and a key reason that we find them so alluring; they allow us to engage vicariously in that most delicious of forbidden pleasures: unveiling the secrets of others. In the Victorian world, this project seems to take on a kind of exigency.

As I have argued above, both in fiction and in real life secrecy is part of the architecture of subjectivity. However, secrecy, and hence subjectivity, is historicized. We can identify a component in the history of informational exchange (and the mental and social states associated with that exchange) that can be called Victorian secrets, and consequently, there are historical forms of subjectivity and mentality that we can term "Victorian."

To accomplish my aim, I will examine versions of the dynamics of secrecy and disclosure as detailed by a variety of English novelists from the 1830s to the century's end. Drawing on Simmel, I hope to have found a credible contemporary counterpoint to Freud as a theorist of personality. In tracing Simmel's influence through Goffman I am aligning myself with a group of current scholars who are turning to mid-twentieth century theorists as alternatives to Freud and psychoanalytic theory in seeking to understand modern subjectivity as constructed in, and by, fictional representation (e.g., Eve Sedgwick's use of the work of Sylvan Tomkins, and Heather Love's use of Goffman),[11] whose projects are related to the current interest in "surface reading." Simmel and Goffman offer a framework for analysis that is neither paranoiacally "symptomatic" nor simplistically "surface."

Several generations of British readers were particularly fascinated with the idea of secrecy, and the novels themselves provide documentation of that near obsession. A large number of readers were willing to part with more than a few coins to get their hands on these novels because these books did indeed plumb the depths of the role of secrecy and dissimulation in social and individual realms – an interest of humans at every period of history, according to Simmel, but one that becomes peculiarly passionate in the nineteenth century. Readers became emotionally and intellectually involved with the novelistic treatment of desperate efforts to protect secrets and the sensational attempts to reveal them. In some respects, readers associated this theme with their own individual situations, but in other ways nineteenth-century readers of fiction believed that secrecy was class based, and that they could only imagine from afar the secret lives of persons in social worlds beyond their own. That too became a source of obsession, going beyond the universal fascination with the secrets of others and the revelation of those secrets that Simmel posited as normal. Social psychologist Karl Scheibe, speaking about the relation between secrecy and class-based power, writes:

> The right to hold secrets is traditionally distributed in a way that corresponds to social power and prestige. The poor and weak are not expected to hold

secrets from the rich and strong. The destruction of the right to secrecy is one of the main means by which the mighty can be brought low.[12]

Scheibe takes note of G. K. Chesterton's observation that detective stories are always about the wealthy. Chesterton accounts for this fact in terms of the social distribution of the right to hold secrets. "Who ever read a detective story about poor people? *The poor have crimes; but the poor have no secrets.* And it is because the proud have secrets that they need to be detected before they are forgiven."[13]

In examining the dynamics of secrecy and disclosure in certain examples of nineteenth-century British fiction, I am not claiming that the level of secrecy to be found in the Victorian world was more considerable there than elsewhere, but I am arguing that it had its own unique form, content, and intensity, and that the interest in it was extreme. We will see shortly a formula emerging from the social sciences suggesting that the amount of secrecy in different societies is roughly the same always and everywhere; only the topics change. I will add to this formula that the cultural differences in the structure and content of secrecy can influence the structure and content of the conception of selfhood as well. Furthermore, I will stress the feature of the formula that emphasizes the historicity of the content of secrets; that is, I will argue that in certain significant ways, the secrecy I study in this book is a distinctively Victorian phenomenon, as are both the strategies for its protection and its divulgence.

I have conceded that the revelation of hidden information is part of *every* story,[14] but I claim that even the investigation of these ever-present plot-driven secrets – what Alfred Hitchcock called "MacGuffins"[15] – is important in terms of both substance and form. However, my study by no means restricts itself to the analysis of MacGuffins. Additionally, I try to demonstrate that in literature we find the deployment of kinds of secrets that are not strictly plot associated but rather are part of the narrative strategy, or found in the nooks and crannies, fissures, cracks, and silences of the plot. Here we would find veiled information, misleading information, misinformation, dissimulation, and lies, as well as the discoveries, unveilings, and revelations of those types of hidden information. As Simmel claims, these forced silences are often psychologically and sociologically creative (as well as being narratologically and artistically creative in works of fiction).

In its most literal definition, the Victorian period lasted sixty-four years, from Queen Victoria's coronation in 1837 to her death in 1901. However, it is well known that we find dramatic social, economic, political, and artistic changes in Britain during these years, some of them slowly developing and others of a seismic nature. There is, therefore, an obvious danger (the danger of essentializing and of monolithic conceptualization) in any attempt to use the word "Victorian" as part of a definition of any cultural phenomena beyond the calendar-based definition. Indeed, the adjective "Victorian" is sometimes used in almost meaningless ways, often having been given too much weight to carry. I respond to the challenge of characterizing my use of the phrase "the Victorian period" not by saying with Humpty Dumpty, "When I make a word do a lot of work like that, I always pay it extra,"[16] but rather by appealing to the Wittgensteinian notion of "family resemblances."

An earlier type of logical analysis would have addressed this problem by demanding a definition of the word "Victorian" in terms of necessary and sufficient conditions, a demand that probably would produce only tautologies (e.g., "X is Victorian if X took place in Britain or its colonies and protectorates at any time during Queen Victoria's reign, or if X occurred elsewhere or at later times and was influenced by any feature of British culture during her reign"). Definitional criteria in terms of necessary and sufficient conditions are certainly appropriate in mathematics and science, but I have been convinced by Wittgenstein's writings that many meaningful concepts in ordinary language can be justified with a less formal logic. Wittgenstein's most oft-cited example is his analysis of the term "game," for which he finds no successful exhaustive definition: not all games involve winning and losing, or competition; skill and luck play different roles in different games, and one is still playing Monopoly whether or not one finds it amusing or fun. To say simply that "games are what people play" is tautological, and to say that all games are rule guided is probably true but insufficient as a definition because many other activities are also rule guided (such as pleading a case before a judge and jury, or taking a quiz in a classroom). According to Wittgenstein, an inspection of the great variety of activities we call games reveals "similarities that crop up and disappear." Wittgenstein concludes:

> I can think of no better expression to characterize these similarities than "family resemblances"; for the various resemblances between members of a family . . . overlap and criss-cross in the same way. – And I shall say: "games" form a family.[17]

I will approach the concept "Victorian" with this model in mind. Certain social, economic, political, ideological, imperial, aesthetic, moral, stylistic, and religious features of the period "overlap and criss-cross" like "the various resemblances between members of a family: build, features, colour of eyes, gait, temperament, etc. etc. in the same way" (§ 67), creating an historical period – the Age of Victoria. This Wittgensteinian approach is applicable not only to the question of meaning but sociologically as well. In a critique of certain movements within New Historicism, John Maynard writes, "there is no reason to have a firm belief in the coherence of [a] culture." He cites Samuel C. Wheeler, who calls the concept of culture "a masking term, . . . referring to a loose assortment of coexisting, overlapping, and interacting groups and individuals."[18] If Maynard and Wheeler are right (as I believe them to be), then the phrases "Victorian culture" and "Victorian secrecy" are masking terms, as is the word "games." This observation serves as cautionary advice but is not a call to cease and desist. (In fact, Wheeler's warning about the imprecision of the word "culture" appears in a book called *The Interpretive Turn: Philosophy, Science, Culture.*)

Therefore, I conclude that during the Victorian period certain kinds of secrecy were prominent, both in terms of structure and content, and that these kinds of secrecy form a family. I will designate some of the particular members of this specific family of secrets as: "secrets of the self," "secrets of the family," "secrets of class membership," "secrets of empire," "secrets of madness," and "secrets of cultural repression" (that is, cultural-historical forces that individuals did not want to think about or wanted to discuss only with selected others in secret). In addition, there are what I term "orientalized secrets" – secrets whose contents are associated with characteristics that British readers often attributed to "the Orient" (forbidden sexuality, promiscuity, opulence, riches, magic, despotism, indolence, caprice, cruelty, treachery, deceit, and conspiracy). This last category stands in a special relation to all the others, thereby infusing the very notion of secrecy with exotic and erotic spices. Then there is the "secret of sex" – a secret that, according to Michel Foucault, is primarily a nineteenth-century invention.[19] In arguing that there is a peculiarly Victorian component of secrecy in nineteenth-century British fiction, I am not, of course, claiming that the kinds of secrets that will be investigated here never appeared before or after that epoch; rather, I argue that these categories are related to each other in peculiar ways that endow them with a kind of periodic unity. I mentioned that the orientalization of secrecy bled into the other Victorian ideas about secrecy, transforming them into kinds of hybrids. But, indeed, most of these categories exert influence on each other – as members of real families influence one another – so that, for example, secrets of madness may be tainted by the impact of other categories, such as secrets of class membership.

In addition, the intensity exhibited by defenders of fictional secrets in the pages of these novels is particular to the period, as is the force of the curiosity of those individuals who were anxious to have these fictional secrets revealed. I assume that one reason for this intensity was a belief held by the reading public that fiction does indeed reflect the kinds of real secrets in the social world that are protected desperately in individual closets, behind the walls of those little secret societies called families, and behind closed doors in the offices of business and government, and in military compounds. In a strict, class-based society, a thrill was produced by peering into other people's secret business – particularly if those secrets were held by people in a higher social stratum than that of the reader, and toward whom one felt both bitterness and awe.

The primary fictional works I treat in this book are Charlotte Brontë's *Villette*; William Makepeace Thackeray's *Vanity Fair*; Mary Elizabeth Braddon's *Lady Audley's Secret*; Edward Bulwer-Lytton's *Leila: or, The Siege of Granada*; and Arthur Conan Doyle's *The Adventures of Sherlock Holmes*. Brontë's proto-sensation fiction exhibits especially secrets of the self and secrets of the family. Braddon's novel features secrets of madness and secrets of class membership. Thackeray's novel also specializes in secrets of class membership, but does so by showing how they are related to secrets of selfishness. Conan Doyle's stories expose secrets of cultural repression while at the same time declaring the end of secrecy. Bulwer-Lytton's *Leila* specializes in orientalized secrets, but according to my argument, all of these novels show the influence of this kind of secrecy, just as Foucault implies that they all suppress the secret of sex.

Because "the paradox of secrecy" structures Victorian novels as a whole, I have chosen some that particularly highlight different aspects of the relationship between secrecy and the self. However, if the thesis of this book holds, then its principal claims should apply to the great majority of Victorian novels.[20] Some will miss Dickens's *Bleak House* as a representative of secrets of the self and of the family.[21] Indeed, almost any Dickens novel could have filled the bill. Secrets of madness could have been revealed by *Jane Eyre, The Woman in White, Dracula, Jekyll and Hyde,* or *The Picture of Dorian Gray.* What I have called secrets of cultural repression (that is, secret or semi-secret fears about the intervention of certain destructive Victorian social forces in one's life) could be teased out of virtually every novel of the period; *The Beetle* or *The Moonstone* could easily exemplify orientalized secrets. In fact, almost every novel dealt with in this book does so as well. Secrets of class membership could also be revealed by most Victorian novels. If we included all the hidden deleterious effects of egoism in the category secrets of selfishness, then any number of novels of the period would qualify – notably, *A Christmas Carol*, or indeed, *all* of Dickens's novels, again. But, as will be seen, Thackeray's narrator seems to posit that no moralizing against selfishness will work. He claims to reveal to the Victorian world the dreadful secret that everyone is motivated primarily by egoism (he calls it "letting the cat of selfishness out of the bag of secrecy"); therefore perhaps the only novel that fits squarely into this category as so defined is *Vanity Fair.* Yet, according to my argument, Thackeray's version of egoism is specifically Victorian, so the category secrets of selfishness as exhibited here proves to be a Victorian one.

The secrets that dominate Victorian fiction are often known and guarded by the novel's protagonist. This is in contrast to the bulk of eighteenth-century fiction, where secrets are MacGuffins that lurk in the background of the plot, usually unknown by the protagonists themselves. Consequently, in novels such as *Pamela* and *Clarissa*, transparency is the ideal. In Victorian fiction, on the other hand, withholding information about oneself – not only from characters in the novel, but from readers and, paradoxically, sometimes from oneself – is a new narrative strategy, one that stands in contrast to earlier periods. By the early twentieth century, secrets will often prove to be psychological in nature: main characters will not know themselves, and novels will track their journeys of self-discovery – everything from *Ulysses*, through *To the Lighthouse*, to *The Loneliness of the Long-Distance Runner*.[22]

Before concluding this introduction with brief summaries of each chapter, I will say something about the method I will employ as I approach my subject, which in turn will lead me to the question of relative methodologies. The sociologists whose theoretical framework has been the initial inspiration of my project (primarily Simmel and Goffman) think of themselves as describing and theorizing real social conditions in the Western world. Because I use vocabulary, concepts, and theories from their sociological discourse, I am committed to the view that the fiction under study here is a kind of "realism" insofar as fiction is able to mirror secrecy as it functions in actual socio-historical contexts. Nevertheless, fiction about social worlds – even *realistic* fiction – is still fiction, and therefore merits (or requires) a narratology as well as a sociology. Therefore, I will be obliged to discuss the role of secrecy in Victorian fiction in terms of narrative strategy as well as social strategy. (It may turn out that these two strategies are not far apart. As D.A. Miller writes, "the social function of secrecy [is] isomorphic with its novelistic function.")[23] My general discussion of narrative theory will appear at the end of chapter 1, but certain narratological factors will first come into focus as I compare and contrast the approach I take in my project to possible alternative approaches to the same material. Most of these alternative methodologies involve *symptomatic readings*, as narratology sometimes terms them.[24] Symptomatic readings are often revisions, challenging earlier, more "standard" readings that now appear naive to the symptomatic interpreter. Symptomatic readings often conclude that what is most important about the novels in question cannot be derived from the conscious intentions of the author or characters in them, nor of the "presumed author," nor from the conscious mental states of the characters in the novels. Rather, this importance is derived from biases, pathologies, conscious or unconscious, or are controlled by the ideologies of the authors of the novels, or of the characters in them, or of the cultures within which these stories were written. Typically, symptomatic readings do not look for a coherent teleology, neither in the story nor the narration of the story, because they believe that what is most important about the novel is precisely what escapes apparent coherence and teleology. The secret to be revealed by critics performing symptomatic readings characteristically involves the unveiling of these sometime political biases, or on other occasions, unconscious biases as motives for fictional thought and action. It is for this reason that Paul Ricouer has dubbed this form of interpretation "the hermeneutics of suspicion."[25]

Psychoanalytic approaches to secrecy represent paradigm cases of symptomatic reading. The problem of secrecy seems to provide a perfect target for psychoanalytic study, because psychoanalysis *just is* the study of secrets. (The Oedipus myth is already the history of a family secret.) Yet, Freud himself wrote no treatise on the concept of secrecy.[26] There are indeed a number of good psychoanalytically oriented analyses of some of the novels I treat.[27] The same is also true concerning Lacanian studies of Victorian works. Lacanian studies are numerous, but none is dedicated to the problem of secrecy itself, nor did Lacan write such a treatise.[28]

Marxist readings of Victorian fiction are usually symptomatic in the same way that psychoanalytic readings generally are, and roughly for the same structural reason – namely, the conviction that there are forces determining art's form or content, or both, that are not under the artist's control. To understand the work of art we must understand these forces that the artist herself failed to understand. There are well-known Marxist critics who have participated in forms of symptomatic reading of Victorian literature as well. A good example is Fredric Jameson's concept of a "political unconscious," according to which "all literature must be read as a symbolic meditation on the destiny of community."[29] More recently, what we had been calling Marxist criticism seems to have evolved into two other broader and overlapping categories: cultural studies and materialism. Both are related to earlier Marxist criticism insofar as their analytical methods involve revealing the function of the material forces of economics both in the production of literature, its narration, and its content, agreeing with Marx that much of the power that these forces exert on the construction of public life and on subjective life in literature and life remain hidden. Like psychoanalytic and Marxist criticism, these newer studies engage primarily in symptomatic readings. Certain well-known critics have excelled in this field, such as Mary Poovey, whose interest in secrecy seems centered primarily on deceit in economic and political contexts.[30] I think of my own work as in some ways ancillary to theirs. However, I will take issue with materialist readings of nineteenth-century fiction that I find to be overstated (for example, Sally Shuttleworth's claim that Charlotte Brontë considered herself to be a materialist,[31] and Nicholas Dames's decision to build upon that premise).[32]

Another interpretive approach employing symptomatic readings of the literature in question would be what I call "destabilizing" narrative theory – destabilizing both in the sense of undermining traditional narrative theory and in the sense of being a theory of destabilized narratives. This category would be dominated by deconstruction[33] but would also include other postmodern narrative studies, such as Andrew Gibson's *Towards a Postmodern Theory of Narrative*. Because of the primary insistence of these theories on symptomatic reading, they too differ structurally from my own project. However, such destabilizing theories often provide convincing accounts of how language escapes the control of authors, implied authors, narrators, and characters in novels. Therefore sometimes I borrow from them, as when I follow D.A. Miller's claim in *The Novel and the Police* that it is difficult for the idea of narrative secrecy not to become a self-defeating concept, or his demonstration in *Narrative and its Discontents* that even successful closures at the end of Victorian novels leave unrevealed secrets behind them.

In my own study, I do not shy away from the insights of symptomatic readings when I find them perspicacious, but my sociological approach keeps me closer to what narratology sometimes calls *intentional reading* – namely, "[a]n interpretation that seeks to understand a text in terms of the intended meaning of its *implied author*" (Abbott, 235), where an "implied author" is not necessarily the real author, but "a single creative sensibility [that] lies behind the narrative" (Abbott, 102).[34] I think of myself as a feminist, and that stance will be evident in my book, but I am unaware of any concentrated feminist study of secrecy with which I can compare my project. Secrets abound, and therefore virtually every possible critical stance confronts the problem of secrecy in one way or another, but I am not cognizant of any sustained investigation in the name of new historicism, queer theory, or post-colonial theory. Certainly in these fields many of the issues I treat here do come to the fore: for example, colonial "mimicry" does seem to be a kind of productive duplicity, and many of my ideas overlap the theorization of public-private spheres in queer theory,[35] hence, as far as I can see, these ideas are not in opposition to the theories in my book. On the other hand, the work of Michel Foucault presents a special challenge. Critic Albert Pionke, referring to Foucault's *Discipline and Punish* (1975 in France, English translation 1979), argues that we must choose between Foucault and Simmel, because the latter claims that secrecy can harbor resistance to power while the former finds that strategies of secrecy "merely contribute to the regimes of power that provoked them."[36] In this debate, I will tend to side with Simmel;[37] however, volume 1 of Foucault's *The History of Sexuality* (1976 in France, English translation 1978) is most closely related to my project, and I will engage his theory concerning sex and secrecy in a number of instances throughout. As is well known, according to Foucault, there was not much secrecy about sex until the Victorians designated it as a secret – precisely in order to be able to talk more about it. We shall follow this idea throughout the remaining chapters, with some degree of skepticism on my part.

Another feature of my approach that may already be obvious is that, in addition to the inspiration I take from certain sociological doctrines, I incorporate a number of strategies borrowed from the history of Western philosophy: from the modern period, initiated by Descartes, into the analytical period known as "ordinary language philosophy," particularly philosophers such as Ludwig Wittgenstein and J. L. Austin. There is a new attention to Anglo-American philosophy within literary criticism now that I find stimulating. I am thinking of such wide-ranging books as Andrew H. Miller's *The Burdens of Perfection: On Ethics and Reading in Nineteenth-Century British Literature*, based on certain ideas developed by Stanley Cavell,[38] and Kent Puckett's *Bad Form: Social Mistakes and the Nineteenth-Century Novel*, which brings together sociology, psychology, and narrative theory to examine the integral role of social and narrative blunders. There also exist organizations such as Duke University's PAL (Philosophy, Art, Literature) program, initiated by Toril Moi, wherein graduate students receive a PAL diploma after completing a certain number of courses in philosophy and art history, and attending and participating in the various meetings where literary critics, art historians, and philosophers from Europe and America read papers and lead discussions.[39] In fact, I think it would be correct to say that the job I assign to Simmel and Goffman is more philosophical than sociological. I see them as offering new metaphysical perspectives from which to regard Victorian fiction, and therefore I am not unduly concerned that, among sociologists, the writings of Simmel and Goffman are sometimes considered controversial.[40] We can benefit from Simmelian and Goffmanian perspectives (or Cartesian, Nietzschean, and even Freudian perspectives) without being required to swear allegiance to them. In any case, I do not claim that the methods I employ in my study produce results superior to those produced by alternative methods, only that my methods will disclose different features of secrecy in Victorian fiction than those revealed in thoroughly symptomatic interpretations. I hope to show how the creative use of secrecy in the fiction I study generates idiosyncratic forms of Victorian subjectivity and sociation, and how overuse of secrecy or under-appreciation of its value results both in narrative infelicities and destructive social relations in the plots.

I have chosen to reject a chronological presentation of the novels I study in order to expose the workings of the dialectic between the two contradictory Victorian discourses about secrecy, one side most clearly defended in Brontë's *Villette* and the other in Conan Doyle's *Adventures of Sherlock Holmes*, each undermining their stated principles (and their main principles as well) by incongruent examples. I think of this feature of my argument as structuralist only insofar as it lays itself out synchronically rather than diachronically.⁴¹ I will close my introduction by presenting a short summary of each of the chapters to follow.

Chapter 1, "Dialectics of Secrecy and Disclosure: Sociology and the Narratology of Secrecy," sets out the theoretical grounding of my arguments, appealing primarily to the hypotheses of sociologists Georg Simmel and his disciple Erving Goffman, as well as to those of social psychologists J.A. Barnes and Karl E. Scheibe. Each of these theorists agrees that secrecy can be individually and socially destructive, but because these social theorists all appear to be committed to a conflict model of society, they deduce from that model the conclusion that secrecy (including its prosthetic devices – withholding of information and lying) is a necessary structure of any possible social relationship and is indispensable for individual safety and sanity. Throughout the book I claim that the application of twentieth-century theories of secrecy and privacy provides insights into our reading of many Victorian novelists, clarifying our understanding of how the Victorian novel represents subjectivity as negotiating between the pains of privacy and the stings of sociality. Conversely I argue that these novels anticipate and offer evidence and clarification of the later sociological theories, and in some ways offer a critique of them. I conclude the chapter with suggestions about the function of secrecy in narrative theory at large, and about its special role in Victorian narrative.

Chapter 2, "Lost in Labassecour: *Villette* and the Privatization of Secrecy," traces how Charlotte Brontë's account of a young, orphaned Englishwoman's attempt to create a life for herself as an expatriate in an alien Continental world requires that she wage a battle to protect deep secrets about her past, and the even deeper secrets of her soul. Many of the first group of secrets concern a period that is long behind Miss Snowe when, as an old lady, she sits down to write, so she can now safely reveal many of them to her readers. However, I also study the barriers that Lucy builds to prevent her readers from fathoming the secrets that she still chooses not to reveal to them. There is, according to Miss Snowe, a certain depth and sanctity in selfhood, and this sanctity would be vulgarized if the self's deepest secrets were made public. Readers of Brontë's novel get only partial glimpses of secrets guarded by her soul in a place buried so deeply within her and so remote and protected that some of those secrets are not accessible even to her own consciousness. All of these secrets are Victorian secrets in their own way, being secrets of a certain kind of selfhood and personality that had not been seen in earlier British literature and would not be seen again. Yet, by an ironic twist, we will discover that the very model of a universal deep, secret, inviolable private Victorian self promoted by Brontë and other authors of the period is in fact undermined by Lucy Snowe's own powerful and nearly foolproof strategies to discover the secrets of others, one that foreshadows the *fin-de-siècle* attempt to eliminate secrecy that we will find in the adventures of Sherlock Holmes.

Chapter 3, "Selfishness and Secrecy in the 'Howling Wilderness': Thackeray's *Vanity Fair*," offers a Goffmanian analysis of the role of secrecy and disclosure in Thackeray's novel of 1847–48. After citing the narrator's pride about his discretion in telling his tale, and his warning that the impropriety of "peering into everyone's private life" would turn Vanity Fair into a "howling wilderness" (Thackeray, 603), I argue that the function of this novel is in fact to do precisely that. Some of the secrets of Vanity Fair (that is, the secrets of London society in the early and mid-nineteenth century) are those MacGuffins about sentiment and unrequited love, but many secrets in this novel are structural and as such are part of the pattern of "criss-crossing and overlapping" that give them the identity of "Victorian secrets": shameful genealogies, bankruptcy, false family façades, illicit love, fraudulent social climbing, and hereditary madness.

As in the other chapters of the book, in addition to examining this material through the lenses provided by Simmel's theory of secrecy, and Goffman's theory of performance, I bring in as an additional lens the theory of society created by Thackeray's countryman, Thomas Hobbes. Just as a major medical secret will be the foundation of *Lady Audley's Secret* – the secret that not only the characters in the novel but we readers as well are all prone to madness ("sane to-day, mad tomorrow") – two metaphysical secrets support the action in Vanity Fair, and, indeed, predestine it to be the howling wilderness that it truly is. The first of such secrets is that of a nearly universal egoism, whose revelation we have seen the narrator call "letting the cat of selfishness out of the bag of secrecy" (222), from which it follows that virtually everybody in the novel is Becky Sharp – and hints are left that this is true of the novel's readers as well. The second is even more disturbing, disclosing as it does a secret Victorian nihilism that the narrator either reveals to his readers, or confirms what they had already suspected: that beneath the surface, we are all evil, our demon-like tails out of vision's sight are "down among the dead men . . . writhing and twirling, diabolically hideous and slimy, flapping amongst bones, or curling around corpses" (760). Is this unspeakable human evil that to which the narrator alludes when he says, "There are things we do and know perfectly well in Vanity Fair, though we never speak of them" (759)?

Chapter 4, "Madness and Class Conflicts: *Lady Audley*'s Sensational Secrets," demonstrates that an analysis of Braddon's sensation novel of 1862 supports Simmel's thesis that the kinds of lives lived by characters in and out of novels require a certain corresponding form of secrecy that produces and maintains those "forms of life."[42] However, in a modification of another Simmelian theorem, the data in this study appear to suggest that, in a society that is at war with itself, secrecy does not promote social harmony but social strife. The two principal characters in Braddon's text – Robert Audley, effeminate and indolent heir apparent to the fortune of his uncle Sir Michael Audley of the *petite aristocratie*; and the lower-middle-class *arriviste* Lucy Graham, who has recently become Lady Audley by virtue of her marriage to the widowed Sir Michael – engage each other in a deadly conflict. In particular, Lady Audley must protect her class-based secret world from disclosure by her step-nephew's investigation, while he must defend his own secrets and those of his social class if he is to overturn her shocking usurpation. These secrets include all the unspoken "Goffmanian" artifices that foster survival and advancement of their classes, and, in Lady Audley's case, all the unspoken strategies that middle-class women had to deploy in order to avoid despair, madness, or suicide. Their secret worlds are also each distinctly idiosyncratic, though peculiarly Victorian in form and content. Lucy Graham hides the shame of having abandoned her child, and the daring, sinister, desperate, and murderous acts in which she has had to engage in order to insinuate herself into the upper ranks of society and gain the wealth and privilege provided there. Robert Audley hides the abandonment of decency and honor that he has undertaken: prevarication, dissembling, intimidating inquisitional tactics, abusing the privilege of rank, and – not least of all – committing to an asylum a woman diagnosed as sane. All this he must do in order to eject the invader from her occupation of the sanctified space of family and class, and do so as secretly as possible without calling attention to the humiliating near-triumph of the invader or to the illegal force required to disguise the damage.

Behind all the military secrets of class warfare, the novel's narrator confirms an ontological secret that she seems to think all her readers have always suspected: a propensity for madness is part of human nature. This, our deepest secret fear – that of impending madness – is not a paranoid apprehension but is wholly justified. The fear of madness and of institutionalization are distinctively Victorian, as are the class-based secrets that motivate the action in this story. The paradox is that the narrator reveals this secret while implying at the same time that civilization would be impossible if this secret were revealed.

Chapter 5, "Veiled Secrets, Veiled Subjects: Scheherazade and the Orientalizing of Victorian Secrecy in Bulwer-Lytton's *Leila: or, The Siege of Granada*," sets forth my theory concerning the nineteenth-century propensity to exoticize and eroticize secrecy. I begin by discussing the profound impact of the various nineteenth-century English translations of *Arabian Nights* on the general public of Britain, and especially on the literary mind; I then "theorize" the veil, not from the perspective of Middle Eastern individuals who actually don the veil, but from the perspective of Western observers of the veil – would-be voyeurs. Toward the end of the chapter, I turn to Sir Edward Bulwer-Lytton's *Leila: or, The Siege of Granada* (1838) as my prime example of an intentionally orientalized Victorian novel, apply my theory of the orientalizing of secrecy to that novel, and show how the orientalist presuppositions both of *Leila*'s author and its readers participate in determining the meaning of the novel. In addition, I take advantage of the specific genre of Bulwer-Lytton's book in order to investigate the paradoxical role of secrecy in the Victorian historical novel, both in terms of plot and narration. Finally, I reveal an historical secret about the battle for Granada that, had he known it, may in fact have prevented Bulwer-Lytton from writing his novel.

Chapter 6, "The End of Secrecy? *The Adventures of Sherlock Holmes*," brings the century and the book to a close, but does it bring an end to secrecy in its many guises (concealment, lies, misinformation, semblance, fraud, and deception)? If the methodology that Holmes claims to employ works, then it certainly should make sustained secrecy impossible, at least in theory. He attributes to himself a method derived from the metaphysical view that every fact in the world is logically related to every other fact, in such a way that a perfect logician could deduce any fact from any other fact. This theoretical stance would indeed make deception a logical impossibility and signal the end of secrecy. A study of the plot-driving secrets that the heroes of all detective fiction must unravel exposes, in Holmes's case, the specifically late-Victorian nature of those MacGuffins, but also the secret (and sometimes not-so-secret) anxieties of the age. Conan Doyle is able to profit, literally, from the orientalizing of secrecy that was, I have argued, a touchstone of his century, taking advantage of his audience's fascination with what was taken to be the opulence, the sensualism, the barbarism, and cruelty of the East. In doing so, Conan Doyle provided a cover story for the imperialism associated with orientalism, but he also gave his readers glimpses of the secrets behind the mask of imperialism, if they cared to look.

Though Conan Doyle's readers may well have realized that Holmes represented the advent of transparency and the end of secrecy, they must have recognized the contradiction that his practical method was flawed (as he admitted) and that he himself used fraud and illegality to pry secrets from both his clients and their tormenters. Moreover, he used his skills to protect the secrets of his benefactors. Indeed, even as Conan Doyle wrote about the end of secrecy, he himself slipped ever further into a secret world of spiritualism inhabited by ghosts with supernatural powers and fairies with dragonfly-like wings. His own parallel secret world (the creation of which was a benefit of the logic of secrecy, according to Simmel) was deeper and more populated than that of most of his readers.

My book, then, will have traced an ironic circle. It commences with Brontë's *Villette*, a novel that defends a highly exaggerated form of Simmelianism, arguing that substantive selfhood and personal identity are impossible without deep and sometimes dark secrets of the soul that are withheld not only from other characters in the story but from readers themselves. Then the novel proceeds to dismantle that Simmelian thesis as Brontë creates a cluster of central characters whose detective skills are so powerful that virtually no secret remains unveiled, and the very concept of secrecy is put at risk. My book concludes with the greatest detective imaginable, Sherlock Holmes,[43] who generates a metaphysical theory proving the impossibility of secrecy, fraud, and all forms of dissimulation, thereby refuting a principal sociological theory of Georg Simmel, whose work has been the keystone to my own theory. Then Conan Doyle allows Holmes to deconstruct his own metaphysics, both by having Holmes use his skills to protect the secrets of his well-heeled clients, and by making that activity possible only by Holmes's own use of secrecy, prevarication, and criminality. At the end of the nineteenth century, most of Simmel's theory of secrecy seems safe even from Sherlock Holmes.

Notes

1 "I think transparency should always be substituted for what is secret, and I can quite well imagine the day when two men will no longer have secrets from each other, because no one will have any more secrets from anyone, because subjective life, as well as objective life, will be completely offered up, given." (Jean-Paul Sartre, "Sartre at Seventy: An Interview," interviewer Michel Conant, trans. Lydia Davis and Paul Auster, *New York Review of Books* [August 7, 1975]: web).

2 "[T]he influence of Sartre's kind of existentialism on Goffman's work is one of the most often discussed topics in the critical literature on Goffman" (Greg Smith, "Introduction: Interpreting Goffman's Sociological Legacy," in *Goffman and Social Organization: Studies in Sociological Legacy* [New York and London: Routledge, 1999], 1–18, 41n3). Goffman quotes Sartre several times in *The Presentation of Self in Everyday Life* – one quotation being more than a page long (New York and London: Anchor Books Doubleday, 1959), 75–76. Future references to this work will be cited parenthetically in the body of the text.

3 "Kant infamously maintains that it is wrong to lie even to a would-be murderer in order to protect his intended victim" (Allen W. Wood, *Kant's Ethical Thought* [Cambridge and New York: Cambridge University Press, 1999], 2). Future references to this work will be cited parenthetically in the body of the text.

4 Immanuel Kant, "Lectures on the Philosophical Doctrine of Religion" [Vorlesungen über die philosophische Religionslehre], quoted and translated by Wood, in *Kant's Ethical Thought*, 167.

5 Immanuel Kant, "Anthropology from a Pragmatic Standpoint" [Anthropologie in pragmatischer Hinsicht], quoted and translated by Wood, in *Kant's Ethical Thought*, 200.

6 Compulsive lying may be an exception: the liar may not be motivated by the hope of gaining an advantage, but may be acting out of a pathological necessity.

7 "Sociation" is Kurt H. Wolff's translation of Simmel's *Vergesellschaftungsform* and *Vergesellschaftung*. Earlier translators used "sociality" or "societalization." See Wolff's explanation of his choice in Georg Simmel, *The Sociology of Georg Simmel*, trans. and ed. Kurt H. Wolff (New York: Free Press, 1964), lxiii. Future references to this work will be cited parenthetically in the body of the text.

8 Kant, "Anthropology from a Pragmatic Standpoint," quoted and translated by Wood, in *Kant's Ethical Thought*, 267.

9 Immanuel Kant, "Religion within the Boundaries of Mere Reason" [Religion innerhalb der Grenzen der bloßen Vernunft], quoted and translated by Wood, in *Kant's Ethical Thought*, 267.

10 William Makepeace Thackeray, *Vanity Fair: A Novel without a Hero* [1847–48], ed. Peter Shillingsburg (New York: Norton, 1994), 507.

11 Sylvan Tomkins, *Shame and Its Sisters*, ed. Eve Kosofsky Sedgwick and Adam Frank (Durham: Duke University Press, 1995); Heather Love, *Feeling Backward: Loss and the Politics of Queer Theory* (Cambridge, MA: Harvard University Press, 2007).

12 Karl E. Scheibe, *Mirrors, Masks, Lies and Secrets: The Limits of Human Predictability* (New York: Praeger, 1979), 101.

13 G.K. Chesterton, *A Miscellany of Man* (New York: Dodd, Mead, 1912), 283 (quoted by Scheibe, *Mirrors, Masks, Lies and Secrets*, 100), emphasis added.

14 In this study I am avoiding the problem of whether there can be *knowledge* of facts and events that are fictitious. That is, I am not tackling the issue of the truth-conditions of fictitious propositions. In my view, a successful solution to this serious problem has been suggested by A.P. Martinich and Avrum Stroll in *Much Ado about Nonexistence: Fiction and Reference* (Lanham, MD: Rowman and Littlefield, 2007), showing how and why the rules of the "language game" called fiction allow attributions of truth conditions to fictitious propositions.

15 According to the *Oxford English Dictionary*, Hitchcock introduced the term "MacGuffin" in a 1939 lecture at Columbia University.

16 Lewis Carroll, *Through the Looking-Glass* [1871], in *The Annotated Alice: Alice's Adventures in Wonderland & Through the Looking Glass*, intro. and notes, Martin Gardner (New York: Bramhall House, 1960), 270.

17 Ludwig Wittgenstein, *Philosophical Investigations*, trans. G.E.M. Anscombe (New York: Macmillan, 1964), § 67. Future references to this work will be cited parenthetically in the body of text.

18 John Maynard, *Literary Intention, Literary Interpretation, and Readers* (Peterborough, ON: Broadview Press, 2008), 80, n162, 221–22. Wheeler's passage is found in David R. Hiley, James F. Bohman, and Richard Shusterman, eds., *The Interpretive Turn: Philosophy, Science, Culture* (Ithaca and London: Cornell University Press, [1991], 208). Future references to Maynard's book will be cited parenthetically in the body of text.
19 Michel Foucault, *The History of Sexuality*, vol. 1, *An Introduction*, trans. Robert Hurley (New York: Vintage Books/Random House, 1980).
20 In fact, I believe that the sociological perspective I have assumed here could be the basis of a study of the role of secrecy in other forms of creative expression, such as poetry, drama, and the visual arts. (In fact, I do occasionally make some gestures in this direction in the current text.) I expect that my form of analysis could also be extended to cover nonfictional discourse, such as advertisements, customer and patient billing, communications among divisions of industrial enterprises and governmental offices, and certainly of political speeches. However, in this book, I will restrict myself primarily to a study of the novel.
21 For example, Esther Summerson is a repressive narrator, much like Lucy Snowe, but perhaps not in such an aggressive fashion as Lucy, and for the purposes of this chapter, precisely the passive aggression of the secrecy of the aging Miss Snowe is more revealing than the less aggressive forms employed by the young Miss Summerson. Also, Brontë's conception of the secret self seems deeper than Dickens's.
22 I am indebted to Deborah Wyrick for this idea.
23 D.A. Miller, *The Novel and the Police* (Berkeley and Los Angeles: University of California Press, 1989), 206.
24 The term was coined by Louis Althusser. H. Porter Abbott defines it thusly: "Decoding a text as symptomatic of the author's unconscious or unacknowledged state of mind, or of unacknowledged cultural conditions. Generally opposed to *intentional reading*" (H. Porter Abbott, *The Cambridge Introduction to Narrative*, 2nd ed. [Cambridge and New York: Cambridge University Press, 2008], 242). Page numbers of future citations from this book will be included in the body of the text.
25 Paul Ricouer, *Freud and Philosophy: An Essay on Interpretation*, trans. Denis Savage (New Haven: Yale University Press, 1970). Some recent critics have argued that the dominance of these hermeneutics during the last decades should now be called into question. Rita Felski began this campaign with an article titled "After Suspicion" (in *Profession* [January 2009]: 28–35), which inspired a one-day conference at Duke University called "Beyond Critique: Reading after the Hermeneutics of Suspicion," held on September 10, 2010. Felski gave the keynote address, arguing that the hermeneutics of suspicion was tantamount to a paranoid approach to literature. Other speakers were Sharon Marcus, Stephen Best, and Kate Hayles. Toril Moi was the moderator.
26 As far as I have been able to determine, no work of Freud's has the word *Geheimnis* in its title. The German word *Unheimlich* (uncanny) seems curiously close to the word *Geheimnis* (secret), and Freud's essay of 1919, "The 'Uncanny,'" may be the closest thing to a theory of secrecy that Freud ever wrote. For Freud, the sense of uncanniness is experienced when certain everyday events remind us of material repressed into the unconscious, or to similarities with childhood psychology that we falsely believe we have left behind. Freud cites Schelling with approval: "According to him everything is uncanny that ought to have remained hidden and secret" (Sigmund Freud, "The 'Uncanny,'" in *The Standard Edition of the Complete Psychological Works of Sigmund Freud*, vol. 17, ed. James Strachey [London: Hogarth Press, 1955], 224).
27 See, for example, psychoanalytic readings from such critics as Peter Brooks, Steven Connor, Helene Moglen, Julia Moynihan, and Diana Sadoff.
28 See, for example, Lacanian readings of Victorian fiction by critics such as David Collins, Mark Hennelly, James Kavanagh, and Pricilla Walton.
29 Fredric Jameson, *The Political Unconscious: Narrative as a Socially Symbolic Act* (Ithaca: Cornell University Press, 1985), 70. According to Jameson, Marxist criticism

must reveal ideology as a "*subtext*" (81), but it must go beyond this traditionally Marxist project and reveal the cultural object's "simultaneously Utopian power as symbolic affirmation of a specific historical and class form of collective unity" (291).
30 See Mary Poovey, *Genres of the Credit Economy: Mediating Value in Eighteenth and Nineteenth Century Britain* (Chicago and London: University of Chicago Press, 2008).
31 "Brontë offers, in *Villette*, a thorough materialization of the self" (Sally Shuttleworth, *Charlotte Brontë and Victorian Psychology* [Cambridge: Cambridge University Press, 1996], 240). Future references to this work will be cited parenthetically in the body of the text.
32 "Shuttleworth's work is a crucial piece of research and theorizing, most worthwhile for its demonstration that Brontë's references to phrenology are more than epiphenomenal; I am indebted to it throughout my reading of Brontë" (Nicholas Dames, *Amnesiac Selves: Nostalgia, Forgetting, and British Fiction, 1810–1870* [Oxford: Oxford University Press, 2001], 258n9).
33 According to David Herman, the shockwaves created by the explosive arrival of deconstruction seemed to herald the death knell of narratology, but after those waves subsided, narratology proved to be reinvigorated by the crises, resulting in what Herman calls a renaissance in the field. The essays in Herman's anthology, *Narratologies: New Perspectives on Narrative Analysis*, along with his introduction to the book, are meant as demonstrations of his thesis (Columbus: Ohio State University Press, 1999).
34 "Implied author" or "inferred author": "Neither the real author nor the narrator. . . . In an *intentional reading* . . . that sensibility and moral intelligence that the reader gradually constructs to infer the intended meanings and effects of the narrative" (Abbott, Glossary in *The Cambridge Introduction to Narrative*, 235). More will be said about this concept at the end of chapter 1.
35 For example, Love's *Feeling Backward* can be read as an invitation to discuss secrecy.
36 Albert D. Pionke, "Victorian Secrecy: An Introduction," in *Victorian Secrecy: Economies of Knowledge and Concealment*, ed. Albert D. Pionke and Denise Tischler Millstein (Farnham: Ashgate, 2010), 1–15, 8.
37 As does Richard A. Kaye who, contrasting Foucault and Simmel, writes: "Simmel offers, I would suggest, a more complex theory of modernity, especially in its newly urbanized forms, and one that provides a more suggestive means of exploring erotic relations in the nineteenth century novel" (*The Flirt's Tragedy: Desire without End in Victorian and Edwardian Fiction* [Charlottesville and London: University of Virginia Press, 2002], 9).
38 Discussing the experimental nature of his text, Miller writes,

> One important feature of that experiment, I should say, is its engagement with recent writing in Anglo-American philosophy. We draw unevenly on sources of inspiration: the crowd circling some waterholes is several scholars deep day and night, while nearby springs bubble unnoticed. There have been good reasons for the neglect of Anglo-American philosophical texts; often they treat literature as merely ornamental and illustrative. But many questions posed by recent work in ethics and philosophy of mind (especially) press with surprising force on the literary texts we share. (*The Burdens of Perfection: On Ethics and Reading in Nineteenth-Century British Literature* [Ithaca and London: Cornell University Press, 2008], 27)

39 Moi, of course, is well known for her writing on French feminist theory, and is currently engaged in Wittgensteinian studies.
40 For example, Greg Smith begins his introduction to *Goffman and Social Organization* by calling Goffman "[a]lways a controversial figure" (1).
41 As when Lévi-Strauss analyzes the myth of Oedipus in terms of two sets of self-contradictory denials and affirmations: "Man is *not* born of the earth"/"Man *is* born of the earth," and "Ties of blood are *less* important than social relations"/"Ties of

blood are *more* important than social relations." This is my simplified reconstruction of Lévi-Strauss's presentation of two primary antinomies in the myth of Oedipus (*Structural Anthropology*, trans. Claire Jacobson and Brooke Grunfest Schoepf [New York: Basic Books, 1963], 213–18). Lévi-Strauss concludes his discussion of this and similar myths, writing, "[T]he purpose of myth is to provide a logical model capable of overcoming a contradiction (an impossible achievement if, as it happens, the contradiction is real)" (229).

42 The phrase "a form of life" is often associated with Wittgenstein, who contends that different language-games produce different forms of life: "And to imagine a language means to imagine a form of life" (*Philosophical Investigations 1*, § 19). I would argue that the different forms of secrecy defended help generate different language-games.

43 Saint Anselm might argue that if such a detective is conceivable, he must exist – a new twist on the ontological proof of God's existence.

1 Dialectics of secrecy and disclosure

Sociology and the narratology of secrecy

> There is no action possible without a little acting.
> —George Eliot, *Daniel Deronda*

My fascination with the project of secrecy in Victorian fiction was inspired in part by the work of a number of social scientists who have studied the function of secrecy in their respective fields: sociology, social psychology, and anthropology. It is recognized that secrecy in the Victorian world played a significant role, and I have come to believe that the application of sociological theories of secrecy to British fiction in the Victorian period provides insight into Victorian sociation and subjectivity. Therefore, in this chapter I will set forth in more detail the two primary sociological theories of secrecy that I will employ throughout, those of Georg Simmel and Erving Goffman (who could be called "Simmel's bulldog").

Simmel was born in 1856 and died seventeen years after Queen Victoria's demise. The near contemporaneity of the professor and the Queen might make the former's theories particularly well suited for use in analyzing literature written during Victoria's reign. Their overlapping life spans are indeed convenient for my theses, but in fact Simmel surely meant for his theories to be generalized. He formulated his theory of secrecy in such a way as to acknowledge the historicity of secrecy, allowing the components of his formulas to shift relative to time and place. Goffman's theory often seems tightly tied to the first half of the twentieth century. Some of his examples now feel dated (London chimney sweeps "dress in white," "American college girls" play down their intelligence when in the presence of "datable boys," American wives "leave *The Saturday Evening Post* on their living room end table but keep a copy of *True Romance* in the bedroom").[1] The second chapter in Freud's *Psychopathology of Everyday Life* is called "Forgetting of Foreign Words," and the primary example is of someone forgetting a word in Virgil's *Exoriare*. It is fair to say that Freud's example is dated. This particular *parapraxis* is one that most of us in today's world are in no danger of making. The fact that this and many other examples in Freud's book are dated does not in itself refute Freud's theory; I have no doubt that we could still test the truth of either Freud's or Goffman's theory, replacing dated examples with newer ones. If I am treating the theories of Simmel and Goffman as if they were transhistorical, it is only in this sense.

Sociologists, like literary critics, do not always agree with one another. Therefore, having presented the theoretical bases of my argument, I will tidy up a bit around the sociological edges, anticipating possible objections to my thesis (imagined criticisms by Judith Butler and, in a note, by Stanton K. Tefft). From there I will attempt to establish a connection between my work and that of John Kucich in his *The Power of Lies: Transgression in Victorian Fiction*, a book I consider to be essential to any discussion of secrecy in Victorian fiction. Kucich appeals to Simmel's authority only briefly, but at a propitious juncture in his book, thereby placing himself in the Simmelian tradition. Because I intend my book to make a contribution to literary criticism rather than to sociology, I will end this chapter with a brief discussion of the role of secrecy in narrative theory and in narrative strategies as they apply to the fiction of the Victorian period.

Georg Simmel and the constitutional role of secrecy

Georg Simmel (1858–1918), *Privatdocent* and *ausserordentlicher Professor* at the University of Berlin, wrote his doctoral dissertation on the philosophy of Immanuel Kant. In addition to the sociology classes he taught, he gave occasional lectures on philosophy, especially on Kant. He wrote an essay with the very Kantian title of "How is Society Possible?"[2] But rather than seeing this and similar problems as primarily logical and ethical, as Kant had done, Simmel sees them as structural. Unlike Kant, Simmel does not consider prevarication and other forms of deception as always socially destructive. To the contrary, Simmel sees a socially valuable creativity in the dynamics of the veiling of the truth. In *The Secret and the Secret Society*, composed in 1908, he writes: "All social relations among individuals are based on their knowing something about one another. . . . Our relationships thus develop upon a basis of reciprocal knowledge."[3] But he complicates this formula when he adds that all social relationships also "presuppose . . . a measure of mutual concealment" (314). Indeed, according to him, "We simply cannot imagine any interaction or social arrangement or society which are *not* based on this teleologically determined non-knowledge of each other" (311–12). There is a further twist:

> all of human intercourse rests on the fact that everybody knows somewhat more about the other than the other voluntarily reveals to him; and those things he knows are frequently matters whose knowledge the other person (were he aware of it) would find undesirable.
>
> (323)

This means that there are elements of deception and self-deception woven into the fabric of social life. I take pleasure in knowing more about you than you think I know, but apparently it does not seriously occur to me that you must know more about me than I think you do. Furthermore, these deceptions are a precondition of sociality.

Even though we know more about others than they want us to know, we certainly do not know everything about them, and we are often highly motivated to find out more. In fact, Simmel's most important contribution to the sociology and social psychology of secrecy is his articulation of the role of concealment in social relationships and interactions – the roles played by silence, secrets, lies, misinformation, disrupted information, disinformation, deception, duplicity, manipulated ignorance, illusion, and all other forms of veiled information. In the exploration of the social history of concealment, all paths lead back to Simmel. According to him, both sociologically and psychologically, "secrets are necessary" as means to personal and social ends (332).

Were Simmel writing today, he might or might not have been pleased to discover neo-Darwinian support for his theory about the roles of secrecy and deception, on both the social and individual levels. In a recent book, biologist and evolutionary anthropologist Robert Trivers argues that both the capacity for deception and the capacity for the detection of deception (closely related to what I am calling the dialectics of secrecy and disclosure) are part of our genetic inheritance, both having survival value. All animals, including humans, are born "into a world saturated with deceit."[4] Survival and reproductive success require that biological organisms inherit skills both in deceiving and detecting deceit. Moreover, as these skills become more sophisticated they promote the evolution of intelligence itself: "The evidence is clear and overwhelming that both the detection of deception and often its propagation have been major forces favoring the evolution of intelligence" (5). Trivers continues: "An important part of understanding deception is to understand it mathematically as an evolutionary game, with multiple players pursuing multiple strategies with varying degrees of conscious and unconscious deception" (48).

Simmel arrives at similar conclusions, derived from sociological rather than biological premises. He catalogues some of the socially teleological necessities that are achieved through secrecy. First, concealment is universally necessary because complete revelation is psychologically impossible: if we revealed all aspects of our inner life, it "would drive everybody into the insane asylum" (312). Second, even the most intimate relationships would founder without "distances and intermissions," whose success presupposes "a certain ignorance and a measure of mutual concealment" (315–16). Indeed, Simmel is convinced that many marriages fail because of a "lack of reciprocal discretion" (329). He argues that these necessary silences can often be arranged by mutual if unspoken consent, but sometimes "aggressive techniques" (315–16) are in order to achieve this end – that is, sometimes lies are appropriate. In this context, Simmel suggests that the "ethically negative value of the lie must not blind us to its sociologically quite positive significance for the formation of certain concrete relations" (315–16). Third, information that is withheld shapes the "intensity and nuance" (307) of relationships. Without concealment of information these important human subtleties could not exist, and the social world would be too one-dimensional to be tolerated. Fourth, without the ability to withhold information, the inner life of the individual is at risk, especially our self-respect, because it is closely related to the respect we receive from others, and respect requires social distance. We cannot always afford to be recognized as what we are. This need adds yet another reason to believe that deception is psychologically and socially necessary. Finally, another socially necessary feature of secrets appears when we consider the function of *shared* secrets, which create "we" groups by excluding outsiders. The concept of "we" that is thus developed is based on the idea of exclusive possession.

According to Simmel, the secret itself is an impressive psychosocial artifact. He says, almost reverentially, that the ability to keep secrets "is one of man's greatest achievements." The secret

> produces an immense enlargement of life; numerous contents of life cannot even emerge in the presence of full publicity. The secret offers . . . the possibility of a second world alongside the manifest world; and the latter is deeply influenced by the former.
>
> (330)

One experiences "the sensation of the ego as that which is absolutely 'one's own.'"[5] Such a conception of the ego involves the feeling of radical uniqueness that escapes physical, social, and moral determinations. One's secret world and one's imaginative world (often the same) produce that feeling of uniqueness, and hence are components of subjectivity. The very idea of subjectivity presupposes secrecy.

Simmel says that we all understand why secrets are necessary, but besides the instrumentality of secrets, there is in addition the universal fascination that secrets generate. However, the value of the secret is only as good as the ability to resist the temptation to reveal secrets through gossip or confession. It turns out that the fascination with secrets is partly the fascination with the possibility of betrayal. Simmel writes:

> The secret, too, is full of the consciousness that it *can* be betrayed; that one holds the power of surprises, turns of fate, joy, destruction – if only, perhaps, of self-destruction. For this reason the secret is surrounded by the possibility and the temptation of betrayal.
>
> (333)[6]

When Simmel says that we know more about the other than the other wants us to know, he implies that we know some of the secrets of the other, but that we often keep secret this knowledge of secrets. There is, in fact, a significant sociological role played by these secrets that are not secret. Simmel says, "what is intentionally or unintentionally hidden is intentionally or unintentionally respected" (330). Part of the reason that these open secrets are respected is, as we have already seen, that we are only capable of dealing with a certain amount of information. It is for this reason that partners in modern business dealings want to know "only exactly *that* and no more about their partner which they *have* to know for the sake of the relationship they wish to enter" (319). I am discreet about the cashier's acne problem not only for her sake but for mine. Discretion, however, is not merely a convenience but also a moral duty. The weight of this duty varies from one society to another. This duty is related to the fact that privacy (a space in which one can guard one's secrets) is a partial determinant of selfhood. To violate the field of privacy allotted to each individual "constitutes a lesion of the ego" (322).[7] Apparently for Simmel the role played by the allowance of privacy in the construction of the ego is culturally determined, often along the lines of social class. In more conservative societies, there is a pronounced "ideal sphere around every human being," differing in size and extension depending on certain social contingencies. This sphere is created by the amount of privacy allotted to the individual, or to the number of apparent secrets (*apparent*, because many of them are known to almost everybody) to which the individual can claim a right. This sphere cannot be breached without destroying the "personality value of the individual." The radius of this sphere marks "the distance whose trespassing by another person insults one's honor" (320–21).[8] In the case of "great personages" such as some kings and queens, penetrating this circle by even taking notice constitutes a violation (322). With the exception of children and convicts, every individual has the right to some discretion, even in less conservative societies. But in social interactions there are certain things that *must* be made known, and the individual has no moral right to demand protection from inquiry into those spheres. The "duty of discretion – to renounce the knowledge of all that the other does not voluntarily show us – recedes before practical requirements" (323). But of course even when there is a social need to pry into the affairs of others, often the keepers of secrets do not give them up without a fight.

As mentioned earlier, though Simmel clearly believes that his investigation reveals a number of universal functions of secrecy as a determinant in human interactions, he is well aware of the historicity of even these universal functions. The closest he comes to stating a theory relating to secrecy's vicissitudes from culture to culture and from one historical period to another is what he calls his

> paradoxical idea that under otherwise identical circumstances, human collective life requires a certain measure of secrecy which merely changes its topics: while leaving one of them, social life seizes upon another, and in all this alternation it preserves an unchanged quantity of secrecy.
> (335–36)[9]

This seems to contradict his assertion that earlier societies needed less secrecy and had available to themselves fewer opportunities for it than in modern societies, but it does suggest the interesting idea that secrecy is an ever-present protean cipher of absence – an unspecified X whose value in quotidian social practice can only be determined historically, even though its analytical value remains more or less constant. Simmel's pioneering attempt to create a sociology of the secret still remains some of the best work on the subject, and I will borrow from it liberally as I develop my own theory of the dynamics of concealment and revelation as represented in the nineteenth-century British novel.[10] Similarly, I will be employing

Erving Goffman's sociology of performance

> All the world's a stage,
> And all the men and women merely players;
> They have their exits and their entrances,
> And one man in his time plays many parts.
> —*As You Like It*, Act II, Scene VII

The Presentation of Self in Everyday Life, by Erving Goffman (1922–82), is generally thought of as the pioneering attempt to understand social relations using a performative model. He writes: "The perspective employed in this report is that of the theatrical performance; the principles derived are dramaturgical ones" (xi). In the preface to his book, Goffman admits that the dramaturgical perspective is not the only possible viewpoint from which to regard sociology, but he justifies this approach in an exclusively pragmatic manner, saying that its "illustrations together fit into a coherent framework that ties together bits of experience the reader has already had and provides the student with a guide worth testing in case-studies of institutional social life" (xii). (In an aside, Goffman mentions that these are the same tests that justify Simmel's approach.) Far from touting his model's superiority, Goffman admits "its obvious inadequacies" (xi). One weakness is that his use of the dramaturgical model forces him to say that the same individual often moves rapidly back and forth between being performer and audience, a mutability that does not exist in genuine theatrical situations; another is that, on stage, "unlike ordinary life, nothing real or actual can happen to the performed characters" (254). It turns out, however, that these are not "crucial" distinctions. Goffman writes: "All the world is not, of course, a stage, but the crucial ways in which it isn't are not easy to specify" (72). The ambiguity between the real case and the staged one is what allows Goffman's model the success it achieves. Sometimes Goffman seems to forget that there is an ambiguity at all. He quotes approvingly a line of Robert Ezra Parks: "everyone is always and everywhere playing a role" (19). Yet, at the end of his book Goffman reconsiders his theatrical model, reminding us that it is only one of several perspectives. As such, he says, this model provides merely a point of view, and "orders facts" as seen from that standpoint (240). Indeed, on the last page of his book Goffman writes, "And so here the language and mask of the stage will be dropped. Scaffolds, after all, are to build other things with, and should be erected with an eye to taking them down" (254).[12]

I have opened my book with an appeal to sociology, claiming it can afford an insight into fiction; conversely, Goffman opens his sociological treatise with an appeal to fiction, claiming it offers an insight into sociology.[13] If Goffman's theory is correct, this reciprocity is logical; the reason it is possible for novelists to create realistic characters is that the real self – or at least the self presented in everyday life – is fictive in exactly the same sense as are the selves of those characters in novels, according to Goffman. In the first few pages of his book Goffman illustrates his main theme by quoting a long passage from the pages of a novel by William Sansom.[14] Goffman's theory about sociality as performance benefits from this humorous exposition. Sansom's Mr. Preedy is a vacationing Englishman who makes his first appearance at a Spanish beach adjacent to his hotel:

> But in any case he took care to avoid catching anyone's eye. First of all, he had to make it clear to those potential companions of his holiday that they were of no concern to him whatsoever. He stared through them, round them, over them – eyes lost in space. The beach might have been empty. If by chance a ball was thrown his way, he looked surprised; then let a smile of amusement lighten his face (Kindly Preedy), looked round dazed to see that there *were* people on the beach, tossed it back with a smile to himself and not a smile *at* the people, and then resumed carelessly his nonchalant survey of space.
>
> (*Self* 4–5)

Sansom carries us through Preedy's entire repertoire. There is "the Ideal Preedy," who institutes a little parade down the beach in such a way that anyone who wishes can get a peek at the title of the book he is reading – a Spanish translation of Homer – and there is the presentation of "Methodical and Sensible Preedy," who wraps his towel and bag into a neat, sand-resistant pile; there is "Big-Cat Preedy," stretching with ease his large frame; there is "Carefree Preedy, after all," who tosses aside his sandals in a wanton manner; and there is "Local Fisherman Preedy," who turns his eyes to the sky, "gravely surveying portents, invisible to the others, of weather" (5). There is also "the marriage of Preedy and the sea":

> There were alternative rituals. The first involved the stroll that turns into a run and a dive straight into the water, thereafter smoothing into strong splashless crawl toward the horizon. But of course not really to the horizon. Quite suddenly he would turn on to his back and thrash great white splashes with his legs, somehow thus showing that he could have swum further had he wanted to, then would stand up quarter out of the water for all to see who it was.
>
> (5)

We have seen Preedy, and he is us.

Goffman proceeds to define various social behaviors in terms of theatrical categories: "performance" (15), "part," or "routine" (16), "stage," with a "front region" (107), and "backstage" (112), and "character" (252). A large part of this thesis – and one that reflects the book's title – is captured in his assertion:

> A correctly staged and performed scene leads the audience to impute a self to a performed character, but this imputation – this self – is a *product* of a scene that comes off, and is not a *cause* of it. The self, then, as a performed

character, is not an organic thing that has a specific location, whose fundamental fate is to be born, to mature, and to die.

(252–53)

There is a direct relationship between Goffman's dramaturgical model and the Simmelian model of society as a dynamic of concealment and revelation. Where there is society, there are veiled secrets. Goffman writes:

> we must be prepared to see that the impression of reality fostered by a performance is a delicate, fragile thing that can be shattered by very minor mishaps. . . . As members of an audience it is natural for us to feel that the impression that the performer seeks to give may be true or false, genuine or spurious, valid or "phony."
>
> (56, 58)

In referring to the performance, "the crucial concern is whether it will be credited or discredited" (253). The actors try to influence this judgment by maintaining as much control as possible over the performance, but in fact not all expressions are governable, and experienced audiences (i.e., most of us, most of the time) "use what are considered to be the ungovernable aspects of . . . expressive behavior as a check upon the validity of what is conveyed by the governable aspects" (7). The actors (i.e., most of us, most of the time) know this, and try to manipulate the so-called ungovernable aspects of their expressive behavior to support the authenticity of the whole performance. This dynamic between performers and audience "sets the stage for a kind of information game – a potentially infinite cycle of concealment, discovery, false revelation, and rediscovery" (8). One of the most radical features of Goffman's theory can be detected in his account of this "information game." The reader comes to realize that, for Goffman, all performances – or presentations of the self – are deceptive, and cannot be otherwise. Goffman is offering us Simmel's main idea in its most extreme expression. The performer sometimes sees through his own act – being in an excellent position to do so – but sometimes he dupes even himself. Goffman says, rather mischievously I believe, that we reserve "the term 'sincere' for individuals who believe in the impression fostered by their own performance," and we call those who don't "cynics" (18).

Is Goffman's theory cynical itself, as many readers come to believe? Or, to pose the question differently, in the same way that one can associate Goffman's theory with Shakespeare's lines from *As You Like It* ("All the world's a stage . . ."), can one also associate his theory with Shakespeare's other terrifying analogy between life and theater?

> Life's but a walking shadow, a poor player,
> That struts and frets his hour upon the stage,
> And then is heard no more. It is a tale
> Told by an idiot, full of sound and fury,
> Signifying nothing.
>
> *Macbeth*, Act V, Scene V

Sociologist Anthony Giddens says that in *The Presentation of Self in Everyday Life*

> Goffman tends to concentrate on situations in which performances are manipulated in such a way as to conceal the true motives of those who carry them out, and where such performances are deliberately staged – no doubt the view that Goffman portrays a cynical world of self-concerned agents, in which appearance counts above all else, derived from this.[15]

In their introduction to *Erving Goffman: Exploring the Interaction Order*, editors Drew and Wootton write, "some have been misled into believing that for Goffman we are all manipulative con men, indeed that interaction itself is a con." Goffman studies "con men" so much because of his technique of engaging in "investigation of the normal through the abnormal. Here, as elsewhere, serious exegesis of Goffman's work is needed as a corrective" (7, 9). This "corrective" is mirrored somewhat by literary critic Jenny Davidson, who asks: "If hypocrisy simply means playing a part, might not the sufficient repetition of a given action allow the hypocrite a kind of functional sincerity?" Davidson associates this defense of hypocrisy with Goffman, but also with La Rochefoucauld, Johnson, Swift, Burke, Wordsworth, William James, Francis Bacon, and Machiavelli.[16]

Goffman is particularly interested in what he calls "team performances." He provides several examples of teams: medical staffs in hospitals, hotel staffs, governmental agents, theatrical, musical, and dance productions, department store staffs, police departments, members of military units, religious officials, baseball teams, university staffs, funeral home staffs, and service staff in upper-class homes. Sometimes the secret behind a team performance is simply "the extent and character of the co-operation" that made the performance possible (104). But this is more important than it may seem, because the point of a team performance is "to maintain a particular definition of the situation" (105), therefore the amount of preparation that goes into a performance must be kept secret so that the sustained definition appears natural and convincing. As we have seen, the reality of the social situation defined is fragile, according to Goffman, and can be lost if the performance is discredited. Sustaining this definition involves over-communication of some facts and under-communication of others. The information that is veiled in team performances Goffman calls "destructive information" (141), because if it is revealed the performers lose their power to define the social situation. Goffman catalogues several types of secrets that teams must guard according to the function those secrets perform. Sometimes these categories overlap. First, there are "*dark secrets*." These are facts "which are incompatible with the image of self that the team attempts to maintain before its audience" (141). There are "*strategic secrets*" that a team conceals to prevent the audience from protecting itself against "the state of affairs the team is planning to bring about" (142). These are the secrets that "armies and businesses employ in designing future actions against the opposition" (142). There are "*inside secrets*," whose content may be fairly arbitrary and harmless, but their possession "marks an individual as being a member of a group and helps the group feel separate and different from those individuals who are not 'in the know'" (142). There are *"entrusted secrets,"* those secrets "which the possessor is obliged to keep because of his relation to the team to which the secret refers" (143), exemplified by lawyers and priests who do not reveal secrets about their clients and confessors. Goffman also speaks of *"latent secrets"* (144), which are not truly secrets because they involve facts that are available to the public, but facts that, were they gathered systematically and presented in a clear manner to the public, would discredit the presentation and undermine the team's effort to define the situation, an imposed definition whose achievement is the goal of the performance.

Indeed, to "maintain the definition of the situation" appears throughout Goffman's book as a constant motive for performance. A good part of social life is participation either as performer or audience in team performances (carried out by small or large "secret societies") that have this goal of maintaining "the stability of some definition of the situation." Goffman's picture implies that life is a process of negotiated power struggles whose strategies are secret – though they are "open secrets" (because we are all familiar with the secrets of our own teams, hence on one level we all know that society works by manipulating forms of deceptions). Goffman maintains that "often the real secret behind the mystery is that there really is no mystery; the real problem is to prevent the audience from learning this too" (70). This important point is also made by the social psychologist Karl E. Scheibe in his work *Mirrors, Masks and Lies*, who writes:

> One of the most powerful employments of secrets as a means of control involves a concealment of a lack of secrets – the secret of having no secrets. The Wizard of Oz had no secrets, no magic, but while he concealed this lack behind a veil, the citizens of Oz were under his control.[17]

These views provide a strong defense of Simmel's argument for the necessity of secrets, misinformation, and disinformation. In Goffman, the main secret is not that of one's true identity, but that one has no identity other than the protective and intrusive set of performances that is one's battle armor. (Self as onion, not as artichoke.) The self seems to be in an even worse predicament for Scheibe, who compares faces and the masks that are meant to hide them. According to Scheibe, the face itself can become a mask, in that facial expressions are "commonly a form of misrepresentation" (80). Then, taking advantage of the etymology of "person" – which derives from *persona*, meaning "mask" – Scheibe makes two conjectures: "the mask produces the person behind the mask, . . . the trait must first be assumed, then acquired" (78); and, if the mask *is* the person, then, at least in the human realm, "the distinction [between reality and appearance] should be collapsed" (78). Scheibe takes the second conjecture to be the more radical one, but it seems to me that this conjecture is simply an endorsement of behaviorism. The first conjecture, when combined with the claim that the face "is commonly a form of misrepresentation," asserts that personhood itself is "a form of misrepresentation," and that assertion seems more radical than mere behaviorism, and in fact sounds like Goffman at his most radical.

We have already seen that, for Goffman as for Simmel, the need for secrecy and deception is endemic to the very structure of social interaction. In Goffman's case, this is because of the fragility of social reality and of the fictions needed to sustain its development. As with audiences at theatrical performances, a certain "willing suspension of disbelief" is required to ratify the reality of the social fact. Because this cooperative effort is carried out within a framework of conflict[18] – different interests struggle to impose their own "definition of the situation" – individuals and groups take advantage of the implicit structure of deception to create benefits for themselves. (Some actors "misrepresent themselves for private psychological or material gain" [60].) It should be mentioned that, for Goffman, this conflict and struggle is not entirely unpleasant; there is, of course, the pleasure taken in triumph, but also we "all carry within ourselves something of the sweet guilt of conspirators" (105). Moreover, the dialectics of secrecy provide a certain amount of *Schadenfreude*: people enjoy an "aggressive pleasure they can obtain by discovering someone's dark, entrusted, inside, or strategic secrets" (235). These pleasures too must be counted among the motives for action operating in Goffman's system.

In addition to the general *a priori* structural causes just mentioned, there are other specific sources of the veiling of information in social encounters, according to Goffman's theory. First, semiology itself reveals an inherent tendency toward representational slippage. On the first page of his book, Goffman refers to humans as "carriers of information," and then further as "sign-vehicles" (1). The theoretically infinite list of signs that can be deployed include: "insignia of office or rank; clothing; sex, age, and racial characteristics; size and looks; posture; speech patterns; facial expressions; bodily gestures; and the like" (24). It is notoriously the case that "there are few signs that cannot be used to attest to the presence of something that is not really there" (58).

Furthermore, because by their very nature representations necessarily "vary in some degree" from that which they represent, they therefore "inevitably misrepresent it." The individual must resort to and rely upon signs even to represent himself to himself; therefore, "the image he constructs, however faithful to the facts, will be subject to all the disruptions that impressions are subject to" (65). Because all actions take place in a semiotic framework and must be part of a narrative, there will always be a discrepancy between the activity and its presentation – namely, every action will be alienated into the vicissitudes of semiotics. And all of this is in addition to the fact that individual actors intentionally manipulate the system of signs to feign, dissimulate, deceive, lie, and bullshit[19] their way across the social map.

According to Goffman, another cause of misrepresentation is the discrepancy between bodily and social reality. "As human beings we are presumably creatures of variable impulse with moods and energies that change from one moment to the next" (56), but the performances that we are required to give – and indeed the selves that we are required to present – must be coherent, consistent, and constant. Disinformation is required to bridge the gap. Other causes of misinformation are the inconsistencies among the plurality of roles that we must play in everyday life. Goffman quotes William James to make the point: "We do not show ourselves to our children as to our club companions, to our customers as to laborers we employ, to our own masters and employers as to our intimate friends."[20]

These, then, are some of the reasons for performance. But there are so many ways that the performance can break down – so many ways offense can be given.

> First, a performer may accidentally convey incapacity, impropriety, or disrespect by momentarily losing muscular control of himself . . . [trips, burps, farts, etc] . . . Secondly, the performer may act in such a way as to give the impression that he is too much or too little concerned with the interaction [he stutters, appears nervous, forgets lines, etc.] . . . Thirdly, the performer may allow his presentation to suffer from inadequate dramaturgical direction [bad timing, embarrassing lulls, etc.].
>
> (52)[21]

We can conclude our overview of Goffman's theory with his tart observation that "performers have ample capacity and motive to misrepresent the facts; only shame, guilt, or fear prevent them from doing so" (58).

Some readers may be surprised to see that so much of my argument concerning performance is based on the work of Erving Goffman rather than on that of Judith Butler, whose name is now so closely associated with performance theory because of her influential book of 1990, *Gender Trouble: Feminism and the Subversion of Identity*. In the preface to that work, Butler does indeed say that her argument will be based on "a performative theory of gender acts."[22] However, there is in fact very little about performance theory in her book. In the index, under "performance," the sole entry is: "performance, see gender." It is not until the final section of her book that any serious attention is paid to theory of performance (pages 136–41 of a 149-page book), and then, as promised, her discussion covers only gender issues. Earlier she had touched on the discussion of this topic, saying, "There is no gender identity behind the expressions of gender; . . . identity is *performatively* constituted by the very 'expressions' that are said to be its results" (25, emphasis added). She follows up this idea at the end of her book, asserting that the origin of gender is "the tacit collective agreement to *perform*, produce, and sustain discrete polar genders as cultural fictions," entailing "punishments that attend not agreeing to believe in them" (140, emphasis added). In *The Presentation of Self in Everyday Life* Goffman has little to say about gender, and nothing to say about feminism, but he might well agree with Butler's assertion, if only because, according to him, *all* identity – not just gender identity – is performed. This may be the reason that Goffman's name does not appear in Butler's book: his general thesis may appear to swallow up her specific one. If all identity is performed, then the news that gender is performative is perhaps not as dramatic as Butler hoped it would be.

In an article published shortly after *Gender Trouble*, Butler attempts to distinguish her theory from his:

> As opposed to a view such as Erving Goffman's which *posits a self which assumes and exchanges various "roles"* within the complex social

expectations of the "game" of modern life, I am suggesting that this self is not only irretrievably "outside," constituted in social discourse, but that the ascription of interiority is itself a publically regulated and sanctioned form of essence fabrication.[23]

Butler attributes to Goffman the idea that there is a substantive self prior to role-playing that then engages in the "game" of role-playing, while Butler's view is that the self – or at least the gendered self – simply is the totality of its (gendered) performances. But earlier we saw that for Goffman the "self" that exists prior to the performed self is not substantive, nor of any interest to sociology. In fact, his view does not appear to be far from that articulated by Butler in her article – a view that I do not find in *Gender Trouble*. Butler also appears to chide Goffman for depending too much on the idea of interiority; however, in *The Presentation of Self in Everyday Life* Goffman has no substantive discussion of interiority, except to call attention to the actor's awareness of the secrets that he or she is withholding as part of the performance. Simmel might well call these secrets forms of interiority.

Goffman's work, then, supports Simmel's initial thesis that secrecy – the withholding of information from others with whom one interacts at all levels of social structure – can sometimes be socially and individually destructive, but at the same time there is in general a formative role for secrecy to play in the construction of social and individual reality.[24] In the following chapters I will examine how that insight plays out as I look at a number of Victorian novels written from the mid-nineteenth century to the turn of the twentieth. In doing so I hope to supplement John Kucich's 1994 book, *The Power of Lies: Transgression in Victorian Fiction*.[25]

John Kucich: lies as rungs in the ladder of social climbing

Kucich's work on "the power of lies," which critics generally have found to be compelling,[26] presents a theory of major significance, and I hope that the arguments that I develop in future chapters will complement his ideas, ideas that employ a specifically historicized version of Simmelian logic, but with an original twist. His thesis is that in Victorian culture certain groups gained advantage in the internal competition among middle-class factions by blurring the line between honesty (a superior Victorian virtue) and dishonesty (a detestable Victorian vice) and, appropriating the new deceitfulness, made it socially and symbolically productive, and fashioned it in their own interest. To the extent that dishonesty is a form of lying, which entails the disguising of secrets, this thesis is Simmelian in nature. Kucich dedicates only two pages to Simmel's theory, but he does so early in his book and stresses one of Simmel's most pungent and startling ideas, his qualified praise of lying cited earlier: "The ethically negative value of the lie must not blind us to its sociologically ... positive significance" (Kucich 20; Simmel 316). Kucich does not deny the high value accorded to honesty in Victorian culture. In fact, he says, "The Victorian lofty regard for honesty [is] too obvious for comment" (4). Nevertheless, according to Kucich, certain elements in middle-class society were able to appropriate creatively to their own advantage a shadow-obsession with dishonesty. These groups were able to see lying

> as a fundamental form of resistance to social control, as a way to deepen norms of subjective development, as a way to recognize the presence and the force of desire, and – most important for purposes of this study – as a way to rethink the distribution of power across the lines of social or sexual difference.
>
> (15)

There was, says Kucich, a perfectly arbitrary over-investment of lying with libidinal force in Victorian writing, an equation of lying with desire that is out of all proportion to any normative model of psychic functioning. One of the general claims of Kucich's book is that, precisely because of the centrality of honesty in "official" Victorian culture, writers were incapable of thinking about desire apart from dishonesty (31).

According to Kucich, the lie became prestigious among certain groups, and provided a new ladder for social climbing that was appropriated by "professionals, social initiates, aesthetes, and others" (34) to promote upward mobility *within* the various rungs of the middle class. From the title of Kucich's book to its final sentence, it is clear that Kucich's primary concern is not secrecy itself but lying. However, as I stated earlier, even though not every secret entails a lie, every lie entails at least two secrets: the truth that the lie denies must remain secret, and the fact that the liar takes it to be to his benefit that the listener believe the lie must also be veiled. Therefore, Kucich's work falls well within the Simmelian tradition of the sociology of secrecy. Lies do indeed have power, and John Kucich has revealed for us a particularly Victorian instantiation of that power.

Narratology and secrecy

Finally, I return to the question of the role of secrecy in narrative theory. In fact, here too the secret generates sociality and individuality. As historian and narratologist Luise White asserts about secrecy, "continual decisions about whom to tell, how much to tell, and whom not to tell describe social worlds," worlds of "alliance and allegiance," and depict the "shape and weight of interactions therein." When a speaker or a storyteller hides a secret, that individual is assigning a higher worth to the secret than to the information she is willing to circulate. The secret is "so charged that its value and importance is unlike that of other information."[27] Not only is the veiled information charged with value but so is the veil. "A world of social and narratological expectations is revealed in any cover story," that is, in lies, misinformation, non-sequiturs, and silences (White, 19). The decision to withhold information has creative consequences in the world. Therefore, White's account of secrecy too is Simmelian, whether consciously so or not. Again, narrative strategy mirrors social strategy.

Story and narrative are not the same. H. Porter Abbott warns us,

> Story should not be confused with narrative discourse, which is the telling or presenting of a story. A story is bound by the laws of time; it goes in one direction, starting at the beginning, moving through the middle, and arriving at the end. . . . Narrative discourse does not have to follow this order.[28]

Yet, it seems that our only access to story is through narrative.[29] In this case, the medium really is the message, and the messenger is in charge: as Humpty Dumpty says to Alice, "The question is, which is to be master." This is worrisome, because we now know that Humpty Dumpty was not the only "unreliable narrator" (a term apparently coined by Wayne Booth),[30] nor even the first of a long line of them, both inside fiction and beyond. Not only do narrators have biases (biases sought out by symptomatic readings), but they also may have malevolent intentions. As Abbott says, "narrative can be used to deliver false information; it can also be used to keep us in darkness and even encourage us to do things we should not do" (12). When we hear or read a narrative, we seek – consciously or unconsciously – a "sensibility behind the narrative that accounts for how it is constructed, a sensibility on which to base [our] interpretations" (Abbott, 84). As I mentioned in the introduction, this sensibility is called by some narrative theorists the *implied author*[31] (or sometimes the *inferred author*), a term designating "that combination of feeling, intelligence, knowledge, and opinion" that accounts for the narrative (Abbott, 84–85) – that is, a sensibility that is consistent with all of the features of the narrative that we can grasp. We also try to reveal whatever secrets the "implied author" withholds from us. Following Booth and Abbott, when I refer to a reading as "intentional" rather than "symptomatic," I refer to the intentions of the implied author rather than the real author. In fact, the real author often puts much of his or her own "feeling, intelligence, knowledge, and opinion" into the voice of the implied author, but, as John Maynard insists, we readers ourselves often deserve at least as much credit as the author for this creation – which we mistake, perhaps, for a discovery. In this case, the secrets that we believe the implied author is withholding are at least as much our own creation as they are the author's, implied or real. Symptomatic readings often discard the intentions of the implied author while searching for symptoms of the real author, or such readings attribute the symptoms of the implied author to the real author (e.g., when the symptoms and secrets of Lucy Snowe are attributed to Charlotte Brontë).

Narrative secrets can involve either what theorists call "kernels" or "satellites."[32] Kernels are a story's main events, linked in a causal sequence that heads toward a closing, the resolution of an enigma, or an uncertainty. Satellites elaborate the outline of a sequence "by maintaining, retarding, or prolonging the kernel events they accompany or surround" (Cohen and Shires, 55). One narrative strategy is to suppress a kernel event or personage. This creates a substantive secret in the narrative, what Hitchcock would call a MacGuffin. The "maintaining, retarding, or prolonging" of kernel events gives the narrator control over the story, and can create an air of mystery or secrecy, delaying the story's resolution. Pausing, decelerating, or accelerating the narration allows the storyteller to prioritize narrative power over story power, according to Cohen and Shires.

In his *Narrative and Its Discontents: Problems of Closure in the Traditional Novel*, D.A. Miller holds that "the normal" itself is "nonnarratable"; a story can exist only when there is some kind of disruption of the quiescence of the *status quo ante*, involving "instances of disequilibrium, suspense, and general insufficiency."[33] Miller does not discuss this disruption in terms of secrecy; however, the key idea of suspense, which is a consequence of the rupture of the normal, entails something unknown, withheld, and I would say, something secret. The subtitle of Miller's book, "*Problems of Closure in the Traditional Novel*," refers to his theory that closure is never completely successful; the hidden instabilities remain "as undercurrents," and "threaten the very possibility of the definitive, 'finalizing' state of affairs" (x). "The narratable" – and with it, the narrative – "inherently lacks finality" (xi). However, the disruption that narrative detests and hopes to expunge is precisely "what it cannot do without" (8). The normal – "socially given reality" – discovers that it needs narratability for its sustenance, needs a secret, a secret to be "revealed" and "expelled," but really to be "incorporated." At the end of a story transparence is implied ("They lived happily ever after"), but the social cannot do without something hidden. "Closure is fraught with self-betraying contradictions" (281). Simmel or Goffman could have written these lines.

In this study, my general thesis will be that in both social worlds and narrated worlds, secrets are required; in both the social reality and in fiction secrecy necessarily has roles to play, sometimes creative, sometimes destructive. The moral dream of total transparency will prove to be a fantasy. In addition, I hope to demonstrate that there are not only peculiarly "Victorian secrets" but that there is a particular narratological fashion of controlling those secrets that we can identify as "Victorian."

Conclusion

I am well aware that not all social scientists would accord Simmel, Goffman, social psychologist Karl Scheibe, sociologist J.A. Barnes, and anthropologist Robert F. Murphy the dominant status I have granted them in my study, and many would not accept as the most appropriate schema for examining human behavior the conflict model of society that I attribute to them. Nor do I know that the dramaturgical model of human interaction is the best one to use for the study of social relations. I do claim, however, that if we assume the stance of these students of society and view the "narrative worlds" (Abbott's term) created by the authors of the novels I have chosen from a sociological perspective we will see these Victorian worlds with new insight. For example, in chapter 2 of this book, as we watch the young, orphaned, friendless Lucy Snowe step off the boat onto the foreign soil of Labassecour – where neither language spoken there is familiar to her, where she is considered a heretic, and where she must find employment despite her lack of good education and skills – it is easy to think of the world she enters as a Goffmanian one in which the maintenance of Simmelian secrecy will be almost her sole defense against those who try to shame her. And all the while that she tries to protect her own inner psychological sanctum against assault by others, she must try to penetrate theirs, both for her own safety and, it must be said, for her quest for power and pleasure. I make similar claims in the cases of the social worlds created in the other novels to be examined here – the "howling wilderness" of Thackeray's London in *Vanity Fair*, the sinister countryside of Braddon's *Lady Audley's Secret*, the Victorianized fifteenth-century Granada of Bulwer-Lytton's *Leila*, and "the great wilderness" of Conan Doyle's London ("London, that great cesspool"). As to the question of whether these fictitious worlds correctly mirror real social worlds, I will take the Goffmanian dodge and say, "What reality really is can be left to other students" (66).

Notes

1 Erving Goffman, *The Presentation of Self in Everyday Life* (New York and London: Anchor Books Doubleday, 1959), 26, 39, 42. Future references to this work will be cited parenthetically in the body of the text.
2 This title is Kantian rather than Humean because, while Hume asks such questions as "Is X possible?" (where X is, say, knowledge, truth, or society), Kant avoids Hume's skepticism by assuming that because X is actual (knowledge, truth, and society do exist), therefore X is logically possible. Kant's investigation then becomes the question of what preconditions are necessary for X to be logically possible. In a Kantian fashion, Simmel concludes that the preconditions for any possible society include both a certain amount of knowledge about the other on the part of each individual member, *and* a certain amount of knowledge withheld from the other by each individual.
3 Georg Simmel, *The Sociology of Georg Simmel*, trans. and ed. Kurt H. Wolff (New York: Free Press, 1964), 307, 309. All future references to Simmel will be to this work unless otherwise indicated. The page numbers of *The Sociology of Georg Simmel* will be cited parenthetically in the body of the text.
4 Robert Trivers, *The Folly of Fools: The Logic of Deceit and Self-Deception in Human Life* (New York: Basic Books, 2011), 329. Future references to this work will be cited parenthetically in the body of the text.
5 Georg Simmel, "Group Expansion and the Development of Individuality" [1908], in *On Individuality and Social Forms: Selected Writings*, ed. Donald N. Levine, trans. Richard P. Abares (Chicago and London: University of Chicago Press, 1972), 249–93, 292.
6 Recently, journalist David Gramm has expressed this Simmelian thought eloquently, writing: "every secret is embedded with the possibility of betrayal" ("A Murder Foretold: Unraveling the Ultimate Political Conspiracy," *New Yorker* [April 4, 2011]: 42–61, 56). Gramm is also the author of *The Devil and Sherlock Holmes: Tales of Murder, Madness, and Obsession* (New York: Vintage, 2011).
7 Erving Goffman quotes this phrase in full the long passage in which this phrase appears (*Interaction Ritual: Essays on Face-to-Face Behavior* [New York: Pantheon Books, 1967], 65–66). Future references to this work will be cited parenthetically in the body of the text as *Ritual*.
8 Goffman quotes this passage from Simmel as well (*Interaction Ritual*, 16).
9 Though this is the only theoretical formula that Simmel offers in his theory of secrecy, there are a number of examples in his writings of the historicity and cultural relativity of secrecy. For instance, Simmel says that in the nineteenth century, "what is public becomes ever more public, and what is private becomes ever more private" in contrast with the eighteenth century (337). This passage is quoted by Karen Chase and Michael

Levinson in *The Spectacle of Intimacy: A Public Life for the Victorian Family* (Princeton: Princeton University Press, 2000), 7.

10 This is not to say that there has been no criticism of it. In 1950, Kurt Wolff, editor and translator of *The Sociology of Georg Simmel*, summarized the critical literature that had appeared since Simmel's death in 1918. Alexandrovitch Sorokin's critique appears to be the most damaging, claiming that

> Simmel's sociological method lacks scientific method. . . . [It] entirely lacks either experimental approach, quantitative investigation, or any systematic factual study of the discussed phenomena. . . . [It involves] pure speculation, metaphysics, and a lack of scientific method. (xlvi, note 32)

Though Wolff defends Simmel against this charge, Wolff's own criticism of Simmel's work has to do essentially with what he takes to be Simmel's confused and contradictory conception of sociology as a science. However, Wolff has only praise for Simmel's discussion of secrecy.

11 Sociologist E.C. Hughes calls Goffman "our Simmel" (quoted by Greg Smith in his introduction to *Goffman and Social Organization: Studies in Sociological Legacy*, ed. Greg Smith [New York and London: Routledge, 1999], 28). Sociologist Philip Manning remarks, "Goffman's projects . . . resemble Simmel's work, as Goffman himself implied in a fugitive remark prefacing *The Presentation of Self in Everyday Life*" ("Ethnographic Coats and Tents," in Smith, *Goffman and Social Organization*, 104–18, 104).

12 In later works Goffman continues using the word "actors" to name the agents whose behavior he describes, but as far as I can tell, he never returns squarely to the "dramaturgical perspective" of *The Presentation of Self in Everyday Life*. But there are continuities. Sociologist P.M. Strong begins an essay on Goffman saying, "Goffman may have changed his terms but he rarely changed his tune" (P.M. Strong, "Minor Courtesies and Macro Structures," in *Erving Goffman: Exploring the Interaction Order*, ed. Paul Drew and Anthony Wootton [Boston: Northeastern University Press, 1988], 228–49, 228). Similarly, Drew and Wootton write, "[T]he emphasis on the moral character of the face-to-face domain persisted throughout [Goffman's] writing" (*Erving Goffman*, 1–13, 7).

13 In *The Presentation of Self in Everyday Life* Goffman quotes passages from a number of well-known novelists, including Franz Kafka, George Orwell, Herman Melville, Daniel Defoe, and Mary McCarthy. Three times in *Asylums* he quotes long passages from Melville's *White Jacket* as evidence for his claims about the conditions of inmates, and he finds numerous occasions to cite Melville again in that volume (*Asylums: Essays on the Social Situation of Mental Patients and Other Inmates* [New York: Anchor Books Doubleday, 1961], 34, 50, 55, 80, 100, 194, 208, 231, 234, 255, 310). In a book published two years after *The Presentation of the Self in Everyday Life*, Goffman quotes another long passage from *White Jacket* to illustrate a sociological point about competing claims for priority in certain kinds of encounters (*Behavior in Public Places: Notes on the Social Organization of Gatherings* [New York and London: Macmillan, 1963], 94–95).

14 William Sansom, *A Contest of Ladies* (London: Hogarth, 1956), 230–32. Apparently Goffman finds that Sansom's fiction complements and exemplifies some of his own sociological theories. Goffman quotes Sansom's *A Contest of Ladies* in his book of 1963, *Behavior in Public Places: Notes on the Social Organization of Gatherings* (New York & London: Macmillan, 1963), 85, along with another of Sansom's novels, *The Face of Innocence* (157–58). He also quotes Sansom's *A Touch of the Sun*, in *Encounters: Two Studies in the Sociology of Interaction* (Indianapolis: Bobbs-Merrill, 1961), 83–152, 135–37. In the same book Goffman quotes Sansom's short story, "The Kiss," in Sansom's collection, *Something Terrible, Something Lovely* (40n37). In Goffman's essay, "Where the Action Is," in a book with the same title, he quotes a whole

page of Sansom's novel, *The Cautious Heart* (*Where the Action Is: Three Essays* [London: Penguin Press, 1969], 190–91).
15. Anthony Giddens, "Goffman as a Systematic Social Theorist," in Drew and Wootton, *Erving Goffman*, 250–79, 260.
16. Jenny Davidson, *Hypocrisy and the Politics of Politeness: Manners and Morals from Locke to Austen* (Cambridge: Cambridge University Press, 2004), 5–6.
17. Karl E. Scheibe, *Mirrors, Masks, Lies and Secrets: The Limits of Human Predictability* (New York: Praeger, 1979), 94. Future references to this work will be cited parenthetically in the body of the text.
18. Sociologist Stanton K. Tefft does not see Goffman as employing a model of social conflict. In Tefft's article "Secrecy, Disclosure and Social Theory," in an anthology edited by Tefft (*Secrecy: A Cross-Cultural Perspective* [New York: Human Sciences Press, 1980]), he criticizes Goffman for stressing team-held secrets but failing to explain why members of a team "may keep secrets from each other as well as from outsiders." If the name "Conflict Theory" designates a sociological school that emerged in the 1970s, as Tefft asserts, obviously Simmel could not be a member. But we could nevertheless call him a conflict theorist (without the capital letters) based on his essay, "Conflict as Sociation," where he argues that "While antagonism by itself does not produce sociation, it is a sociological element almost never absent in it" (Georg Simmel, *Conflict and the Web of Group-Affiliations*, trans. Kurt H. Wolff and Reinhard Bendix [Glencoe, IL: Free Press, 1955], 25).
19. Let us add "bullshit" to our list of deceptive practices. Philosopher Harry Frankfurt published a very small book simply called *On Bullshit* (Princeton: Princeton University Press, 2005) that was received with acclaim. According to Frankfurt, bullshitting is not the same as lying; it is a kind of fakery, more like bluffing or phoniness. The bullshitter "does not care whether the things he says describe reality correctly. He just . . . makes them up to suit his purpose" (56). This idea touches on themes that appear throughout *The Presentation of Self in Everyday Life*.
20. William James, *The Philosophy of William James* (New York: Modern Library/Random House, n.d.), 129. Quoted by Goffman in *The Presentation of Self in Everyday Life*, 48–49.
21. In a discussion about radio announcing, Goffman, perhaps appealing to the Rev. Mr. Spooner – or, in this case to Dr. Freud – later adds one more category of ways that performances can go wrong. He quotes an announcer saying, "Stay tuned now for a dramatization of Dickens's immortal *Sale of Two Titties*. Uh! I mean *Tale of Two Cities*" ("Radio Talk: A Study of the Ways of our Errors," in Erving Goffman, *Forms of Talk* [Philadelphia: University of Pennsylvania Press, 1981], 197–330, 305).
22. Judith Butler, *Gender Trouble: Feminism and the Subversion of Identity* (New York and London: Routledge, 1990), xii.
23. Judith Butler, "Performative Acts and Gender Constitution: An Essay in Phenomenology and Feminist Theory," in *Performing Feminisms: Feminist Critical Theory and Theatre*, ed. Sue Ellen Case (Baltimore: Johns Hopkins University Press, 1990), 270–82, 29, emphasis added.
24. As will the work of the social psychologists, J. A. Barnes and Karl Scheibe, and anthropologist, Robert P. Murphy, to whose theories I will appeal elsewhere in my study.
25. John Kucich, *The Power of Lies: Transgression in Victorian Fiction* (Ithaca and London: Cornell University Press, 1994). Future references to this work will be cited parenthetically in the body of the text.
26. See, for example, Ivan Kreilkamp's review in *Novel: A Forum on Fiction* 29.2 (Winter 1996), as well as Judith Wilt's "Recent Studies in the Nineteenth Century," *Studies in English Literature* (SEL) 35.4, Nineteenth Century (Autumn 1995): 807–86; Margaret Sonser Breen, "Review of *The Power of Lies: Transgression in Victorian Fiction*, by John Kucich," *George Eliot-George Henry Lewes Studies* 30–31 (April 1996): 87–90.

27 Luise White, "Telling More: Lies, Secrets, and History," *History and Theory* 39.4 (December 2000): 11–22, 14–15.
28 H. Porter Abbott, *The Cambridge Introduction to Narrative*, 2nd ed. (Cambridge: Cambridge University Press, 2008), 241 (Glossary). Future references to this work will be cited parenthetically in the body of the text.
29 "[T]he events making up a story are only available to us through a telling" (Steven Cohen and Linda M. Shires, *Telling Stories: A Theoretical Analysis of Narrative Fiction* [New York and London: Routledge, 1988]), 1. Future references to this work will be cited parenthetically in the body of the text.
30 Wayne Booth, *The Rhetoric of Fiction* (Chicago: University of Chicago Press, 1983).
31 Wayne Booth and H. Porter Abbott, for example.
32 This is the term of Steven Cohen and Linda Shires; H. Porter Abbott calls them "constituent events" and "supplementary events."
33 D.A. Miller, *Narrative and Its Discontents: Problems of Closure in the Traditional Novel* (Princeton: Princeton University Press, 1989), ix. Future references to this work will be cited parenthetically in the body of the text.

2 Lost in Labassecour

Villette and the privatization of secrecy

> The self is most itself at the moment when its defining inwardness is most secret.
> —D.A. Miller, "Secret Subjects, Open Secrets"

"*Who are* you, Miss Snowe?"[1] When Ginevra Fanshawe, a frustrated, angry, annoyingly superficial acquaintance of Lucy Snowe blurts out this impolite question to the heroine and narrator of Charlotte Brontë's *Villette*, she unknowingly and uncharacteristically asks the deepest question in the novel. By the end of the story, she still does not know the answer to her question, nor do we readers know it 150 years after Brontë chose to leave this secret concealed.[2] I will argue in this chapter that the primary secret of Charlotte Brontë's last novel is the identity of the hidden self of the odd Miss Snowe. Narratologically, this secret is the novel's "kernel," and the whole novel consists of "satellite events" whose job it is to prolong indefinitely the reader's ignorance of this kernel truth. This secret will be discussed in this chapter and shall be considered as the foundational enigma of the story, meaning that all of the other structural secrets of the novel are based on this one or derived from it.

By structural secrets I mean those that are themselves not plot-driving secrets yet are semi-concealed frameworks that are presupposed in the formulation of all such MacGuffins. As such, structural secrets are ever-present but not something whose revelation would bring closure to the narrative. Often, these are versions of what Goffman calls "latent secrets" (144):[3] information that is subliminally available but which has not been gathered and presented publicly in a systematic form. (We shall see in chapter 5, the dread[4] of the Orient will count as a structural secret behind large parts of Victorian discourse; in chapter 6, the cruelties and abuses of British imperialism will count as a structural secret behind many of the Sherlock Holmes stories.) Often the foundational and structural secrets are analytically deeper and more important for the student of culture than the plot-driving concealments that we expect to find in any fictional narrative, deeper than those memories, events, facts, and ideas that are hidden from readers and characters alike, waiting to be revealed in order to bring closure to the tensions, conflicts, and mysteries of the narrative. This is not to say that MacGuffins (Who? What? Where? Why? When?) are of no theoretical interest to scholars. Because of the preponderance of domestic issues in so many Victorian novels, the principal MacGuffins in such fiction often concentrate on the family secrets that are commonly at the heart of the plot: past sexual indiscretion, illegitimate heirs, bigamy, incestuous liaisons, betrayals, hereditary madness, falsified genealogies, criminal behavior in a long-ago past, vicious infighting among family members, illegitimate acquisition of family fortune, new money posturing as old, inglorious or cowardly behavior in imperial wars, disguised poverty, imminent bankruptcy, or hidden class or ethnic origins. There is something recognizably Victorian about these domestic secrets, and many of them will make appearances in this study. However, in Charlotte Brontë's *Villette* none of these shameful categories comes into play, as far as we are allowed to know. Typically, structural secrets will be social or institutional, but in *Villette* they are *personal*, parts of Lucy Snowe's trove of memories – usually painful ones – that are determinants of the plot-driving secrets in Lucy's narrative, but they are secrets she never reveals, and we try to divine them at our own risk.

There is indeed a mysterious domestic secret in *Villette*, one that would count as a major MacGuffin if finally it were revealed and its revelation resolved conflict in the text. But this domestic secret remains concealed throughout the novel, and is clearly seen by Lucy Snowe as being related to the foundational secret of her self-identity, an identity that would be compromised if the secret of her lost domesticity were betrayed, and it is therefore structural in the sense outlined earlier. Virtually everything in Lucy Snowe's narrative is framed by a secret tragedy that, by the time we meet Miss Snowe, now well into old age, long ago decimated her family and left her in her early days as a young woman bereft of roots, purpose, and prospects. Whoever reads for the first time the beginning of the novel must expect that eventually the shocking details of this secret tragedy will be revealed in ways that must resolve mysteries that otherwise puzzle the reader; but it will not be so. Lucy allows her reader at the beginning of her story to guess at these devastating events and their meaning, and she will not disabuse readers of their desire to find some redeeming qualities in her darkened childhood – "the amiable conjecture does no harm and may therefore be safely left uncontradicted" (39) – just as, on the last page of her tale, she allows her readers to imagine a possible happy ending to her sad story: "Trouble no quiet, kind heart; leave sunny imaginations hope. . . . Let them picture union and a happy succeeding life" (546). But in this novel there is never an unveiling of this important mystery nor a serious hint of the usually requisite happy ending that is often the consequence of such an unveiling. Lucy is secretive about both of the tragedies between which her story is sandwiched: a metaphorical shipwreck and a real one. She refuses to reveal any literal information about the first one, expressing only the provocative metaphor about a disaster at sea, and toying with our emotions at the end by leaving open the unlikely happenstance that the second tragedy was averted – "unlikely" but not impossible. If Brontë intentionally ends her narrative ambiguously, the supposition that M. Paul survives must be both logically and materially possible (that is, the story of his survival must not generate logical contradictions with the rest of the text, nor with any natural laws of causality). Jolene Zigarovich has made a laudable effort to defend Paul Emanuel's survival. Her best evidence is biblical. Saint Paul is Monsieur Paul's namesake. Saint Paul also is shipwrecked (Acts 27:18–19, King James Version) but survives: "And so it came to pass that they [the crew] escaped all safe to land" (Acts 27:44). Zigarovich concludes: "no one perishes in biblical shipwrecks, proving the important clue to Brontë's allusion."[5] I find her thought-experiment ingenious and tempting, but, finally, not wholly compelling. Basing our conclusion on the same biblical evidence, would we go so far as to say that Paul Emanuel, like his namesake, would suddenly be dazzled by a vision on his journey and find the true religion (in this case, Protestantism), and be beheaded by the Romans (or Roman Catholics)? Zigarovich quotes Brontë's humorous letter to her publisher concerning M. Paul's fate:

> it was designed that every reader should settle the catastrophe for himself, according to the quality of his disposition, the tender or remorseless impulse of his nature. – Drowning and Matrimony are the fearful alternatives. The merciful [reader] will of course choose the former and milder doom – drown him and put him out of pain. The cruel-hearted will on the contrary pitilessly impale him on the second horn of the dilemma – marrying him without ruth or compunction to that – person – that – that – individual – "Lucy Snowe."[6]

Brontë's whimsical second alternative would require a sequel to *Villette*, depicting a surprise reversal in the very old age of Lucy and Paul, *Geriatric Love: The Return of Paul Emanuel*. Brontë does not consider a third alternative, the one preferred by Zigarovich, that Paul chooses not to return to Lucy: "Lucy has been tragically abandoned" (Zigarovich, 52). In allowing Lucy Snowe's future husband to die at sea, Charlotte Brontë demolishes the dream of domesticity to such a degree that we cannot seriously consider categorizing her novel as domestic fiction – this despite Tony Tanner's assertion, "The world of *Villette* is indeed from one point of view a very domestic one."[7]

When the twenty-two-year-old narrator and protagonist of the novel crosses the English Channel on her way to the city of Villette (a fictional Brussels) in the country of Labassecour (a fictional Belgium), she says, "If I died far away from – home, I was going to say, but I had no home – from England, then, who would weep?" (110). Her woeful reflection is, alas, true. Nowhere in the novel is she represented in a domestic scene among members of her family. Later in the narrative, Lucy is unable to deny Ginevra Fanshawe's cruel challenge: "[Y]ou are nobody's daughter, . . . [Y]ou have no relations" (160). Yet, apparently there once was some semblance of domestic bliss in Lucy's life. At one point, Lucy thinks back on her "hearth of old England," but she quickly cancels the thought: "But no. I knew the fire of that hearth burned before its Lares no more – it went out long ago, and the household gods had been carried elsewhere" (188).

For my own purposes, I will regard *Villette* as a domestic novel *manqué*. It is the story of a missing domesticity on two levels: first, a tale that, from its initial moments, disallows the memory of the original domestic scene that was lost; second, a tale of a failed attempt to reconstitute the lost family and household. It contrasts notably with *Jane Eyre*, in which unsuspected family members (uncles, cousins) do, in fact, turn up out of nowhere to create the protective family Jane lacks for most of the novel.[8] However, in a chapter of *Villette* titled "Auld Lang Syne" there is one mysterious scene in which it first appears that Lucy has magically achieved this recovery. She awakens from a swoon and finds herself in bed in a strange but at the same time uncannily familiar room where she recognizes every item as if from a dream of her childhood. She soon realizes that the small items of domesticity that surround her are indeed ones with which she was familiar as a child in the house of her godmother at Bretton, and that she has awakened in the house in Villette, which unbeknownst to Lucy is the new abode of her now expatriate godmother and godbrother, the physician John Graham Bretton (sometimes called Graham, sometimes Dr. John).[9] It will be he with whom Lucy falls fervently, but altogether secretly, in love. Years before, Lucy had lived among these knick-knacks in the Bretton's house in England after the disappearance of her own family, and therefore the household items that she sees – items that, like Lucy herself, have been uprooted from their native soil – provide a Proustian bridge to the last remnants of her lost state of domesticity. Therefore, this nearly hallucinatory moment could easily be the harbinger of a successful *recherche à la vie de famille perdue*. But, alas, it is not to be so. Graham will marry another, and it will be his new wife, not Lucy, who surrounds herself with these household items. Lucy will fall in love again, but her passion for her strange new lover will be cut short by a disaster far away on the high seas. She will have her own home, thanks to the generosity of her drowned lover's will, but, because of the cruel operations of fate, she will never have a family. Therefore, one of the most important secrets that Lucy Snowe withholds from us – and one closely related to the missing answer to Miss Fanshawe's question – is why domesticity was lost in the first place. The fact that this is never resolved is significant. It will be part of the private store of secrecy that has fashioned her now disguised personhood. Therefore, Lucy will never release this information; she will only provide cryptic hints to her readers.

When the novel opens, Lucy remembers herself at fifteen years of age and away from home staying at her godmother's. She writes:

> In the autumn of the year . . . I was staying at Bretton; my godmother having come in person to claim me of the kinfolk with whom at that time was fixed my permanent residence. I believe she then plainly saw events coming, whose very shadow I scarce guessed; yet of which the faint suspicion sufficed to impart unsettled sadness, and made me glad to change scene and society.
>
> (8)

Who are the "kinfolk" with whom she is staying? It is not obvious that they are her parents; but if not, what has become of her mother and father? As an aside, Lucy later mentions "two uncles, Charles and Wilmot" (53), who frequented London when Lucy was eight years old. But they disappear from the story no sooner than they are mentioned. What became of them? Why can she not appeal to them for help? Lucy knows, but does not tell. What events did Mrs. Bretton see plainly and Lucy only sense? We are never told. The undisclosed story clearly contains facts that, if known, would help us understand the curious person who withholds them from us, but we can only guess at them.

Critic Nicolas Dames seems to believe that Lucy Snowe does not reveal her past to us because she and Charlotte Brontë have self-induced memory problems they share with the rest of the mid-Victorian world. According to Dames,

> The absence of memory from much of Brontë's fiction has been thoroughly noted by various critics; *Villette*, most famously, is often noted as an instance of narrative repression, for we are aware throughout Lucy Snowe's narration of what is being withheld. We do not know anything about Lucy Snowe's childhood or parents.[10]

I think it matters that the last two sentences in this passage appear to contradict one another. Dames adds that both Brontë's fiction and the science of phrenology "can be considered parallel discourses illustrating a general early to mid-Victorian tendency: the elision of memory that contributes to the 'amnesiac self' and the replacement of memory by the legible body."[11] Dames makes an interesting case for his thesis as applied to Victorian fiction in general, but I see no reason to believe that Lucy Snowe has repressed or in any other way forgotten the story she refuses to tell. Indeed, there is good textual evidence that she knows perfectly well the facts that she is loath to reveal. In addition, there is an episode during which, the night before her death, Miss Marchmont pronounces a long discourse upon the value of memory: "I love Memory tonight. . . . I prize her as my best friend" (43–44). Rather than seeing this panegyric upon memory as evidence against his theory, Dames seems to claim that Miss Marchmont's love of Memory kills her. He calls this passage "an object lesson . . . as if the flood of painful recollections she evokes is linked to, if not a cause of, mortality" (114). Finally, I call attention to the fact that the whole of the novel – except for one sentence on page 51 ("I speak of a time gone by: my hair which till a late period withstood the frosts of time, lies now at last, white, under a white cap, like snow beneath snow"), and the last two short paragraphs of the book – comprises the memories of an old woman thinking back upon her youth some fifty years earlier. Some readers might think this key feature of *Villette* would be an embarrassment to Dames's argument, but he disposes of it in one eye-opening sentence: "While the old Lucy Snowe, with white hair underneath her cap, withholds memories, the young Lucy Snowe avoids them by searching out new faces and new ways of seeing faces" (114). The old Lucy does indeed withhold memories (which, again, is not the same as being *amnesiac*), but, thankfully, she does record 500-plus pages of them.

Lucy's compromised narrative continues, containing the passage in which Lucy allows her readers to imagine a story happier than the one she is about to tell:

> On quitting Bretton – little thinking that I was never again to visit it: never more to tread its calm old streets – I betook myself home, having been absent

six months. It will be conjectured that I was of course glad to return to the bosom of my kindred. Well! the amiable conjecture does no harm, and may therefore be safely left uncontradicted.

(39)

This passage is followed by the much-discussed strange, long, nautical metaphor, and a mixed metaphor at that, initially describing herself as a boat, and then as a passenger *on* a boat: "picture me . . . as a bark" and, a few lines later, "Picture me then idle, basking, plump, and happy, stretched on a cushioned deck, warmed with constant sunshine, rocked by breezes indolently soft" (39). This metaphor terminates in a shocking reversal of fortunes that anticipate the shipwreck at the novel's close: "we cast with our own hands the tackling out of the ship; a heavy tempest lay on us; all hope that we should be saved was taken away. In fine, the ship was lost, the crew perished" (39).

This is the calamity that the godmother foresaw, but what is it? To whom does the pronoun "we" refer in the description of the shipwreck? Lucy describes herself at the end of the eight years following her departure from Bretton as "bereaved" (40) and as wearing a "mourning-dress" (41). She does not tell us who has recently died, nor whether this death is related to the "shipwreck." She announces that she lost her relationship to the Bretton household "years ago" because of "impediments raised by others" (40). What were these impediments, and who were "the others"? At what point, and why, do the "kindred" disappear, never to be mentioned again? Did they literally perish, or was there some kind of domestic disaster or scandal that definitively rules out Lucy's continued residence at "home"? If so, what was the disaster or the scandal, and how was Lucy involved in it? And if not this, what explains the oddity of Lucy's character? We as readers would like to know; how will we decide?[12] Do we look for textual hints of some kind of anomaly in her personality?

Recalling that Lucy Snowe is the narrator of her own story, let us look at an especially curious case of *narratological* secrecy in *Villette*, one that is of greater interest than the many kinds of plot-bound secrets that motivate the resolution of the narrative. On a particular afternoon early in the novel, Lucy Snowe, who is now employed as a teacher at Madame Beck's "Pensionnat de Demoiselles" in the city of Villette, finds herself in Madame's private quarters, staring at the young English doctor who is treating an obviously simulated "disease" manufactured by the hypochondriacal little Désirée, daughter of Madame Beck, a Goffmanian delight in her own way. Lucy cannot understand why the doctor is willing to spend so much time at the house for no obvious purpose. (She does not yet know that Dr. John has a secret of his own, viz., that he is smitten with one of the school's inmates, Ginevra Fanshawe, and, much as little Désirée believes she is manipulating Dr. John, he is in turn manipulating Madame Beck, taking advantage of the opportunity to be near Miss Fanshawe.) As is her wont, Lucy studies the physician carefully as he tends the little girl. Lucy suddenly realizes that Dr. John, at whom she is staring, is her long lost godbrother – Graham Bretton – whom she has not seen for ten years (and in whose house she will awaken after her first fainting spell). Yet the action proceeds for eighty-six pages before Lucy reveals this discovery to Dr. John. Moreover, Lucy as narrator reveals this secret to her reader only after the same long delay. Why does Lucy keep this secret both from Dr. John at the moment of recognition, and from her reader for six chapters? The concealment of the information and its belated revelation is "explained" by the narrator when she writes:

> To *say* anything on the subject, to *hint* at my discovery, had not suited my habits of thought. On the contrary, I had preferred to keep the matter to myself. . . . As to spontaneous recognition – though I, perhaps, was still less changed than he – the idea never approached his mind, so why should I suggest it?
>
> (196)

Concerning this episode, Mark Lilly, editor of Tanner's earlier Penguin edition of *Villette*, remarks, "It is not only Madame Beck and M. Paul whose activities have the aura of secrecy. Time and again Lucy's reticence (not merely towards the other characters but towards us, the readers) is tantamount to deception" (Tanner 607n2). This seems correct, but incomplete. Lucy herself gives as her motive a certain secretive "habit of thought," and indeed, she usually (but not always!) is discreet and retiring. However it is also clear that her silence gives her a certain power over Dr. John – and perhaps over her readers. Her decision is motivated by a heady sense of that power, as well as by resentment, spite, and a desire to punish Dr. John. (*I* recognized him, but he did not recognize *me* – "though I, perhaps, was still less changed than he.") As Ali Behdad observes, "Lucy seems to realize with Foucault that 'le silence et le secret abritent le pouvoir.'"[13] On this occasion, and on others, Lucy takes a certain *pleasure* in her secrets, and this is yet another motive for her to guard her secrets. On the first anniversary of her arrival in Villette, Lucy recalls that she had briefly met Dr. John on that first night, a year ago. "Had I ever reminded him of that rencontre, or explained it? I had not, nor ever felt the inclination to do so: it was a pleasant thought, laid by in my own mind, and best kept there" (254).

The sexualization of secrecy

The last in the series of eight types of Victorian secrecy that I catalogued in the introduction to this book was "sexual secrets," though I added it to my list with some trepidation. Is there a deeper secret whose revelation would resolve the mystery of the lost domesticity, perhaps some sexual secret whose disclosure would explain the impossibility of a domestic solution and happy ending to this story: child abuse, incest, seduction, infidelity, rape?[14] One does not need to be a critic in the classical Freudian mold to find this possibility worth considering. Ever since the publication in 1976 of Michel Foucault's *La volonté de savoir* (volume 1 translated into English in 1980 as *The History of Sexuality*), questions about Victorian sexuality seem more urgent, as Foucault's book profoundly reframed much of the scholarly discussion of sex and secrecy in the nineteenth century. Even Foucault's detractors felt obliged to approach these subjects on his terms. As is well known among Victorianists, Foucault rejects what he calls the Repressive Hypothesis,[15] according to which in the nineteenth century "sexuality has been repressed, silenced, and deadened"; rather, according to him, sex experienced "a veritable discursive explosion" (17), commencing at the eighteenth-century *fin-de-siècle*, an interest that is "the opposite of Victorian puritanism" (22). Apparently, according to Foucault, the "explosion" was one of *discourse* about sex, rather than an explosion of sexual activity itself.[16] Some passages in *The History of Sexuality* may seem to suggest that in the Victorian period people talked about sex all the time.[17] However, it becomes clear that part of the "discursive explosion" included not only warnings, mental obsessions, and confessions, but an economy of strategic silences:

> Silence itself – the things one declines to say, or is forbidden to name, . . . [is] an element that functions alongside the things said. . . . There is not one, but many silences, and they are an integral part of the strategies that underlie and permeate discourses.
>
> (27)

Another important twist in Foucault's theory is found in a rather startling idea: "What is peculiar to modern societies, in fact, is not that they consign sex to a shadow existence, but that they dedicated themselves to speaking of it *ad infinitum*, while exploiting it as *the* secret" (35). Then, for Foucault, sex in the nineteenth century is *not* a secret, but much of the incessant discourse about sex derives from its being treated as if it were not only *a* secret but *the* secret of the century.[18]

Foucault's challenging thesis seems to me only barely to escape indictment by Karl Popper's "principle of falsifiability," according to which a proposition is scientifically meaningful only if the empirical conditions of its falsifiability could be recognized – that is, only if there is an answer to the question, "what facts or events established as existing in the world would count as a refutation of the theory?"[19] If Foucault's thesis were simply, "There was a great increase in sexual discourse in the nineteenth century; people were encouraged to talk about sex incessantly, and they did so," then, if submitted to Popper's principle, the thesis would be scientifically meaningful, but probably false. However, as was shown, the thesis is complicated by the claim that sexual discourse comprises not only words and gestures (shameful looks, etc.) but also *strategic silences* that emphasize those words and gestures. This is the feature of Foucault's thesis that might invite Popperian concerns: we do not want the thesis to be reducible to the tautology, "People talked incessantly about sex, except when they didn't."

Foucault offers as evidence for his hypothesis the fact that the pornographic works of the Marquis de Sade at the end of the eighteenth century and the anonymous pornographic Victorian novel *My Secret Life* "use the format of confession as their guide" (23). Otherwise, he has little to say about how this new ubiquitous sexual discourse shows up in fiction. I will now turn to *Villette* with this question in mind. If Foucault's claim is true, it seems to me that there should be some strong evidence supporting it in the fiction of one of Britain's most adept novelists writing during the period in which Foucault fixes his thesis.

It is well known that Lucy Snowe, as narrator and main character of the novel, enters into two romances – unusual in Victorian fiction – both of which fail for very different reasons. In addition, there are several tangential romances with various results: Miss Marchmont's fiancé is killed in an accident on the eve of their marriage, and she spends the rest of her life in mourning; Justine Marie marries Heinrich Mühler; Ginevra Fanshawe marries Col. De Hamal; Paulina Home marries Dr. John. There are flirtations and courtships preceding the marriages, and babies that follow them, but no more than in many other works of fiction since the beginning of the sixteenth century, and no "long-winded, . . . immense verbosity" (33) about sex is evident in the novel.

Is there, then, any *indirect* sexual discourse in *Villette*, figurative language that might invite a sexual reading, or are there "silences . . . functioning alongside things said"? Of course there are. One of the most likely candidates involves several letters to Lucy Snowe from the two men who in succession become the object of Lucy's desire. Lucy describes these letters as life-sustaining food, but at least in one dramatic case, it is easy enough to think that this is not merely food for the soul. At a point halfway through the novel, when Lucy is still in love with Dr. John and is not yet consciously infatuated with Monsieur Paul Emanuel, the latter, with great annoyance, delivers to Lucy a long-promised letter from Dr. John that has just been delivered at the Pensionnat – a letter whose extended delay has thrust Lucy into a state of anguish and despair. Lucy's thoughts as she clutches the letter deserve full attention:

> I experienced a happy feeling – a glad emotion which went warm to my heart, and ran lively through all my veins. For once a hope was realized. I held in my hands a morsel of real solid joy: not a dream, not an image of the brain, not one of those shadowy chances imagination pictures, and on which humanity starves but cannot live; not a mess of that manna I drearily eulogized awhile ago – which, indeed, at first melts on the lips with an unspeakable and preternatural sweetness, but which, in the end, our souls full surely loathe; longing deliriously for natural and earth-grown food, wildly praying heaven's spirits to reclaim their own spirit-dew and essence. . . . It was neither sweet hail nor small coriander seed – neither slight wafer, nor luscious honey, I had lighted on; it was the wild savoury mess of the hunter, nourishing and salubrious meat, forest-fed or desert-reared, fresh, healthful, and life sustaining.
>
> (266)

Lucy's enthusiasm for the "wild, salubrious meat" of the hunter, which outperforms the "mess of manna" provided by Jehovah – a mess that finally "our souls sure fully loathe" – seems to border on impiety. It is as if the desire for sexual love finally overwhelms the desire for the divine, a divinity that heretofore in the novel has been primary. But Brontë does not allow such an abandonment of faith to take place. Lucy writes: "I inwardly thanked God who had vouchsafed [the letter]. Outwardly, I only thanked man, crying 'Thank you, Monsieur!'" (266). An irony – intentional on Brontë's part, I suspect – is that "the man" whom Lucy thanks for "the wild, savoury mess of the hunter" is M. Paul and not Dr. John, the latter being presumably the "hunter" in the metaphor. This may be the beginning of the transfer of erotic desire from an object that does not acknowledge nor deserve that desire to an object that does, a transfer that is necessary for the story to work. Later, when M. Paul leaves for his three-year obligatory work in Guadeloupe – a journey that surely will cost him his life – Lucy finds that *Paul's* letters also "were real food that nourished" (544).

Does the foregoing interpretation – the enjoyment of letters equals the enjoyment of nutrition equals the anticipation of sex – count as evidence for Foucault's thesis, or, to the contrary, could we expect to find equally suggestive passages in earlier authors (e.g., Cervantes, Shakespeare, Marvell), whose work Foucault would place in a different *épistème*? And does the otherwise apparent absence of a "discursive explosion" of sex in *Villette* count as examples of the "silences" that participate in the structuring of that discourse, according to Foucault? It does not appear to me that even the sexual interpretation I have proffered of Lucy's letters supports Foucault's thesis about the "great increase in sexual discourse in the nineteenth century," even if we include the component of "strategic silences" about sex that actually strengthen and organize that discourse.

Or, in Brontë's novel, is the "open secret" that is so important to Foucault's thesis revealed only in the love that dares not speak its name? Certainly one category of secret dealt with in Victorian literature, either by revealing the secret or suppressing it, is the fear of homosexuality. This fear, then and now, can take on various forms: fear on the part of an individual that she or he is homosexual, or that another member of the family is homosexual; fear that one's own homosexuality will be discovered; fear that society's condemnation of homosexuality will consign one to a lifetime of unhappiness; or in more extreme cases, fear of a homosexual conspiracy by others as an active social force that will somehow negatively impact one's own wellbeing.[20] Is any such secret being protected or revealed in *Villette?* Would the discovery that Lucy is a closeted lesbian explain her reticence toward unveiling her secrets? Sharon Marcus, in *Between Women: Friendship, Desire and Marriage in Victorian England*, writes: "Critics often interpret *Villette* as an account of repressed desire, but remarkably few have suggested that the desires its heroine denies include lesbian ones."[21] This observation seems to imply that there is at least a *prima facie* case for such a suspicion. In fact, critic Kathryn Bond Stockton leaves a hint – but only a hint – of lesbian desire on Lucy's part, basing it on a look exchanged between Lucy and her Parisian colleague, Mlle. St. Pierre. Stockton describes that gaze that appears on the surface as exceedingly antagonistic, and she concludes, "The innuendoes here . . . all point to lesbianism."[22] Marcus continues:

> This is, after all, a novel in which the first-person narrator, Lucy Snowe, has passionate responses to several other female characters, takes immense

pleasure in partially dressing as a man and flirting with a woman during the course of the school play, and is haunted by a nun – a figure for lesbian sex since Diderot.

(102)

After careful consideration, however, Marcus concludes,

> The novel's failure to end in marriage has less to do . . . with the heroine's desire for women than with her idiosyncratic rejection of female friendship. Lucy's queerness is distinctly Victorian: it inheres in an anomalous distaste for other women's amity, not in a transgressive preference for women's love.
>
> (102)

One of the main claims of Marcus's book is that there is "[n]o female friendship without marriage in the Victorian novel . . . , no marriage without female friendship" (102). This thesis has a corollary: "the Victorian novel shows the paradigmatic importance of female friendship in courtship narratives" (2). *Villette* follows that rule: no female amity, no marriage. Hence, according to Marcus, there is no suppressed secret lesbianism in *Villette*, though perhaps "the secret" that is there is in fact related to Lucy Snowe's "queerness."[23] But even so, such queerness would not explain Lucy's refusal to reveal past secrets, and would seem to be a secret more easily revealed retrospectively from the vantage point of the twenty-first century than from that of the nineteenth. In this nineteenth-century novel there is little or no evidence for Foucault's claim that, in that period, sex was treated as *the* secret, and talked about "*ad infinitum.*"

Secrets of an Orient expressed

In *Villette*, the nun that haunts the school is described both as masked and veiled. Masking and veiling involve concealment, and therefore secrecy, but veiling, particularly in Victorian culture, connotes Oriental exoticism and eroticism, thereby linking these characteristics with concealment. The veiling of the nun curiously eroticizes her, but doing so works well in this case because, first, the ghost's identity is a secret, and second, the ghost has already been associated with the story of a nun who, in the middle ages, had been buried in the garden of the cloister that would become the Pensionnat de Demoiselles, guilty of some sexual sin.[24]

When the aged Lucy Snowe recalls the first meeting between her sixteen-year-old godbrother Graham Bretton and "little Polly," the six-year-old child who will eventually become Graham's wife, she characterizes Graham as being "more than the Grand Turk" (28) in little Polly's eyes. In using this phrase, Lucy expresses the erotic power Graham already has over the little girl. (The reference to the Ottoman Emperor places this erotic power in an ideational concatenation of despotism, grandeur and exotic splendor, and the context in which old Lucy produces this simile associates these characteristics with her painful and, so far, secret memories.) Lucy follows up this orientalist reference by saying that Polly herself seems to be "a little Odalisque, on a couch, half shaded by the drooping draperies of the window near" (33) – a six-year-old Odalisque: originally a slave to the wives and concubines of a Muslim man, and hence, by extension, a woman of the harem. Miss Lucy Snowe, at the time of writing these stories, knows a secret that will only be revealed to her readers later: namely, that this Grand Turk and this little Odalisque will wed, and will break Lucy's heart. We see that this secret too has been orientalized. Many readers will recall that in chapter 24 of *Jane Eyre* Brontë has Rochester declare that the "Grand Turk's harem" is less appealing to him than "this one little English girl," as he prepares for their marriage. It should be noticed that as Rochester is saying this he is hiding a secret from Jane – the secret that, if Jane does marry him, she will indeed be added to Rochester's small harem. This secret, surely the most damaging one in the novel, is associated with orientalist imagery. All of this is part of a narrative strategy whose result is the orientalizing of secrecy. If we view this process as it develops in *Villette* from the perspective of Simmel's claim about the generative function of secrecy, we see that it participates in the creation both of a certain cultural "globalization" (though a false one) and a certain feature of subjectivity (one that succeeds in making the world and one's own life more interesting, if in this case painfully so). If we regard the process from the perspective of Goffmanian performance theory, we see that as secrecy becomes orientalized it indeed becomes performed. Fifteen-year-old Lucy Snowe is watching a staged performance from which she is at the moment excluded and will in fact be forever excluded. Yet the performance is only in her own mind; it is unlikely that at that moment Polly is consciously playing the Odalisque or that Graham is intentionally playing the Grand Turk. It is also possible that Miss Snowe, as the elderly narrator of our story, is imposing on a scene of fifty years ago an Oriental character that she did not discern during the actual performance. In that case, it is not only secrecy that is being orientalized (surely these memories were kept secret by Lucy for all these years and are only now being revealed) but memory itself.

Did the elderly Miss Snowe more than fifty years later still feel a pang of heartsickness when thinking of Graham Bretton's choice of the little Odalisque over herself? If so, this secret that Lucy still withholds from her readers is disguised in orientalist images. At a moment later in the story, Lucy, observing Polly Home (now called Paulina Mary Home de Bassompierre), says, "we so rarely meet with our double that it seems a miracle when that chance befalls" (308). If Lucy truly sees Polly as her double then it is no stretch to think of Lucy as approvingly imagining herself as a resident in a harem, an Odalisque herself.[25] If so, then we readers may have discovered an orientalized secret about Lucy of which she herself is unaware: that at some level she still imagines herself as the prima donna of Dr. John's harem.

On one occasion we find little Désirée Beck, the thoroughly spoiled daughter of Mme. Beck, home sick in her bed, where she too "lounged like a Turk amidst pillows and bolsters" (107). This passage again hints at a metonymical association between the Orient, the sensuality of the bed, and little girls of the nineteenth century. The "secret" that Désirée does not hide well is that she is only playing sick to get Dr. John's attention. But Madame Beck also has a poorly veiled secret. Not only does she think that the troublesome Désirée is less of a nuisance in bed than out, but she is preparing Dr. John to inhabit her own bed, or so rumor has it ("the whole house – pupils, teachers, servants included – affirmed that she was going to marry him" [111]). Dr. John sees through both plots, and has his own secret plot, which is advanced by Désirée's "illness" and by Madame's matrimonial strategies. By attending to the little Turk, he gains access to this "demi-convent" (108), to be closer to one of its inmates, Ginevra Fanshawe, with whom he is secretly smitten. Ginevra, for her part, at one point turns on Lucy and accuses her of being an Oriental despot. She hisses at Lucy, "Nobody in this world was ever such a Turk to me as you are" (342).

There are myriad references in the novel to *Arabian Nights*, a work that was known to have made a deep impression on Charlotte Brontë.[26] I will not catalogue all of them, but will mention a few that are related to the principal structural and plot-driving secrets of the novel. As was mentioned earlier, after collapsing on the street of Villette, Lucy is brought unconscious to the home of Dr. John and his mother, Mrs. Bretton. Lucy wakes up, believing for a moment she has been brought back to her godmother's home in England. She immediately associates this time-travel with the magic transport of Bebreddin Hassan from *Arabian Nights*, "transported in his sleep from Cairo to Damascus." She asks herself:

> Had a Genius [Genie] stooped his dark wing down the storm to whose stress I had succumbed, and gathering me from the church-steps, and "rising high into the air," as the eastern tale said, had he borne me over land and ocean, and laid me quietly down beside a hearth of Old England? But no; I knew the fire of that hearth burned no more.
>
> (188)

So, the secret past that Lucy refuses to reveal to any character in the book or to her reader, is associated in her own mind with images from *Arabian Nights*. Another significant allusion to the *Nights* in *Villette* is linked to Lucy's secret despair. For weeks she has received no new letter from Dr. John. So each night she sneaks to the hiding place of her old letters to reread them, which she likens to feasting on the "crust from the Barmecide's loaf" (297) – an illusionary loaf of bread fed to a starving man in "The Barber's Tale of his Sixth Brother."[27] On another occasion, still thinking about the five letters sent to her by Dr. John, she speaks of the "few kind words" in the letters, "scattered here and there – not thickly, as the diamonds were scattered in the valley of Sinbad, but sparely" (325). (Sinbad the Sailor discovers the extravagant luxury of the Valley of Diamonds and stuffs his pockets on the second of his seven voyages.) On another occasion, late in the book, when M. Paul's passion for Lucy is becoming more obvious, he inquires into Lucy's "plans of life." She tells him of her dream of one day running her own school. He makes her repeat it several times, but calls it "an Alnashar's dream" (488).[28] According to Mark Lilly's notes to the 1979 Penguin text, there are as many allusions in the novel to *Arabian Nights* as there are to Greek mythology. Although a few of these references seem arbitrary, most of them occur in the context of the pursuit of the principal plot-driving secrets in the novel.

No discussion of orientalism in *Villette* can omit the two-page description of a large painting of Cleopatra at "a certain gallery," full of orientalist allusions. Jill Matus, discussing this episode, writes:

> With the rise of orientalism in the nineteenth century, the figure of Cleopatra lends itself to representation as the acme of exotic Oriental sexuality. Part of the developing nineteenth-century discourse of the Orient was the construction of the sexualized Eastern woman.[29]

But this construction was not merely a masculine project; women too are mimetically participating in it, perhaps with mixed feelings of pleasure and guilt, and even if deriving their inspiration only from a form of voyeurism, much of it, indeed, in art galleries. If Matus is right, as I believe she is, Victorian desire itself is enhanced by orientalism, and where, in the Victorian world, there is desire, there is secrecy. At the art exhibit, M. Paul arrives and finds Lucy staring at the large work. He is outraged, not at the painting, but that Lucy should be looking at it – alone! He rushes her off to see quite a different group of paintings (226). M. Paul himself glances quite frequently at Cleopatra but prohibits Lucy from doing so, even though half the crowd observing her are ladies. When Lucy objects to her exclusion M. Paul explains the women observing the painting are "'des dames,' and it was quite proper for them to contemplate what no 'demoiselle' ought to glance at." Lucy objects, "I assured him plainly that I could not agree with this doctrine" (226).

It turns out that Graham is also at the exhibition. "Dr Bretton, too, gazed on the Cleopatra" (229). He does not ask for Lucy's judgment, but ejaculates: "Pooh! . . . My mother is a better-looking woman. I heard some French fops, yonder, designating her as 'le type du voluptueux'; if so, I can only say, 'le voluptueux' is little to my liking." The revelation of secret Oriental voluptuousness is not for him. "Compare that mulatto with Ginevra!" he says to Lucy (230). Graham escapes the siren-like appeal of Oriental exoticism, aided in his resistance by a mote of racism. Whom does he prefer to Cleopatra? At one moment, Ginevra; at another, his mother. (One might think that the secret here must wait a few years to be revealed by a different physician who took up residence at Berggasse 19 in Vienna.) Lucy's revulsion toward Cleopatra is deeper than Graham's, but apparently her disgust is not anti-orientalist. Later in the novel she contrasts negatively the image of Cleopatra in the painting to the art of Vashti, an aging but fiery actress, who is giving what will be one of her last performances – an orientalist one at that – at the theater in Villette. Lucy writes: "Place now Cleopatra, or any other slug, before her as an obstacle, and see her cut through the pulpy mass as the scimitar of Saladin clove the down cushion" (287). Here, Lucy's literary mind attacks the "acme of exotic Oriental sexuality," but she uses orientalist weapons to do so.[30]

In this novel, the concepts of pleasure, desire, and fantasy, like the concept of secrecy, are often orientalized. Though there are no strict logical connections between these four concepts, they are very often combined in the Victorian period, and certainly in *Villette* (and, as I will show shortly, in *Vanity Fair*). Lucy recalls pleasures, desires, and fantasies that were her secrets in the far distant past, and in writing about them she orientalizes them. She exposes these secrets to us now, but apparently did not reveal them to her contemporaries at the time, many of whom would be dead by the time she finally makes these disclosures.

Similar secrets are divulged years after the fact in Lucy's account of perhaps the most remarkable event in her narrative. Mme. Beck has deciphered Lucy's attempts to keep secret her new liaison with M. Paul, for whom Mme. Beck herself has plans. Mme. Beck feigns recognition of a malady in Lucy that must be treated. She secretly administers a sedative, "a strong opiate" (496) to keep Lucy in her bed at the Pensionnat. Although the opium – a potion already associated with the Orient – does not put Lucy to sleep, it does have a powerful and strange effect: it energizes her. She slips out to the fête, and, through the opium-induced haze, the cheap decorations are transformed into an Oriental delight:

> In a land of enchantment, a garden most gorgeous, a plain sprinkled with colored meteors, a forest with sparks of purple and ruby and golden fire gemming the foliage; a region, not of trees and shadow, but of strangest architectural wealth – of altar and of temple, of pyramid, obelisk, and sphinx, incredible to say, the wonders and the symbols of Egypt teemed throughout the park of Villette.
>
> (500)

Lucy sees Dr. John and his party at the fête, but she pulls her hat brim down to hide her face. The secret is that even in that moment of anguished despair over her love for M. Paul Emanuel, she still harbors feelings for Dr. John. At this point she refers to the space where this sentiment still abides as "the tent of Peri-Banou" (505), a magic tent given to Prince Ahmed by Peri-Banou, a beautiful genie in *Arabian Nights*, as a reward for Ahmed's having rescued her. This tent could be so small as to house a flea, or so large as to encamp an army. Her dreamy enjoyment of these thoughts is suddenly interrupted when she spots "the secret junta," Mme. Beck and the conspirators who are plotting to keep M. Paul and Lucy apart. Among the junta is Mme. Walravens, as "hideous as a Hindoo idol" (509), to whose estate on the island of Guadeloupe they have implored Paul Emanuel to sail on the pretext of putting the untended land back into production. As Lucy writes her narrative, looking back perhaps fifty years to this moment, she knows that Mme. Beck had her own "secret reason" for urging her cousin to comply: "*The thing she could not obtain, she desired not another to win; rather would she destroy it*" (510, emphasis added). This is a rather amazing secret guarded by Mme. Beck. How did Lucy discover it? Was the revelation made at the moment of the fête or did Lucy deduce it years later? In any case, the discovery results in a harsh accusation. Madame Beck, who shortly before had wished to marry her cousin, Paul Emanuel, may now be wishing for his death. We might hope that Miss Snowe means that Mme. Beck wishes to destroy the love M. Paul has for Lucy rather than destroy M. Paul himself, but this less sinister possibility is made unlikely by the passage at the end of this same paragraph. Lucy, speaking of thoughts entertained about M. Paul by Père Silas, Mme. Walravens, and Mme. Beck, writes, "one of the number, perhaps, wished that in the meantime he might die" (510). We see that this shocking element, totally new to the plot, and hence a secret to us readers until this moment, has been veiled in orientalist allusions.

One final reference to orientalism in the novel is interesting in the light of Brontë's religious proclivities. Lucy, still under the influence of her opiate, comments on the effect of a thick snowfall on Villette: "it petrifies a living city, as if by eastern enchantment; it transforms a Villette into a Tadmor" (429). In 2 Chronicles, 7:4, King Solomon builds this great city in the wilderness. Brontë collapses an orientalist image ("eastern enchantment") with a biblical one. This maneuver shows how, in Brontë's mind, the world of the Old Testament is linked metonymically with the Orient. And, of course, the events that are described in the Bible – both Old and New Testament – do take place in the Near East. Yet, certainly Victorian Christians and Jews did not want to "orientalize" the Bible – i.e., did not want to find sexuality, promiscuity, opulence, riches, magic, despotism, indolence, caprice, cruelty, treachery, deceit, and conspiracy as being key biblical themes (not that the biblical stories fail to touch on any of these subjects) – but the unconscious bridges between biblicism and orientalism allowed some slippage by Brontë and other Victorian writers. For them, biblical signifiers did bleed into thoughts about the Orient, achieving a form of capillarity, in which the liquid of the one is sucked into the liquid of the other. It will not do to explain away the scandal of the "orientalist" Old Testament by saying that such an offense is overcome because in Christianity the New Testament redefines the various exoticisms and eroticisms of the Old Testament, especially not in the case of Charlotte Brontë's *Villette*, where the New Testament does not tame the Old. A perusal of Lilly's excellent notes on *Villette* indicates that there are at least twenty-four references to the Old Testament in the novel. It is noteworthy that, according to Tanner's research, there are only five direct references to the New Testament (one each from Luke, John, and Revelation [the reference to Revelation 17:5 concerns the Whore of Babylon], and two from Acts). These biblical references too are often presented in the context of the guarding or the revelation of secrets.[31]

Secrets of the soul, and their hiding places

All of these secrets that Lucy, as narrator, keeps from her readers and, as actor in the story, she keeps from the other characters, are structurally related to the most important of secrets for Lucy Snowe, her hidden soul. The soul, which is spirit and hence supposedly intangible, is nevertheless treated spatially by Brontë's narrator: it is a secret *place*.[32] William A. Cohen shows that this spacialization of the spirit is a tendency of Brontë's from the beginning. He observes that in her first novel, *The Professor*, she creates a "literary depiction of ethereal inner qualities in a language of tangible objects." According to Cohen – but not to me – this practice "collapses dualistic conceptions of mind and body (or body and soul) by making subjective inwardness and bodily innards stand for each other."[33] My view is that, by using spatial language to describe interiority, Brontë does "collapse dualistic conceptions of mind and body," but she does so only metaphorically. She does not thereby become a materialist nor does she solve the mind/body problem with which she is dealing; she merely disguises it.

Indeed, Lucy associates all of her secrets with the places in which she keeps them. She reads secret letters, and has her most private thoughts in secret places along "dark, narrow, silent landing[s]"; she enters a space behind "a worm-eaten door." She keeps secrets in her soul, but also in a "deep, black, cold garret," a space that is metonymically equated with her soul. Lucy exults: "Here none would follow me – none interrupted – not Madame herself" (272). "None" would follow? But immediately after saying this a "nun" *does* follow, a ghostly figure interrupting and violating her private[34] space. Lucy ends her narration in chapter 22 ruminating on the nun: "I was left secretly and sadly to wonder, in my own mind, whether that strange thing was of this world, or of a realm beyond the grave" (280). However, she dramatically alters her tone when she commences the new chapter with a reference to the last sentence of the preceding chapter:

> To wonder sadly, did I say? No: a new influence began to act upon my life, and sadness, for a certain space, was held at bay. Conceive a dell, deep-hollowed in forest secrecy; it lies in dimness and mist: its turf is dank, its herbage pale and humid. [This is the space of secret sadness.][35] A storm or an axe makes a wide gap amongst the oak-trees [Graham Bretton cuts into the secret space]; the breeze sweeps in; the sun looks down; the sad, cold dell, becomes a deep cup of lustre; high summer pours her blue glory and her golden light out of that beauteous sky, which till now the starved hollow never saw.
>
> (281)

Secrecy throughout is in a private space, and again, that space is Lucy Snowe's soul itself. But it is a space that can be violated (for example, by Graham's letters, by the prying of Madame Beck and Monsieur Paul Emanuel, and by the nun's ghost). Surprisingly, in this case and elsewhere, such violation is sometimes welcome.[36]

Perhaps one of the most noteworthy examples of secrets in secret places is offered in the very rich scene of Lucy's swoon, when she drops unconscious onto the rain-soaked portico steps of the church, after running away from her encounter with Père Silas in the confessional. Upon awakening from her faint, she says:

> Where my soul went during that swoon I cannot tell. Whatever she saw, or wherever she traveled in her trance on that strange night, she kept her own secret; never whispering a word to Memory, and baffling Imagination by an indissoluble silence.
>
> (185)

The soul is the deepest secret, and it has its own secrets even from the agent, as well as its own secret places. There is a place that offers absolute privacy – so secret and private that even she, Lucy Snowe, does not have full conscious cognizance of it even in those rare moments when she occupies it. And yet, for Lucy, this secret space is somehow her most real place – the site of her being, where she comes closest to touching God ("show Him the secrets of the spirit" [200]). This secret site is tremendously Cartesian in its conceptualization, being more real and more certain than any other kind of public reality, and being one that ought to be absolutely inaccessible to the other – and, as we just saw in the last example, at its deepest level, it is inaccessible to components of the conscious self. A major source of Lucy's vitriol against Catholicism appears to be her belief that its system of churchly interventions conspires against the cultivation of this secret, private space. At one moment, knowing that M. Paul has been to see his confessor, she complains that he must have been "permitted to withhold nothing; suffered to keep no corner of his heart sacred to God and to himself" (458). We see in this illuminating comment that Miss Snowe's private Simmelian parallel world is more valuable to her than is any other feature of her being, and, by implication, it would be one withheld forever from M. Paul, no matter how deep her love for him nor how long Lucy and Paul Emanuel were to remain together, if she is to remain true to her own metaphysics of selfhood. Indeed, it must be said that Lucy's conviction that selfhood itself must remain secret (i.e., that the answer to the question, Who is Lucy Snowe really? must remain unanswered) far outstrips Simmel's requirement for secrecy as a presupposition of selfhood.

It is clear that the veiling of Lucy's secrets is intentional on Brontë's part. Tim Dolan in his introduction to the Oxford World Classics edition of *Villette* points out that Brontë's editor urged her to add more information about Lucy's past; but instead, in the late revisions of the manuscript, Brontë removed what few details she had originally provided.[37] Sally Shuttleworth, in her influential work, *Charlotte Brontë and Victorian Psychology*, asserts, "The question of Lucy's actual instability must remain unanswered." In view of this clearly purposeful secrecy, it is curious to see that Shuttleworth goes on to say that Lucy Snowe has "no dark secrets to be unearthed" (Shuttleworth 229, 243).

I am suggesting in this chapter that Charlotte Brontë withholds vital information from her readers not merely in order to create an aura of mystery around her fictional character, Lucy Snowe, but that she also intentionally uses a Simmelian-like theory of the role of secrecy in the construction of personal and social identity. True selfhood and sociality do require privacy and secrecy. When Simmel writes that secrecy provides a second world to the individual that is both parallel to the manifest world and an influence on it, he is implying that one's secrets are instrumental in one's agency – one's ability to act and the manner in which one does so. Though Lucy Snowe exaggerates this Simmelian insight, the novel itself is proof that she – and probably Brontë with her – subscribes to this theory of selfhood. In keeping Lucy's secrets from us, Brontë is making Lucy more human rather than less so, and protecting her as if she were a real person, possibly because of the rather autobiographical nature of her story.

Inner outings

The very title of R.A. York's *Strangers and Secrets: Communication in the Nineteenth-Century Novel* informs us that novels – at least Victorian novels – are about "interrupted and distorted communication, about hidden and suppressed facts."[38] York suggests that one reason Victorian readers were willing to put up with the "distortion" in every novel of the period (and why we are still willing to do so) stems from a curiosity about other people, real or fictional. York appeals to Simmel to justify this hypothesis (18). This curiosity may involve "a feeling that the real self of the other person lies precisely in his or her unwillingness to tell us everything" (York 18). Readers may suspect that the reason certain individuals resist revealing their "real self" is that such a self is a shameful one whose scandalous characteristics or histories must be shielded from public view to avoid condemnation, ostracism, exile, imprisonment, or even execution. Certainly in Mary Elizabeth Braddon's *Lady Audley's Secret* this concern will prove to be the title character's motivation in concealing her true self. We see these same kinds of shameful, if not sensational, secrets held by many other important characters in novels of all periods; however, there are motives behind the desire for secrecy about one's true self other than shame. There are individuals – real and fictional – who for philosophical reasons believe that public revelation of the truths of one's selfhood is dangerous in that such disclosure damages or destroys the very identity that one chooses to reveal.

If secrecy is necessary for the establishment of true selfhood, then full transparency is incompatible with true selfhood. Lucy Snowe, and possibly Charlotte Brontë, seems to hold an extreme version of this metaphysical view: the act of self-disclosure dissolves a certain important aspect of the very self that one is attempting to reveal. Therefore, because of the high value attributed to the secret self by these philosophically inclined individuals, extreme wariness must be practiced to protect it. Such a view was not uncommon in the nineteenth century. Albert Pionke refers to certain poets of the period who in fact believed not only in the impossibility of such a revelation but in the *danger* of even attempting to reveal in speech or writing basic secrets about the self, subscribing as they did to "an expressive aesthetics of the pre-linguistic secret."[39] However, Pionke reminds us that other well-known Victorians did not share this aesthetic. He declares that Christina Rossetti's poem, "Winter: My Secret," mocks such a conceit. Rossetti opens the poem with a question and an answer: "I tell my secret? No indeed, Not I." But the poem's second stanza has something different to say about the secret:

> Or, after all, perhaps there is none.
> Suppose there is no secret after all,
> But only just my fun.

Pionke's discussion of Rossetti's poem reveals that the belief that the secret self is the real self may be a *sufficient* condition of the Victorian mind, but not a *necessary* condition (Pionke 4).

Nevertheless, many Victorian readers and writers were fascinated by the idea of the secret self. This conception of selfhood appears in Mary Elizabeth Braddon and in Wilkie Collins, and it certainly appears in *David Copperfield*, as D.A. Miller demonstrates in *The Novel and the Police*.[40] But this conception of selfhood is problematic in various ways. After establishing that this conception is indeed the one to which Lucy Snowe is passionately committed, I hope to show that one of the (surely unintended) consequences of her narrative is the empirical demonstration of the impossibility of this "secret self" to whose defense Brontë's heroine is committed. Miller arrives at a conclusion about secret subjectivity in *David Copperfield* that is similar to the conclusion I reach in *Villette*, except that I argue that Lucy Snowe undermines her metaphysical project with specific empirical actions that falsify her theory of selfhood, while Miller presents what he takes to be an *a priori* proof that David Copperfield's metaphysical project – and all like it – deconstructs itself. In fact, Miller tries to demonstrate that the very idea of thinking or writing about secrecy is self-defeating. I would maintain, however, that Miller's argument is not the *a priori* proof that he thinks it is: he has an easier time showing the logical inconsistency of Mr. Copperfield's discourse than he would of Miss Snowe's because, unlike her, Copperfield cannot resist the temptation to tell his readers the very secrets he claims to be withholding from the world.[41] Brontë solves Dickens's dilemma by entering into the discourse of secrecy without betraying either the idea of secrecy or the secret itself. Miller, perhaps correctly, judges David Copperfield's project to be a failure because in defending his secret he betrays it. Miller generalizes from this case and sees all Victorian characters with "secret selves" as "pathetically reduced beings" (207), and claims that David Copperfield has a "damaged life" (208). Readers of *David Copperfield* who find the characters in the novel to be a source of "great charm" rather than "grotesque" are accused by Miller of seeking guilty pleasures. He writes: "The charm we allow Dickens's characters, I submit, is ultimately no more than the debt of gratitude we pay to their fixity for giving us, in contrast, freedom" (207–8).[42] In addition, Miller judges as "paranoid" David Copperfield's perception that "the social world is a dangerous place to exhibit the inner self," along with "the aggressive precautions that must be taken to protect it from exposure" (203).

Both Simmel and Goffman, however, will find features of the social world that would justify David's concerns, and, although Lucy's dedication to secrecy is overwrought,[43] it is based on an intuition about personal and social reality that anticipates the theories of these sociologists. If, as Catherine Belsey claims, the classic realist text is constructed on the basis of enigma – information initially withheld on condition of a "promise" to the reader that it will finally be revealed, bringing the story to an end[44] – then the story that Lucy Snowe tells must necessarily subvert the principles of realism. Moreover, if, following J.L. Austin, speech-act theory requires that a promise can only be made if the agent intends to fulfill the contract to which her promise commits her,[45] then Lucy Snowe cannot make the promise required by realism. Yet, Lucy's "deception" does not stem from dishonesty. She establishes early on and forever that she is not an Elizabeth Bennett, who, by the end of Austin's narrative, is transparent to the reader, her story having provided to the reader the pleasure of closure.[46]

Contrary to my view, some critics argue that Lucy Snowe does indeed reveal her "secret self," if only elliptically. Adrian Wisnicki, reviewing Joseph Boone's anti-Foucauldian and anti-Millerian defense of Lucy Snowe's successful evasion of the powers of surveillance,[47] asserts that those same evasive strategies allow Lucy to express her feelings via non-traditional venues. Wisnicki appeals to the work of Janice Carlisle, Penny Boumelha, and Robert Polhemus to support his claim. Carlisle views deflection and irony as allowing "Lucy to express feelings that would otherwise remain hidden."[48] Boumelha and Polhemus assert that Lucy reveals herself through acts of displacement: other characters become "doubles and alter egos, projections and fragments of Lucy herself" (Wisnicki 116).[49] Wisnicki and his colleagues do indeed succeed in demonstrating that Lucy reveals much more about herself than would be obvious in a *prima facie* reading of the novel, but she reveals exactly as much as she chooses to, and little more. Wisnicki's thesis is undermined when he admits that Lucy herself encourages misinterpretation (130–31). When Lucy claims that only Polly (Paulina Home) really knows her, Wisnicki seems to approve of Boumelha's revealing remark that "Polly lacks the knowledge Lucy ascribes to her: the concession here appears to be but another of Lucy's ruses" (Boumelha 115). If this is true – as it appears to be – this confirms that the "doubles, alter egos, projections and fragments" can also be pieces in Lucy's game of dissimulation. Nevertheless, Wisnicki concludes, "Lucy shares her feelings and makes herself visible. . . . The moments of disclosure may seem infrequent, but they *are* there and their presence counter-balances those times when Lucy is less forthcoming" (132–33). It is as if Wisnicki has forgotten that he had written only a page earlier,

> The figure of Lucy . . . demonstrates that to be a Vanishing Subject, i.e., a subject that subverts the Inaccessible Authorities, is only to mimic the positioning of the authorities by constructing the self as a site that evokes the projections of others and so returns others to themselves.
> (132)

To occupy such a refractory site is hardly the same as revealing one's secret self.

Lucy Snowe: a material girl?

I am certainly not the first critic to emphasize the metaphysics of spiritual interiority in *Villette*. Charlotte Brontë has long been considered one of the nineteenth century's foremost psychologists of inner spiritual being. Accordingly, she is viewed as a staunch defender of the need for privacy in the personal worlds in which she places her protagonists. Such a view of Brontë's metaphysics was attacked forcefully by Sally Shuttleworth in her influential work *Charlotte Brontë and Victorian Psychology*, where Shuttleworth attributes to Brontë a materialistic psychology derived from Brontë's interest in new advancements in the psychology and physiology of her day, and especially from her commitment to phrenology. Shuttleworth's claim, if true, would undermine my thesis concerning the role of secrecy in Brontë's conception of selfhood, because the goal of phrenology is to make public all that was private. Elsewhere I have challenged Shuttleworth's attribution of a materialist metaphysics to Brontë;[50] here, I will simply set forth my two most basic objections to Shuttleworth's argument. Before doing so, I will summarize what I take to be the main points of Shuttleworth's argument. Then, having opposed Shuttleworth's provocative view, according to which Brontë is depicted as having arrived at a materialistic conception of the self, I will argue that Brontë is clearly a dualist, and that her dualism is both as intentional and as radical as René Descartes's in the seventeenth century. In fact her version of dualism is very similar to his, not only in content but functionality – each having as their goal the defense of inner selfhood against its occupation and erasure by the new sciences of their times. Because Brontë's novel anticipates the sociological theories of Simmel and Goffman her view is not as antiquated as Descartes's in all respects, though dualism is currently out of favor today.

Shuttleworth does not deny that Brontë, like so many other Victorian writers, believed in a "concealed realm of interiority" (29) – indeed, Shuttleworth calls *Villette* Brontë's "seemingly most inward text" (219) – but Shuttleworth sees Brontë as probing this concealed realm through physiognomical and, more importantly, phrenological examinations. Shuttleworth ultimately seems to acknowledge that, if such inquiries succeeded, they would eliminate the secret spirituality that Brontë wished to defend. Shuttleworth writes at the end of her study that, as a result of these investigations, the "fictional status" of "inner mental life" is revealed (241). (I will argue later that, ironically, Brontë manages to eliminate such spirituality all by herself, without any help from the new pseudo-sciences.) According to Shuttleworth, "Brontë offers, in *Villette*, a thorough materialization of the self" (240), and she claims that those critics are wrong who have "hailed Brontë as the high priestess of the truth of the soul, . . . revealing the inner mysteries of a secret, interior realm of essential selfhood" (244). This claim signifies a major misstep in Shuttleworth's otherwise indispensable study of Charlotte Brontë. I am sympathetic to scholarly critiques of Brontë's work from a materialistic perspective, but Brontë herself never abandoned her dualism. On the other hand, Brontë does unintentionally slip toward behaviorism – a form of materialism – by making the novel's progress depend upon the astonishing detective skills of the three main characters who inhabit Rue Fossette, skills that would be equally at home at 221B Baker Street later in the century.

My first thesis against Shuttleworth's position is that, contrary to her insistence that Brontë's infatuation with phrenology directed her into a form of materialism, I claim that there is very little in *Villette* that testifies to the author's supposed celebration of phrenology. Although there are occasional phrenological references in the novel,[51] they are not named as such. The word "phrenology" does not appear in the text, yet the word "physiognomy" shows up on a number of occasions.[52] Given Shuttleworth's insistence on the profound influence of phrenology on the author of *Villette*, and her claim that Brontë understood the distinction between phrenology and physiognomy, choosing the former over the latter, it is startling to discover how many references there are to physiognomy in *Villette* (some of which are clearly jokes) and that there are no references by name to phrenology. Of the few cases where there are allusions to phrenology, none appears at an important moment of character judgment, and some seem to me also to be jokes on Lucy Snowe's part. It is especially surprising to notice that, early in the novel, when Madame Beck calls Monsieur Paul into her office to participate in her interview with Lucy, she does not ask for a *phrenological* study of Lucy's head but says: "We know of your skill in *physiognomy*; use it now" (73, emphasis added). Shuttleworth refers to this episode, saying:

> While physiognomy merely recast in verbal terms the unambiguous statement imprinted in the features, phrenology delved below the surface, examining the secrets of a psyche which was no longer figured as one uniform essence, but rather a contradictory, fragmented system. A phrenological reading would explore not only present attainment, but also potentiality (hence M. Paul's rather enigmatic decipherment of Lucy's character in *Villette*), and would offer an emphatic judgment on the position each individual should hold within the social hierarchy. Reading the inner self had become an overtly political act.
>
> (69)

But M. Paul's judgment is much more enigmatic than emphatic, and seems hardly political. And, if Brontë thought much more highly of phrenology than of physiognomy, why is M. Paul made out by Mme. Beck to be an expert in physiognomy and not phrenology? (It is a compliment he does not reject.) If M. Paul exemplifies phrenology's ability to "offer an emphatic judgment" on an individual's theory of latent potentiality, why is his prognosis so vacuous?

Lucy describes her interrogation by Monsieur Paul:

> The little man fixed on me with his spectacles. A resolute compression of the lips, and gathering of the brow, seemed to say that he meant to see through me, and that a veil would be no veil for him.
> "I read it," he pronounced.
> "Et qu'en dites vous?"
> "Mais – bien des choses," was the oracular answer.
> "Bad or good?"
> "Of each kind, without doubt," pursued the diviner.
> . . . .
> Still he scrutinized. The judgment, when it came at last, was as indefinite as what had gone before it.
> "Engage her. If good predominates in that nature, the action will bring its own reward; if evil – eh bien!"
>
> (73–74)

If we had not already been convinced of the importance of phrenology (or "phrenology/physiognomy") in Brontë's work, we might think Lucy Snowe is mocking the new sciences here. Certainly, Lucy's humorous report of M. Paul's words indicates that we are meant to question his honesty later when he claims that during his inspection of Lucy he had seen in Lucy's skull her talent for acting.[53] However, Shuttleworth apparently finds nothing but phrenological seriousness here. She interprets M. Paul's words after the interview to mean: "if Lucy is to succeed, it must be by a process of *self*-control, subduing her 'evil' propensities, and encouraging the good" (223, emphasis original).[54]

There are more than 175 occasions when Lucy or other characters in the novel observe individuals while assessing their character, and on five of these occasions physiognomy is mentioned by name. Only two occasions are unquestioningly motivated by an interest in phrenology: one speaking of "the sympathetic faculty" (212), and the other of "the organs of reverence and reserve" (391).[55] The other 168 examples make no obvious reference either to phrenology or physiognomy. Yet in almost all these cases, someone's character is being judged. I believe it is fair to say that the skills and techniques that Lucy Snowe deploys to make these judgments are the same ones that Charlotte Brontë deployed as well, and that possession of these tools constitutes a large part of Brontë's success as a writer. We still find more insight in her writings than in all the writings of the phrenologists and physiognomists combined, and to attribute her insights to them is to give credit where credit is not due.[56]

My second objection to Shuttleworth's position stems from her failure to justify with textual evidence her claim that Charlotte Brontë had embraced a metaphysics of monistic materialism by the time she wrote *Villette*. Virtually all of the textual evidence points rather to a radical form of dualism defended by Charlotte Brontë, or at least by Lucy Snowe. For Shuttleworth, the theory of phrenology that had so deeply influenced Brontë had a common denominator with the views of Victorian psychiatrists. Their new theories of madness had led to certain dramatic conclusions: "No longer was the mind viewed as an immaterial or spiritual essence, but was placed firmly within workings of the body" (42). She concludes, "Cartesian man ceased to exist. In his place theorists suggested a model of the individual grounded entirely in physiology" (51). In *Villette*, Brontë does indeed forcefully defend the model of the interiorized self, as Shuttleworth argues – and as hardly anyone would deny – but, *pace* Shuttleworth, Brontë strongly repudiates the self's materiality. If "Cartesian man" was now dead, Brontë had not heard of his demise.

Indeed, "Cartesian" is a singularly appropriate term for describing Brontë's view of the mind. According to both Descartes and Brontë, the true self is a spirit accessible to no one, and certainly to no doctor. The radical dualism that got Descartes into so much trouble was originally conceived by him to protect the mind (or soul, or self)[57] against the intrusions of science – the very science to which Descartes himself was a major contributor. According to Descartes, no one has access to my mind except me. My mind is a secret, private, spiritual place, and no quantitative analysis of it can ever succeed.[58] This is strikingly similar to the view that Brontë defends, and it explains one aspect of Lucy Snowe's resistance to Dr. John's attempts to penetrate her inner self (though, it must be said, it does not explain Lucy's apparent disappointment when he fails in his attempt). The difference between the ontological stance taken by Descartes and the one Brontë writes into Lucy Snowe's character is that in the former the division between body and mind (or "soul," as we have seen Descartes sometimes call it) is absolute and unbridgeable, while in the slightly paranoid vision that Brontë bestows on Lucy, the protection of the soul from the intrusion of attempts by others to penetrate its deepest recesses requires constant vigilance and stealth.[59] There is also a problem with Lucy's consistency: she sometimes seems to invite the very kind of intrusion against which she normally struggles, nor does she always respect the secret space of others. However, if the physiological account of the mind were correct, then the first person to understand the mind would be the scientist – whether the scientist be Dr. John Graham Bretton, Dr. Franz Joseph Gall (the founder of phrenology), or Dr. Sigmund Freud – and the last person, if at all, would be the individual herself. This is certainly not Lucy Snowe's opinion of the case, nor was it Descartes's, and it almost surely was not Charlotte Brontë's.

Rather than accepting Shuttleworth's innovative view that Brontë's goal is to promulgate a materialistic model of the self, it appears to me that the older view of her conception of the self is the correct one, and that Brontë's understanding of her mission would better be described as one similar to Descartes's – namely, that of waging a rear-guard action to preserve spiritual interiority from an onslaught by modernity. Earlier we saw Lucy's poetic account of the divorce between her soul and her body at the time of her fainting spell. Indeed, when we look at the remainder of Lucy's commentary about that event, I believe we see something quite different from the posture Shuttleworth attributes to Brontë:

> She [my soul] may have gone upward, and come in sight of her eternal home, hoping for leave to rest now, and deeming that her painful union with matter was at last dissolved. While she so deemed, an angel may have warned her away from heaven's threshold, and, guiding her weeping down, have bound her, once more, all shuddering and unwilling, to that poor frame, cold and wasted, of whose companionship she was grown more than weary.
>
> (185)[60]

Shuttleworth writes that Brontë "decisively . . . imbibed the notion that physiological, psychological and social pathology are all interconnected" (48). If she did, this passage proves that she did not pass that notion on to her creation, Lucy Snowe. What we have in the foregoing poetic exaltation is a distinct form of dualism that prioritizes the spiritual component of the duality (as in Plato). It is the exact opposite of any physicalism. Indeed, the passage we have just read continues in a virtual paraphrase of Plato: "she [my soul] re-entered her prison with pain, . . . The divorced mates, Spirit and Substance, were hard to re-unite" (185). Unless Shuttleworth is able to demonstrate that this passage does not express Brontë's own philosophy, or that it does not say what it seems to say – that is, that it does not entail a radical form of dualism that prioritizes the spiritual over the material –

this passage alone is enough to refute Shuttleworth's attribution of materialism to Charlotte Brontë; yet Lucy's amazing declaration about her soul's "painful union" with her body gets no mention in Shuttleworth's discussion of *Villette*.

Lucy conceptualizes the true self as a secret inner spirituality that is the wellspring of all the individual's action, and which, if known, would explain the individual in totality. Lucy associates it, or perhaps equates it, with the soul. It seems that, with the exception of Shuttleworth and Nicholas Dames,[61] critics have largely been in agreement in attributing to *Villette* one version or another of this Cartesian thesis involving a deep, hidden, secret self. However, many critics also seem to be in agreement concerning the *illusory* status of this supposed deep interiority. Its delusionary state has been most recently discussed by Eva Badowska, who says, "Brontë – like her protagonist, Lucy Snowe – jealously guarded an imaginary space of privacy" (1510). For Badowska, this space is imaginary because it is an ideological site that fashions itself as a refuge from the "things" of the world of commodities produced by capital; but for that very reason, this imaginary space is itself the product of precisely the things from which it claims to offer asylum. Obviously, Brontë would reject Badowska's deflationary analysis of the putative inner sanctum that Brontë takes to be very real and of utmost importance, and would instead approve of Simmel's view that secrecy can provide for the individual "the possibility of a second world alongside the manifest world." And when Simmel adds that the first world "is decisively influenced" by the second world (330), he is making the point that Erving Goffman would later expound: namely, that the subjectivity created by secrecy is not an illusory one.

Sleeping with the enemy

I have argued that in *Villette* we see a model of the self whose major component is a secret spiritual element roughly equivalent to the soul. But now in the final portion of my discussion the worm turns, as I am forced to conclude that, despite Lucy's major investment in the idea of a Cartesian-like dualism, and despite the efforts of some of her latter-day supporters to defend her view of interiority,[62] it must after all be admitted that Lucy shows tendencies to aid the enemy camp. Primarily, she undermines her own metaphysical argument concerning the inaccessibility of the private self by exercising her exquisite skills as a detective of the soul.[63] Moreover, Brontë has bestowed similar powers of surveillance, observation, and penetration upon the other two most important characters in her narrative, Mme. Modeste Beck and M. Paul Emanuel, to such an extent that no secret at all is safe from them. As Joseph Boone writes, "if ever there were a novel filled with spying eyes, knowing gazes, and significant glances, it is *Villette*" (21–22). One of the most startling examples of such a penetrating gaze in the novel occurs as M. Paul sits in class as his students are writing and examines one of the assistant teachers, Mademoiselle Zélie St Pierre:

> He would sit and watch her perseveringly for minutes altogether. I have seen him give her a quarter of an hour's gaze, while the class was silently

composing, and he sat throned on his estrade, ... [I]n some cases, he had the terrible unerring penetration of instinct, and pierced in its hiding-place the last lurking thought of the heart, and discerned under florid veilings the bare, barren places of the spirit: yes, and its perverted tendencies, and its hidden false curves – all that men and women would not have known – the twisted spine, the mal-formed limb that was born with them, and far worse, the stain and disfigurement they have perhaps brought on themselves. ... He could ... show them all naked, all false – poor living lies – the spawn of that horrid Truth which cannot be looked on unveiled.

(373–74)

This is perhaps the clearest example in the book of the sociological assumption that everything is on view to the trained eye. No private spirituality here, no clandestine sensations nor secrets are possible under M. Paul's gaze. What happens here to the inner/outer distinction? Is this ability to see into the naked soul of young women the quality that causes Lucy to fall in love with this somewhat questionable character? Moreover, the soul that is seen here is scarcely akin to the soul alluded to earlier by Lucy Snowe, one that aspires to higher things and longs to unite with God. We are never told how Lucy, who is watching M. Paul watch Zélie, knows what M. Paul's gaze discerns, but if Lucy's description is correct, the soul of Mlle. St Pierre is more a tortured body than an anguished spirit, and it is prone to all of the disfigurement risked by material things.[64] In the final analysis, it is also anything but private. In fact, Lucy is often angered by many of M. Paul's Jesuitic manipulations, but she does not seem outraged by his penetration into Zélie's private places. Indeed, Lucy's attitude toward her own highly valued privacy is surprisingly uneven. She seems veritably giddy when she discovers that Mme. Beck has purloined the letters written to her by Dr. John. On another occasion, Lucy arrives quietly in the dormitory and sees Madame bent over Lucy's desk, and for the second time catches Madame sneaking through her belongings. Lucy reports: "it was with a secret glee that I watched her. Had I been a gentleman, I believe madame would have found favour in my eyes" (131). Later, when she discovers M. Paul also rifling through her possessions, and realizes that he too has removed her precious letters in order to examine them, she makes no move against him. She says about her feelings as she watches him sift through her things: "My heart smote me. ... I did not dislike Professor Emanuel" (381–82). Lucy *enjoys* the violation of her private space by her rival, Mme. Beck, and by her future lover, and sexualizes both of them.

The case of Mlle. Zélie St Pierre is only the most dramatic of scores of such examples on the part of M. Paul Emanuel, Mme. Beck, and Lucy Snowe herself. Cataloging the many other instances of the penetrating gaze in *Villette* is beyond the scope of this discussion, but I trust that readers of the novel will recognize this tendency throughout, a tendency that is so overwhelming as to undermine Lucy Snowe's own metaphysics that imply the absolute necessity of privacy and secrecy for anyone desiring a fully human life. Madame Modeste Maria Beck, the owner and director of the Pensionnat de Demoiselles at Rue Fossette, is of course presented as the case *par excellence* of a spy. Lucy soon learns to appreciate Madame Beck's formidable administrative skills concerning purloined information. She "ruled by espionage." She is not only a spy but a spy-master: she has "her staff of spies" (81), and offers a perfect example of what sociologist J.A. Barnes calls "Machiavellian intelligence,"[65] capable of using honesty, guile or deceit to her advantage, creating a kind of realm of omniscience that "poses a threat to social life" (Barnes 163). Indeed, Lucy's list of Madame's virtues could be taken directly from the pages of *The Prince*: "Wise, firm, faithless; secret, crafty, passionless; watchful and inscrutable; acute and insensate – withal perfectly decorous – what more could be desired?" (Brontë 82).[66] But Lucy's talents trump those of Madame Beck. We are told that the fourteen-year-old Lucy residing with her godmother was already skilled in the art of scrutiny. Just as the young Lucy has used this talent to her advantage at Bretton, so does she at Rue Fossette, where her gaze penetrates the perpetual mask worn by the harsh matron, Madame Beck. Despite "Madame's face of stone" (77), Lucy says, "her habitual disguise, her mask and her domino,[67] were to me a mere network reticulated with holes" (494). There is of course a price for Lucy to pay. Knowing so much about others is often quite maddening, just as Simmel predicted it would be. (Recall that, according to Simmel, if each person revealed everything, it "would drive everybody into the insane asylum" [312].) It also provokes ethical dilemmas. Psychologist Paul Ekman has written of what he learned from "the legendary sociologist Erving Goffman," who said, "part of what it means to be civilized is not to 'steal' information that is not freely given to us."[68]

Lucy Snowe, a thief who wishes that someone would steal from her (and if he did, would that be theft?), is not the only one whose gaze robs from the soul of others. M. Paul, despite his bumbling physiognomic/phrenological investigation of Lucy in her initial job interview, is normally an expert at extracting information by observing the everyday behavior of his students and colleagues, as we have seen. Paul Emanuel admits to Lucy that he has rented "a room with a view" high above the schoolyard from which he secretly observes the school's inmates: "My book is this garden; its contents are human nature – female human nature. I know you all by heart. Ah! I know you well – St Pierre the Parisienne – cette maîtresse-femme, my cousin Beck herself" (403). Lucy is shocked to learn of M. Paul's Panopticon,[69] and of his deceptive ways. She cries out:

"It is not right, monsieur."
"Comment; it is not right? By whose creed? Does some dogma of Calvin or Luther condemn it?"

(403)

Of course, as we all know, Lucy too likes to watch – although, arguably, her observations reflect more of a desire for an "enlargement of life" (the product of secrecy, according to Simmel) than does M. Paul's voyeurism. She admits to having her own Panopticon, her "watch-tower of the nursery, . . . whence," she says, "I . . . made my observations" (83). Lucy knows what Erving Goffman (that fourth "Jesuit")[70] would come to know a hundred years later – that all social events, no matter how public they are, conceal "secrets" that are already known by everybody, and that social conventions exist that disallow direct gazes upon them. Lucy dispenses with these conventions, refusing to honor them. In this way, she plays the same game as Madame Beck, M. Paul, and Goffman himself, and she becomes Goffman's "thief of information." She admits that since girlhood she has exhibited "a *staid manner* of my own which ere now had been as good to me as *cloak and hood of hodden gray*," that allowed her to gather information "with impunity, and even approbation" (49, emphases added). This "staid manner," this "cloak and hood," are clearly a set of protective performances in Lucy's strategic armamentarium. This prophylactic device may seem to provide Lucy with a secret space from which her gaze can penetrate the soul of the other, but, according to my argument, it is no longer clear what this cloak will protect. It seems that an attentive scrutiny from any of the expert detectives at Rue Fossette ("Dimple Street" – or, in a stretch, a "Small Septic Tank Street," or a "Common Grave Street") undoes the inner/outer distinction.

Lucy often tries to prevent others from seeing into her own soul by engaging in deceptive performances (even though she attempts to avoid performing at the school play). She takes pleasure in knowing that others misattribute roles to her (334); in mock anger, she tears up the essay of a rebellious student, and locks her co-conspirator in a closet, before resuming the class as if nothing had transpired (88–89) – thereby showing herself to be well aware of the goal of all performances according to Goffman: "to sustain a particular definition of the situation" (Goffman 85). She is pleased to discover later that Mme. Beck, watching the episode through the keyhole, approves of the performance. Lucy responds to an insult from M. Paul by play-acting a rejection of his newly expressed interest in her, with, she tells us, "consummate chariness and frostiness I could not but applaud" (354). Lucy becomes her own audience, and congratulates herself on the successful performance. The pleasure that Lucy takes in this act is identical to the pleasure she experiences when she successfully lies to M. Paul – when she pulls off her "neat, frosty falsehood" (354). These are only a few of many examples of what John Kucich calls her "performative psychological organization" (Kucich 927). Kucich also comments on the enjoyment Lucy takes in the successful deployment of her skills. She may well enjoy them as long as they work. What is important, says Goffman, is that the performance not be discredited (140). Lucy's performances are contrived, and she seems to know it – to an extent. She also knows that all performances are deceptive, as Goffman would later argue,[71] and that often what seem to be mysteries are only secrets in broad daylight.

Conclusion

We thus see in Charlotte Brontë's *Villette* confirmation of Simmel's theory that the participation in the dialectics of closure and disclosure plays a major role in the construction of individuality (and by extension, the construction of social reality). Brontë's fictional account of a young, orphaned Englishwoman's attempt to create a life for herself as an expatriate on the European mainland depicts great efforts on the part of a variety of agents to protect secrets whose revelation would be injurious to them, and to penetrate secrets of others that would benefit them. Therefore, these agents employ deception, lies, dissimulation, and misinformation to protect against the discovery of their vulnerabilities and the intrusion upon them, or to gain advantage over others. The dissembling Goffmanian performances of these agents become necessary features of the form of life that Brontë has imagined for us – one that, by implication, generates a conflict theory of society. Without dissimulation both individuality and sociality would be impossible. Along with the usual cast of MacGuffins in the novel, we see the pleasure that the elderly virginal woman who narrates her story takes in her secrets, sometimes admitting that she has concealed information out of a sense of sheer *ressentiment*, and other times because of the heady sense of power it gives her. Moreover, she keeps secrets from her readers, and never reveals them, such as those family secrets that have made Lucy the strange person she is, and the secret of why domesticity was lost in this failed attempt to recover a lost domesticity. The idea of secrecy is also conscripted into the service of what we may perhaps now see as an ideological requirement for a "deep self" unavailable to political and economic forces of materiality. The implication in this novel is that the model of the secret self can be universalized; we all potentially have such secret places to which we can and should repair, and only superficial people – or Roman Catholics – fail to do so.

On the other hand, at the same time that this model of a universal, deep, secret, inviolable private self is championed, it is countered and undermined in two ways as Lucy Snowe tells her story: first by a wish on Lucy's part that her secret inner self be penetrated by a male other than God, and second by the presence in the novel of highly skilled people-watching "Jesuits," including Lucy herself, who unveil the deepest secrets of others by scrutinizing their faces, gestures and language as signs of their inner selves. Except on the rare occasions that these Jesuits err, it seems that no secret is safe from their gaze, and that therefore there is no inviolable secret self. Yet the multifaceted performances whose function is to disguise this destructive information from people who already have it (the secret in broad daylight) play a major constitutive role in "the show that must go on." If Lucy Snowe is a material girl, she is one *malgré elle*. The implication of my argument is that the conclusion about the materiality of the "inner self" drawn by Shuttleworth and Dames is in an ironic way almost correct after all – but for the wrong reasons. It is not the "phrenological gaze" that subverts the interiority that Brontë seeks to defend, but the very nature of the gaze itself. When the Protestant Lucy Snowe enters the deeply Catholic world of Villette, she finds herself confronted by a Simmelian secret society whose rituals and hidden meanings she must essay to penetrate in the name of her own survival. Lucy also intuits Simmel's later disconcerting discovery that

> all of human intercourse rests on the fact that everybody knows somewhat more about the other than the other voluntarily reveals to him; and those

things he knows are frequently matters whose knowledge the other person (were he aware of it) would find undesirable.

(Simmel, 323)

With this information in hand, Lucy therefore is able to compete relatively successfully in what Goffman calls the "information game – a potentially infinite cycle of concealment, discovery, false revelation, and rediscovery" (8). In the name of privacy and depth, she develops her own "strategically located points of reticence" (64) – that is, she guards her own secrets – thereby declaring herself an enemy of the secret society that produces the Catholic soul while inhabiting the center of that society.

Lucy Snowe discovers by the end of her story a truth about the mysteries of the Catholic soul that we readers are in a position to discover about Lucy's own mysteries: namely, Goffman's secret – the secret that there is no secret, and that each actor's job is to prevent the audience from learning this too. Perhaps Eva Badowska is right to say, "*Villette* may well be read as Brontë's *Vanity Fair*" (1509). In *Vanity Fair* there are persons, plots, and secrets in broad daylight, but no souls – and there, in the figure of Rebecca Sharp, the true material girl dwells.[72]

Notes

1. Charlotte Brontë, *Villette*, ed. and introduction by Helen Cooper, Penguin Classics (London: Penguin Books, 2004), 341. Future references to this work will be cited parenthetically in the body of the text, unless otherwise indicated.
2. Caveat emptor! If Miss Snowe's and Miss Brontë's conception of the self entails the claim that, *by definition*, no one ever truly knows any one else, then it may be a mere tautology to assert that neither Miss Fanshawe nor Brontë's readers know who Miss Snowe is. Later I will contend that while Lucy Snowe's metaphysical claim is problematic, it is not tautological.
3. In this chapter all citations from Goffman are from *The Presentation of Self in Everyday Life* (New York and London: Anchor Books Doubleday, 1959).
4. "Dread" in the Kierkegaardian sense: a "sympathetic antipathy and an antipathetic sympathy," i.e., a desire of what one fears and a fear of what one desires (Søren Kierkegaard, *The Concept of Dread* [1844], trans. Walter Lowrie [Princeton: Princeton University Press, 1957], 38).
5. Jolene Zigarovich, *Writing Death and Absence in the Victorian Novel: Engraved Narratives* (New York: Palgrave, 2012), 1. Future references to this work will be cited parenthetically in the body of the text.
6. Letter to George Smith; Haworth, March 26, 1853.
7. Charlotte Brontë, *Villette*, ed. Mark Lilly, intro. Tony Tanner (Harmondsworth and New York: Penguin Books, 1984), 12. If the novel is domestic only "from one point of view," then there is at least one other point of view from which it is not domestic. I am occupying the latter perspective, and claiming it gives us a more accurate panorama of the landscape as a whole.
8. I am grateful to John Kucich for this observation in a personal communication.
9. Sally Shuttleworth points out that Dr. John's name most surely derives from that of Thomas John Graham, a medical doctor who authored *Domestic Medicine*, a book that had a prominent position in the library of Charlotte Brontë's father (*Charlotte Brontë and Victorian Psychology* [Cambridge: Cambridge University Press, 1996], 10–11). Future references to this work will be cited parenthetically in the body of the text.

10 If Brontë had wanted Miss Snowe to reveal her past, she could have done so in the first chapter of the novel called "Bretton," which is the name of one side of her family, and the name of the place where they lived.
11 Nicholas Dames, *Amnesiac Selves: Nostalgia, Forgetting, and British Fiction, 1810–1870* (Oxford: Oxford University Press, 2001), 78. Future references to this work will be included parenthetically in the text. For a full development of my argument against Dames's treatment of *Villette*, see my "How Lucy Snowe Became an Amnesiac," *Brontë Studies* 34.3 (November 2009): 220–33.
12 Linda Hunt writes:

> In order to evoke Lucy's alienation from a social world in which she has no place, Brontë uses a method which is highly experimental for the time. While characters in a traditional novel are carefully defined in terms of family background, financial history, and class position, Lucy virtually moves in a void. ("*Villette*: The Inward and the Outward Life," *Victorians Institute Journal* 11 [1982–83]: 23–31).

This is another way of saying that Brontë knowingly builds her plot around secrets that will never be revealed (but, then, the first sentence of the first modern novel exhibits a similar plan: "Someplace in La Mancha, whose name I do not wish to remember, . . . ").
13 Ali Behdad, "Visibility, Secrecy, and the Novel: Narrative Power in Brontë and Zola," *LIT* 1 (1999): 253–64, 261, quoting Michel Foucault, *Histoire de la sexualité*, vol. 1 (Paris: Editions Gallimard, 1976), 133.
14 These possibilities will probably seem unlikely to readers familiar with Charlotte Brontë and her novels, yet Jean Rhys's interpretation of *Jane Eyre* in *Wide Sargasso Sea* finds them lurking everywhere in the backdrop of that novel.
15 Michel Foucault, *The History of Sexuality*, vol. 1, *An Introduction*, trans. Robert Hurley (New York: Vintage Books/Random House, 1980), 15–35. Future references to Foucault's work will be cited parenthetically in the body of the text.
16 Why did this development take place? Foucault seems less interested in causal analysis than most historians. For example, consider the well-known opening of *Madness and Civilization*: "At the end of the Middle Ages, leprosy disappeared from the Western World" (3). Epistemes happen.
17 For example: there was an "institutional incitement to speak about it, and to do so more and more" (18), and the assertion that institutions such as medicine, psychiatry, and police became sites that "radiated discourses aimed at sex, intensifying people's awareness of it as a constant danger, and this in turn created a further incentive to talk about it" (31).
18 For Foucault, it turns out that the *real* secret is the secret of power. In a well-known passage he asserts: "Power is tolerable only on condition that it mask a substantial part of itself. Its success is proportional to its ability to hide its own mechanisms" (86). Ironically, this sounds like Schopenhauer talking about sex.
19 Karl Popper, *The Logic of Scientific Discovery* [1935] (London: Routledge, 2002).
20 I can think of no cases in Victorian fiction where there is a fear of a "homosexual agenda" that seeks to recruit children. This seems to be an anxiety of the twentieth- and twenty-first centuries.
21 Sharon Marcus, *Between Women: Friendship, Desire and Marriage in Victorian England* (Princeton and Oxford: Princeton University Press, 2007), 102. Future references to this work will be cited parenthetically in the body of the text.
22 Kathryn Bond Stockton, *God between Their Lips: Desire between Women in Irigaray, Brontë, and Eliot* (Stanford, CA: Stanford University Press, 1994), 136. The passage in question appears in *Villette*, 138–39. Future references Stockton's book will be cited parenthetically in the body of the text.
23 As it was for Anne Weinstone, "The Queerness of Lucy Snowe," *Nineteenth-Century Contexts* 18.4 (1995): 367–84. Marcus cites Weinstone, saying that she "argues for an 'anti-straight' rather than lesbian reading of the novel" (*Between Women*, 283n38).

Katie R. Peel follows Weinstone's lead. She writes, "Here I apply the term 'queer' to any practice that challenges the normative, be it the heteronormative or not. Lucy's performative acts critique more than the categories of gender and sexuality" ("The 'Thoroughly and Radically Incredible' Lucy Snowe: Performativity in Charlotte Brontë's *Villette*," *Victorians Institute Journal* 36 [2008]: 231–44, 231).

24 The fact that the veiled ghost proves to be a fraud might be interpreted by some readers as an indication that, in this story, Brontë is mocking orientalism. Or that, because the ghost is a spirit, she is mocking religious sentiment. But because of the proliferation of orientalist references and religious references throughout *Villette* – sometimes overlapping each other – I doubt the validity of either inference.

25 Eleanor Salotto, Mary Jacobus, and Patricia S. Yeager provide additional arguments that Lucy identifies herself with Polly. Salotto sees Paulina Home's last name is as a reference to the domestic scene Lucy has lost ("*Villette* and the Perversions of Feminine Identity," in *Gender Reconstructions: Pornography and Perversions in Literature and Culture*, ed. Cindy L. Carson, Robert L. Mazzola and Susan M. Bernardo [Aldershot and Burlington, VT: Ashgate, 2002], 53–75, 59). Both Salotto and Yeager present arguments going beyond the quoted passage to define Polly as Lucy's double (Patricia S. Yeager, "Honey-Mad Women: Charlotte Brontë's Bilingual Heroines," *Browning Institute Studies* 14 [1986]: 11–35, 20). Jacobus shows how Lucy borrows Paulina's grief at the temporary loss of her father as her own grief at the loss of her domestic nest (*Women Writing and Writing about Women*, ed. Mary Jacobus [London: Croom Helm, 1979], 44).

26 Eva Badowska cites a letter written by Brontë to her father after she had visited the great Exhibition at the Crystal Palace in June of 1851, telling him that the place resembled "a Bazaar or Fair . . . as eastern Genii might have created. It seems as if magic only could have gathered this mass of wealth from the ends of the Earth." Badowska says that the letters "showcase the hypnotic power of the exhibition, as Brontë dreamily slips into an Orientalist rhetoric that echoes the Orientalism of the display." But, says Badowska, "[To] describe commodities as conjured up by a genie is to mask the movements of capital that really make things happen" ("Choseville: Brontë's *Villette* and the Art of Bourgeois Interiority," *PMLA* 120.5 [October 2005]: 1509–23, 1511).

27 Brontë 297; *Arabian Nights: The Marvels and Wonders of the Thousand and One Nights*, ed. Jack Zipes, trans. Richard F. Burton (New York: Dutton Signet, 1991), 414–18. In his edition of Burton's translation, Zipes has changed "barmecide" to "nobleman." Burton's original translation uses "barmecide." Lane's translation does not contain this story, but it is found in Jonathan Scott's translation of 1811, where "barmecide" occurs. Perhaps this translation belonged to the Brontë household when she was a girl.

28 Alnashar, in "The Barber's Tale of His Fifth Brother" in *Arabian Nights* hopes to multiply his small inheritance by investing in glassware. He buys the glasses, but, while daydreaming about the great wealth he will obtain from his sales, he foolishly breaks all of the glasses before he is able to sell them.

29 Jill L. Matus, "Looking at Cleopatra: The Expression and Exhibition of Desire in *Villette*," *Victorian Literature and Culture* 8 (1993): 345–67, 348.

30 "Orientalist" rather than Oriental: the Scimitar of Saladin to which she refers is not the one that beheaded the many Christian knights and soldiers who were Saladin's prisoners of war after the battle of Hama in 1178; rather it is the scimitar featured in Walter Scott's *The Talisman*. There, in a confrontation between Richard Lionheart and Saladin, Richard cuts an iron bar in two with his sword, to prove the superiority of Christian weapons. Saladin stands a silk cushion on end and cuts it in two with his scimitar, something that the iron sword could not do, much to Richard's chagrin. In real life, Richard's army did fight Saladin's, but apparently Richard Lionheart's meeting with Saladin took place only in Walter Scott's imagination.

31 Not all biblical references in *Villette* are presented in the context of secrecy, but most seem to be: for example:

Genesis 5:27: evoked in a discussion of the secret of the buried nun (117).
Exodus 18:7: in the context of Mme. Beck's secret surveillance of Lucy's possessions (108).
John 5:4: in the passage in which Lucy discusses "secrets of the spirit" (200).
2 Samuel 1:20: in the context of trying to prevent Mme. Beck from discovering the truth (85).
Judges 4:1–24: in the context of Lucy's painful (but unshared) memories of childhood (121).
Matthew 11:30: a second secret visit by Mme. Beck in order to rifle through Lucy's possessions (131).
Exodus 17:7: Lucy penetrates Mme. Beck's secret thoughts, and is delighted to have done so (131–32).
Daniel 3: in the context of M. Paul's attempt to silence Lucy's opinion of the painting of Cleopatra (228).
Exodus 13:21: in the context of Lucy's private struggle with the thought of "destiny and her decrees" (257).
Deuteronomy 34:1–5: same private wrestling with the concept of destiny (257).
Genesis 27:7: in the context of Lucy's erotic excitement provoked by the arrival of a long-awaited letter from Dr. John – an excitement she has surely shared with no one all these years except with us, her readers (266–67).
2 Kings 5:1–18: in the context of describing a secret letter she writes to Dr. John, a letter she does not send (281–82).
Daniel 4:7: in the context of Lucy's describing her repressed thoughts about her pain and misery, which she cannot express publicly (303–4).
1 Samuel 4:19–21: in the context of thinking about letters from Dr. John that she has hidden (327).
2 Chronicles 8:4: in the context of the opium fog through which she views Villette (429).

32 Kate Brown makes a similar point when she asserts that in *Villette* Brontë is "translating the architectural structure of the boarding school into the space of Lucy's psyche" ("Catastrophe and the City: Charlotte Brontë as Urban Novelist," *Nineteenth-Century Literature* 57.3 [December 2002]: 350–80, 357).

33 William A. Cohen, "Material Interiority in Charlotte Brontë's *The Professor*," *Nineteenth-Century Literature* 57.4 (March 2003): 443–76, 445. Future references to this essay will be included parenthetically in the text.

34 In this study I distinguish between the concepts of secrecy and privacy, but I maintain a close association between them. (Often, but not always, a desire for privacy involves a desire for secrecy.) I must point out that in his 1981 study, "The Paradox of Secrecy," sociologist Beryl L. Bellman is at great pains to distinguish conceptually between "secrecy" and "privacy" and to discourage discussions that connect them. I will rest my case by quoting philosopher Sissela Bok. According to her, if privacy is defined as "the condition of being protected from unwanted access by others," then there is a direct connection between secrecy and privacy. They overlap "most immediately in the private lives of individuals, where secrecy guards against unwanted access by others – against their coming too near, learning too much, observing too closely. *Secrecy guards, then, the central aspects of identity*" (Sissela Bok, *Secrets: On the Ethics of Concealment and Revelation* [New York: Vintage/Random House Books, 1989], 13, emphasis added).

35 For a rather more specific interpretation of this "secret dell," see Kathryn Bond Stockton, who calls it a "figure for female genitals and genital pleasure." Similarly, she

claims that Lucy's decryption of "l'allée défendue" (the forbidden alley behind the Pensionnat) "trace[s] a genital cleft." When Lucy says of this allée, "I became a frequenter of this strait and narrow path" (*Villette*, 119), Stockton interprets this as a report of autoeroticism (148).
36 Clearly Graham Bretton might penetrate Lucy's private spaces using more than his letters, if he wished to do so. William Cohen asserts, "bodily penetration is Brontë's dominant metaphor for access to human interiority." He adds, "an important psychological component of the process is the subject's willing submission" (458).
37 See Beth Newman's contribution to the debate concerning Brontë's reasons for this decision (*Subjects on Display: Psychoanalysis, Social Expectation, and Victorian Femininity* [Athens: Ohio University Press, 2004], 158n36.) Future references to this work will be cited parenthetically in the body of the text.
38 R. A. York, *Strangers and Secrets: Communication in the Nineteenth-Century Novel* (London and Toronto: Associated University Presses, 1994), 18. Future references to this work will be cited parenthetically in the text.
39 Albert D. Pionke, in his introduction to *Victorian Secrecy: Economies of Knowledge and Concealment*, ed. Denise Tischler Millstein and Albert B. Pionke (London: Ashgate, 2010), 2–3. Future references to this work will be included parenthetically in the body of the text.
40 See the opening epigraph of this chapter, in which D. A. Miller, speaking of Dickens's novels, writes: "The self is most itself at the moment when its defining inwardness is most secret" (*The Novel and the Police* [Berkeley and Los Angeles: University of California Press, 1989], 200). Future references to this work will be cited parenthetically in the body of the text as "Miller, 1989."
41 Recall that Simmel mentions that a secret is only as good as resistance to the temptation to betray it: "The secret . . . is full of the consciousness that it *can* be betrayed. . . . [It] is surrounded by the possibility and the temptation of betrayal" (Simmel 333).
42 James Eli Adams comments on this aspect of Miller's work, saying, "[T]his reading exposes a curiously puritanical strain in [Miller's] Foucauldian tactics. . . . In his insistence that [novels offer] no innocent pleasures, Miller reproduces a very Victorian suspicion" (*Dandies and Desert Saints: Styles of Victorian Masculinity* [Ithaca and London: Cornell University Press, 1995], 204).
43 Eugenia Delamotte refers to Lucy's "pathological reserve" in "*Villette*: Demystifying Women's Gothic," chapter 7, *Perils of the Night* (New York: Oxford University Press, 1990), 229–89, 250.
44 Catherine Belsey, *Critical Practice*, 2nd ed. (London and New York: Routledge, 2001), 97–98.
45 J. L. Austin, *How to Do Things with Words* [1962], ed. J. O. Urmson and Marina Sbisà, 2nd ed. (Cambridge, MA: Harvard University Press, 1975), 9.
46 In chapter 1, I discussed D. A. Miller's *Narrative and Its Discontents: Problems of Closure in the Traditional Novel*, according to which narrative by its very nature is unable to provide successful closure, and therefore it produces anxiety and "discontent." If so, Miller should be prepared to admit that Lucy Snowe develops one of the few honest narratives in Victorian fiction. Perhaps the anxiety and discontent that her honesty provokes is not as bad as Miller would suggest. H. Porter Abbott asserts that the failure to achieve closure may indeed cheat readers of the gratification of experiencing the resolution of conflict, but he claims that such a failure can also have its own satisfactions (*The Cambridge Introduction to Narrative*, 57). Abbott might well have been thinking of *Villette*. There is something quite pleasurable about the never-ending tricks that Lucy Snowe plays on us.
47 Joseph Allen Boone, *Libidinal Currents: Sexuality and the Shaping of Modernism* (Chicago: Chicago University Press, 1998), 34–37. Future references to this work will be cited parenthetically in the body of the text.

48 Janice Carlisle, "The Face in the Mirror: *Villette* and the Conventions of Autobiography," *ELH* 46 [1979]: 35–36, quoted in Adrian S. Wisnicki, *Conspiracy, Revolution, and Terrorism from Victorian Fiction to the Modern Novel* (London and New York: Routledge, 2008), 129. Future references to this work will be cited parenthetically in the body of the text.
49 Penny Boumelha, *Charlotte Brontë* (London: Harvester Wheatsheaf, 1990); Robert M. Polhemus, *Erotic Faith* (Chicago: University of Chicago Press, 1990).
50 Leila S. May, "Lucy Snowe, a Material Girl? Phrenology, Surveillance, and the Sociology of Interiority," *Criticism* 25.1 (Winter 2013): 43–68.
51 For example, speaking of Dr. John, Lucy remarks: "the sympathetic faculty was not prominent in him" (212). This clearly recognizable phrenological reference occurs in a long passage in which Lucy is discussing Dr. John's character in detail, but none of the other descriptions in the passage appears to be particularly phrenological. The passage does not seem to have been written by someone who was obsessed with phrenology. Other passages in the novel that can be read as references to phrenology are on pages 79, 93, 111, 147, 344, 391, 395, and 539. I see some of these as phrenological jokes on Lucy's part (e.g., speaking of the way children in this country boss around their parents, Lucy writes: "The Labassecouriens must have a large organ of philopregenitiveness" [111]), and none of them occurs as a feature of important developments in the novel.
52 Viz., 17, 73, 111, 171, 178, 212 and 245.
53 "I read your skull, that night you came; I see your moyens: play you can; play you must" (147).
54 Similarly, Nicholas Dames – under the influence of Shuttleworth – finds no irony in Brontë's words. He writes: "The vagueness of M. Paul's verdict ('bien des choses') should not invalidate his process of reading, for it mirrors the deliberately unlimited scope of phrenology's reformist aims" (84). In my view, this justification, along with Shuttleworth's, simply repeats the tautological form of M. Paul's verdict after his scrutiny of Lucy, and rivals that of Winnie the Pooh, who occasionally explains the odd actions of other creatures by declaring, "Some do; some don't."
55 The latter case appears when Lucy responds to some rather crude words spoken by Rosine, an unsophisticated servant girl: "The terms were precisely such as Rosine – a young lady in whose skull the organs of reverence and reserve were not largely developed – was in the constant habit of using" (391). Here, too, I think readers will have to decide for themselves whether to read this passage as evidence of Brontë's support for phrenology, or as a joke on her part. Dames assumes it is the former.
56 In 1853 Brontë was certainly aware of the vast amount of criticism that phrenology had engendered. David de Giustino, in *Conquest of Mind: Phrenology and Victorian Social Thought* (London: Croom Helm and Totowa, NJ: Rowman and Littlefield, 1975) asserts,

> By the early 1840s, the downfall of phrenology as an intellectual study was apparent almost everywhere. . . . The decline through the 1840s went unchecked. . . . The novelty of phrenology had worn away, and it was increasingly regarded as a form of entertainment. . . . [T]he dominant style was now a variety of fortune telling. (91, 100)

Despite the titillation phrenology might have provoked in her, Brontë was not above poking a little fun at it in *Villette*.
57 Descartes treats "mind" and "soul" as interchangeable terms ("I am . . . a mind or a soul" [*Med. II*, 173]). Lucy Snowe – probably along with Brontë – seems to conceive of an overlap between the soul and the deepest part of the mind. Lucy would not be likely to interchange the word "soul" with "mind" in a phrase such as "not one soul [was] present" (239), but she does equate mind and soul when she says, "All her

thoughts turned on this difficulty; her whole soul was occupied with [it]" (96), and she equates them when she refers to "my inner self . . . , my spirit . . . , my soul" (53). Also, when speaking of M. Paul Emanuel, she writes, "He believed in his soul that . . ." (393).

58 The beauty of this model is somewhat tarnished, of course, by the risible image of one's mind having access to one's body and hence to the rest of the physical world only through one's pineal gland.

> I had clearly ascertained that the part of the body in which the soul exercises its functions immediately is in nowise the heart, not the whole of the brain, but merely the most inward of all its parts, to wit, a certain very small gland which is situated in the middle of its substance. (*The Passions of the Soul*, in *The Essential Descartes*, 362).

Brontë's version of Descartes's problem is that she seems incapable of describing the soul, self, or spirit as anything other than a spatial entity. The difficulty is that whatever takes up space seems to be physical, and hence measurable. Descartes's dilemma appears to be the same: if the soul meets the body any *place*, the soul becomes a body by virtue of exhibiting the capacity of *location*, a capacity that, according to Descartes, only bodies have.

59 In note 2, I mentioned that some versions of the secret-self thesis are capable only of producing empty, tautological defenses of their case. In fact, I think Brontë's version of this thesis escapes circularity better than does Descartes's. Descartes defines mind as private (secret) and body as public, while Brontë realizes that without concentrated effort, the mind's privacy (and secrecy) can be made public, so certain *actions* and *strategies* are required in Brontë's formulation of the thesis, while in Descartes's mere definitions are sufficient.

60 Louise Penner, in her article "'Not Yet Settled': Charlotte Brontë's Anti-materialism," *Nineteenth-Century Gender Studies* 4.1 (Spring 2008): 1–27, responding both to Shuttleworth's analysis of *Villette* and a similar view expressed by Athena Vrettos in her *Somatic Fictions: Imagining Illness in Victorian Culture* (Stanford, CA: Stanford University Press, 1995) – a year before the publication of Shuttleworth's book – agrees with Shuttleworth and Vrettos that Brontë was indeed influenced by her reading of the scientific materialists of her day, but Penner poses a question similar to mine: "But did Brontë herself accept the apparent implication of this scientific work that all references to mind, soul, and the spiritual life can in principle be eliminated in favour of talk of brain, nerves and matter?" The thrust of Penner's argument is two-pronged: first, to show that Brontë was reading from many more sources than just the materialistic writers on whom Shuttleworth and Vrettos concentrate, including some who were attempting to demonstrate compatibility between spiritualism and science; second, that many of the examples that Shuttleworth presents to support her view that Brontë had become a materialist are open to alternative interpretations. I agree with Penner but go beyond her in my criticism, arguing that there is virtually no good reason to hold that Brontë had become a hard-core materialist. In commenting on the passage in *Villette* that begins, "Where my soul went during that swoon I cannot tell" (*Villette*, chapter 16), Penner writes, "On the one hand, Lucy's narrative insists on the utter separation between an independently existing body and soul. At the same time, Brontë has shown us time and again the unreliability of Lucy's own claims about her psychic states." My own view is that the fact that sometimes Lucy veils herself in the portrait she paints for us (to use Penner's felicitous metaphor) is no reason to think that in this passage Lucy is also veiling her materialism.

61 Apparently Dames believes the critical obsession with interiority in *Villette* is the result of an anachronistic intervention by theorists who have been too much influenced by postmodern concerns regarding visuality and "the gaze." He writes:

> I will suggest that attention to a different model of visuality – the clinical project of phrenology and physiognomy – compels us to revise, or nuance, our more usual

privileging of depth over surface. . . . If Brontë's investment in the phrenological enterprise is taken seriously, . . . then our habitual (and ritually asserted) claims for the "interiority of the Other" must seem less secure. (86)

Dames has got it half right. As I will attempt to show, an analysis of the fruits of surveillance in *Villette* concludes that the outer is the inner; but an analysis of the idea of subjectivity concludes that the surveillance of the outer can never gain entrance to the inner. These two forcefully contradictory views in *Villette* stand side by side, and generate much of the energy that drives Brontë's narrative.

62 John Kucich has supported Lucy's defense of her interiority in his "Passionate Reserve and Reserved Passion," *ELH* 52.4 (Winter 1985): 913–37. There, he discusses a number of overlapping dialectical systems employed by Brontë: "master/slave" (934), "self-concentration/self-disruption" (935), "expression/reserve" (934), "reserve/performance" (927), and "histrionic passion/reserve" (916). He argues that none of these systems is so deterministic, either individually or collectively, as to become determinants of the self; to the contrary, in combination they "become the fulcrum for inward variation," making Lucy's "inwardness mercurial and fluid" (934). Kucich restated his ideas in a new form in his *Repression in Victorian Fiction: Charlotte Brontë, George Eliot, and Charles Dickens* (Berkeley, Los Angeles, and London: University of California Press, 1987; see especially p. 112). Joseph Boone has also written an apologia of Lucy's conception of subjectivity. (See Joseph A. Boone, "Depolicing *Villette*: Surveillance, Invisibility, and the Female Erotics of 'Heretic Narrative,'" *Novel* 26.1 [Fall 1992]: 39, 42.)

63 Lucy also undermines her metaphysics of unique private individuality by conceptualizing the soul as a kind of spiritual *spaciality* – as mentioned earlier – and perhaps by leaving metaphorical and metonymical traces that show a figurative equation between Lucy's story and the legend of the nun, a nun whose ghost (= spirit) proves to be a fraud. A number of critics discuss this fusion of identities, including Shuttleworth (283n14) and Eleanor Salotto (55, 63). See also Christina Crosby, "Charlotte Brontë's Haunted Text," *Studies in English Literature* 24 (1984): 701–15, 705, and Eva Badowska, 1513. Toni Wein complicates this equation by reminding us of the figurative equation made several times in the novel between Lucy Snowe and Polly Home. Wein then demonstrates that Polly herself is described in imagery that connects her to the ghostly nun. A syllogism emerges: Lucy equals Polly, Polly equals the nun; therefore, Lucy equals the nun (Toni Wein, "Gothic Desire in Charlotte Brontë's *Villette*," *Studies in English Literature 1500–1900* (*SEL*) 39.4 [1999]: 733–49, 740–41).

64 I am indebted to Sharon Setzer for this idea.

65 J. A. Barnes. A Pack of Lies: Towards a Sociology of Lying (Cambridge: Cambridge University Press, 1994), 149. Future references to this work will be cited parenthetically in the body of the text.

66 Machiavelli, discussing the virtues of integrity, mercy, faithfulness, sincerity, religiosity, humanity, and charity, says, "It is not, therefore, necessary for a prince to have all the above-named qualities, but it is very necessary to seem to have them" (93).

67 A domino is a "hooded cloak with a mask, worn at masquerades" (*Webster's New Universal Unabridged Dictionary* [New York: Barnes and Noble, 1996]).

68 Malcolm Gladwell provides a summary of the work of Paul Ekman and other psychologists who study unintentional facial expressions for insight into hidden motives (Malcolm Gladwell, "The Naked Face," *New Yorker* [August 5, 2002]: 49).

69 Beth Newman correctly points out that the use of the term Panopticon in the sense in which I am employing it does not have the strictness of Foucault's "Panopticism" (Newman, *Subjects on Display*, 49) because, according to Foucault's interpretation of Bentham's invention, the function of the Panopticon is to make the inmate ever aware of the possibility of surveillance ("the inmate must never know whether he is being looked at any one moment; but he must be sure that he may always be so" [Newman, *Subjects on Display*, 201]). The inmates of the Pensionnat do not know about

M. Paul's tower, but, I suggest, they *do* realize in a chillingly mysterious way that he knows ever so much about them; thus his Panopticism is in some ways more sinister than that of Bentham's warden. On the other hand, Lucy too has Panopticons of sorts, as we will see, yet virtually no one knows of Lucy's spying. This still counts as a case of Benthamite Panopticism because Bentham wrote that the key virtue of that structure is that it provides methods of "seeing without being seen" (Bentham quoted by Shuttleworth in *Charlotte Brontë and Victorian Psychology*, 46).

70   Or perhaps I should say she is the fifth Jesuit. Mme. Beck is called a Jesuit three times in the novel; M. Paul is called a Jesuit six times. Père Silas *is* a Jesuit. I have accused Lucy herself of being a virtual Jesuit (in the spirit of her own usage of the term: having the "crafty glance of a Jesuit-eye" [436]).

71   Goffman writes,

> At one extreme, one finds that the performer can be fully taken in by his own act; he can be sincerely convinced that the impression of reality which he stages is the real reality. When his audience is also convinced in this way about the show he puts on – and this seems to be the typical case – then for the moment at least, only the sociologist or the socially disgruntled will have any doubts about the "realness" of what is presented. (17)

72   Barbara Baines, Antony Harrison, John Kucich, Sharon Setzer, Toni Wein, and Deborah Wyrick have read earlier versions of this chapter. I am grateful to them for their helpful suggestions, and to Donald D. Palmer for his discussions with me concerning Descartes's ontology, as well as for his chapter on Descartes in his *Visions of Human Nature* (Mountain View, CA, London, and Toronto: Mayfield, 2000).

3 Selfishness and secrecy in the "howling wilderness"
Thackeray's *Vanity Fair*

> I love acting. It is so much more real than life.
> —Oscar Wilde, *The Picture of Dorian Gray*

The howling wilderness

Secrets abound in William Makepeace Thackeray's *Vanity Fair*, yet the novel contains no deep souls to hide those secrets, no secret selves, and few narrative secrets that will be withheld from readers. In this respect it differs from many novels written by his contemporaries – most certainly from *Villette*. Georg Simmel knew that even surface secrets can have their effects. As we have seen, Simmel claimed that if each individual revealed everything it "would drive everybody into the insane asylum," and from this thesis alone it follows that secrecy is a necessary ingredient in both private and public life. In the light of that assertion by the German sociologist we see that there is an extraordinary Simmelian moment in Thackeray's *Vanity Fair* when, in an aside, the narrator claims: "if we are to be peering into everyone's private life, speculating on their income, and cutting them if we don't approve of their expenditure, why, what a howling wilderness and intolerable dwelling Vanity Fair would be!"[1] This passage is replete with intentional irony but also framed in an impeccable if perverse logic. First, the function of the novel *is* to pry into everyone's business, and most certainly into Becky Sharp's. Second, Vanity Fair, as the narrator describes it, *is* a howling wilderness and an intolerable dwelling. He asserts that, if we really understood society, we would see that we "live in a world that we should be glad to quit, and in a frame of mind and in a constant terror" (304). Indeed, before his story concludes, Thackeray's narrator will have convinced his readers that life in Vanity Fair is one steeped in despair, and he will have raised the question in the reader's mind as to whether "Vanity Fair" names only London society of the early nineteenth century or is an exposition of human social nature at large. He also will have revealed virtually all of Becky Sharp's secrets, both the plot-driving MacGuffins and the structure of social and private secrecy in terms of which Becky and each of her fellow conspirators operate.

Despite his shocking revelations, the narrator claims to be proud of the discretion he practices. He refuses to tell us the causes of old Miss Crawley's final illness because of their "unromantic nature" (140) – old Miss Crawley, whose nephew young Miss Sharp will marry, incorrectly expecting Miss Crawley's fortune to be willed to Rebecca's future husband.[2] The narrator also excuses himself from informing us about the events that take place when Becky meets King George in private rooms, even mockingly warning us not to exercise our imagination.

> The dazzled eyes close before that Magnificent Idea. Loyal respect and decency tell even the imagination not to look too keenly and audaciously about the sacred audience-chamber, but to back away rapidly, silently, and respectfully, making profound bows out of the August Presence.
>
> (478)[3]

The narrator brags that he has not reveled in the seamier side of the behavior of Becky Crawley (née Rebecca Sharp), but has presented it in a guarded manner – "we must pass over a part of Mrs. Rebecca Crawley's biography with that lightness and delicacy which the world demands" (637) – and he asks his reader, "has not everything been proper, agreeable, and decorous?" (638). Even Jos Sedley's death is presented in a circumspect manner. Despite pointed hints that he is murdered by Becky Sharp, we are not given enough information to determine with certainty her innocence or guilt.

These instances of the narrator's discretion fit the Simmelian mold, despite their being jokes on Thackeray's part. The narrator explains why propriety requires him to withhold some features of Becky's biography, saying, "There are things we do and know perfectly well in Vanity Fair, though we never speak of them" (637). So if we are not told what Rebecca and the King did in his chambers, nor what illicit acts Becky engaged in that would be improper to recount, nor how Jos died, we are invited to guess. Surely these secrets will reveal themselves to our imagination, despite the narrator's exhortation that we not let the imagination "look too keenly and audaciously about."

The novel occasionally alludes to dark, destructive family secrets of the type with which the middle-class, mid-Victorian world was familiar and whose public revelation delighted its inhabitants. Often these secrets have to do with genealogy. Becky, furious with George Osborne for convincing Jos Sedley not to marry her because she is a nobody, says to him:

> What an honour [for me] to have had you for a brother-in-law, you are thinking? To be sister-in-law to George Osborne, Esquire, son of John Osborne, Esquire, son of – what was your grandpapa, Mr. Osborne? Well, don't be angry. You can't help your pedigree.
>
> (149)

In fact, in Vanity Fair – as in the mid-Victorian world at large – there appears to be a marked prevalence of amnesia about class backgrounds: a very Victorian kind of secret that one keeps even from oneself. Miss Violet, daughter of the first Sir Pitt, believes that governesses should know their place, forgetting that she herself "had a coal scuttle in her scutcheon" (416). At another point, Tom Eaves, the eavesdropper, speaking about Lady Gaunt, tells the narrator, "depend on it, there's a mystery in her case," which provokes the narrator to muse, "it is very likely that this lady, in her high station, had to submit to many a private indignity and to hide many secret griefs under a calm face," and he imagines an aristocrat who, like Damocles,

> has an awful sword hanging over his head in the shape of a bailiff, or an hereditary disease, or a family secret, which peeps out every now and then from the embroidered arras in a ghastly manner, and will be sure to drop one day or other in the right place.
>
> (467)

This standard list of Victorian secrets is presented to Thackeray's middle-class readers with no small degree of class-based *Schadenfreude*, and we are soon to learn that Lady Gaunt's secrets are those of bankruptcy and hereditary madness,[4] both of which are given loving attention by the narrator, though not as knowledge but only as hearsay, coming as it does from Tom Eaves.

Tom Eaves and the narrator are not faithful guardians of the secrets of their "betters" (467), but neither does it seem that others in the service classes are. Simmel's disconcerting claim about the destructive knowledge that others have about one's self would certainly include one's servants. Becky herself, as governess to Sir Pitt's children, "became inducted into most of the secrets of the family" (90), secrets that she uses to her own advantage; then, as only seems fitting, later in her life, Becky's secrets become known to *her* servants. The narrator exclaims to his protagonist,

> Bon Dieu! it is awful, that servant's inquisition. . . . Madame, your secret will be talked over by those men at their club at the public-house tonight. . . . Some people ought to have mutes for servants in Vanity Fair – mutes who could not write.
>
> (444–45)

What about the lawyers; are they more discreet? "Ye gods, what do not attorneys and attorneys' clerks know in London! Nothing is hidden from their inquisition, and their families mutely rule our city" (264). And the money-lenders? Here at last are people who can keep a secret. And why not? They benefit from their silence. The "Israelites" know plenty about Lady Gaunt's financial circumstances (486), and they – the "Hebrew gentlemen" – know how Lord Bareacres could afford his trip abroad (616). The narrator worries about these secrets in the hands of others:

> But Mr. Joseph Sedley, lucky for his own peace, no more knew what was passing in his domestic's mind than [we know] what John or Mary, whose

wages we pay, think of ourselves. What our servants think of us! – Did we know what our intimates and dear relations thought of us, we should live in a world that we should be glad to quit, and in a frame of mind and in a constant terror, that would be perfectly unbearable.

(303–4)

Then it is not just our servants who possess embarrassing or destructive knowledge about us but also "our intimates and dear relations"! And they judge us accordingly. Indeed, what "an intolerable dwelling Vanity Fair" must be (507).

As in a preponderance of the novels of the period, a great number of the secrets that appear in *Vanity Fair* are the secrets of lovers: Jos's secret love for Becky, Becky's secret marriage to Rawdon, Dobbin's secret love for Amelia. In addition, there are such secrets as "the mysteries" of "female fashion and its customs" (373), the "mysteries" of the ladies' drawing-room (417), the secrets that women hide from their husbands (477), and what mothers hide from the rest of the world about their daughters (339). There are secret tears, secret agonies, secret sentiments, and secret prayers ("Have we the right to repeat or overhear [Amelia's] prayers? These brother, are secrets, and out of the domain of Vanity Fair, in which our story lies" [262]), as well as secret thoughts ("Amelia did not answer, . . . and how do we know what her thoughts were?" [282]). But these thoughts and these prayers – whatever they were – are not deep. This superficiality cannot be blamed solely on the simplicity of various characters. Thackeray does not seem to believe that any form of depth psychology is needed to explain the behavior of the inhabitants of Vanity Fair.

Vanity Fair, like all social worlds, can exist only if its citizens have mutual knowledge of each other, and also if its citizens keep different kinds of secrets from each other. Yet, most of these secrets are "mysteries in broad daylight," to use Sartre's perspicacious phrase once again. And the secrets – both those that are hidden and those that are known by everybody, are socially constructive. They help construct the social world that is Vanity Fair, for better or for worse. At one point, the narrator refers to "the mysteries of freemasonry," which he suspects of being mere "humbug" (503). It is as if he feels the same way about the secrets *and* the revelations that are the constitutive elements that form Vanity Fair – they too are all humbug. Masonry's secrets are humbug because they are all artifices; there is really nothing to be known. The secrets of Vanity Fair are simply masks hiding negatives (we are not who we want you to think we are) – but they are "secrets" known by all. Recall that Goffman asserted that often the secret is the fact that there is no secret (the secrets of the Wizard of Oz again). Thackeray is a proto-Simmelian, but a cynical one: "*Vanitas Vanitatum!*" (689).

I will now turn to a secret that so far has been left out, a very large secret that Thackeray through his narrator manages to reveal to his reluctant reader: that the source of virtually all motivation, or at least all motivation in Vanity Fair, is self-interest. I call this a secret, as does Thackeray's narrator, because most readers in Thackeray's day and in ours would deny that this claim were true of themselves, though they would suspect it applied to certain annoying individuals, real or fictitious, with whom they were acquainted (including Becky Sharp). If this *is* a secret – that is, if this is true – it is one of the few *natural* secrets in the novel, a secret that is not the product of some social deviation, not the effect of breaking some promise, contract, agreement, rule, or social expectation. Thackeray accepts what I call a Simmelian thesis – that secrecy is necessarily a part of all human interaction – and another Simmelian thesis – that people engage in constant attempts to discover the secrets of others. However, Thackeray holds this opinion because he judges that, at the individual level, people see secrecy as being in their own best interest, and that individuals try to discover the secrets of others because they believe that knowing them is also to their personal, familial, or class advantage. Clearly Thackeray believes he knows something that most of his readers do not: namely, that self-interest is the primary motive in human interaction.[5] This, perhaps the primary factual revelation of the novel, is what Thackeray's narrator calls, "*letting the cat of selfishness out of the bag of secrecy*" (194). I will turn now to that revelation.

Selfishness

The novel that William Makepeace Thackeray eventually published in 1847–48 as *Vanity Fair* was first meant to have the title of *Pen and Pencil Sketches of English Society*. It has been pointed out that, unless one treats this original title as an ironic gesture, it "is ludicrously inadequate to the novel."[6] One of several layers where its deficiency is obvious is the theoretical level. Thackeray employs (or even generates) a wholesale theory of human nature; an artist's sketchbook does not promulgate such a theory. Even Thackeray's letter to Robert Bell misses the mark in this respect: "My object . . . is to indicate, in cheerful terms, that we are for the most part an abominably foolish and selfish people."[7] In fact, Thackeray's novel is predicated on an egoistic theory of human nature that in most respects is similar to that of his countryman, Thomas Hobbes.[8] Thackeray's revision of Hobbes's theory of the social contract propels him into the arena in which Simmel and Goffman would later work out their own theories. Thackeray's theory differs from Hobbes's by being on the one hand more ambiguous, and on the other more disenchanted. Curiously, the theory's ambiguity is what makes it logically superior to Hobbes's; its disenchantment makes it more modern.

Hobbes did not have a name for his theory of motivation; today philosophers call it "psychological egoism."[9] According to this theory all voluntary acts – as opposed to accidental events and bodily functions – have as their motive a benefit to the agent. Hobbes presents his view in *Leviathan*, where he writes:

> Of the voluntary acts of every man, the object is some good to *himself*.[10]
>
> For no man giveth, but with intention of good to himself; because gift is voluntary; and of all voluntary acts, the object is to every man his own good.
> (100)
>
> Every man by nature seeketh his own benefit, and promotion.
> (126)

84 *Selfishness and secrecy*

Psychological egoism therefore rejects the possibility of altruism, if by altruism one means the sacrifice of one's own interests for the interests of another. According to Hobbes, I can sacrifice my own interests for yours only if I believe – correctly or incorrectly – that it is in my interest to do so. A standard objection to Hobbes's psychological egoism is that it is tautological;[11] rather than creating a theory that can be tested observationally, Hobbes simply defines human motivation *a priori* in terms of selfishness. The easy defense of such a closed theory allows one to ignore potential evidence against it. If a person leaps in front of another to take a bullet meant for her friend, a Hobbesian does not have to consider the possibility of such an act's being altruistic. Clearly, the "heroine" believed that such an action was to her advantage – by definition. (It is, of course, possible to mistake a disadvantage for an advantage.) Thackeray's informal statement of his theory ("we are for the most part an abominably foolish and selfish people"), vague as it is, at least avoids Hobbes's logical problem. The phrase "for the most part" allows that altruism – or at least unselfish behavior – is logically possible. The question of what counts as such an unselfish act, however rare, as opposed to the much more common selfish acts, will be an empirical one rather than a definitional one.[12] What evidence is there in the world of *Vanity Fair* that we are all primarily egoists in this sense?

The examples presented by Thackeray are of course legion, some less ambiguous than others. It scarcely seems necessary to establish that Becky Sharp is always motivated by self-interest, unless of course one ignores the narrator's sometimes unsubtle attempts at irony ("poor, innocent creature" [17], "the simple girl" [26], "a poor, artless girl" [142],"this artless little creature" [440]), each of which is countered by a more straightforward judgment, even though these judgments too are covered with a thin coat of sugar: "the little artful minx" (47), "the little schemer" (523). Consider Rebecca's attentive and solicitous nursing of Miss Crawley during the old lady's final illness. Does Miss Crawley see through her? The narrator suspects so:

> And I am not sure that . . . the shrewd old London lady, upon whom these treasures of friendship were lavished, had not a lurking suspicion all the while of her affectionate nurse and friend. It must have often crossed Miss Crawley's mind that nobody does anything for nothing.

The narrator continues:

> Like many wealthy people, it was Miss Crawley's habit to accept as much service as she could get from her inferiors; and good-naturedly to take leave of them when she no longer found them useful.

Then the narrator addresses his reader:

> Nor have you, O poor parasite and humble hanger-on, much reason to complain. Your friendship for Dives is about as sincere as the return which it usually gets. It is money you love and not the man; and were Croesus and his

footman to change places you know, you poor rogue, who would have the benefit of your allegiance.

(144)

This passage seems to imply that both the victim and the victimizer are manipulative egoists. Apparently everyone is a Becky Sharp; she's just better at it than most of us.[13]

There is one significant act of generosity on Becky's part that appears to be a counterexample to the allegation of Becky's pan-egoism. Becky has saved the note that George Osborne slipped to her at the ball (the night before his death) in which he asked Becky to abandon her husband and run off with him. Near the end of the novel, after Amelia has perhaps terminally alienated Major Dobbin over what she takes to be an offense against the cherished memory of her dead husband, Becky brandishes the letter before Amelia's horrified eyes. Because this act is purposefully designed to bring about Amelia's disenchantment with her rogue of a husband, Amelia is able to return to the faithful Dobbin and eventually to find (a modicum of) happiness in her marriage to him.

I find no textual evidence indicating that Becky's act is motivated exclusively by self-interest. Rebecca had been annoyed at the salacious attention paid to Amelia by two officer-friends of Jos Sedley's and was protecting her from them. The narrator says, "Rebecca, *to do her justice*, never would let either of these men remain alone with Amelia" (679, emphasis added). On the day she reveals her knowledge of George's true nature to Amelia, Becky thinks to herself: "She shan't marry either of these men. . . . No, she shall marry the bamboo cane. I'll settle it this very night" (880). The "bamboo cane" is of course Becky's enemy, Major Dobbin. And he *is* her enemy, but, again, "to do her justice," we must note that, according to the narrator, "She admired Dobbin; she bore him no rancour for the part he had taken against her. It was an open move in the game, and played fairly" (670). Therefore, it is reasonable to say that, in this case – and perhaps only in this case – Becky is motivated by the best interest of another rather than by her own egoism. As such, her demonstration of sympathy is an anti-Hobbesian act. Even Becky Sharp is thus capable of acting in the interest of another at least once in her life. (I have avoided saying that she acts in the interest of *her friend* because there is textual evidence that she considers herself to be a friend to no one.) The narrator calls it "a rare mark of sympathy" (682), and indeed it is not only rare, it is startling. It is so atypical as to be the exception that proves the rule. Even so, Rebecca's intention does not seem to be an altruistic act, if by altruism we mean an act in which one's own interests are sacrificed to the interests of another. In the context of a discussion concerning Becky's decision to have Dobbin and Amelia marry, the narrator makes it clear that Becky will attend to her matchmaking only after satisfactorily attending to her own affairs, Becky "being by no means so much interested about anybody's welfare as about her own" (672). Her kind act is described as a respite from her usual marauding:

> The halt in that roving, restless life was inexpressibly soothing and pleasant to her. So, pleased herself, she tried with all her might to please everybody;

and we know that she was eminent and successful as a practitioner in the art of giving pleasure.

(673)

Moreover, Becky seems to enjoy the control she has over the situation, as well as her obvious intellectual superiority over Amelia. Before commencing her annihilation of Amelia's love for George, Becky surveys her friend "with a sort of *contemptuous kindness*" (680, emphasis added). She then calls Amelia to her face a "silly, heartless, ungrateful little creature" and a "fool." Rebecca Sharp is clearly enjoying herself, as the illustration accompanying this episode demonstrates (680).

Do any other characters in the novel – particularly other main characters – exhibit convincing evidence of non-egoistic motivation? What about George Osborne, Amelia Osborne (née Sedley), and Rawdon Crawley? And what about lesser characters such as Jos Sedley, Lord Steyne, the two Sir Pitts, and Miss Crawley? Certainly George Osborne cannot be placed in such an anti-Hobbesian category (who, having just tried to seduce Becky on the night before his death, contemplates his situation: "Hope, remorse, ambition, tenderness, and selfish regret filled his heart. . . . [H]ow selfish, brutal, and black with crime!" [292]). We see that, according to the narrator (who "knows everything" [329]), even George's regret is selfish. Similarly, the narrator makes no bones about attributing the motivation of Jos Sedley, Lord Steyne, and the Sirs Pitt, elder and younger, exclusively to egoism. The narrator twice refers to Sir Pitt the younger as "Machiavel" (344). The narrator's oxymoronic benediction at Miss Crawley's death scene is: "Peace to thee, kind and selfish, vain and generous old heathen!" (351).[14]

Despite *Vanity Fair*'s subtitle, *A Novel without a Hero*,[15] Thackeray's narrator sometimes refers to Amelia Sedley as "our heroine" (95, 96, 391). It might be hoped, therefore, that of all the characters in the novel, she can be found to be motivated by something other than selfishness. Indeed, when the narrator discusses the "nature and instinct of women," he writes: "Some are made to scheme, and some are made to love" (122). The referents are clearly Becky and Amelia, so upon reading this we are prone to consider Amelia's love as the basis of a non-selfish motivation. But in the next sentence we are told that, because of her love for George Osborne, Amelia "neglected her twelve dear friends at Chiswick most cruelly, as such selfish people commonly do" (122). Much later in the novel, the narrator says, "This woman had a way of tyrannizing over Major Dobbin" (663). The Major himself has the same thought, referring to Amelia as the "little heedless tyrant" (677). The notion that this accusation is merely another of the myriad examples of the narrator's idea of irony must evaporate before the well-known painful scene near the end of the novel, in which Amelia is on the verge of losing her faithful friend and not-so-secret lover, William Dobbin, who prepares to abandon her in frustrated disgust. The narrator says: "She didn't wish to marry him, but she wished to keep him. She wished to give him nothing, but that he should give her all. It is a bargain not unfrequently levied in love" (670). U. C. Knoepflmacher correctly infers:

> While Becky disregards all considerations beyond the self, Amelia's love is presumably directed at others. And yet her childlike and naive obsession with

love resembles Becky's adult and cynical obsession with money. . . . Amelia's love, like Becky's, thus is self-love. . . . Like Becky, she takes without offering a return.[16]

More than thirty years ago John Halperin derided Amelia's selfishness, calling it

> another strain of villainy – less pronounced, less conscious than Becky's, but just as virulent and just as destructive. . . . [Becky's egoism is] unscrupulous, clever, and sentient – Amelia's is a concomitant of stupidity. But it is neither less destructive nor more excusable than Becky's, and therefore it is of equal importance in the novel.[17]

Halperin points out that Amelia has been too self-absorbed to appreciate Dobbin's merit even as much as Becky, his enemy, does (44). He concludes,

> Although Amelia is meek and passive where Becky is aggressive, in her own fashion she is as self-centered as Becky. . . . War rages "all over Europe," but Amelia thinks only of George and her own relationship with him.
> (39–40)

By contrast, Halperin calls William Dobbin "the only character who manages to combine generosity and selflessness with intelligence and strength" (55). Does Dobbin, then, exhibit a motivation unlike the other egoistic characters in the novel? More than a dozen times the narrator refers to him as "honest William," "honest Dobbin," or "our honest Major."[18] In context none of these appellations appears to be ironic. (Thackeray is certainly capable of using the word "honest" in a mocking way, as when he uses the term to describe Rawdon Crawley [373, 487, 502], or when he calls young James Pitt "honest James" [344] after the young man drunkenly says the first self-indicting foolish thing that comes into his mind.) On the other hand, it is more difficult to determine the status of Thackeray's intentions when he has his narrator say such things about Dobbin as: "his selfishness was punished just as such odious egotism deserved to be" (300); or when he calls him "the most selfish tactician" and "this Machiavellian captain" (223), "the heartless man" (437), "this artful Major," a "rogue . . . [who] was urged by . . . hypocrisy" (575), "like a hypocrite as he was" (626), and "this odious, artful Major" (657). The contexts in which most of these condemnations appear indicate that they are most likely meant to be read as irony. Indeed, because we have come to believe that Dobbin's motivations are all governed by honesty and love for Amelia, we are taken aback when, exasperated, he responds to her in a fashion not seen before: "'This manner toward me is one which scarcely becomes you, Amelia' the Major answered haughtily" (668).

In the same letter of September 1848, in which Thackeray stated the object of his novel was to demonstrate that we are "an abominably foolish and selfish people," he says, "if I had made Amelia a higher order of woman there would have been no vanity in Dobbin's falling in love with her." Does the vanity that Thackeray attributes to Dobbin constitute a kind of egoism, and does Thackeray feel the need to attribute it to him in order to demonstrate that even the best of the principal characters is ultimately motivated by selfishness? Even if this is Thackeray's intention, Dobbin's boundless capacity for self-sacrifice makes it clear that he is not a truly Hobbesian character. As has been shown, Thackeray's assertion that we are all egoists is qualified by the phrase "for the most part." There is no conclusive textual evidence that Dobbin is "for the most part" selfish, though there is compelling evidence that he is foolish.[19] (There is even less evidence that the long-suffering, faithful Miss Briggs – "honest Briggs," [249, 251, 521, and 526] – lesser character though she may be, is ever motivated by selfishness, though she too is certainly foolish. Indeed, we might say – recasting a formula from John Halperin – that in the same way Amelia's selfishness is a concomitant of her stupidity, so Miss Briggs's *altruism* is a concomitant of her stupidity.)

A number of Thackeray scholars offer indirect support for the hypothesis that Thackeray attributes to all of us a modified version of universal egoism. These critics find a significant association, parallel, identity, collusion, or sympathy between Rebecca Sharp and Thackeray, or in some cases Thackeray's narrator.[20] Barbara Hardy, in fact, goes so far as to declare that Thackeray "could certainly have adapted Flaubert and said, 'Becky Sharp, c'est moi.'"[21] But because Thackeray's narrator clearly identifies with his middle-class readership ("Ah, my beloved readers and brethren" [503]),[22] if Thackeray can say, "Becky Sharp, c'est moi," then *we* can say, "Becky Sharp, c'est nous." If this conclusion is the one intended by Thackeray, and if he was right, then a rather shocking secret has been revealed to his nineteenth-century readers, many of whom surely read the novel in a state of righteous indignation at the amoral selfishness of Becky Sharp, and would be offended to be placed in the same category as she. Thackeray's secret was as radical as Darwin's, which would be revealed a decade later. Many a Victorian citizen wished to dismiss both of these secrets as mere fiction. Perhaps the kind of secret we are dealing with here is akin to Goffman's "latent secrets," which are secrets based on information that is available in scraps, but these scraps "might not have been gathered and presented publicly in a systematic form" (Goffman 144). In the cases of Darwin's and Thackeray's secrets, the evidence was available and, they might have said, staring people in the face; however, these are the faces of people in denial. But now, in the case of Thackeray, no more. The cat of selfishness has indeed been loosed from the bag of secrecy.

It is well known that Hobbes solves the question of how a social world can be possible if it is made up of individuals who are all egoists. He does so by developing a theory of social contract in which each individual theoretically (as opposed to actually) realizes that in the long run it is in her best interest to compromise her immediate self-interests by accepting social rules that are cognizant of the interests of others, even if these rules oppose one's *immediate* self-interest. Hobbes opposes this world governed by a social contract to an imagined "state of nature" in which each of us follows our own untrammeled egoistic impulses at the expense of the interests of others. Hobbes analyzes what human relations would be like in such a "state of nature," and infamously concludes that it constitutes a condition of "continual fear, and danger of violent death; and the life of man, solitary, poor, nasty, brutish, and short" (84). According to Hobbes, by entering into the social contract we leave behind us "the war of each against all," even if there is always the threat of the collapse back into that horrible state.

Thackeray seems to accept Hobbes's depiction of human nature, and Hobbes's claim that the social contract (or systems of performance, as I will soon call them) save us from the worst degradations of our own selfish, foolish nature. However, he parts from Hobbes when the latter says that by entering into a formal social arrangement we leave the war of each against all behind us. The social contract for Thackeray does not supersede that war: rather it brings it forward into society in a new, ameliorated and therefore less dangerous if more disguised form. As Robert Lougy writes, "Thackeray suggests . . . that civilization . . . rests upon a tacitly accepted hypocrisy and aggression" (260). The aggression – Hobbes's "time of war, where every man is enemy to every man" (101) – is ongoing, but it is "disguised," sometimes thinly, sometimes densely, by a set of performances that are recognized by all, at some level, as performances. Another secret in broad daylight. Lougy continues, claiming that the world Thackeray shows us "is defined by aggression – on the battlefield, in the marketplace, in the drawing room – and while the rules of the game vary, the prizes sought and the prices paid are similar" (260). Thackeray's narrator says, "The nods between Rawdon and Dobbin were of the very faintest specimens of politeness" (282). But the performance – the nods – are all that stand between the antagonists and the state of nature. And what about home and hearth, the supposed Victorian refuge from the battlefield of the competing captains of industry and their mignons? Judith Weissman astutely observes:

> The home, in Thackeray's view, no more than the country, is a haven. . . . [T]he family is as full of cruelty and exploitiveness as the business world in *Vanity Fair*. Thackeray shows us competition and viciousness within the Osborne, Steyne, and Crawley families, and he draws his readers into his cruel circle, refusing to allow us to imagine that we are different from his corrupt characters. . . . The middle-class leisured readers of Thackeray's novel are presumed to be in the camp of the victimizers, along with the majority of the characters.[23]

No surprise that one critic has declared, "Of the early Victorian novelists, Thackeray . . . was certainly the most disconcerting, if only because he offered so few consolations."[24] Thackeray offered fewer consolations than Hobbes as well, because he showed that in Vanity Fair we do not leave behind the state of nature and its war of each against all; we simply sublimate it into something barely more supportable. At the end of the novel, Thackeray's narrator gives us the last glimpse of Becky Sharp: "She has her enemies. Who has not?" (689). Again, who indeed?[25]

I have argued here that there is not only one cat in the bag of secrecy that Thackeray lets escape but two. The first represents the nearly universal egoism that motivates all of us in Vanity Fair. Most adults with a propensity to philosophize must sometimes consider this Hobbesian/Thackerayan "secret," if only in their darker moments. The second represents another secret, a purely Thackerayan one, a secret that goes beyond Hobbes's pessimism and into cynicism, and is therefore more stunning than the first: the secret that the only way that Hobbes's "war of each against all" can be kept at bay is by entering into a permanent theatrical game of performances that involve deceptive (and therefore secretive) practices at every turn. If this is true, then the success of performativity – and therefore of sociality – depends on its secrets. Thackeray thought seriously about this possibility. Goffman wrote a book about it.

The war of each against all

One of the strategies of war is to gather intelligence concerning the enemy's condition and intentions. That is, as if in a military deployment, each of us must constantly attempt to penetrate the secrets of the other. Let us revisit in its totality the curious passage in *Vanity Fair* whose beginning we saw earlier concerning the prying into the secrets of others, one that seems on its surface to indicate the narrator's disapproval of such a procedure. He writes:

> if we are to be peering into everybody's private life, speculating upon their income, and cutting them if we don't approve of their expenditure – why, what a howling wilderness and intolerable dwelling Vanity Fair would be! Every man's hand would be against his neighbor in this case, my dear sir, and the benefits of civilization would be done away with. We should be quarrelling, abusing, avoiding one another. Our houses would become caverns, and we should go in rags because we cared for nobody. Rents would go down. Parties wouldn't be given any more. All the tradesmen of the town would be bankrupt. Wine, wax-lights, comestibles, rouge, crinoline-petticoats, diamonds, wigs, Louis-Quatorze gimcracks, and old china, park hacks, and splendid high-stepping carriage horses – all the delights of life, I say, would go to the deuce.
>
> (507)

The language is similar to Hobbes's description of the state of nature (especially "the howling wilderness," and "every man's hand would be against his neighbour ... and the benefits of civilization would be done away with"). Still, Thackeray's list of horrors – merely bemoaning the loss of petticoats, precious stones, and wigs – does not seem quite as depressing as Hobbes's, which includes

> no ... industry, ... no culture of the earth; no navigation, nor the use of commodities that may be imported by sea; no commodious building, no instruments of moving; ... no knowledge of the face of the earth; no account of time; no arts; no letters; no society; and which is worst of all, continual fear.
>
> (84)

Yet, despite his obvious mockery, the issue here for Thackeray is the centrality of secrecy in the social fabric. Therefore, the sentiment in this passage is as much Simmelian as Hobbesian.

According to Simmel, as we saw in chapter 1, even the most intimate relationship requires "distances and intermissions" (315). The necessary withholding of information is most often achieved "by mere secrecy and concealment" (316), but lying – a more "aggressive technique" (316) for achieving the same end – is common. This means that lies, though morally negative, can have a certain social value. Even though lies sometimes destroy relationships, lying is "an integral element" (316) of all relationships, just as is the secrecy that lying protects. Recall that for Simmel, there could exist no relationships or societies "which are *not* based on this teleologically determined non-knowledge of each other" (312). If Vanity Fair exists at all as a social unity removed even slightly from the state of nature, it is because social relations are cemented by secrets, lies, misinformation, manipulated ignorance, illusion, and all the other forms of veiled information.

We saw that, despite the need for secrecy in all relationships, we always know things about the other that the other believes he has withheld; and those things we know "are frequently matters whose knowledge the other person (were he aware of it) would find undesirable" (Simmel 323). In other words, in every fairly close relationship, the other has always already penetrated some of our secrets, and therefore possesses destructive information about us. If this feature of Simmel's theory applies to *Vanity Fair*, as surely it must, then in Thackeray's version of Hobbesian egoism – that is, a version in which the war of each against all is brought forward from the state of nature into the commonwealth itself, into Vanity Fair – discovering the secrets of the other becomes a primary tool of protection from and power over the other. The marriage of the insights of (Thackerayan) Hobbesism and Simmelian sociology implies that society itself – Vanity Fair – is anti-social. No wonder there is so little hope offered in Thackeray's novel.

Performing self(ishness)

It has been noted that Hobbes envisions a civil society based on a recognition by all egoists (i.e., by everybody) that the only way their individual welfare can be maximized is to behave in ways that tend to maximize the welfare of others (though Hobbes knows very well that many people will be more immediately motivated to behave civilly by their fear of punishment by the authorities). Thackeray, on the other hand, imagines not a replacement of the state of nature by a civil society in which most individuals recognize that it is in their best interest to behave civilly but a system of *competitive performances* that will disguise (always from others and often from the performers themselves) both the motives and the anxiety of the performers.

Earlier, I implied that Thackeray's novel anticipates the sociological writing of Erving Goffman. Goffman, like Thackeray, commences his book with the metaphor of life as a stage. As we saw in chapter 1, Goffman says, in the preface to *The Presentation of Self in Everyday Life*, "The perspective employed in this report is that of the theatrical performance: the principles derived are dramaturgical ones" (xi). In his preface to *Vanity Fair*, called "Before the Curtain," Thackeray's narrator presents himself as the "Manager of the Performance" (x). By insisting at the beginning and end of the novel that the performers are all marionettes, the Manager seems to be placing himself in the role of puppeteer (although, if this is so, as many commentators have noted, he soon loses control of his puppets), but he also characterizes himself as a mere observer of others' performances.

If there is a performance, then there is a performer. (I include puppeteers as performers; Thackeray seems to agree.) As I showed in the first chapter, Goffman always gazes hard at the performance but rarely at the performer behind the roles, and when he does, not much information is forthcoming. Late in his book he writes:

> Let us turn now from the individual as character performed to the individual as performer. He has a capacity to learn, . . . He is given to having fantasies and dreams, some that pleasurably unfold a triumphant performance, others full of anxiety and dread. . . . He often manifests a gregarious desire for teammates and audiences, a tactful consideration for their concerns; and he has a capacity for deeply felt shame, leading him to minimize the chances he takes of exposure.[26]

Recall that Goffman adds, "Behind many masks and many characters, each performer tends to wear a single look, a naked unsocialized look, a look of concentration, a look of one who is privately engaged in a difficult, treacherous task" (234). But Goffman does not seem interested in providing a substantive theory concerning the pre-theatrical individual. Thackeray, by contrast, is much less reticent on this theme than Goffman. For him, each individual is indeed an actor, and behind the performing actor is a quasi-Hobbesian organism (with, perhaps, touches of Schopenhauerian perversion) whose essence expresses itself in behavior organized to maximize survival, power, and pleasure – which, in Vanity Fair, means to maximize material wealth, or at least the appearance of it. To achieve these goals, each organism becomes a dissembler, and each performance is a weapon, offensive or defensive, in a larger armamentarium.

By the middle of Thackeray's novel, the narrator seems to have slipped from his roles of Manager/puppeteer/sociologist and has become one more performer (actor? marionette?) among the others, as he relates conversations and encounters he has had with various characters in the novel ("as Captain Dobbin has since informed me . . ."; "I was told by Dr. Pestler . . ." [389]), and indeed, he has descended to the role of mere gossiper ("do you suppose, I say . . . that the Marchioness of Steyne, the haughtiest woman in England, would bend down to her husband so submissively if there were not some cause? Pooh! I tell you there are *secret reasons*" [467]).[27] And if, in a novel in which the actions of virtually every character are accused of being mere performance, and if the narrator himself is simply another character in the novel, hence another actor, can we not say that Thackeray's theory of performance is itself a performance? There are signs that this is indeed the case. Lisa Jadwin observes that, as the novel progresses, "The narrator . . . increasingly draws attention to his narrative as a theatrical spectacle staged to manipulate the reader."[28] In a similar vein, Wolfgang Iser observes that the narrator

> is continually donning new masks: at one moment he is an observer of the Fair, like the reader; then he is suddenly blessed with extraordinary knowledge, . . . then, toward the end, he announces that the whole story was not his own at all, but that he overheard it in a conversation.[29]

If one's motives are selfish, and if one must disguise those motives – for whatever reason (because denial is part of the performance, or even only because "there are certain things one does not discuss in Vanity Fair") – then performance (and performance as dissimulation) will be *de rigueur*. There is little doubt that virtually all of Rebecca Sharp's actions are theatrical acts that involve dissimulation. We do not need to scan the novel for examples; rather, we should look for counterexamples. We find these particularly in the case of expressions of emotions, but even there, rarely. Already as a child she was not given to exposing her feelings. "Miss Rebecca Sharp never blushed in her life – at least not since she was eight years old, and when she was caught stealing jam out of a cupboard by her grandmother" (28). Still, as a nineteen-year-old Becky is shown a drawing by her dead father "which caused her to burst into tears and leave the room, ... her eyes red with weeping" (25–26). On a couple of occasions emotions threaten to emerge during moments of friendship with Amelia. Calming Amelia on the night before the Battle of Waterloo, "'He will come back, my dear,' said Rebecca, touched in spite of herself" (310). On a later occasion she expresses gratitude to Amelia, with an emotion that "for a moment was almost genuine" (659). Much later still, having caught her small son spying on her as she sings for Lord Steyne, Becky "came out and struck him violently a couple of boxes on the ear." Before little Rawdon flees to the kitchen, "bursting in an agony of grief," he hears Lord Steyne laughing, "amused by the free and artless exhibition of Becky's temper" (444).

Although many of Becky's performances are simply the required roles of social intercourse (as governess, as wife, as hostess), they almost always have a quality of wiliness about them, consciously involving "the art of deceiving" (17), as well as "arts and cajoleries" (241). She is a "little artful minx" (47), she "writhes and twists about like a snake" (286), she is a "little schemer" (523), while at the same time being "a perfect performer" (64). As in the case of real actors on stage, the audience is complicit in the artifice and in the attempt to pass off illusion as reality. Indeed, members of real audiences are critical of the actors if they fail in their attempt at deception. But in Vanity Fair many members of the audience are much less consciously aware of the forms of fraud and imposture required in what Goffman calls "the show that must go on" (252), and less adept at seeing through them. Amelia Osborne is the main case in point. Becky is easily able to take Amelia in. When Becky tells Amelia an outrageous, complicated lie concerning the reason that she has been separated from her son, Amelia bursts into tears over the

94 *Selfishness and secrecy*

way Becky has been so shamefully treated. The narrator says, "the consummate little tragedian must have been charmed to see the effect which her performance produced on her audience" (661). But even such a hardened and experienced old actor as Lord Steyne can be overpowered by Becky's skills. Consider the scene in which Becky relates to Lord Steyne how Miss Briggs has been ruined by Becky's inability to repay her debt to Miss Briggs: after breaking down, she begins to "cry bitterly" (481). She convinces him that her husband will kill her if he finds out how much debt she is in. When a deeply moved Lord Steyne leaves to write a draft to Becky for the amount of the debt (which Becky has overstated by double), "she rose up with the queerest expression of victorious mischief glittering in her green eyes" (481).

Hobbes calls those who refuse to see that the social contract is in their own interest "Fooles." David Gauthier, a modern-day defender of Hobbes, calls those Fooles – that is, those who seek only to maximize their own interests – "straightforward maximizers," and those who realize that it is in their interest to honor the interests of others he calls "constrained maximizers." Gauthier makes the following observation:

> If we fall into a society – or rather into a state of nature – of straightforward maximizers, the constrained maximization, which disposes us to justice, will indeed be of no use to us, and we must then consult only the direct dictates of our own utilities. . . . In a world of Fooles, it would not pay to be a constrained maximizer, and to comply with one's agreements. In such circumstances, it would not be rational to be moral.[30]

It seems that Vanity Fair is a world of Hobbesian Fooles who believe that it is in their interest to *feign* commitment to the social contract, but, because either they think that they cannot trust others enough to abide by the contract's constraints, or they believe they can benefit from breaking its rules while pretending to play the game, they continue to be covert straightforward maximizers. Even Thackeray's narrator sometimes seems to hold this view, and therefore he occasionally justifies Rebecca Sharp's aggressive pursuit of self-interest. In chapter 10, titled "Miss Sharp Begins to Make Friends," the narrator writes: "and, if there entered some degree of selfishness into her calculations, who can say but that her prudence was perfectly justifiable?" (92). Therefore, unlike the cases in Hobbes and Goffman, in *Vanity Fair* the performances, rather than being forms of cooperation, become competitive with winners and losers, as we saw with Becky's lies vanquishing both Amelia and Lord Steyne. And, as Becky moves up in society, she cuts people whose friendship she had once sought. She explains: "One must, my dear, show one is somebody. One mustn't be seen with doubtful people" (478).

When Goffman attempts to define his concept of "performance" in terminology not taken from theatrical lexicons (thereby avoiding the circularity of so many definitions), he says, "A 'performance' may be defined as all the activity of a given participant on a given occasion which serves to influence in any way any of the other participants" (15).[31] This seems almost too broad to be useful. More helpful is an earlier example of a performance, but not a definitional one, that Goffman described as "a kind of information game – a potentially infinite cycle of concealment, discovery, false revelation, and rediscovery" (8). This characterization brings in the Simmelian component of Goffman's theory of performance (recall that Simmel is the only sociologist mentioned in Goffman's preface to *The Presentation of Self in Everyday Life*) because we see that such a performance always has secrets to hide. Indeed, a scrutiny of Goffman's examples reveals that *all* performances intentionally involve concealment. This is because performance is always a kind of "impression management" (238); a performance always fosters a "definition of the situation," which is a "reality which is dramatized" (141). The performer must suppress any reality that is at odds with the one she wishes to "foster" or "define." According to Goffman, "a performer tends to conceal or underplay those activities, facts, and motives which are incompatible with an idealized version of himself and his products" (48). Keeping secrets is not the same as lying, but because control over the situation is at stake, "many performers have ample capacity and motive to misrepresent the facts; only shame, guilt, or fear prevent them from doing so" (58). Still, Goffman makes it clear that he is not claiming that the performed reality, even if it is the product of withholding or misrepresenting information, is less real than another reality. It is through performance that social reality comes about (65).[32] Vanity Fair is a real place. It is an artifice, but it is not artificial. It is what real social interaction is like. Without secrets there would be no social life, only "the state of nature." But how much worse could such a state be than this "howling wilderness"?

Orientalized secrecy in the howling wilderness

Vanity Fair, whose author was born in India, is a book in which orientalist subplots are never far below the surface – though often the function of these subplots is to mock the orientalism that so fascinated much of the British reading public. One of the most sustained of these subplots is also probably the least significant one – namely, the recurring references to Joseph Sedley, "who was in the East India Company's Civil Service, and his name appeared . . . in the Bengal Division of the East India Register, as collector of Boggley Wollah, an honorable and lucrative post, as everyone knows" (33). Jos is certainly swathed in orientalist signifiers. Though he seems to be a minor player, as we approach the end of the novel, we begin to realize that one of the biggest mysteries that Thackeray leaves unresolved is the cause of Joseph Sedley's death, a mystery that seems to point to Rebecca Sharp as a secret murderess. This is a mystery placed squarely in the center of a faux-orientalist context. Most often these signs are indications of luxurious self-indulgence, a typical orientalist fantasy. Occasionally Jos's Oriental signifiers are preludes to escape, as such signifiers often are. These evasions sometimes serve as small escapes from his shy awkwardness (much to Becky's annoyance, he rushes off to see a production of *"The Forty Thieves"* [37] rather than deal with Rebecca's flirtatious gratitude after he recovers the handkerchief that she has allowed to fall to the floor); sometimes they are large escapes, as when, shortly before his mysterious death, he plots his escape from Rebecca Crawley's murderous hand ("He would go back to India. He would do anything, only . . . they mustn't say anything to Mrs. Crawley – she'd – she'd kill me if she knew it. You don't know what a terrible woman she is" [820]). Here, Jos's secret is his desire to escape Becky's sinister control over him, and what better imaginary escape than into the Orient? If Jos had managed to flee to India, would his life and money be safe from the machinations of Rebecca Sharp?

Sometimes the proliferation of orientalist signs are Thackeray's jokes mocking the Jos Sedleys of Vanity Fair, which, as I noted earlier, is to mock British orientalism itself, as when the guests at a party given by Becky include His Excellency "Papoosh Pasha, the Turkish Ambassador, attended by Kibob Bey" (599), or that the ignorant, pompous Miss Pinkerton was "the Semiramis of Hammersmith" (11), that she wore a turban that she "tossed . . . indignantly" (17), and that the foolish Irish Lady O'Dowd also showed up in public places in a turban (818). Though Miss Pinkerton and Lady O'Dowd may have had secrets that these orientalist signifiers were meant to conceal, Thackeray's narrator makes certain that all of them are revealed. He is also recording fictitious examples of how orientalism was intervening in Victorian subjectivities.

As in so many of the novels of the period, *Arabian Nights* makes multiple appearances in *Vanity Fair*. Becky refers to the tales at dinner, to make light of her embarrassing response to the red pepper that she has swallowed whole: "I ought to have remembered the pepper which the Princess of Persia puts in the cream-tarts in the *Arabian Nights*" (34). We had been informed early on of Becky Sharp's familiarity with these tales:

> She had a vivid imagination; she had, besides, read the *Arabian Nights* . . .; she had arrayed herself in an infinity of shawls, turbans, and diamond necklaces, and had mounted upon an elephant to the sound of the march in *Bluebeard*, in order to pay a visit of ceremony to the Grand Mogul. Charming Alnashar visions! It is the happy privilege of youth to construct you, and many a fanciful young creature besides Rebecca Sharp has indulged in these delightful day-dreams ere now!
>
> (32–33)

The parallel world into which secrecy allows us to slip is here an orientalized one, for children as for adults. Although the tone of this passage is one of frivolity, we should note, as does Micael Clarke, that "[t]he Bluebeard and Scheherazade motifs from *Arabian Nights*, both narratives about murderous husbands, are linked (in a chapter titled 'Rebecca is in Presence of the Enemy') to Becky's dreams of marriage to Jos Sedley."[33] The orientalist signifiers here may well be omens of a secret murderous plot that will unfold before Becky's tale is done.

But if the tales of *Arabian Nights* inspire much of Becky's immoral and even murderous secret plots, we must recognize a more noble inspiration as well in the novel. As a youngster, William Dobbin – the closest thing to a hero that we find in the novel – also has a passionate relation to *Arabian Nights*. In school, during the play period, we find William lying on his back under a tree, lost in a trance as he reads "a favourite copy" of the tales (a line that seems to imply that he had several copies). Young William

> had for once forgotten the world, and was away with Sinbad the Sailor in the Valley of the Diamonds, or with Prince Ahmed and the Fairy Peribanou in that delightful cavern where the Prince found her, and whither we should all like to make a tour.
>
> (55)

This is a clear case of the orientalizing of the imagination, and, by extension, of secrecy. In this same episode, the narrator refers to "those feelings and thoughts which are a mystery to all," in particular, the feelings and thoughts of a child before his mind has been tainted by the ideas of "the dull and world-corrupted person who rules him" (parents? King?) (55).

Young Dobbin's reverie in the school yard is broken by the shrill cries of little George Osborne who is being beaten by the school bully.

> Dobbin looked up. The Fairy Peribanou had fled into the inmost cavern with Prince Ahmed: the Roc had whisked away Sinbad the Sailor out of the Valley of Diamonds out of sight, far into the clouds: and there was everyday life before honest William; and a big boy beating a little one without cause.
>
> (56)

Robert Lougy, while recognizing that the episode foreshadows what Dobbin will become in adult life, resists the temptation to dismiss as a frivolity the power of *Arabian Nights* over the imagination. For Lougy, this episode, along with a few others in the novel, sets up an opposition to the frivolity of the world of Vanity Fair – a world that Thackeray surely condemns. Lougy writes:

> Thackeray returns to the cavern of Fairy Peribanou, . . . This cavern becomes for him a repository of memories of the "expression of youth," usually relived or recaptured as an adult. When such memories are regained, if only for an instant, they stand apart from and opposed to the present moment and represent a plane of experience more intense and more real than the world of *Vanity Fair* makes possible. But because they also create a heightened awareness of the disparity between the world the person now possesses and the world he or she once loved, these moments provoke a profound sense of loss as well.
>
> (265)

I would like to emphasize that this secret space – this cavern of youthful memories – is an orientalized space. Lougy recognizes this as well. He talks about young Dobbin

> during those moments when he had "for once forgotten the world": a sanctified and solitary realm within which mysterious feelings and thoughts remain

inviolate, it is a domain, like those magic lands in *The 1001 Arabian Nights*, where desire and fulfillment merge.

(264)

And, as I keep insisting, where there is desire, there is usually secrecy, especially in the Victorian world.[34]

We should recall that at the end of the novel, Dobbin, who has spent the greater part of his life in a state of misery over his unrequited love for Amelia, is discovered to be slightly but unquestionably dissatisfied when he finally achieves his desire. He has a recompense, however; he is writing a *History of the Punjaub*, "which," even as the narrator tells his story years later, "still occupies him" (819). Indeed, there is a hint on the last page of the novel that perhaps William is fonder of his *History of the Punjaub* than he is of Amelia. The secret pleasures of the Orient are an antidote to the flatness of Victorian matrimony.

Scheherazade, after all, tells her tales to save her head from the executioner's sword. There is in *The 1001 Arabian Nights* violence, brutality, tyranny and fanaticism, as there was in the Victorian idea of the East. No surprise that the orientalizing of fantasy and secrecy in *Vanity Fair* sometimes take on more unseemly or even sinister inferences. When George Osborne goes against his father's wishes and promises the now disgraced Amelia that he will marry her, she cries, kisses his hand "humbly, as if he were here supreme chief and master." George is flattered.

> He saw a slave before him in that simple yielding faithful creature, and his soul within him *thrilled secretly* somehow at the knowledge of his power. He would be generous minded, Sultan as he was, and raise up this kneeling Esther, and make a queen of her.
>
> (226, emphasis added)

Again, we see here the orientalizing of secrecy and fantasy. We find also in *Vanity Fair*, as elsewhere in Victorian racial categorizing, that biblical Jews have much of the same glory as the heroes of *Arabian Nights*, but contemporary Jews, while still somewhat exoticized, are "dingy guests of Oriental countenance" (191); the references are all either to "Solomon's glories, and all the wardrobes of the Queen of Sheba" (132) or "those inexorable Israelites" (577).

On one occasion, *Vanity Fair*'s Lord Steyne rages at the women of his family and commands them to obey his request that Mrs. Crawford be invited to a party where only the high and mighty will be in attendance. This was the way "Lord Steyn treated his 'Hareem' whenever symptoms of subordination appeared in his household" (576). On another occasion the narrator interrupts his story to comment:

> We [men] are Turks with the affections of our women. . . . We let their bodies go abroad liberally enough, with smiles and ringlets and pink bonnets to disguise them instead of veils and yakmaks. But their souls must be seen by

only one man, and they obey not unwillingly, and consent to remain at home as our slaves – ministering to us and doing drudgery for us.

(202)

This is a very interesting observation, and goes a long way in explaining why the performances of women are all hypocritical – that they are so we have on good authority, from our narrator, who tells us that "The best of women (I have heard my grandmother say) are hypocrites. . . . A good housewife is of necessity a humbug; and Cornelia's husband was hoodwinked, as Potiphar was – only in a different way" (197).

Notice the final biblical/orientalist reference in this revelation of the secret of women's character. One can only surmise that men's performances are also all hypocritical, and the hypocrisy is also motivated by fear. In a war of each against all, in which every male begins with an unfair advantage against that half of the population that happens to be female, there must be masculine fear of losing that unmerited privilege. It must be a secret that cannot be admitted; yet the narrator of *Vanity Fair* does so, and casts that secret in terms of orientalist imagery.

Another example of the orientalizing of fantasies of violence occurs in a story told to the narrator by Tom Eaves, the town eavesdrop and gossip, concerning the relationship among brothers in noble homes where legacies are at stake. Tom asserts to our narrator:

> My dear sir, you ought to know that every elder brother looks upon the cadets of the house as his natural enemies, who deprive him of so much ready money which ought to be his by right. I have often heard George Mac Turk, Lord Bajazet's eldest son, say that if he had his will when he came to the title, he would do what the sultans do, and clear the estate by chopping off all his younger brothers' heads at once; and so the case is, more or less, with them all. I tell you, they are all Turks in their hearts.

(556)

Here, even the war of each against all has been orientalized – a war that has been a secret war, until the narrator of *Vanity Fair* lets "the cat of selfishness out of the bag of secrecy."

In another sinister if humorously introduced reference to Britain's colonial reach, we are told that when Jos returns from India, he buys a house in a "comfortable Anglo-Indian district. . . . [W]ho does not know these respectable abodes of the retired Indian aristocracy?" (711). Jos purchased furniture from a certain "Mr. Scape, lately admitted partner into the great Calcutta House of Fogle, Fake, and Cracksman, . . . taking Fake's place." Then the narrator casually mentions that eventually this great agency "failed for a million and plunged half the Indian public into misery and ruin" (712).[35] The White man's burden was to promote ruin among the natives, another secret in broad daylight – daylight from which Thackeray will not let his reader look away. A similarly disturbing passage about the relation between West and East takes place in the German town of Pumpernickel – on the River Pump – where, on a bridge built by the unheralded (and now impoverished) Victor Aurelius XIV, on which his own statue rises,

> surrounded by water nymphs and emblems of victory, peace, and plenty; he has his foot on the neck of a prostrate Turk. ... [Q]uite undisturbed by the agonies of that prostrate Mohametan, who writhes at his feet in the most ghastly manner, the Prince smiles blandly and points with his truncheon in the direction of the Aurelius Platz, where he began to erect a new palace that would have been the wonder of his age had the great-souled Prince but had the funds to complete it.
>
> (748–49)

It is difficult not to see this passage as another example of Thackeray's mocking nineteenth-century orientalism.[36] But Thackeray is not merely a satirist. He shows how British orientalist fantasy hides Oriental fact – the ugly realities of colonial rule. This is yet another way in which orientalism is connected with secrets in the Victorian world.

In *Vanity Fair*, the most striking metaphors that purport to reveal the hidden truth about Rebecca Sharp's character are those of Clytemnestra (who murders her husband, Agamemnon) and Circe (who turns men into swine). But there is a third one, almost as devastating, and it is an orientalist one – that of a marauding Arab. Toward the end of the novel, as Becky once again focuses on the benighted, vulnerable Jos Sedley, first taking advantage of his hospitality, then sinking her claws into him. The narrator makes an observation about Becky's decision to move in with Sedley once more:

> As the most hardened Arab that ever careered across the desert over the hump of a dromedary likes to repose sometimes under the date trees by the water, or come into the cities, walk into the bazaars, refresh himself in the baths, and say his prayers in the mosques, before he goes out again marauding, so Jos's tents and pilau were pleasant to this little Ishmaelite. She picketed her steed, hung up her weapons, and warmed herself comfortably by his fire. The halt in that roving, restless life was inexpressibly soothing and pleasant to her.
>
> (803)

Here we see that the secret of Becky's personality, which the narrator has claimed to be hiding from us, is exposed in orientalist imagery: she is a marauding Ishmaelite, a secret that she manages to keep from many of her victims, but one that is revealed to us by the narrator.

Finally, let us turn to the greatest orientalist episode of the novel, the charades at Gaunt House, which have been prepared to entertain a very aristocratic audience that included His Royal Highness. Lord Steyne was "incited by Becky" to stage a set of charades, new entertainment recently arrived from France, knowing as she did that these games would allow "the many ladies amongst us who had beauty to display their charms, and the fewer number who had cleverness to exhibit their wit" (604) (thereby literalizing Goffman's metaphor about sociality as theater). The point of the charade is for the audience to guess the word that is being acted out. The first charade opens with a Turkish dignitary in full costume languishing on a divan in obvious boredom.

> He claps his hands and Mesrour the Nubian appears, with bare arms, bangles, yataghans, and every Eastern ornament – gaunt, tall, and hideous. He makes a salaam before my lord the Aga. A thrill of terror and delight runs through the assembly. The ladies whisper to one another. The black slave was given to Bedwin Sands by an Egyptian pasha in exchange for three dozen of Maraschino. He has sewn up ever so many odalisques in sacks and tilted them into the Nile.
> "Bid the slave-merchant enter." . . . [H]e brings a veiled female with him. He removes the veil. A thrill of applause bursts through the house. . . . She is in a gorgeous Oriental costume; the black braided locks are twined with innumerable jewels; her dress is covered over with gold piastres. The odious Mohametan expresses himself charmed by her beauty. She falls down on her knees and entreats him.
>
> (605)

By the end of this first charade, the clever members of the audience realize that the name Agamemnon has been acted out, and it is in the second charade that Rebecca plays Clytemnestra for the first time.

> Clytemnestra glides swiftly into the room like an apparition – her arms are bare and white – her tawny hair floats down her shoulders – her face is deadly pale – and her eyes are lighted up with a smile so ghastly that people quake as they look at her. A tremor ran through the room. "Good God!" somebody said, "it's Mrs. Rawdon Crawley."
>
> (606–7)

Thus, we have witnessed a double instantiation of the orientalization of secrecy. First, there is the small secret that one finds in any game of charades – in this case, that the charades depict Agamemnon, the husband of Clytemnestra, who will soon be murdered by his wife. However, the secret is not revealed in terms of Greek references but is discharged in orientalist images. Then there is the larger secret known by the narrator but not to us readers so far. Later, with hindsight, we will recognize the secret that was insinuated here – that Clytemnestra, aka Rebecca Sharp, not only will be instrumental in the death of her own husband, Rawdon Crawley, but it will be almost certainly she who takes the life of the man she has twice tried to make her husband, Joseph Sedley. And the hint of the revelation of this secret will prove to have been cloaked in orientalist signifiers.

102 Selfishness and secrecy

We must acknowledge that Becky's seductive orientalist performance has conquered the royal personage, who declares with an oath that she was perfection, and engaged her again and again in conversation.

> Little Becky's soul swelled with pride and delight at these honours; she saw fortune, fame, fashion before her. Lord Steyne was her slave, ... Papoosh Pasha himself would have liked to dance with her if that amusement had been the custom of his country. . . .
> The greatest triumph of all was at supper time. She was placed at the grand executive table with his Royal Highness the exalted personage before mentioned, and the rest of the great guests. She was served on gold plate. She might have had pearls melted into her champagne if she liked – *another Cleopatra.*
> (611–12, emphasis added)

However, unfortunately for Mr. and Mrs. Rawdon Crawley, and for Lord Steyne – as readers of *Vanity Fair* know well – this evening is the apogee of her story, but not its end. We had been warned. When the narrator introduced the reader to "this brilliant *réunion*," he said that it would be a "melancholy welcome too, for it will be among the very last of the fashionable entertainments to which it will be our fortune to conduct" (604). Despite the victory over the Turkish Aga and the executioner in his service, and despite being positioned before the king as a new Cleopatra, the current of Rebecca Sharp's fortune inclines from this point on in the novel and dissipates like a powerful river from the Atlas Mountains disappearing into the sands of the Sahara.

I will connect my earlier discussion of secrecy and orientalism in *Villette* to that here about *Vanity Fair*, arguing that the textual evidence supports the development of a fusion of these two concepts in these novels. Most allusions to orientalist imagery or ideas here involve some story or other about secrecy. In the nineteenth century the association between orientalism and secrecy becomes so familiar that it often works the other way as well – namely, the thought of secrecy often leads to orientalist images. There is a smooth transition between the idea of keeping secrets and veiling. Often the second is used as a metaphor for the first. In this period, the distinction between metaphor and fact became blurred, thereby orientalizing the fact. This may be partly the result of a collusion between the mentality provoked in the thousands of British readers, young and old, who had read *Arabian Nights*, and the images of veiled Eastern women provided by tourists, traveling journalists, merchants, imperial occupiers, and colonial officials returning from duty. Victorian fashions that employed the veil supported the fusion of orientalism and secrecy. The Indian director Mira Nair had good reason to interpret Thackeray's story as an orientalist morality play in her 2004 cinematic rendering of *Vanity Fair*.

Conclusion

Thus far I have argued that the motivations of the characters in *Vanity Fair* are unified by a general theory of egoism that underlies (and sometimes gives the lie

Selfishness and secrecy 103

to) our normal everyday appeals to a variety of motivations. According to this theory, all actions – or at least almost all actions – are stratagems to gain benefits for the actor himself. However, the claim I have made appears to be in conflict with a well-known if puzzling feature of the novel, the infamous "monster's hideous tail" passage. This passage constitutes a philosophical outburst by Thackeray's narrator that complicates any attempt to derive a consistent theory of motivation from *Vanity Fair*, because the explanation of the passage in terms of mere selfishness would be inadequate. The passage is introduced calmly enough, in terms of the narrator's self-congratulations regarding his proto-Simmelian discretion in not revealing the secrets of others and his "delicacy" and "inoffensive manner" in avoiding them:[37]

> There are things we do and know perfectly well in Vanity Fair, though we never speak of them. . . . It is only when their naughty names are called out that your modesty has any occasion to show alarm or sense of outrage, and it has been the wish of the present writer, all through this story, deferentially to submit to the fashion at present prevailing, and only to hint at the existence of wickedness in a light, easy, and agreeable manner, so that nobody's fine feelings may be offended. I defy anyone to say that our Becky, who has certainly some vices, has not been presented to the public in a perfectly genteel and inoffensive manner. (637)

Then suddenly we are blindsided by what may be the most startling idea of the book. The narrator writes:

> In describing this Siren, singing and smiling, coaxing and cajoling, the author, with modest pride, asks his readers all round, has he once forgotten the laws of politeness, and showed the monster's hideous tail above water? No! Those who like may peep down under waves that are pretty transparent and see it writhing and twirling, diabolically hideous and slimy, flapping amongst bones, or curling around corpses; but above the water-line, I ask, has not everything been proper, agreeable, and decorous . . . ? When, however, the Siren disappears and dives below, down among the dead men, the water of course grows turbid over her, and it is labour lost to look into it ever so curiously. . . . and we had best not examine the fiendish marine cannibals, revelling and feasting on their wretched pickled victims.
>
> (637–38)

This passage is accompanied by Thackeray's woodcut of Becky as a siren, tail visible beneath the waves. Thirty years ago Robert Lougy thought that this passage was easy enough to interpret. According to him,

> we need not be especially subtle to see that Thackeray is describing a particular sexuality, one that is perverted and employed in the service of death. . . . [T]he

siren's world is *Vanity Fair*'s civilization wherein sexuality, beauty, and grace become forces of death.

(262–63)

It is true that, out of context, this passage can be viewed as a proto-psychoanalytic intervention – or more precisely, a Schopenhauerian intrusion[38] – but this intrusion goes against so much else in the book.

In *Vanity Fair* there are secrets that individuals, couples, or small secret societies (families) try to keep from the rest of society; there are also social "secrets" that everyone knows but ignores. But there are no deeply held, private secrets, not even a deep, secret, private self. There are only surfaces and subcutaneous surfaces, but, with the exception of this notorious passage, no "depths" hiding "fiendish marine cannibals, revelling and feasting on their wretched pickled victims." In fact, there are no depths at all. I take it that, likewise, in Hobbes's theory of human nature, no "depth psychology" is required to explain individual or group behavior. Therefore, if we choose to attribute theoretical importance to the "monster's hideous tail" passage, then *Vanity Fair* must be taken as a monstrously hideous tale. Just as the narrator of *Lady Audley's Secret* will reveal a deep and dreadful secret to her Victorian readers – namely, we are all mad – so does the narrator of *Vanity Fair* reveal yet another deep and horrible secret: we are not, after all, simply "an abominably foolish and selfish people"; we are all of us deeply evil, and thus the idea that we are all Becky Sharp is even worse news than we thought.

Notes

1. William Makepeace Thackeray, *Vanity Fair: A Novel without a Hero* [1847–48], ed. Peter Shillingsburg (New York: Norton, 1994), 507. Future references to this work will be cited parenthetically in the body of the text.
2. Thackeray's narrator explains why he refuses to reveal Miss Crawley's secret:

    For how is it possible to hint of a delicate female, living in good society, that she ate and drank too much, and that a hot supper of lobsters profusely enjoyed at the Rectory was the reason of an indisposition which Miss Crawley herself persisted was solely attributable to the dampness of the weather? (140)

3. Georg Simmel remarks that there is a compulsion to keep at a distance from "great individuals," saying that in the presence of such a person even "taking notice" constitutes "a violation of . . . personality" ("The Secret and the Secret Society," *The Sociology of Georg Simmel*, ed. Kurt H. Wolff [New York: Free Press], 321). Future references to this work will be cited parenthetically in the body of the text.
4. The secret madness of the Gaunt family is covered extensively by Robert E. Lougy in "Vision and Satire: The Warped Looking Glass in *Vanity Fair*," *PMLA* 90.2 (March 1975): 256–69; see especially 260–61. Future references to this article will be cited parenthetically in the body of the text.
5. I say "Thackeray" and not "Thackeray's narrator" because of the passage in Thackeray's letter to Robert Bell (discussed in the next paragraph), in which he says that his goal in writing the novel is "to indicate . . . that we are . . . an abominably . . . selfish people." There is the possibility that Thackeray was joking with Bell, and really meant that he had created a *narrator* who would hold that view (perhaps in the way that Dostoevsky created a narrator in *Notes from the Underground* who claims that individuals

can be free only when they are motivated by spite, even though Dostoevsky himself does not necessarily hold that view). If such were the case I would have to exchange "Thackeray" with "Thackeray's narrator" throughout this section of my argument.
6 Kathleen Tillotson, "Vanity Fair," first published in Tillotson's *Novels of the Eighteen-Forties* (London: Oxford University Press, 1954), 224–56. Reprinted in *Thackeray: A Collection of Critical Essays*, ed. Alexander Welsh (Englewood Cliffs, NJ: Prentice-Hall, 1968), 65–86, 65.
7 Letter to Robert Bell, September 1848. Edgar F. Harden, ed., *Selected Letters of William Makepeace Thackeray* (New York: New York University Press, 1996), 154. A problem with Thackeray's comment – in addition to the problem I raised in note 5 – is whether the word "we" designates Londoners, city-folk, the English, or the human race. If it designates any group smaller than the human race, then Thackeray's indictment is much less sweeping than I believe.
8 I am not claiming to demonstrate the influence of Hobbes over Thackeray, even though it is not unlikely that Thackeray was familiar with Hobbes's views. Rather than a genealogical analysis, I offer here a comparative conceptual analysis of the ideas Thackeray used in his novel. Similarly, I am not emphasizing the line of influence that runs from Hobbes into modern sociology, though such a line certainly exists. It must be said that the line it traces is tortuous – sometimes one of direct influence, sometimes of family resemblance, while other times the connection to Hobbes proves to be one of open resistance. (For a more extended discussion of these issues, see Leila S. May, "The Sociology of Thackeray's 'Howling Wilderness': Selfishness, Secrecy and Performance in *Vanity Fair*," *Modern Language Studies* 37.1 [Summer 2007]: 18–41).
9 Even Bernard Gert, one of the few philosophers who claims that Hobbes is *not* a psychological egoist, admits that Hobbes is "almost unanimously" taken to be one. Rather than calling Hobbes a psychological egoist, Gert calls him a "tautological egoist" ("Hobbes and Psychological Egoism," in *Hobbes*, ed. Robert Shaver [Brookfield, VT: Dartmouth, 1999], 255–72, 259).
10 Thomas Hobbes, *Leviathan: Or the Matter, Forme and Power of a Commonwealth Ecclesiasticall and Civill* [1651] (Oxford and New York: Oxford University Press, 1988), 88. Future references to this work will be cited parenthetically in the body of the text.
11 In this respect, Gert was right about Hobbes (see note 9), but a theory can prove to be tautological and still make the claim that all motivation is egoistical.
12 Judith Fisher concludes that Thackeray is "highlighting the dangers of egoism, whether it be as author of a novel or of a life" (*Thackeray's Skeptical Narrative and the "Perilous Trade" of Authorship* [Burlington, VT: Ashgate, 2002], 18). But if I am right, Thackeray's narrator holds a view much closer to Hobbes, according to whom egoism, like the laws of gravity, cannot be avoided. All we can do is accept both egoism and gravity, working within their constraints, and behave in ways that prevent them from damaging us as much as they are capable of doing. For Hobbes, there are no exceptions to this law of nature; for Thackeray's narrator, there may be rare exceptions; it is an empirical question, but the narrator is not certain that he has detected any such exceptions.
13 Recently Peter Capuano has demonstrated one of Rebecca's idiosyncratic specialties: her hand gestures as depicted in the illustrations to the novel drawn by Thackeray himself, gestures that express her passive-aggressive politeness – a form that remains barely within "permissive aggressiveness." For example, in the illustration on p. 148 depicting the moment when George Osborne expects to fluster Rebecca by forcing upon her a masculine handshake, Becky merely offers her little finger to him, pointing it roughly in the direction of his crotch. Capuano says that her hand "operates as a powerful, but camouflaged, sexual and social appendage." Here and elsewhere, her hand becomes her "primary physical agent in the battle for social advantage that Erving Goffman refer[s] to as 'impression management'" (Peter J. Capuano, "At the Hands of

Becky Sharp: [In]Visible Manipulation and *Vanity Fair*," *Victorians Institute Journal* 38.1 [2008]: 167–91, 175).

14 Notice that whatever else we can say about the virtues of kindness and generosity in this novel, they must be understood as being compatible with selfishness and vanity.

15 According to Rachel Pietka, Thackeray's subtitle "ridicules the ideal [Victorian] man," just as the novel "challenges the impossible standards to which Victorian women were held" (Rachel Pietka, "Thackeray's *Vanity Fair*," *Explicator* 68.4 [2010]: 239–41, 240).

16 U. C. Knoepflmacher, "*Vanity Fair*: The Bitterness of Retrospection," in *Laughter and Despair: Readings in Ten Novels of the Victorian Era* (Berkeley and Los Angeles: University of California Press, 1971), 50–83, 76–77.

17 John Halperin, *Egoism and Self-Discovery in the Victorian Novel: Studies in the Ordeal of Knowledge in the Nineteenth Century* (New York: Burt Franklin, 1974), 34, 36. Future references to this book will be cited parenthetically into the body of the text.

18 E.g., 186, 241, 285, 288, 434, 572, 582, 596, 608, and 609.

19 As Arnold Kettle noted more than half a century ago: "How any man of such sense and character could remain utterly in love, in quite an adolescent way, with Amelia all those years Thackeray can neither explain nor convince us" (*An Introduction to the English Novel* [London: Basil Wiley, 1951], 166).

20 E.g., Catherine Peters, *Thackeray's Universe: Shifting Worlds of Imagination and Reality* (New York: Oxford University Press, 1987), 164, 167; Cynthia Griffin Wolf, "Who Is the Narrator of *Vanity Fair* and Where Is He Standing?" *College Literature* 1 (1974): 190–203 (see esp. 196); Lisa Jadwin, "Clytemnestra Rewarded: The Double Conclusion of *Vanity Fair*," in *Famous Last Words: Changes in Gender and Narrative Structure*, ed. Alison Booth (Charlottesville and London: University of Virginia Press, 1998), 35–61 (see esp. 40). Also, Lisa Jadwin, "The Seductiveness of Female Duplicity in *Vanity Fair*," *Studies in English Literature, 1500–1900* 32.4 (Autumn 1992): 663–87 (see esp. 679, 682, 683–84). Jadwin remarks on the book's final illustration, where children are shutting the case in which the puppets have been replaced. She writes:

> Yet the illustrator does not "shut up" the Becky puppet at all. To the right of the toy box, the narrator's jester's stick lies side-by-side with the Becky puppet, its motley flung over her in an ambiguous embrace that suggests both partnership and conquest. (683–84)

Jadwin attributes this insight to U. C. Knoepflmacher.

21 Barbara Hardy, *The Exposure of Luxury: Radical Themes in Thackeray* (London: Peter Owen, 1972), 68.

22 Michael Wheeler writes, "In satirizing the aristocratic world of the silver-forked novel, Thackeray indicates that he places himself and his readers in the middle ranks of society: 'Dear Brethren, let us tremble before those august portals'" (*English Fiction of the Mid-Victorian Period* [New York: Longman, 1985], 50).

23 Judith Weissman, *Half Savage and Hardy and Free: Women and Rural Radicalism in the Nineteenth-Century Novel* (Middletown, CT: Wesleyan University Press, 1987), 148. Future references to this work will be cited parenthetically in the body of the text.

24 David Morse, *High Victorian Culture* (New York: New York University Press, 1993), 207.

25 Because of my conclusion that in *Vanity Fair* the war of each against all is brought forward into the civil state, I must disagree with Sambudha Sen, who, contrasting Dickens and Thackeray, concludes that Dickens expresses the social contradictions of the city of London that Thackeray fails to deal with. (Dickens learns from the "city sketch" its "capacity to express urban contradictions" and Thackeray learns its "ability to manage them.") Sen discusses Thackeray's "focus on the internal world of a socially homogeneous group of characters" (Sambudha Sen, "*Bleak House*, *Vanity Fair*, and the Making of an Urban Aesthetic," *Nineteenth-Century Literature* 54.4 [Mar. 2000]: 480–502, 481, 487). For similar reasons I disagree with Nicola Minott-Ahl's conclusion about

the novel in her article "Dystopia in *Vanity Fair*: The Nightmare of Modern London," *Literary London: Interdisciplinary Studies in the Representation of London* 7.2 [September 2009]: electronic journal). Minott-Ahl quotes a letter written by Thackeray in which he expresses his wish that the novel "leave everybody dissatisfied and unhappy at the end of the story." From this wish, she deduces that "Thackeray sees opportunities for something better" (sec. 46, p. 11). She continues: "One can have a good society in spite of human nature and the distortions to it that modern life permits if people abandon their obsession with money and ownership and focus on living well and not causing anyone else pain" (sec. 46, p. 12).

26 Erving Goffman, *The Presentation of Self in Everyday Life* (New York and London: Anchor Books Doubleday, 1959), 253. Future references to this work will be cited parenthetically in the body of the text. In this chapter, all references to Goffman are to passages in this book.
27 The narrator wishes not to be taken as a gossip, warning us, "the reader must bear in mind that it is . . . Tom Eaves who speaks," but he who repeats gossip is a gossip.
28 Jadwin, "Clytemnestra Rewarded," 38.
29 Wolfgang Iser, "The Reader in the Realistic Novel: Esthetic Effects in Thackeray's *Vanity Fair*," in *William Makepeace Thackeray's "Vanity Fair,"* ed. Harold Bloom (New York, New Haven, and Philadelphia: Chelsea House, 1987), 37–55, 41.
30 David Gauthier, "Morals by Agreement," in *Contractarianism/Contractualism*, ed. Stephen Darwall (Oxford and Malden, MA: Blackwell, 2003), 108–37, 129–30.
31 Later, as we have seen, Goffman writes,

> I have been using the term "performance" to refer to all the activity of an individual which occurs during a period marked by his continuous presence before a particular set of observers and which has some influence on the observers. (22)

Here we see that the term "participant" from the first definition is interchangeable with the term "observer" in the second.
32 The "performers" we call the Founding Fathers may or may not have misrepresented the facts when they wrote that there are certain God-given rights. Even if there is no God, we who follow in the wake of that *ex nihilo* performative utterance do have certain rights that had not been honored before.
33 Micael M. Clarke, *Thackeray and Women* (DeKalb: Northern Illinois University Press, 1995), 95.
34 Secret desires in the nineteenth century are not necessarily sexual (even if sex is "*the* secret," according to Foucault). Consider the opening of *Dr Jekyll and Mr Hyde* [1886], where we are told that Mr. Utterson never discusses his desire for vintage wines (rather, he drinks gin when alone to suppress that desire!), nor does he discuss his yearning to attend the theater – another suppressed desire. The narrator tells us: "he had not crossed the doors of one for twenty years" (Robert Louis Stevenson, *The Strange Case of Dr Jekyll and Mr Hyde*, ed. Martin A. Danahay [Peterborough, ON: Broadview, 2005], 31).
35 It might seem that this small but biting intrusion into the plot of a British business venture that fails, plunging "half the Indian public into misery and ruin," could be seen as a forerunner of what Edward Said calls "contrapuntal reading" of colonialist literature, meaning by that phrase,

> reading a text with an understanding of what is involved when an author shows, for instance, that a colonial sugar plantation is seen as important to the process of maintaining a particular style of life in England. . . . The point is that contrapuntal reading must take account of both processes, that of imperialism and that of resistance to it.

However, apparently Said does not see this aside about "the Indian public" and "misery and ruin" as an example of contrapuntal reading, because he says, "Hardly ever is the novelist interested in doing a great deal more than mentioning or referring to India, for example, in *Vanity Fair* and *Jane Eyre*" (Edward Said, *Culture and Imperialism* [New York: Alfred A. Knopf, 1993], 66, 74). It seems to me that Said errs here. Thackeray's usual irony should not disqualify him from participation in this form of discourse that Said has astutely identified. Even an intentionally understated demonstration of the consequences of British imperialism – both on its victims and on the psyches of the imperialists themselves – is surely a form of resistance to that imperialism.

36 This episode too might well count as "contrapuntal" in Said's sense. It is surprising to me that Said did not see it that way.

37 Recall that, according to Simmel, "discretion consists by no means only in the respect for the secret of the other, . . . but in staying away from the knowledge of all that the other does not expressly reveal to us" (320–21), and,

> To penetrate this circle [of privacy] by taking notice, constitutes a violation of his personality. . . . [This] violation effects a lesion of the ego in its very center. Discretion is nothing but the feeling that there exists a right in regard to the sphere of the immediate life contents. (322)

38 The "will" of *The World as Will and Idea* is surely the progenitor of Freud's id. But what makes Thackeray's depiction more Schopenhauerian than Freudian is that in Freud's account, the perversion of the unconscious is the result of the collision between the demands of the id and those of civilization. In Schopenhauer and Thackeray, if we can talk of perversion at all, it will be a natural perversion, not nature perverted.

4 Madness and class conflicts
Lady Audley's sensational secrets

> Nothing can be more slightly defined than the line of demarcation between sanity and insanity. . . . [I]f all the passionate, prejudiced and vain people were to be locked up as lunatics, who is to keep the key to the asylum?
>
> —*The Times*, 1853

An environment of secrecy

No one will be surprised to learn that a book with the title *Lady Audley's Secret* is a book about secrecy and dissimulation, about attempts to veil and counter-attempts to unveil dangerous information. In fact, the genre of Braddon's work – the sensation novel – is defined by the dialectics of concealment and the revelation of scandalous secrets, but always secrets that are "at our own doors."[1] It is reasonable to ask whether that genre, including the novels of Mary Elizabeth Braddon, wildly exaggerates the role of secrecy in the construction of the peculiar mentality of Victorian England's middle classes, or if it offers a special insight into it. I will attempt to show that *Lady Audley's Secret* does indeed expand the role of secrecy in everyday human interaction, both in content and form, but does so in a way similar to that of a magnifying glass enlarging its object of investigation in order to make visible its otherwise hidden features. However, the heat produced by magnification can burn the object of investigation to ashes. Something similar to that destructive event nearly takes place in this novel, because Braddon stresses the *negative* features of secrecy rather than its generative components. Yet, I will argue, precisely by stressing the negative Braddon will end up accentuating the positive by showing how the dialectics of concealment and revelation produce a new and perhaps more just social world. Therefore, I claim, Braddon's and Simmel's treatment of secrecy are part of a single intellectual tradition. Indeed, the novel proves to be a virtual Simmelian study of both the social creativity of secrecy and of the cultural fascination with secrecy as these two forces relate to nineteenth-century middle-class England. In addition to illustrating the reciprocity between Braddon's use of secrecy in her fiction and Simmel's treatment of it in his sociology, I will demonstrate that Braddon, like Brontë, entwines the concept of secrecy with that of selfhood in ways that once again evoke the solipsism of neo-Cartesianism. Moreover, just as Brontë's *Villette* and Thackeray's *Vanity Fair* each reveal a dramatically idiosyncratic secret – a secret that their respective narrators claim everyone has always known (in *Villette*, the secret that secrecy itself is a sanctified requirement for the salvation of the soul; in *Vanity Fair*, the secret that selfishness is the basis of all motivation) – so does Braddon's narrator make a similarly idiosyncratic revelation. According to her,[2] the very essence of consciousness in its relation to the external world determines that madness is an inevitable natural condition: we are all mad. As will be seen at the end of this chapter, this is arguably the real secret of *Lady Audley's Secret*.

From its opening pages, *Lady Audley's Secret* creates an environment of secrecy. There is an architecture, a landscape, and a psychology of secrecy, adding up to what either is or isn't a paranoid suspicion of the defining characteristics of everyday life. (If it is reasonable to entertain and act on these suspicions, they are not paranoid; if it is unreasonable, they are paranoid.) The principal door of the Audley mansion "wished to keep itself a secret," as if "it were in hiding from dangerous visitors"; there are "secret chambers," a "secret drawer," and "a secret passage," all of which play roles in the plot.[3] Large oaks "circled in the house and gardens with a darkening shelter" (7), and a lime-tree walk was "so screened from observation by the thick shelter of the over-arching trees that it seemed a chosen place for secret meetings or for stolen interviews; a place in which a conspiracy might have been planned" (9).[4] Even the bucolic surroundings of the Audley mansion – "[t]he lowing of a cow in the quiet meadows, the splash of trout in the fish-pond, the last notes of a tired bird, the creaking of wagon-wheels upon the distant road" (26) – which might bring to mind a poem by Thomas Gray or a painting by John Constable, here become sinister: "The very repose of the place grew painful from its intensity, and you felt as if a corpse must be lying somewhere within that gray and ivy-covered pile of a building – so deathlike was the tranquility of all around" (26).

When we turn to human interaction, we find a social world in which despair and alienation are avoided only by acting on obsessive concerns about concealment and revelation; we find a conspiratorial, inquisitional culture where children must be interrogated to pry loose the plots of small secret societies, where individuals of a lower social class are intimidated into submission by the power wielded by their social superiors,[5] and where one's days are spent brooding over suspicions about others that one may not whisper even to those one loves best. This mentality is memorialized in an exchange between the novel's hero, Robert Audley, and his new aunt, Lady Audley. Robert asks:

> "What do we know of the mysteries that may hang about the houses we enter? . . . Foul deeds have been done under the most hospitable roofs; terrible crimes have been committed amid the fairest scenes, and have left no trace upon the spot where they were done. I do not believe in mandrake, or in bloodstains that no time can efface. I believe rather than we may walk unconsciously in an atmosphere of crime, and breathe nonetheless freely. I believe

that we may look into the smiling face of a murderer, and admire its tranquil beauty."

My lady laughed at Robert's earnestness.

(124)

We have seen that, according to Georg Simmel, "the secret" creates an entire world alongside the manifest world, and that that secret world gives the manifest world depth and dimensionality. It is this phenomenon that fascinates the readers of *Lady Audley's Secret*, but within the narration itself this same phenomenon intervenes in the manifest world as a kind of morbid obsession and is the source of the eccentric combination of characteristics that comprise Robert's life – apathy, monomaniacal dedication to a mission, superstition, and paranoia.[6]

Lyn Pykett, among others, has correctly pointed out that the sources of the sensation plot spring from the secrets of the family, and she cites Henry James's well-known observation that these are the "most mysterious of mysteries, the mysteries that are at our own doors."[7] Pykett argues that Braddon and other authors of sensation novels "transform the home, in middle-class ideology a domestic shrine, into a prisonhouse of suspicion" (Pykett 1992, 111). She agrees with Elaine Showalter's thesis that the power of sensationalism derives from "its exposure of secrecy as the fundamental enabling condition of middle-class life" (Pykett 1992, 83). This is a Simmelian insight, one that allows us to see that sensation novels do not merely exaggerate and sensationalize the role of secrecy in Victorian England; they frame it in ways that allow its structural details to be observed.[8] Victorian readers may not have consciously walked around in a state of nervous excitation over the notions of concealment and revelation, but the pleasure they took from novelists such as Braddon and Collins contained a *frisson* of recognition. Simmel's assertion that societies differ according to the roles that lying and the evasion of truth play in them can certainly be applied here.[9] For example, Sir Michael Audley, in shock after receiving evidence of his new wife's felonious activities, says to his nephew Robert: "it is my earnest wish never again to hear that person's name. I have no wish to be told the nature of the arrangements you may make for her" (339). Uncle and nephew, members of a family of the *petite aristocratie*, understand each other fully. The wish not to know everything pertaining to the maintenance of family honor is, as Simmel suggests, socially creative: it preserves continuity just as it avoids guilt and shame. Sir Michael requests that certain information be withheld from him. It is very likely that he does not wish to be told what he already knows – that the "mad doctor" will soon make a house call. Selective oblivion is also creative, or at least, life-sustaining.

Lady Audley's Secret, like so many sensation novels, has as its primary scandal the crime of bigamy (not murder, as we are led to believe throughout the bulk of the novel).[10] But the secret of bigamy in England in the 1850s and 1860s is that its "success" is a result of the failure of workable divorce laws. As Karen Chase and Michael Levinson say, "what makes bigamy a compelling alternative is that it is so close to the divorce it replaces."[11] Bigamy is a default solution to a genuine social problem. But one must always remain silent about bigamy, or lie about it. If it *must* be dealt within one's own family circle, it should be done so in secret. Consequently, when Robert Audley seeks a "mad doctor" who can be "trusted with a secret" (314), his quest is not unique. Such physicians covered a multitude of sins in nineteenth-century England – usually sins against women, but not in this case. Robert's friend recommends to him a certain Dr. Mosgrove, who "looked like a man who could have carried, safely locked in his passionless breast, the secrets of a nation, and who would have suffered no inconvenience from the weight of such a burden" (320). Robert gravely asks him: "The revelation made by the patient to the physician is, I believe, as sacred as the confession of a penitent to his priest?" Dr. Mosgrove answers, "Quite as sacred" (319). Robert continues: "A solemn confidence, to be violated under no circumstances?"[12] After having been reassured, Robert recounts Lady Audley's confession, but does not include everything – reveals nothing of his suspicions about George's murder, nor about the fire at the Castle Inn that killed a not-so-innocent victim. The doctor says: "You would wish to prove that this lady is mad, and therefore irresponsible for her actions, Mr. Audley?" Robert answers: "Yes, I would rather, if possible, think her mad; I should be glad to find that excuse for her." "And," says the doctor, "to save the *escandre* of a Chancery suit, I suppose, Mr. Audley" (320). Robert bows, thinking that it is not just a divorce scandal that worries him but a murder trial that haunts his dreams "in an agony of shame" (321).

Simmel and Goffman both remind us that we cannot always afford to be recognized as what we are. Lady Audley is the case *par excellence* of this principle. She is, after all, an impostor and a bigamist, as well as, perhaps, a murderess and/or a madwoman. She protects what Goffman calls "dark secrets" (as opposed to merely "strategic secrets"). These are facts that are "incompatible with the image of the self" that the individual attempts to project before his audience.[13] Robert suspects all of this, and that the public revelation of any part of Lady Audley's secret would destroy her, but also bring shame to his family and his class. It shows that dark secrets do not only bring the downfall of the individual but sometimes damage certain collective interests. He therefore takes things into his own hands in order to bring about a purely *private* (secret) revelation of dangerous secrecy. To do this, he must break the rules of discretion that bind together the social world – rules to which his family and class are particularly committed. Simmel says that discretion is not only a convenience – a convenience because we do not *want* to know everything – but a moral duty. One such Simmelian moral rule is that whatever is "intentionally or unintentionally hidden is intentionally or unintentionally respected" (330). Included in that which is respected is the secret world that each of us constructs alongside the "manifest world" (330). Robert violently intrudes into Lady Audley's secret world because he believes that that world threatens other secret worlds, not only his own but that of his family and of his social class. We are indeed dealing here with the secret world of the *petite aristocratie* and not only with its manifest world. The manifest world of this group, like that of the middle classes, is in many ways determined by its secret world – again, according to Simmelian principles. The idea of a "we" requires the exclusion of outsiders by guarding certain secrets. Servants, of course, know many of these secrets, but can be manipulated not to use them destructively. Strictly speaking, Helen Talboys ("Lady Audley") is not in fact a member of the servant class: she has been previously employed as a governess under the name of Miss Lucy Graham. However, the new Lady Audley is thought of as a servant by another servant: Phoebe Marks, who had worked alongside her at the home of their previous employer, Mr. Dawson. Since Lady Audley's marriage, Phoebe has been taken in by my lady as her maid. But Phoebe Marks still sees her mistress, the former Lucy Graham, as a member of her own class. About her current superior and former colleague, Phoebe says: "What was she but a servant like me? Taking wages and working for them as hard, or harder than I did" (29). Deep down, Lucy too seems to hold that view of her former self: during her confession to Robert she tells him, "what labour is more wearisome than the dull slavery of a governess?" (300).

As a servant of sorts, Lucy has knowledge of the secrets of her superiors and uses that knowledge not simply as a defense but as a weapon in her offensive invasion and occupation of enemy territory. Goffman writes:

> Perhaps the classic type of non-person in our society is the servant. . . . In certain ways he is defined by other performers and audience as someone who isn't there. . . . [However,] we must not underestimate the degree to which the person who is given or who takes such a role [i.e., the person who takes the role of non-person] can use it as a defense.
>
> (151)

Indeed, if "a Cat can look at a Queen" (as Alice reminds the King of Hearts), a servant or a governess can become a Lady. Lucy Graham's fraudulent penetration into a much higher class by means of imposture is not merely a case of *lèse-majesté* but is an anarchic act of class warfare that can be annulled only by secret operations and, eventually, the secret employment of a mad doctor. If a Cat can look at a Queen, how sovereign can a Queen be? And if a governess can perfectly impersonate an aristocrat, then what is it about aristocratic character that justifies its privileges?

Braddon's novel raises questions about the very concept of pedigree. What exactly is it about old blood that justifies privilege and superiority? Despite her crimes and impersonations, Lucy Graham, a woman with no pedigree at all, might have maintained the status of a woman with a noble pedigree for the rest of her life, if only she had been able to protect her secret. In that case, the very idea of a pedigree is devalued and threatened with redundancy. And if those with pedigrees had suffered an assault on their personhood as ferocious as the one suffered by Lady Audley, would their honor survive? Is Lady Audley's staged acquisition of wealth, power, and privilege all that different from that of the play-acting of the pedigreed class? Think of Robert's own dramatic skills,[14] of his fraudulent and unethical activities to bring about "justice." Eva Badowska evokes Charles Dickens's characters, the Verneerings from *Our Mutual Friend*, who "have no pedigree"; rather, they invent one "as a historical object, a faux antique" (Badowska, 161). And what exactly is the substance of a real pedigree as opposed to a false one that would justify such a discrepancy between the lives of Helen Maldon and Lady Audley? If the ancient tradition of privilege is to remain in place, the true answer to this question will have to be concealed from those who ask it. Apparently, this issue worried even members of the lower social classes. Jonathan Loesberg asserts,

> sensation novels evoke their most typical moments of sensation response from images of loss of class identity. And this common image links up with a fear of a general loss of social identity as a result of the merging of the classes – a fear that was commonly expressed in the debate over social and parliamentary reform in the late 1850s and 1860s.[15]

This possibility is not the only anxiety provoked by the novel. The content of the book is disturbing enough, but its avid consumption by members of different social classes caused concern. Lyn Pykett, in her introduction to the newest edition of *Lady Audley's Secret*, writes that there was a

> widespread anxiety among middle-class commentators that not only did sensation novelists adapt the fast-paced and melodramatic narratives enjoyed by lower-class readers for a more affluent and higher-class readership, but that they also produced a form of fiction that was read simultaneously by both classes. These anxieties about the promiscuous mingling of readerships were part of a wider anxiety about the erosion of social boundaries in an age of rapid social change.
>
> (xxiv)

When Robert Audley initiates his violent penetration into Lady Audley's secret world, his acts are still superficially consistent with Simmel's idea that the "duty of discretion – to renounce the knowledge of all that the other does not voluntarily show us – recedes before practical requirements" (Simmel, 323). Robert has arrogated to himself this right, but in the name of a very private urgency, one not justified by Simmel's idea of "practical requirements." Robert Audley has remade himself into a detective and an inquisitor, but a *secret* detective and inquisitor. He does *not* turn the case over to the police. Simmel's concession to practicality addresses itself to public areas: people engaging in business contracts, individuals who seek employment, persons who have been invited as new members into a social circle – these people must accept indiscreet questions. But Robert's abandonment of discretion is an assault on Lady Audley's very self, which he hopes to destroy and finally succeeds in doing. Selfhood, according to Simmel, is partly constructed out of privacy (secret space); hence, to violate the field of privacy allotted to each individual by the rules of discretion "constitutes a lesion of the ego" (Simmel 322). Philosopher Sissela Bok agrees: "Secrecy guards . . . the central aspects of identity" (*Secrets*, 13). Robert believes that he is justified in destroying Lady Audley because, as a bigamist, she is *not* Lady Audley, and he means to expose her impersonation by tearing her mask from her. From a legal perspective, Robert is right, but from a sociological perspective matters may quite look different. His attack is less in the name of justice than in the name of self-interest and, perhaps more importantly, class interest. Yet, when we consider what was at stake in the challenge against the social prerogatives of the ruling class at this moment in the Victorian world, we may see that it was inevitable that such a preemptive assault would be mounted.

Let us consider how Lady Audley, née Helen Maldon, born as a member of the lower middle class, ascends to the ranks of the aristocracy on her own initiative simply by wearing different masks. Social psychologist Karl Scheibe conjectures that "the mask produces the person behind the mask, . . . the trait must first be assumed, then acquired". And, if the mask *is* the person, then "the distinction [between reality and appearance] should be collapsed."[16] A newborn baby had become "Helen Maldon" by having her parents so inscribe her name on a birth certificate. She had become Helen Talboys by marrying George Talboys in a ritual sanctioned by British law. The clergyman standing before Miss Maldon and Mister Talboys had asked, "Will you, Helen Maldon, take this man, George Talboys, as your lawfully wedded spouse?" When she answered, "I will," she voiced the performative utterance with which, in conjunction with the corresponding performative of George Talboys, "I will," and with the terminating performative by the priest, "I pronounce you man and wife," she became Mrs. George Talboys – if and only if those performative utterances were "felicitous," to use J. L. Austin's term to designate successful performatives.[17] A successful performative utterance creates social facts only if the individuals who performed them were "authorized" to do so: if the priest was ordained by Church authorities; if the two candidates for marriage were unmarried and of "sound mind" at the moment of their participation, and if they had remained silent when asked by the priest, "If either of you know any impediment why you may not be lawfully joined together in matrimony, do you now confess it." (Underlining the constructive role of performatives in the social world, Goffman at one point asserts: "The world, in truth, is a wedding" [36].)

The same holds true when, later, Helen Talboys – now choosing to call herself Lucy Graham – submits to the same liturgy with Sir Michael Audley before a different clergyman. We understand that two flies are in the social ointment on this occasion: Lucy's legal name is not Lucy Graham, and she is already married. Concerning the first disqualifier, notice that her crime is not that of impersonation, if that term denotes the fraudulent claim to be an existing person who one is not (e.g., what we now call identity theft); it is simply that of asking to be called by a name that was not bestowed upon her by any authorized performative utterance. (If she had presented herself to the priest as Helen Talboys this specific objection would be defeated, although she certainly had a good personal reason for not doing so.)

The second and stronger disqualifier is the fact that she was already married at the moment that she answered "I will" in response to the question posed by the priest. The name for that "infelicity" is, of course, bigamy. (There is a third disqualifier hardly mentioned by critics: if, at the time of her first marriage, Helen believes herself to be mad – as she admits to believing by the end of the novel – then neither marriage is valid, because she knows she is not of "sound mind.")

There are other extenuating circumstances related to Lucy's first marriage, though not enough to have the marriage annulled or to grant her a divorce in the England of 1862: in addition to the performative utterances that established the social fact of marriage, there are certain behavioral performatives required on the part of the newly married couple, though they are vague, and derived from common law – that is, based not on documented legal decisions but rather on historical precedent. It is questionable whether George Talboys has fulfilled the minimum amount of this requirement. Almost four years after the marriage, while returning by ship to England after three years seeking his fortune in the Australian gold fields, George Talboys admits to a new acquaintance who is a fellow passenger on the ship:

> "Do you know . . . that I left my little girl asleep, with her baby in her arms, and with nothing but a few blotted lines to tell her why her faithful husband had deserted her?"
> "Deserted her?"
> "Yes."
>
> (21)

George realizes that his action will certainly appear to be desertion, even if on another occasion he says, "I did not desert her" (41). He had disappeared into the night, leaving a letter for his young wife, saying that he loved her "never . . . better than now that I seemed to desert her," that he would seek his fortune "in a new world," but that, if he failed, he "should never look upon her face again" (24). He further admits that in the more than three years since his departure he had never sent a letter to his wife until days before his ship to England sailed, nor let her know in any way where he was and that he was still alive (also having admitted to his new friend that he had been suicidal: he states in his own words that, on a cold night shortly before the abandonment, standing on a pier, he had felt "a strong inclination to throw myself into the sea" [23]). He is in fact providing evidence that, before a judge, might have supported a request by Helen for a divorce, or even ameliorated the charge of bigamy against her after she married Sir Michael, while assuming, as she claims she did, that he was dead or had permanently abandoned her and their child. (George can afford to admit all this to his fellow ship passenger, Miss Morely, as he knows that he will never see her again, and hence she can never serve as a witness against him.)

Among those who knew George Talboys and his young family before his sudden disappearance, it was believed that he had left his wife and child permanently. His former landlord, speaking to Robert Audley, refers to George Talboys as "him as deserted her so cruel, and left her with her pretty boy upon her poor old father's hands" (40). The manager of a hotel where the Talboys stayed shortly before the event tells Robert,

> the gentleman ran away to Australia, and left the lady, a week or two after her baby was born. The business made quite a sensation in Wildernsea, . . . and Mrs Talboys was very much pitied by the Wildernsea folks, sir.
>
> (208)

Another resident of Wildernsea says to Robert, "poor little woman! She tried to support herself after her husband's desertion by giving music lessons" (212). In her final confession to Sir Michael before being whisked off to the *maison de santé*, Helen Talboys (now still barely Lady Audley) says:

> Three years had passed, and I had received no token of my husband's existence; for I argued that if he had returned to England, he would have succeeded in finding me under any name and in any place. I knew that energy of his character well enough to know this. I said, "I have a right to think that he is dead, or that he wishes me to believe that he is dead, and his shadow shall not stand between me and prosperity." I said this, and I became your wife, Sir Michael, with every resolution to be as good a wife as it was in my nature to be. I would have been your true and pure wife to the end of time, though I had been surrounded by a legion of tempters.
>
> (301)

Again, these facts, presented in a court of law, would not have established Helen Talboys's innocence on the charges of impersonation and bigamy, but they might well have resulted in a more lenient judgment than that sought by the amateur detective Robert Audley. According to his way of thinking, no public judgment of any sort could bring "justice" because even the most lenient sentence would bring shame, dishonor, and embarrassment to Audley Court, to its current baronet, Sir Michael Audley, and to Robert himself, as future baronet ("I'm heir-presumptive to my uncle's title" [138]).[18] Robert's self-appointed role as police inspector, judge, jury, and executioner would necessarily mete out secret justice – secret but not subjective, being a class-based justice rather than merely a personal one.[19] If public justice had been executed by the processes of law (whether in a sensation novel or in the real social world), the punishment suffered by both Helen Maldon and the Audley family would obviously be a social construction rather than a natural one (natural, or the result of the "forza del destino"). Therefore, even such a powerful drama, either fictional or real, would be tenuous, its authority guaranteed only by socially accepted performative utterances and actions. Most "authorizations" of performatives are themselves based upon or derived from earlier performatives going back either to forgotten sources or to arbitrariness, as in a revolutionary declaration arrogating authority to oneself with a performative assertion such as, "We the people, hereby . . . ."[20]

It is because of this tenuousness of conventional reality that Goffman says that the social world is "a delicate, fragile thing" (56). The self that is presented to the world is a performed self, social relations are also performances, and it is easy to cast doubt on the rules that are supposed to determine the "felicity" or "infelicity" of these performances. Though no Victorian reader had the questionable pleasure of having read *The Presentation of Self in Everyday Life*, many of them had the disquieting pleasure of reading *Lady Audley's Secret*, which delivered a proto-Goffmanian message that many readers began to fear was correct: "All the world is not, of course, a stage, but the crucial ways in which it isn't are not easy to specify" (Goffman 72).[21] In a world in which class and gender rules are taught as natural, absolute, and definitive of one's identity and one's social status in the world, these thoughts could be disturbing to readers – but also perhaps a bit liberating.

Then, in a case such as Lady Audley's, as long as she can carry out what Goffman calls a performance that has not been discredited, or, to use another of his formulas, as long as she can control "the definition of the situation" (19), she *is* Lady Audley in the same way that Robert Audley, Esq., *is* the future baronet of Audley[22] – if and until he is unmasked. (Unmasking can come in many forms. The decapitation of the kings of England and France is the most radical form of demasking, a violent instantaneous decertification, a disbarring, an excommunication, and a depersonalization.) Robert had tried to destroy Lady Audley's ego by revealing her secrets and disclosing that her professed identity was fraudulent, and had taunted her with that most terrible unmasking: hanging publicly from the gallows. But such an event would have unmasked more than the Audley dynasty could tolerate. Indeed, from the perspective of the theories I am employing here, all egos – including Robert's – are based on secrets that, if revealed, would damage them. Hence, all egos are impostures. This was Sartre's discovery, who, after brilliantly analyzing "bad faith," anguished over his inability to depict, either in fiction or philosophy, "good faith."[23] It is Goffman's rediscovery, and the reason he quotes Sartre so frequently.

Is Robert Audley in good faith (legally, morally, or philosophically) when he writes to the incarcerated Lady Audley in Belgium telling her that, after all, it has been discovered that she did not kill George as she thought she had done? "'It may be some comfort to her to hear that her husband did not perish in his youth by her wicked hand,' he thought, 'if her selfish soul can hold any sentiment of pity or sorrow for others'" (368). Helen Talboys is now known to be innocent of intentional homicide, yet she still is imprisoned for life without a trial. Even after discovering that George is still alive, Robert allows her no reprieve from her life sentence. This confirms that, despite Robert's agony provoked by the supposed murder of his friend, Lady Audley's real crime was that of bringing shame to Audley Court. Even George Talboys, Lucy's legal husband, is given no say in her fate. Every feature of the criminal investigation, the arrest, judgment, and imprisonment is left to the future baronet and ruler of Audley Court.

Mary Elizabeth Braddon may well have hoped that at least some readers would catch the irony that the charge of criminality leveled by Robert Audley against his aunt could also be brought against Mr. Audley himself, against him who has single-handedly and illegally condemned a person to life imprisonment, amounting in this case to a death sentence, for *lèse majesté*, defined by Webster as "insolent behavior toward a person to whom deference is due." Another irony is that it is Robert's new father-in-law, Mr. Harcourt Talboys, who thrusts the rapier:

> "It is not for me to blame you, Mr Audley," he said, "for having smuggled this guilty woman out of reach of justice, and thus, as I may say, paltered with the laws of your country. I can only remark that, had the lady fallen into *my* hands, she would have been very differently treated."
>
> (369)

Indeed, Lucy Audley could have been charged in court with imposture, bigamy, intended homicide (against George), and second degree homicide (against Luke);[24] but she cannot be declared guilty until being proved guilty. On the other hand, Robert might well have been found guilty of obstructing justice for his role in this drama and been disbarred.

There is also a moral issue that may have resonated even more deeply with Braddon's readership than the legal one. A paradigmatic case of that issue can be seen when Mr. Maldon, intimidated by the barrister's extralegal inquisitional attack upon him, says to Mr. Audley in fear and trembling but also in an inarticulate rage: "'you come to my house . . . – you take – the – opportunity to – terrify me – and it is not right, sir – it is –' he dropped his face upon the table and wept aloud." Braddon's narrator observes:

> Perhaps in all the dismal scenes of domestic misery which had been acted in those spare and dreary houses – in all the petty miseries, the burning shames, the cruel sorrows, the bitter disgraces which own poverty for their common father – there had never been a scene such as this. An old man hiding his face from the light of day, and sobbing aloud in his wretchedness.
>
> (147)

Nothing illegal happening here, but anyone with a moral pulse must ask: Is Helen Maldon's crime of imposture and *perhaps* bigamy, in any way more outrageous than the crimes that "Father poverty" commits on millions of British subjects in this century? Does the insult done to the rich and privileged baronet demand more reparation than does the crime of poverty that his wealth underwrites?

If Braddon expected or hoped that her readers would feel sympathy for Lucy (the way twentieth-century authors and screenwriters know that American audiences, at least, will have sympathy for the underdog, criminal or not), and if Braddon thought that readers might read this passage with a sense of outrage, then she meant for her novel to be progressive. If she meant for them to be satisfied with Robert's religious explanation for his "monomania" ("the stronger hand of Providence leading him on," etc.), then she meant it to be conservative.[25]

The stronger hand: Robert Audley as secret agent of God

Concerning the question of justice – or perhaps one should say eternal or supernatural justice – there is a curious incongruity at the heart of *Lady Audley's Secret* whose resolution is a secret of narrative strategy. Early in the novel the narrator, using tones that border on the paranoid, seems to deny the guarantee of the certainty of divine justice, promised by Christianity, showing us that we cannot trust any sense of peace or innocence that a particular landscape might instill in us:

> We hear everyday of murders committed in the country. Brutal and treacherous murders; slow, protracted agonies from poisons administered by some

kindred hand; sudden and violent deaths by cruel blows, inflicted with a stake cut from some spreading oak, whose very shadow promised – peace. In the county of which I write, I have been shown a meadow in which, on a quiet summer Sunday evening, a young farmer murdered the girl who had loved and trusted him; and yet even now, with the stain of that foul deed upon it, the aspect of the spot is – peace.

(51)

If we dismiss this warning as simply a well-known narrative strategy of the sensation novel to provoke in readers a thrill of apprehension, and to make them uneasy in any condition of apparent safety and calm, we might miss the fact that the narrator shares this paranoia with her hero, Robert Audley, who we recall tells his aunt, that "terrible crimes have been committed amid the fairest scenes, and have left no trace upon the spot where they were done." He does not believe in "blood stains that no time can erase" (124). Robert's suspicions here are so close to those expressed by the anonymous narrator that we might wonder if the storyteller is not really Robert Audley himself. The metaphysical assumption here is a version of the philosophical contrast between appearance and reality dating at least to the pre-Socratics, but one that in this case is sinister in its Schopenhauerian pessimism: evil may inhabit a landscape that lulls us into a state of peace and tranquility, an evil that might burst forth at any moment, or at least remain forever undetected though forever threatening. However, this metaphysical angst contrasts jarringly with Robert's later pronouncement to Lady Audley, who, according to Robert's fallacious belief at this point, is guilty of murdering his friend and her former husband, George Talboys. Robert says: "there is a Providence above . . . and . . . wicked secrets are never permitted to remain long hidden" (229). Robert's metaphysical view is similar to another belief, expressed by the narrator soon after, who now also seemingly jettisons her epistemological cynicism and embraces a naive optimism: "I cannot believe that an honest man . . . is ever really deceived by falsehood" (300).

The "providential" aspect of this astonishing epistemology is related to the idea that Robert expressed. He claims to believe that in his search for his friend's remains and his murderer, he is "reliant on a stronger hand than his own to point the way which he was to go" (135) – a stronger hand that guarantees that crime will not go unpunished. (Perhaps in Robert's case it is just as well that there is a stronger hand than his own; Robert's physical and moral frailty was clearly exhibited earlier in the novel when, having reluctantly agreed to ice-skate with other members of his party, and, falling to the ice on his first attempt, Robert lay "placidly extended on the flat of his back until such time as the bystanders should think it fit to pick him up" [102].) There are five more references in the novel to this "stronger hand."[26] By implication, it is the hand of God that intervenes in nature (and intercedes in Robert's flaccid moral nature), infusing him with the requisite motivation and strength: the narrator tells us that his newfound purpose (formerly suspected by Robert himself to be his "monomania" [217]) "made him what he had never been before – a Christian" (135). Robert says – or, more correctly, *thinks*[27] – "Surely this awful responsibility has been forced upon me in order that I may humble myself to an offended Providence, and confess that a man cannot choose his own life" (313). And, at the end of the tale, Mr. Audley *thinks* once again, "Who can fail to recognize God's hand in this strange story?" If Robert's "victory" is in fact the result of the hand of a *deus ex machina*, what does this victory say about that *deus*? The beckoning hand does not lead him to a murderer, because there was no murder, hence it does not lead him to his friend's corpse, because there is no corpse. It does not even lead him to his friend, who shows up on his own. It certainly does not direct him toward action to ameliorate the conditions of those victims of the crimes of "Father poverty." Does it lead him to love, marriage, and fatherhood? At one point, the "beckoning hand" transforms into the hand of Clara Talboys: "But amid all, and through all, Clara Talboys, with an imperious gesture, beckoned him onwards to her brother's unknown grave" (216). Clara's hand does not beckon Robert to herself but toward the same error to which God beckoned him, to an empty grave, and hardly the empty grave of Christ.

Before leaving behind the puzzle of the beckoning hand, I will call attention to one last troubling reference to this theme. At the point at which Robert has insinuated himself into the drunken Mr. Maldon's home, and begins a siege of intimidation trying to force Maldon to reveal information (it is at this moment that that the narrator says, "there had never been such a scene as this" [147]), the old man, on the verge of collapse, finally musters enough energy to give the unemployed barrister the "Have-you-no-shame?" lecture mentioned earlier: "– you take – the opportunity to terrify me – and it is not right, sir – it is –" (147). In fact, Robert *is* shamed, and he asks himself, "Why do I go on with this? . . . how pitiless I am, and how relentlessly I am carried on. It is not myself; it is the hand which is beckoning me further and further upon the dark road whose end I dare not dream of" (147). For a moment, Robert wishes he could take back his bitter accusations: "If I had known this, I might have spared him. It would have been better, perhaps, to have spared him." Despite this moment of regret, immediately thereafter Mr. Audley regales Mr. Maldon with a moral lecture that occupies a full page of the novel, again justifying his actions by appealing to the "stronger hand." If the intentional cruelty in which Robert engages is justified religiously, then Robert is indeed more of an inquisitor than a detective. Lucy Snowe may also have had a special relationship with her Lord, a uniqueness that allowed her exemption from common morality (as did Abraham as he prepared to sacrifice his son),[28] but if Lucy did, unlike Robert, she kept it secret from the other characters in her story, and from her readers. This religiosity, if intentional on Braddon's part, gives us reason to conclude that she meant for her story to be a defense of the *status quo ante*.

Beautiful performances and performances of beauty

I have characterized the Victorian self as neo-Cartesian, and will return to that theme insofar as it applies to Braddon's novel. On the other hand, we have also seen the insistence that nothing about another person escapes the prying gaze of the astute agent. A work such as *Villette* is a handbook of strategies for achieving this kind of knowledge. This is what I call a Goffmanian feature of Victorian novels. We will now briefly explore some of the components of *Lady Audley's Secret* that seem to support the claim that, despite the metaphysics of secret interiority, there are no secrets except secrets of performance – secrets understood by all – secrets in broad daylight.[29]

The character that the actress Helen Talboys has played, that of "Lucy Graham," is a fictive personality, an impersonation not of an actual person but of an ideal (which, according to Goffman, is the goal of every performance).[30] However, the sunny, angelic personality she has created is not a complete sham: she turns herself into an excellent governess, and the charm she exhibits in this role is real – that is, she really can charm individuals and groups alike. Her beauty is also real, but for her, it is a military implement. The narrator tells us that she who will soon be Lady Audley did not waste time being proud of her beauty; rather, "she looked upon that beauty as a weapon" (287) – a "strategic armamentarium," in the vocabulary of Karl Scheibe (53). Her sweetness and concern for others are also weapons, even though, unlike her beauty, they are fraudulent. (That is, in other roles she can exhibit viciousness and selfishness with the same skill with which she now brandishes their opposites.) Nevertheless, Lucy Graham does not overact, nor does she step completely out of character with her former roles.

Despite her supremely convincing performance, she does in fact have a critic in the person of Alicia Audley, her new stepdaughter, whose motives are based primarily on jealousy. After all, not all fairy tales lie when they depict stepmothers as evil. Sometimes stepmothers fraudulently claim to replace real mothers. In those cases they usurp not only maternal roles but also depose stepdaughters from their hard-earned position as sole object of fatherly love and attention; and *this* stepmother, Lady Audley, seems to flirt with her new step nephew, who just happens to be the person with whom Alicia Audley is infatuated. I will not dwell further on Alicia Audley, other than to say that throughout the novel she too proves to be a well-practiced performer, though without the consummate expertise of her stepmother.

Robert Audley's suspicions are differently motivated. He puts his new aunt under strict surveillance, waiting for her to blow her cover, and becomes convinced that Lady Audley is an "arch trickster," an "all-accomplished deceiver." "Good Heavens," Robert exclaims, "what an actress this woman is" (219). "She shall look at me," he thought; "I will make her meet my eyes, and I will read her as I have read her before. She shall know how useless her artifices are with me" (185). This strategy of vigilance underscores Robert's anti-Goffmanian conviction that there is a true self behind the performance. Yet at the same time the person-as-text metaphor ("I shall read her") makes it difficult to sustain the "inner/outer" ontological distinction. According to Victorian ideology, the true "inner self" is private and secret. Yet Robert's strategic assumption (like Sherlock Holmes's at the century's end) is that no secret can be protected from strict scrutiny. Sometimes Lady Audley is able to preserve intact her performance in Robert's presence, but is unable to do so in the presence of the narrator (nor, therefore, in the presence of Braddon's readers), given the narrator's near-omniscience. For example, we are told by the narrator that Lady Audley, alone in her room, quickly changes positions upon hearing someone at the door: "She rose, and threw herself into a low chair near the fire. She flung her beautiful head back upon the soft cushions, and took a book from the table near her" (254). The narrator comments on the episode:

> Insignificant as this action was, it spoke very plainly. It spoke very plainly of ever-recurring fears – of fatal necessities for concealment – of a mind that in its silent agonies was ever alive to the importance of outward effect. It told more plainly than anything else could have told how complete an actress my lady had been made by the awful necessity of her life.
> (254)

This is perhaps a rather hyperbolic but otherwise accurate paraphrase of Goffman's central claim about all of our lives. The narrator makes it clear that the fears that motivate this aspect of Lady Audley's act are a consequence of her misbehavior. However, a conflict model of social life of the type employed by Goffman puts everyone in Lady Audley's situation. One must dissemble in order to thrive, or even to survive.

It may seem that, by showing that there is, after all, a true self behind the actor, a self into which we are afforded glimpses when the performance breaks down, these rare breakdowns on Lady Audley's part refute the applicability of a Goffmanian model for an analysis of the novel. But what Robert's strategies produce are shards, fragments of information – usually about emotions – fragments that do indeed prove helpful in Robert's vengeful quest, but they do not produce a picture of a whole self (in the way that the pre-Raphaelite portrait of Lady Audley, so disdained by the narrator, *does* depict a whole self). Lady Audley's self behind the masks and veils is partially captured by Goffman's assertion, "Behind many masks and many characters, each performer tends to wear a single look, a naked unsocialized look, a look of concentration, a look of one who is privately engaged in a difficult, treacherous task" (235). Or perhaps the "self" depicted in the accumulation of these fragments is more like David Hume's troubling characterization of the self as "a bundle or collection of different perceptions which succeed each other with an inconceivable rapidity, and are in perpetual flux and movement." Each individual must forge a credible self out of these fragments through the art of performance. Goffman makes a point similar to Hume's when he writes, "As human beings we are presumably creatures of variable impulse with moods and energies that change from one moment to the next. As characters put on for an audience, however, we must not be subject to ups and downs" (56). Some do this better than others. Lady Audley excels; but nobody is perfect.[31]

I am not the first critic to have tried to generalize Lady Audley's performance of self to a wider group. Elaine Showalter observes that Braddon succeeds in undermining gender stereotypes by revealing that "the dangerous woman is not the rebel or the intellectual, but the pretty little girl whose indoctrination in the feminine role has taught her deceitfulness almost as secondary sex characteristic."[32]

In this case, there is a "feminine role" into which little girls are "indoctrinated." This insight fits nicely with Lyn Pykett's observation that

> by foregrounding Lady Audley's impersonation of proper femininity, the novel does more than simply focus attention on the feminine duplicity in which the entire narrative originates. It also explores and exploits fears that the respectable idea, or proper feminine, may simply be a form of acting, just one role among other possible roles. Even more seriously, the representation of Lady Audley, like that of some of Braddon's other heroines, raises the spectre that femininity is itself duplicitous, and that it involves deception and dissembling.
> (Pykett 1992, 90–91)

Yet another contribution to this discussion is offered by Kimberly Reynolds and Nicola Humble who write about Lady Audley's relation to "the culture of respectability," contending that "[r]ather than undermining its codes of propriety, she threatens bourgeois culture by too closely parodying its ideal, and revealing it as a hollow idol."[33] I see nothing wrong, and everything right, about this concatenation of theses. I only question what may appear to be the implication in some of these arguments that it is only the feminine that is constructed and performed. Whether by choice or indoctrination, everybody in this novel is acting out a role. Idiosyncratic roles overlap team efforts; individual performances veil private secrets; team efforts disguise group secrets. All involve lies – if only lies to oneself. Most of these are creative lies: they engender a certain social world.

We have not yet remarked on the irony that Lady Audley, burdened with secrets as she is, has virtually no sexual secrets – with the exception, mentioned earlier, that she must present herself to Sir Michael as a virgin. The person in the novel who has powerful sexual secrets – even from himself – and sexual secrets that reveal something of a hidden aspect of Victorian sexuality, is Robert Audley. As is well known, Robert Nemesvari has presented this case in a most convincing manner:

> By portraying her putative hero, Robert Audley, as driven by repressed homoerotic desires, Braddon exposes the self-interested and self-protective denial which underlies Victorian patriarchal society. The subtextual revelation of the "unspeakable" secret of male homosocial desire is essential to Braddon's feminist critique of the roles and behaviors forced upon women by men who are unwilling to acknowledge their own motives and insecurities.[34]

Nemesvari goes on to argue that Braddon's hint to her readers of "Robert Audley's Secret"

> is part of her feminist attack on the *status quo* by calling into question male self-awareness, exposing the profound sexual ambivalence at the core of masculine power, and emphasizing that it is women who pay the price for preserving the secret upon which male privilege rests.
> (527)

Following Nemesvari, Ann Cvetkovich observes that Robert

> is indifferent to women as sexual objects and to marriage as an economic benefit. . . . The moment that marks his change is . . . his meeting with George and their homoerotic attraction to one another. . . . [H]e finds new passion and direction in his life.[35]

The novel concludes with an even stranger *ménage-à-trois* than the one in Wilkie Collins's *The Woman in White*, where Walter Hartright, Laura Fairlie, and Marion Halcomb must sort out connubial rights and obligations. What "noble lie" will George Talboys, Robert Audley (soon to be the new Sir Robert, Baronet of Audley), and the new Lady Audley (née Clara Talboys) tell little Georgey about his missing mother? Will the new Lady Audley also have a secret?

Acting mad or dangerous acts?

Many critics agree that the question, What is Lady Audley's secret? cannot be answered with confidence. Of course, she has so many secrets that it is possible to argue about which one is the eponymous secret, but almost all commentators accept that the secret referenced in the title most likely alludes to Lady Audley's fear of the madness passed down from her mother, or the belief that she is and has been in a state of madness by the time we first meet her (as she declares to Robert when her tormenter finally corners her: "I killed him because I AM MAD!" [294]). For a number of well-known reasons, it is possible that neither of these guesses is correct: first, even the narrator – who often, but not always, seems to know everything – appears to waver about whether lunacy is "Lady Audley's Secret."[36] Second, after interviewing Lady Audley, the psychiatrist Dr. Mosgrove declares, "The lady is not mad" (323). Third, her symptoms are not those of insanity, and they are nothing like those of her mad mother in her asylum. In the face of these puzzles, there has been a variety of critical responses. Pykett says: "In fact the question of Lady Audley's madness (is she mad, or is she simply clever and/or wicked?) becomes one of the key secrets of the narrative" (Pykett 2002, 88–89). D. A. Miller writes:

> The "secret" let out at the end of the novel is not, therefore, that Lady Audley is a madwoman but rather that, *whether she is one or not*, she must be treated as such. Robert feels no embarrassment at the incommensurability thus betrayed between the diagnosis and the data that are supposed to confirm it.[37]

Chiara Briganti agrees:

> We cannot confidently say that at the end of the novel we have discovered Lady Audley's secret. Her secret may be one of many: it may very well be related to her mother's legacy, but it may also be, as Elaine Showalter has indicated, that she is not insane.[38]

Finally, Helena Michie expresses a similar view:

> The text does not allow us – or for that matter, Robert – to decide whether Lady Audley is "really" mad or "simply" criminal; this is a secret Lady Audley – if she herself knows the answer – takes to the grave with her.[39]

Sally Shuttleworth would think that all of these approaches involve "category mistakes." She asserts, provocatively, "To try to determine . . . whether Lady Audley was really mad, is to misunderstand the radical workings of the text – its challenge of certainty."[40]

There is also a Goffmanian factor that adds to the confusion. Earlier I mentioned Goffman's fascination with Sartre's inability to define "good faith" (or, as Sartre occasionally calls it, "authenticity" [116]) in a way that would give it a moral standing. If all "presentations of the self" are more or less a form of theater, then the difference between authenticity and inauthenticity is indeed problematical in any moral ontology. And, by extension, the question of authentic madness as opposed to falsified madness becomes critical, especially in Victorian times, when theatricality and authenticity appear to have been seen as diametrically opposed. According to Lynn Voskuil, one reason behind the Victorian suspicion about theatricality was that it "disrupts and disables selfhood, rendering the self multiform rather than uniform, shifting rather than coherent, constructed rather than (at some level) essential."[41] Yet, actresses study what they take to be cases of authenticity in order to reproduce them convincingly on stage. Indeed, Voskuil detects an ambiguity concerning the relation between performance and authenticity in Victorian England. According to her, the two ideas of theatricality and authenticity were not seen as wholly opposed to each other, but rather "each concept shapes the other." They are, she says, "mutually determinative." Voskuil points out that Ellen Terry, preparing for her role as Ophelia, visited a lunatic asylum in order to view firsthand "authentic" madness. Erving Goffman wrote his book *Asylums*[42] after having himself imbedded in such an institution. He concluded not so much that madness was a performance but that the wardens at the asylums would get annoyed at inmates who did not play the roles that lunatics were supposed to play; hence, lunatics (and the odd sociologist) learned to play these roles. One reason Dr. Musgrove concludes that Lady Audley is dangerous is that there is no way to determine whether she is authentically insane or playing with conviction the role of a madwoman. A woman who might suffer occasional short bouts of "acute mania" might on other occasions be intentionally imitating the behavior she exhibited during those bouts, if she thinks it is in her interest to do so. Sartre records all the artificial mannerisms of a Parisian waiter: "His movement is quick and forward, a little too precise, a little too rapid. He comes toward the patrons . . . a little too eagerly; his voice, his eyes express an interest a little too solicitous." Sartre then asks himself: "What game is the waiter playing?" He concludes, "He is playing at *being* a waiter in a café" (Sartre 101–2). And we must remind ourselves that he is not only playing at being a waiter; he *is* a waiter.

There is, then, a mystery about Helen Maldon's madness. It is a meta-secret – a secret about a secret. At the first level, we can possibly say that Lady Audley's secret – her madness – is a plot-driving secret, and is hence, perhaps, theoretically less interesting than secrets at other depths; indeed, that same secret at the secondary level is much more analytically engaging and revealing. In fact, in *Lady Audley's Secret*, the question of madness is the leitmotif of the work, an underlying theme that not only dominates the central plot of the novel but one that swells and recedes within each of the various subplots as well. And wherever there is insanity, or the threat of insanity, there is secrecy, and in this case, a peculiarly Victorian form of secrecy – and often, therefore, of Victorian lying, but one that, consistent with Simmel's insight, is a socially creative form of lying, and not only because it will eventually usher in reformed divorce laws.

Throughout the novel, there are reciprocal accusations of insanity leveled like cannon volleys, and there are threats of institutionalization hurled around like pots and frying pans in the Duchess's kitchen.[43] Consequential to the threats of having others declared mad is the persistent menace of institutionalization. Lady Audley threatens her legal husband, George Talboys – "I told him that if he denounced me to Sir Michael, I would declare him to be a madman" (335) – and when she sees that the threat fails, she pushes him down a well. She threatens to have Robert placed in a madhouse:

> "I would warn you that such fancies have sometimes conducted people, as apparently sane as yourself, to the life-long imprisonment of a private lunatic-asylum." Robert Audley started and recoiled. . . . "She would be capable of using her influence with my uncle to place me in a mad-house."
>
> (233)

The battle between Robert and Lady Audley becomes a struggle over who can get the other institutionalized first, or who will be the cause of the other's death. "He will do it, unless I get him into a lunatic-asylum first; or unless –" (264). Lady Audley knows that if she loses, she will, like her mother, end up in an asylum ("and die – as my mother died" [269]).

It would be easy to conclude from the textual evidence in *Lady Audley's Secret* that Braddon depicts insanity as a purely social construction, one that is manipulated by the upper-middle and aristocratic classes to their own advantage (and in this novel, by at least one member of the "servant class"). But of course in the Victorian world (as in ours), a significant number of mental and behavioral patterns diagnosed as madness were not merely products of social construction: activities of the brain have gone seriously wrong; there are mental and emotional states and events that go awry and behaviors that are unintelligible. Like the early Michel Foucault, Braddon's narrator refers to these behaviors as forms of "unreason," which according to Foucault were primordial, unhistoricized, inchoate, ungovernable, antisocial manifestations that historical societies try to organize and expel as "the other."[44] Braddon's narrator has something to say about this unreason. For instance, after describing Robert Audley's superstitious fear that the ghost of

George Talboys would haunt him for his failure to avenge George's death, or for failing to place his remains in a final resting place, the narrator remonstrates with the reader:

> Do not laugh at poor Robert because he grew hypochondriacal after hearing the horrible story of his friend's death. There is nothing so delicate, so fragile, as that invisible balance upon which the mind is always trembling. Mad to-day and sane to-morrow. ... Who has not been, or is not to be mad in some lonely hour of life? Who is quite safe from the trembling of the balance?[45]
>
> (344)

The images and formulas in this passage are dear to the narrator, as we will see if we examine an earlier passage about the same theme. It deserves to be quoted in full.

> Who has not felt, in the first madness of sorrow, an unreasoning rage against the mute propriety of chairs and tables, the stiff squareness of Turkey carpets, the unbending obstinacy of the outward apparatus of existence? We want to root up gigantic trees in a primeval forest, and to tear their huge branches asunder in our convulsive grasp; and the utmost that we can do for the relief of our passion is to knock-over an easy chair, or smash a few shillings' worth of Mr. Copeland's manufacture.
>
> (175–76)

This rather remarkable passage depicts a kind of rage that the narrator assumes we have all experienced, a rage that, with good luck, we take out on the inanimate material objects of the everyday world that we inhabit. But we do not do so arbitrarily, for the arbitrariness is found not in us but precisely in the maddening orderliness of these quotidian material objects that everywhere surround us, and it is this very arbitrariness that provokes our rage.[46] The narrator continues:

> Madhouses are large and only too numerous; yet surely it is strange that they are not larger, when we think of how many helpless wretches must beat their brains against this hopeless persistency of the orderly outward world, as compared with the storm and tempest, the riot of confusion within – when we remember how many minds must tremble upon the narrow boundary between reason and unreason, mad to-day and sane to-morrow, mad yesterday and sane to-day.
>
> (176)

Here, the narrator derives the source of our temporary but recurring madness from the discrepancy between the inner and the outer. The outer is the same obstinate orderliness of the materiality of the everyday world that we saw earlier, but here that intransigent world is in dramatic tension with the inner world of "storm and tempest, the riot of confusion within," a chaos that the narrator seems to attribute to us all under normal conditions. The terrible opposition between these two worlds throws some (all?) of us into temporary fits of madness – "mad to-day and sane to-morrow." The tone of the passage is such that the narrator appears to take for granted that we all know this truth. It is a profound and secret knowledge – we do not tell our children, and we rarely speak of it – but it is universally known. Another secret in broad daylight, but a terrible one. Is it a particularly Victorian secret? Perhaps only in the sense in which Freud is a Victorian.

Apparently I am one of the few critics who treats this "madhouse" passage as setting forth a major claim by Braddon's narrator about the way the human mind functions. My impression is that most critics handle this and the related passages that I have cited about the danger of universal madness as merely rhetorical flourishes that are part of the hyperbole of the sensation genre. One exception is Lauren Chattman, who takes the idea as seriously as I do. She opens her essay, "Diagnosing the Domestic Woman in *The Woman in White* and *Dora*" with the passage from *Lady Audley's Secret* that begins, "Mad-houses are large" and that ends with the line, "mad yesterday, sane to-day." Chattman reads this passage as evidence of the view that "*all* subjectivity is constructed as irrational during this period" (123). So stated, this puts Chattman's reading close to my own. But Chattman steps away from me as she develops her argument, which contains four main propositions, as I understand it, beginning with that first proposition, which I will number as proposition #1:

1. In the Victorian world, "*all* subjectivity" is understood to be irrational.
2. Proposition #1 is true of "subjectivity before it is gendered" (124).
3. Even after the gendering of subjectivity, "a middle-class professional man [e.g., Robert Audley] might lose his grasp on reality at any moment" (124).
4. "Madness is increasingly figured in terms of undomesticated femininity" (125).

There seems to me to be some logical tension among these four propositions. Proposition #2 conflicts with proposition #1, and proposition #3 seems to undermine proposition #4.[47]

Superimposing Goffmanian social theory onto the psychological theory of Braddon's narrator produces what might be thought of as a decidedly radical result, namely, that the ontological division between the pre-performative self and the performed self places the performances (the "presentations of self in everyday life") in the category of the objective world, along with the quotidian material objects that surround us in everyday life (the infuriating regularity and arbitrariness of the Turkish carpets, chairs, tables, cups, and saucers). This world is in contrast to the subjective world, characterized as "storm and tempest, the riot of confusion" (176), a world that cannot be called mad because apparently it is our natural state. Madness, as in Freud, is the product of the conflict between the two worlds. The surprising news is that the roles we are forced to play in the show that must go on are included in the category of the external objects that tend to drive us mad. A role is a material thing in that world, and it is against that material world that, on occasion, we insanely rage. Each of the items that the narrator lists as objects of our fury (chairs and tables, cups, saucers, and Turkey carpets) is the product of role-playing. If we rage against the roles that sociality demands of us, then ours is truly a mad, mad, mad world. (Similar, though less radical, estimations of our reaction to the roles imposed upon us in civil society are presented by Freud in *Civilization and its Discontents.*)

Some readers of Braddon's novel assume that the narrator's diagnosis of the human condition as one that is never far from insanity is merely a flamboyant exaggeration typical of the sensation genre, but if we treat it rather as a key element of the narration, then we must consider the consequences of this diagnosis for our general understanding of the novel's plot. First, and most evident, is that the question of whether, at any given moment, Lady Audley is or is not mad is less urgent, because the answer by itself does not distinguish her from any other character in the novel (nor, perhaps, from any of Braddon's readers). Nevertheless, the identity of Helen Maldon cannot be established without addressing the question of the state of her mind: Helen *is* the person who will become Lucy Graham, and who will become Lady Audley, and eventually Mrs. Taylor. All of these identities are strung together on a specific accusation of insanity. Helen Maldon's impersonations are associated with her impugned madness. In fact, the question of identity, impersonation, and madness is a theme that is generalized in *Lady Audley's Secret*. Once her impersonation is discovered, both her new husband and her new nephew hope to convince themselves and others that the cause of her crimes is insanity. Her successful penetration of a social status that is not her own is less worrisome if the cause of her outrageous occupation is madness rather than intelligence, ambition and determination. Rebecca Stern urges us "to remember that 'personation' – that is, impersonation – loomed large in Victorian culture, far exceeding the parameters of sanity and entering into many facets of daily life" (35). Jessica Saxon, commenting on Stern's passage, says,

> Victorian culture was concerned about false identities, the ability of people to cross class boundaries, and the difficulty of proving an identity as false. A person who could successfully change his or her identity or assume the identity of another person could change his or her social standing.[48]

Together, these ideas give us a theory concerning one of the anxieties about secrecy that haunt Victorian culture. Even in a phony meritocracy – "phony" because in a real meritocracy being born into privilege is not the same as achieving it through just deserts – there is the fear that stealth freeloaders (here, impersonators) will deplete the resources that constitute the rewards that should be distributed to the meritorious. Then as now, many try to paint the poor as the freeloaders. Worse, *Lady Audley's Secret* hints that it may well prove to be the very wealthy who produce nothing and contribute little, and hence are the least meritorious.

In this novel the problem of identity is associated with the problem of insanity because from the beginning Lady Audley herself links her "personation" to her madness. Moreover, if the "secret" of near-universal madness revealed by the narrator is true, then the answer to the question, "Who am I?" must contain a reference to the uncontrollably fluctuating state of the chaos of my mind, and the rage that builds up in my subjectivity's encounter with the arbitrary stability of the world. A later Victorian logician will understand this, and can produce a syllogism to prove it. In Wonderland Alice asks directions of the Cheshire Cat:

> "In *that* direction,' the Cat said, waving its right paw round, "lives a Hatter: and in *that* direction," waving the other paw, "lives a March Hare. Visit either you like: they're both mad."
> "But I don't want to go among mad people," Alice remarked.
> "Oh, you can't help that, we're all mad here. I'm mad. You're mad."
> "How do you know that I'm mad?" said Alice.
> "You must be," said the Cat, "or you wouldn't have come here." . . .
> "How do you know that you're mad?"
> "To begin with," said the Cat, "a dog's not mad. You grant that?"
> "I suppose so," said Alice.
> "Well, then," the Cat went on, "you see a dog growls when it's angry, and wags its tail when it's pleased. Now *I* growl when I'm pleased, and wag my tail when I'm angry. Therefore I'm mad."
> "I call it purring, not growling," said Alice.
> "Call it what you like," said the Cat. "Do you play croquet . . . ?"[49]

In chapter 2 I argued that privacy, in the sense in which it entails secrecy, is a primary component of a middle-class Victorian conception of selfhood. I maintained (*pace* Shuttleworth) that this posture constitutes a kind of neo-Cartesianism. In Braddon's novel, different features of the Cartesian self are stressed, but the Cartesianism here is even more dramatically expressed than in *Villette*. Descartes had argued that privacy and inaccessibility are the key defining constituents of selfhood; this is the metaphysical view of a great many Victorians who write on the subject of the self. The Cartesianism expressed in *Villette* and in *David Copperfield*, as in so many other Victorian novels, stresses the discrepancy between the inner and the outer, between the private realm and the public, and the secrecy, depth, and inviolability of the true self, as well as the natural connection between that true self and the supernatural. But in *Lady Audley's Secret*, the neo-Cartesianism expressed also emphasizes the more sinister subtext of Descartes's theory of the mind. Descartes saw that the same feature of the mind (= self) that allowed it knowledge of God, namely, the self's solipsistic isolation, also placed the mind in danger of insanity. Descartes's ontological and epistemological foundation – selfhood, expressed as "I am" in the *Discourse*, and "I think, therefore I am," in the *Meditations* – not only failed to guarantee the sanity of the self (even a madman can correctly think "I am") but seemed to Descartes himself to be in danger of insanity. In the Second Meditation, the notorious "dream problem" is a problem of insanity. For Descartes, dreams are madder than madness, and at any particular moment it is impossible to know with certainty whether one is awake or dreaming. Descartes writes: "in my dreams [I] imagine the same things that lunatics imagine when awake, or sometimes things which are even less plausible. ... [Furthermore], there are no conclusive indications by which waking life can be distinguished from sleep."[50] Notice that in this respect the Cheshire Cat is a Cartesian as well.[51] Wonderland is nothing but a dream-world created in Alice's sleep; therefore, according to Descartes, the Cat is the product of a temporarily insane mind, and so is the image of Alice as she appears in the mind of the temporarily mad little girl: "I'm mad; you're mad."

One might object to the use of Descartes in my analysis of Braddon's novel, saying, perhaps, that if I must use philosophy, I should at least use British philosophy. Indeed, it could be done. The conception of the self as it developed in British empiricism also leads to the problem of madness. David Hume (1711–76) saw that the *tabula rasa* of Locke and Berkeley led directly to solipsism, and to a self that proves to be merely "a bundle or collection of different perceptions," "heat or cold, light or shade, love or hatred, pain or pleasure," which "succeed each other with an inconceivable rapidity, and are in a perpetual flux and movement."[52] This is indeed a mad, mad, mad world, and one that Braddon's narrator could have used to her purposes. However, it is clear that Braddon, like many of her contemporaries, including George Eliot, was familiar with Continental metaphysics, and more interested in it than in British empiricism. At one point in *Lady Audley's Secret* the narrator seems to mock the sincerity of philosophers in the schools of German Idealism:

> you may frequently find that the philosopher who calls life an empty delusion is pretty sharp in the investment of his monies, and recognizes the tangible nature of India bonds, Spanish certificates, and Egyptian script – as contrasted with the painful uncertainty of an Ego or non-Ego in metaphysics.
> (208)

We see here that in 1869 the author of *Lady Audley's Secret* is conversant with the latest trends in Continental philosophy, including, possibly the work of Fichte. Also, Alicia Audley indirectly accuses her cousin of Schopenhauerian pessimism when, sarcastically responding to Robert's comment about her not looking well, she says: "What does it matter? I'm growing a philosopher of your school, Robert Audley. What does it matter? Who cares whether I am well or ill?" (191). On another occasion the narrator shares with the readers an extended philosophical meditation of Robert's on what amounts to another summary of Schopenhauerian rational pessimism.

Descartes's even more infamous evocation of "the Evil Genius" is also a problem of insanity (the very idea of an Evil Genius of the dimensions described by Descartes is the most paranoid thought possible for any human to think).[53] Yet, only when he is able to deduce the existence of an all-perfect God from the certainty of selfhood is Descartes able to dismiss the dream problem and the problem of the Evil Genius, that is, to dismiss the problem of insanity. If Descartes's logic in his proofs of God's existence is fallacious – as most philosophers seem to believe it is – then it is impossible to remove the persistent threat of lunacy from the very conception of the self. Braddon's narrator not only does not try to remove that threat but insists that it is a real component of selfhood.

Indeed, the condition of the self as depicted by Descartes, minus the lengthy philosophical argument that leads up to it, appears to be exactly the condition of the self that is revealed in *Lady Audley's Secret*. It is, in a certain sense, the deepest secret of the novel. Yet, it is a condition that follows logically from the general Victorian conception of the self as a mysterious entity existing in a purely private (hence secret) space that is alienated from the external world in an absolute sense. Braddon's narrator has simply cut to the quick and made the (Victorian) self not only susceptible to madness but mad in and of itself. This is one of the most dramatic secrets communicated in Victorian literature – apparently another secret in broad daylight, as Braddon's narrator assumes that her reader will recognize its truth without resistance. The true self is in a state of chaos that, in the narrator's eyes, sometimes allows itself to be contained by the orderliness of the alienated external reality, but sometimes it reacts violently against its natural and social constraints, flowing out into that arbitrary world, engulfing and threatening it. It may not only be the singular voices of Braddon's narrator and the Cheshire Cat that give voice to this secret. Psychiatry itself may have done so. The authors of a book on the history of psychiatry assert: "the aspiration widely entertained in 1800, of curing a relatively small population of lunatics, seemed by 1900 to be in danger of revealing the fundamental craziness of the human mind itself."[54] If this is so, then the narrator has every reason to repeat several times: "sane to-day and mad to-morrow." What I concluded about Preedy in chapter 1 and Becky Sharp in chapter 3 seems also to be true of Lucy Graham: we have met Lady Audley, and she is us.

Conclusion

The two principal characters in Braddon's text, Robert Audley, Esq. and Lady Lucy Audley, are in mortal combat, the former initially trying to discover the fate of his missing school friend – or his murdered body, if such a murder took place. But his quest morphs into a battle to prevent devastating damage to family and class honor from a systematically corrosive invasion by the woman who is now called Lady Audley, who tries to prevent Robert from discovering not the "secret of her life" but the resting place of his friend's body. All this she does to save her own life, and to defend and solidify her successful occupation of enemy terrain. It is not as if the privileges she usurps are war trophies; rather, her triumph is that of being considered by the enemy as one of their own and to have a favored life offered to her that she otherwise could never have. The secret worlds of these two protagonists are each distinctly idiosyncratic, though peculiarly Victorian in form and content. Lady Audley's secret world contains not only powerful ambitions to escape the cycle of poverty and misery into which she was born but also the guilty memories accrued during her escape: the abandonment of her child, and the immoral, desperate, and audacious actions in which she has had to engage in order to penetrate and remain in the upper ranks of society and garner the wealth and security afforded there. Of course, her secret world surely (or perhaps only probably) houses the fear of hereditary insanity, and consequent institutionalization. Robert's secret world hides, though not well, his natural propensity for lassitude and ennui that make him a burden even to his own parasitic class, as well as concealing a homoerotic obsession with a school chum with no apparent redeeming qualities and no inclination or ability to reciprocate Robert's affection. It contains in addition the ruptures with civility and honor that he has undertaken (lying, dissimulation, terroristic inquisitional tactics, abusing the privilege of rank, and – not least of all – the institutionalization of a woman diagnosed as sane) to oust the dangerous interloper from her invasive possession of purloined power. Finally, it also seems to include a fear of insanity – as does that of the woman he hates. Robert Audley's refusal to divulge the world of secret suspicions that torture him is motivated by his fear that this parallel world is a paranoid one. Thus, the fear of insanity and the threat of being declared insane are components of the secret worlds that Lady Audley and Robert Audley share. In fact, they are closely linked to the larger world of Victorian secrecy, requiring a new army of diagnosticians, asylums, and their attendants. Yet, in the case of Lady Audley, the mad doctor's diagnosis, prognosis, and prescription are not medical judgments but more like military engagements as deterrents against insurrection. They too are part of a strategic armamentarium designed for both defensive and offensive assignments.

Selfhood in *Lady Audley's Secret* (never far from madness), as in *Villette*, emerges as a kind of radical neo-Cartesianism, wherein the private world that is the locus of selfhood is profoundly isolated from its embodiment and from the strictures of the social world in which that embodiment finds itself. In *Villette*, that space was like a mysterious secret temple, inaccessible to anyone other than the priest or priestess who is its lonely occupant. In *Lady Audley's Secret*, the private space that is the mind is less a mystical dream than a Freudian nightmare, close to lunacy by its very nature, or at least destined to fall into bouts of madness by virtue of its unavoidable, horrifying daily contacts with the world of materiality. This secret, which the narrator seems to think we (Victorian citizens) all know but do not articulate, is finally publicly revealed by her. In Braddon's novel, it is as though privacy and selfhood are properties only of a certain class of individuals. Or perhaps, in the same way that Lady Audley's selfhood is finally proved to be fictive and vulnerable when subjected to a regime of scrutiny and terror, all selfhood in this novel is doubly fictive, reducible to Goffmanian performances, in which case we have a deconstruction of the much-vaunted Victorian inner/outer (or public/private) distinction, and of its mystical theological source, much like the undoing of that model in *Villette*.

Simmel touted the sometimes socially and individually creative function of secrecy, but in this novel, secrecy's function seems almost always defensive, motivated by fear and vengefulness. The secrets that Robert Audley successfully protects do not so much create a certain kind of individuality and sociality as they sustain already existing forms of individuality and sociality, questionable as these forms may be. If Robert's secrets were revealed – as they *are* revealed by the narrator to a rather wide audience comprising precisely the kinds of real individuals from whom the fictional Robert wishes to hide his secrets – then the family he is protecting and the class of which that family is representative would be damaged. If people suspected that a supposedly superior class of individuals is indistinguishable from frauds who imitate them, then this discovery would damage that privileged class by eroding the willingness of the other social classes to behave as if inferior to them. It is ironic that Lady Audley's secrets also would protect those same upper-class interests if they were not disclosed, and that therefore Robert Audley, even as a fictional character, has damaged the interests of his social class by unveiling those secrets as the novel unfolds. Within the novel he has exposed them only to members of his secret society – some to his uncle, perhaps to his soon-to-be wife, and to the mad doctor – but Braddon's narrator has revealed these fictitious facts to the general reading public as if they were real facts; even as fictions, they indicate something true about the role of secrecy in class structure. Therefore, by revealing the secrets not only of Lady Audley but of Sir Michael and Robert, Braddon's narrator has participated in the eventual undermining of what was once the ruling class. Hence, in a curious manner, Simmel's theory when applied to Braddon's novel remains progressive; it shows how secrets sustain individual and social relationships, and it shows how the unveiling of these secrets can undo those relationships. To recuperate Simmel's progressive reputation as his theory applies to *Lady Audley's Secret* I have had to think of Braddon's readers as real people (as they were and are) and have had to treat the characters in her novel as if they were real people (just as Braddon did and as her readers did). In that case, the fictitious revelation of the secrets of Audley Court (including Lady Audley's secrets) is part of the non-fictitious undermining of aristocratic authority, and is complicit in the middle-class revolution in modern Britain, helping to move the artifacts and artificers of the Audley Courts of the land closer to "the museum of antiquities, by the side of the spinning wheel and the bronze axe."[55]

Notes

1 Henry James, "Miss Braddon," *Nation* (November 1865): 593–95.
2 I, like many other critics, choose rather arbitrarily to treat the narrator as female. In fact, I find no compelling textual evidence one way or the other.
3 Mary Elizabeth Braddon, *Lady Audley's Secret* [1861–62], ed. Lyn Pykett, notes and intro. by Lyn Pykett (Oxford and New York: Oxford University Press, 2012), 8, 31, 62. Future references to this work will be cited parenthetically in the body of the text.
4 A number of critics have commented on the passages I am citing here, though most of them seem less interested in its treatment of secrecy than in the decay revealed in these descriptions. See Aeron Haynie, "An Idle Handle that Was Never Turned, and a Lazy Rope so Rotten: The Decay of the Country Estate in *Lady Audley's Secret*," in *Beyond Sensation: Mary Elizabeth Braddon in Context*, ed. Marlene Tromp, Pamela K. Gilbert, and Aeron Haynie (Albany: State University of New York Press, 2000), 63–74. Haynie argues that Braddon is using the symbolism of decay to indict the Audley family for its useless stagnation. She places much of the blame for the invasion and occupation of Audley Hall by Helen Maldon/Lucy Graham/Lady Audley on the decadent stupor of the Audley family (66). Also see Eva Badowska, "On the Track of Things: Sensation and Modernity in Mary Elizabeth Braddon's *Lady Audley's*

Secret," *Victorian Literature and Culture* 37.1 (March 2009): 157–75, xxxvii. Badowska sees that "here modernity inevitably crumbles to dust" (162), arguing that the novel exhibits modernism's fear of "its own passage and inevitable, impending obsolescence" (158). Future references to this work will be cited parenthetically in the body of the text.

5 Robert, to little Georgey when the boy's grandfather leaves the room:

> "'Now, Georgey, suppose you sit on my knee, and tell me about the pretty lady' . . . 'I'll tell you about the pretty lady,' he said, 'because I like you very much. Grampa told me not to tell anybody, but. . . .'"

Robert claims to have come to help the boy, but he is using him for his own ends. Georgey's caretaker, Mrs. Plowson, hired help of a considerably lower social standing than Mr. Audley, enters the room and tries to take Georgey to bed in order to disrupt Mr. Audley's interrogation of him. "'Suppose you wait till I say so, ma'am, before you stop the little fellow's mouth,' said Robert Audley, sharply" (143).

6 Apathy: "I have shrunk . . . from all the fatigues of this troublesome life" (106); superficiality: "the few ideas which have made up the small sum of the young baronet's life" (112); superstition: "What if [I] were henceforth to be haunted by the phantom of murdered George Talboys?" (342); monomania and paranoia:

> "Why did that uncontrollable terror seize upon me?" he thought. "Why was it that I saw some strange mystery in my friend's disappearance? Was it a monition or a monomania? What if I am wrong after all? What if this chain of evidence which I have constructed link by link is woven out of my own folly? What if this edifice of horror and suspicion is a mere collection of crochets – the nervous fancy of a hypochondriacal bachelor?" (217)

7 Lyn Pykett, *The "Improper" Feminine: The Women's Sensation Novel and the New Woman Writing* (London and New York: Routledge, 1992), 83. Future references to this work will be designated as "Pykett 1992" and will be cited parenthetically in the body of the text.

8 Showalter tends to see secrecy as a pathological response to patriarchal society. In this sense Showalter's "secrecy" seems more Freudian than Simmelian. However, I find nothing in Simmel that disallows the possibility of pathological secrecy being sometimes creative (again, as in Freud's theory of sublimation).

9 "Sociological structures differ profoundly according to the measure of lying which operates in them" (Georg Simmel, *The Sociology of Georg Simmel*, trans. and ed. Kurt H. Wolff [New York: Free Press, 1964], 312–13). All citations of Simmel in this chapter refer to this work will be cited parenthetically in the body of the text.

10 Unless, of course, one counts Luke's death as second degree murder on the part of Lady Audley.

11 Karen Chase and Michael Levinson, "Bigamy and Modernity: The Case of Mary Elizabeth Braddon," in *The Spectacle of Intimacy: A Public Life for the Victorian Family* (Princeton: Princeton University Press, 2000), 203.

12 This is quite a remarkable exchange. Despite positioning himself as if he must reveal to the doctor confidentialities about himself, Robert Audley is *not* the patient, nor the penitent – unless he is obliquely admitting his own guilt, or his own madness. In fact, directly after meeting the doctor, Robert thinks to himself, "He is wondering whether I am the patient . . . and is looking for the diagnoses of madness in my face" (319).

13 Erving Goffman, *The Presentation of Self in Everyday Life* (New York and London: Anchor Books Doubleday, 1959), 141. Except where indicated, in this chapter all future references to Goffman's work will be to this book, and will be cited parenthetically in the body of the text.

14 Rachel Heinrichs argues that Robert Audley is always playing a part.

> It is appropriate to consider Robert's masculinity in terms of scripts, narrative, or staging, because he overtly mediates his identity through fictional and dramatic forms. . . . Braddon questions the autonomy and authority of the middle-class gentleman by calling attention to its innate theatricality. ("Critical Masculinities in *Lady Audley's Secret*," *Victorian Review* 33.1 [2007]: 103–20, 104, 105)

15 Jonathan Loesberg, "The Ideology of Narrative Form in Sensation Fiction," *Representations* 13 (Winter 1986): 115–38.
16 Karl E. Scheibe, *Mirrors, Masks, Lies and Secrets: The Limits of Human Predictability* (New York: Praeger, 1979), 78. Future references to this work will be cited parenthetically in the body of the text.
17 Refuting the claim of the logical positivists that all propositions are either true, false, or nonsense, Austin asserts that performative utterances cannot be "true" or "false" but rather they succeed or they fail; they are "felicitous" or "infelicitous" (J. L. Austin, *How to Do Things with Words* [1962], ed. J.O. Urmson and Marina Sbisà, 2nd ed. [Cambridge, MA: Harvard University Press, 2001], 14).
18 This assertion seems to conflict with another one by the narrator: "Miss Alicia Audley . . . was sole heiress to a very fine estate" (33).
19 Another example in the novel of a class-based sense of justice is found at the end of the novel, moving us several notches lower on the social hierarchy. The servants at Audley Hall detect evidence of a great disaster in the house when Lady Audley disappears and Sir Michael suddenly leaves with his daughter for a lengthy stay on the Continent. The servants try to divine the cause of the upheaval:

> The general leaning was towards the failure of a bank; and every member of the assembly seemed to take a dismal and raven-like delight in the fancy; though such a supposition involved their own ruin in the general destruction of that liberal household. (315)

Here we see a class-based *Schadenfreude* whose glee overrides the fear of the loss of wages for past work and fear of unemployment in the future.
20 Derrida treats the issue of the arbitrariness of the American Declaration of Independence in "Otobiographies: The Teaching of Nietzsche and the Politics of the Proper Name," trans. Avital Ronell, in *The Ear of the Other: Otobiography, Transference, Translation* (Lincoln: University of Nebraska Press, 1988), 1–38.
21 Not every scholar would agree with this assertion. For example, Rebecca Stern, in her brilliant discussion of *The Woman in White*, *Lady Audley's Secret*, and *St. Martin's Eve*, says, "All these novels, albeit to different degrees, highlight the problematic relationship between performance and sanity, ultimately endorsing an antiperformative stance toward the treatment of the mad and toward identity in general" ("'Personation' and 'Good Marking-Ink': Sanity, Performativity, and Biology in Victorian Sensation Fiction," *Nineteenth Century Studies* 14 [2000]: 35–62, 36–37). Future references to this work will be cited parenthetically in the body of the text. My view is that Braddon opens the floodgates to a Goffmanian reading of her story, though perhaps she would not have consciously intended to support a materialistic rendition of the theme.
22 Through most of the twentieth century, a woman in the Catholic Church, – call her Mrs. Smith – who discovered that she was in a bigamist relationship (her husband being in an active state of marriage to another woman) could marry again only if the Church issued an annulment of the first marriage. That is, she was still Mrs. Smith until an official cancelling performative was uttered.
23 For Sartre's primary account of bad faith, see *Being and Nothingness: A Phenomenological Essay on Ontology* [1943], trans. Hazel E. Barnes (New York and London:

138   *Madness and class conflicts*

Washington Square Press, 1956), 86–116. For his failure to treat good faith, Sartre writes:

> If it is indifferent whether one is in good or bad faith, because bad faith reapprehends good faith and slides to the very origin of the project of good faith, that does not mean that we cannot radically escape bad faith. But this supposes a self-recovery of being which was previously corrupted. This self-recovery we shall call authenticity, the description of which has no place here. (116n9)

Apparently, it had no place at all. At the end of *Being and Nothingness* Sartre returns to the issue of good faith. In the last sentence of the book he writes, "All these questions, which refer us to a pure and not accessory reflection, can find their reply only on the ethical plane. We shall devote to them a future work" (798). No such work was forthcoming.

24 Nicole P. Fisk suggests that Luke "is determined to have died more from the 'habits of intoxication' than the fire, since he was 'not much burnt'" (Braddon 347; "Lady Audley as Sacrifice: Curing the Female Disadvantage in *Lady Audley's Secret*," *Victorian Newsletter* 105 [Spring 2004]: 24–27, 25).

25 There is a well-known debate about the question of the political status of Braddon's novel, with Elaine Showalter seen as attributing to Braddon a progressive stance and with Ann Cvetkovich attributing to her a conservative one. The extreme version of the latter view is, I believe, Lillian Nayder, who claims that Lucy's attempted murder of George Talboys by forcing him down a well is meant by Braddon to provoke memories of the massacre by the Indian sepoys against British women and children by dropping them down the infamous well at Campore. Nayder claims that the real threat posed to the British Empire in the 1860s does not come from unruly natives in the colonies but from Englishwomen agitating for their rights" ("Rebellious Sepoys and Bigamous Wives: The Indian Mutiny and Marriage Law Reform in *Lady Audley's Secret*," in Tromp et al., *Beyond Sensation*, 31–42, 39).

26 See 144, 147, 148, 216, and 219.

27 The narrator of Braddon's novel is able to read the thoughts of the characters in her history: e.g., the phrase, "he thought," or "she thought" appears frequently: 37, 47, 78, 79, 104, 117, 127, 128, 139, 143, 147, 154, 173, 174, 178, 179, 180, 181, 185, 193, 195, 197, 202, 204, 206, 211, 213, 215, 217, 223, 224, 226, 233, 234, 248, 263, 264, 269, 284, 289, 326, 336, 337, 338, 341, 345, 367, 368. Occasionally the narrator is privy to the dreams of her characters: 39, 86 and 210. This would not be strange if we simply accepted without question the conventions of an "omniscient narrator," but, contrary to this conceit, this narrator sometimes admits at least partial ignorance of the thoughts and intentions of her subjects: "I doubt . . ." (81); "I do not know . . ." (156); "I have little doubt . . ." (156); "My lady . . . may have thought of many things . . ." (252); "I believe it was . . ." (284); "I think she even took malicious pleasure . . ." (290); "I believe she . . ." (290); "I do not believe . . ." (299); "I cannot believe . . ." (300). Furthermore, she seems to have personal associations with the story's characters, and sometimes gossips about them or tattles on them: "I am ashamed to say that the young barrister [used to read] Paul de Cock and Dumas *fils*" (183); "I am sorry to say . . ." (225, 248 and 372); "I do not say that Robert Audley was a coward, but I will admit that . . ." (233); "I think she even took malicious pleasure . . ." (290).

28 It is the "Victorian" philosopher Søren Kierkegaard, who, in the context of a discussion of Abraham, "the father of us all," poses most dramatically the questions: When is a sacrifice a murder? When is obeying God's commandments an act of insanity? (*Fear and Trembling* [1843], trans. Walter Lowrie [Garden City, NY: Doubleday Anchor Books, 1954].)

29 Alongside the "inner/outer" model that structures selfhood in *Lady Audley's Secret*, there is also at work a quasi-Goffmanian model of performative selfhood. These two models

would be in opposition to each other only if the second were fully Goffmanian, in the sense of implying that the self is exhausted in the totality of its performances. (Once again, a fully Goffmanian model articulates the self as an onion; in a quasi-Goffmanian model the self is an artichoke, but perhaps an artichoke as conceived of by someone who had never peeled an artichoke and had no clear idea of what its interior was like.)

30 [P]erformers often foster the impression that they had *ideal* motives for acquiring the role in which they are performing, [and] that they have *ideal* qualifications for the role. ... A performer tends to conceal or underplay those activities, facts, and motives which are inconsistent with an *idealized* version of himself and his products. (Goffman, *The Presentation of Self in Everyday Life*, 46, 48, emphases added)

31 Still, when Robert feels most dedicated to his mission, when he says such things as "I will read her" (185), or "I will . . . tear away the beautiful veil under which she hides her wickedness" (216), he usually fails. He finds that it is she who reads him. "She reads my pitiful, vacillating soul, and plucks the thoughts out of my heart with the magic of her solemn brown eyes" (221). Earlier (apparently enough time has passed either to cause Robert to forget the color of Lady Audley's eyes or for their color to have actually altered), "she had defied him with her blue eyes, then brightness intensified by the triumph in their glance" (186). He discovers that the "mask that she wears is not to be plucked away" (234).

32 Elaine Showalter, "Desperate Remedies," *Victorian Newsletter* 49 (1976): 1–5.

33 Kimberly Reynolds and Nicola Humble, *Victorian Heroines: Representations of Femininity in Nineteenth-Century Literature and Art* (New York: New York University Press, 1993), 110.

34 Richard Nemesvari, "Robert Audley's Secret: Male Homosocial Desire in *Lady Audley's Secret*," *Studies in the Novel* 27.4 (Winter 1995): 515–16.

35 Ann Cvetkovich, "Detective in the House: Subversion and Containment in *Lady Audley's Secret*," in *Mixed Feelings: Feminism, Mass Culture, and Victorian Sensationalism* (New Brunswick, NJ: Rutgers University Press, 1992), 57. See also Lyn Pykett's discussion of the socializing transition Robert must make away from his attachment to George to one with Clara:

> This relationship [between Robert and Clara] functions to some extent as a displacement of the homoerotic bonding of Robert and George. (There is a great deal of narratorial insistence on Robert's attraction to Clara's close physical resemblance to her brother.) However, its main function is its role in the novel's investigation and satirisation, as well as reproduction and naturalisation, of a particular social construction of masculinity. The movement from male bonding to male-female bonding is presented as part of a process of maturation and socialization. (Pykett, *The "Improper" Feminine*, 103–4)

36 At one point, well into her story, the narrator speaks of Lady Audley's despair, saying: "she was wretched by reason of a wound which lay too deep for the possibility of any solace" (251). By this time, the reader might assume that the "wound" is the memory of her mother's hereditary madness, but the narrator does not seem to mean this at all, confiding rather that the wound is Lady Audley's recognition that she "was no longer innocent, . . . she had wandered out of the circle of careless pleasure-seeking creatures, she had strayed far away into, terror and crime, a desolate labyrinth of guilt and treachery" (251–52). One might deduce that the narrator believes that this guilt is the secret displayed in the novel's title.

37 D. A. Miller, "*Cage aux folles*: Sensation and Gender in Wilkie Collins's *Woman in White*," *Representations* 14 (Spring 1986): 107–21.

38 Chiara Briganti, "Gothic Maidens and Sensation Women: Lady Audley's Journey from the Ruined Mansion to the Madhouse," *Victorian Literature and Culture* 19 (1991): 189–211, 189–90.

140   *Madness and class conflicts*

39   Helena Michie, *Sororophobia: Differences among Women in Literature and Culture* (Oxford and New York: Oxford University Press, 1992), 67.
40   Sally Shuttleworth, "'Preaching to the Nerves': Psychological Disorder in Sensation Fiction," in *A Question of Identity: Women, Science, and Literature*, ed. Marina Benjamin (New Brunswick, NJ: Rutgers University Press, 1993), 192–219, 196. Future references to this essay will be cited parenthetically in the body of the text, designated as "Shuttleworth 1993."
41   Lynn M. Voskuil, "Acts of Madness: Lady Audley and the Meaning of Victorian Femininity," *Feminist Studies* (FSt) 27.3 (Fall 2001): 611–39, 613. Future references to this work will be cited parenthetically in the body of the text.
42   Erving Goffman, *Asylums: Essays on the Social Situation of Mental Patients and Other Inmates* (New York: Anchor Books Doubleday, 1962).
43   Lady Audley accuses Robert of madness (232, 233, 253). Lady Audley and Robert accuse one another of madness (227). Robert worries that he will end up mad (127, 217). Lady Audley tries to convince her new stepdaughter that Robert is mad (237). Lady Audley tries, almost successfully, to persuade her new husband of Robert's lunacy (244–45). Lady Audley accuses Robert of scheming to drive her mad (235).
44   Michel Foucault, *Madness and Civilization: A History of Madness in the Age of Reason*, trans. Richard Howard (New York: Random House Vintage Books, 1973). Future references to this work will be cited parenthetically in the body of the text. (When the later Foucault cuts loose from his structuralist roots, he seems to reject categories such as "the unhistoricized" and "the primordial.")
45   Lady Audley, speaking of her own madness, says: "Again the balance trembled, . . . again I was mad" (302). Why does she use identical language to that of the narrator? Is it possible that Mrs. Taylor escaped from the *maison de santé*, put pen to paper and narrated her own story? It would not be the first time Helen Maldon had arranged a false burial for herself.
46   Shuttleworth says, "Madness . . . is the state that occurs when we let the social mask slip, and the inner self disrupts surface social performance" (Shuttleworth 1993, 212). While masking and performance certainly play a large part in this novel (and in everyday life, if Goffman is right), when we take offense at "the mute propriety of chairs and tables [and] the stiff squareness of Turkey carpets" we are usually quite alone, in the privacy of our own abode, playing in no performance and wearing no mask.
47   Lauren Chattman, "Diagnosing the Domestic Woman in *The Woman in White* and in *Dora*," in *Eroticism and Containment: Notes from the Flood Plain*, ed. Carol Siegel and Ann Kibbey (New York and London: New York University Press, 1994), 123–53, 123. Sally Shuttleworth is another critic who takes seriously the narrator's assertions about the ubiquity of madness. She quotes the pertinent passages in full. However, recognizing the irony that Robert Audley's case rather than Lady Audley's provokes the narrator to make this diagnosis ("mad to-day and sane to-morrow"), Shuttleworth qualifies the case of men in sensation fiction, writing: "The threat of insanity that hangs over them is rarely an inescapable physiological destiny, but rather a partial, temporary form, which can be shaken off through self-discipline and a transformation of lifestyle" (Shuttleworth 1993, 206.) But Shuttleworth seems to subvert her own claim about the temporary nature of male madness when she asserts that, at the end of *Lady Audley's Secret*, Robert has *not* overcome the problem of insanity. The "descriptions of the impact" on Robert by his new wife, Clara Talboys, "suggest something altogether more sinister." Shuttleworth analyzes scrupulously the hidden evidence that leads her to this conclusion: "Although the novel seems to portray the victory of male reason over female madness, and Robert's ascent to true masculinity, it shows in fact his complete overthrow and loss of self-possession" (Shuttleworth 1993, 211).
48   Jessica Saxon, "Secrecy, Trust, Anonymity, and Identity: The Anonymous Narration in Mary Elizabeth Braddon's *Lady Audley's Secret*, and Why the Reader Should Be Concerned," unpublished essay.

49 Lewis Carroll, *Alice's Adventures in Wonderland* [1865], in *Alice's Adventures in Wonderland* [1865] & *Through the Looking-Glass* [1871] (New York: Penguin Signet Classic, 1960), 65.
50 "Meditations on First Philosophy," in *Discourse on Method* and *Meditations* [1637 and 1641], trans. Laurence J. Lafleur (New York: Bobbs-Merrill, 1960), "Second Meditation," 76–77.
51 The same might be said of Lewis Carroll himself. In his diary entry of February 9, 1856, he writes:

> Query: when we are dreaming . . . , do we not say and do things which in waking life would be insane? May we not then sometimes define insanity as an inability to distinguish which is the waking and which is the sleeping life? (quoted by Martin Gardner in his *The Annotated Alice: Alice's Adventures in Wonderland & Through the Looking Glass*, intro. and notes, Martin Gardner [New York: Bramhall House, 1960], 90, n 8)

If we connect Carroll's diary entry with Descartes's line quoted earlier ("there are no conclusive indications by which waking life can be distinguished from sleep"), we arrive at the conclusion of the Cheshire Cat: "We are all mad here."
52 David Hume, *A Treatise of Human Nature* [1739] (Oxford: Clarendon Press, 1941), 252–53.
53 Regarding the Evil Genius, Descartes says:

> I will therefore suppose that, not a true God, who is very good and who is the supreme source of truth, but a certain evil spirit, not less clever and deceitful than powerful, has bent all his efforts to deceiving me. I will suppose that the sky, the air, the earth, colors, shapes, sounds, and all other objective things that we see are nothing but illusions and dreams that he has used to trick my credulity. I will consider myself as having no hands, no eyes, no flesh, no blood, nor any sense, yet falsely believing that I have all these things. I will remain resolutely attached to this hypothesis. ("Second Meditation," 80)

54 W. F. Bynum, Roy Porter, and Michael Shepherd, in the introduction to their anthology, *The Anatomy of Madness: Essays in the History of Psychiatry*, vol. 1 (New York: Routledge, 1988), 9. Also quoted by Laura Chattman in "Diagnosing the Domestic Woman in *The Woman in White* and *Dora*," in Siegel and Kibbey, *Eroticism and Containment*, 125.
55 Friedrich Engels, "The Origin of the Family, Private Property and the State" [1884], in *Basic Writings on Politics and Philosophy: Karl Marx and Friedrich Engels*, ed. and trans. Lewis S. Feuer (Garden City, NY: Doubleday, 1959), 392–94, 394.

5 Veiled secrets, veiled subjects
Scheherazade and the orientalizing of Victorian secrecy in Bulwer-Lytton's *Leila: or, The Siege of Granada*

> The veil at last was rent, and the mystery had vanished.
> —David Urquhart, *Spirit of the East* (1838)

The historicizing of secrecy

This chapter's primary function is to analyze a product of the Victorian mentality that in earlier sections of this book I have called the orientalizing of secrecy. Georg Simmel and Erving Goffman had nothing to say about this particular project, but I argue that it is a specific instantiation of Simmel's general thesis about the historicity of secrecy, and manifests itself often in terms of Goffman's general thesis concerning the performative features of concealment and revelation. Although my appeals to Simmel and Goffman are often less direct here than in other chapters, the arguments I present are usually inspired by the work of these sociologists, and presuppose the viability of their theories.

Michel Foucault has contrasted the widespread belief in what he calls the "repressive hypothesis," presumed by so many to be true about the Victorian world.[1] He maintains that sexual discourse, far from being silenced, censored, suppressed, and/or sublimated by "Victorian puritanism" (22), was encouraged, solicited, and insisted upon in "endlessly accumulated detail" (18). However, paradoxically, in this process sex was not simply declared a secret that had to be revealed but was presented as "*the* secret" of the century (35).[2] In this chapter, I will argue that not only "*the* secret" but the very concept of secrecy itself becomes orientalized[3] in the Victorian world. I will provide examples of this phenomenon, and speculate on how it comes about. Unlike Foucault, I will not exempt fiction from the evidential registers of my thesis; rather, I will see fiction as a primary index of the orientalizing of secrecy. I will offer these cases as a specific example of the historicizing of secrecy, recalling Simmel's formula according to which the amount of secrecy in each social system stays roughly the same, but the form and content of that secrecy changes from period to period and place to place. This collective act during the Victorian period rendered the very concept of secrecy more exotic and sexualized it at the same time. Because of the "parallel world" that secrecy provides each individual (Simmel 335–36), it follows that this orientalizing of secrecy becomes a new component in the production of Victorian subjectivity.

This chapter develops the idea of the orientalizing of secrecy first by recalling the powerful impetus that was given to that already ongoing project by the publication of English translations of the *Arabian Nights* in the British Isles (at first pirated) in the eighteenth century and their proliferation in the nineteenth. I next present a discussion of the function of veils – imagined and real – in the orientalizing of secrecy. Finally, I will briefly look at Bulwer-Lytton's *Leila: or, The Siege of Granada* as an example of an intentionally orientalist novel written by a popular Victorian author.

In addition to the Simmelian axiom concerning the historicization of secrecy, there is another one pertinent to this discussion. Simmel claims that the possession of a common secret by a group of individuals produces a "we" group. About this process Simmel writes: "the strongly emphasized exclusion of all outsiders makes for a correspondingly strong feeling of possession. . . . [W]hat is denied to many must have special value" (332). Those excluded from that group have a natural envy and fascination with the secret, and a desire to penetrate into its interior. Simmel is speaking here primarily of the creation of secret societies, such as the Masons or the Illuminati, but in nineteenth-century Britain a kind of inversion of Simmel's formula takes place: the "we" group – "we British" – whose unity had been established by means other than secrecy (patriotism, colonialism, imperialism, and dedication to the monarchy, all of which somehow became embroiled in and fused with the values of domesticity), became fascinated by the secrets of some of those who were excluded from their group, the "Orientals," who – seen from a distance – were perceived as a kind of secret society from which "*we*" (we Westerners, we Europeans, we British, we English, we Londoners) have been excluded.[4] Those alienated European subjects[5] now thirsted after the imagined Oriental secrets. It is not surprising that in an age of blurred, convoluted, stifled, yet aggressive sexuality (at least, according to Foucault), the supposed secrets of Oriental eroticism would provide a source of fascination. As Joanna Da Groot observes, "images of Oriental sexuality were a feature not only of Western relations with the Middle East but also of discussion of male-female relations in Europe."[6] Da Groot speaks of the many books and paintings about the Middle East "portraying a sexualized Orient and/or orientalized sexuality for a receptive audience" (120). The irony here, according to my thesis, is that the "secrets of the Orient" – or really, *orientalized secrets* as these secrets were more the products of the Western imagination than of Eastern conspiracy – influenced both the British concepts of secrecy and sex.

Stalking Scheherazade

The attraction to the East felt by Victorians did not develop solely because of Britain's geographic expansionism in that century. There was also a literary event whose roots went back at least as far as the end of the medieval world, one that I suspect overlapped and seeped into the geographic expansionism of imperialism and colonialism. If Salomé (whose "beauty and wickedness are inseparable") fascinated the world of the Renaissance, in the beginning of the eighteenth century there was "another prototype of Eastern sensuality [that] took Europe by storm."[7] Her name was Scheherazade.[8] Although it required some time for the tempest to build up, her seduction of all who heard her tale already had a history, as did her seductiveness itself ("Scheherazade . . . came forward swaying from side to side and moved so coquettishly that she ravished the minds and hearts of all present and bewitched their eyes").[9] The book that was eventually called *Arabian Nights* in its English translation derived from a cycle of oral tales that emerged from Indian, Persian, and Arabic sources developed over at least eight centuries. Some of these stories had reached Europe in the late medieval period, but the most significant moment for Scheherazade's Western debut was when the Frenchman Antoine Galland – secretary to the Portuguese ambassador to Turkey – purchased fifty manuscripts in Arabic under the general title of *Alf laila wa laila* (*One Thousand Nights and One Night*) sometime between 1679 and 1688.[10] Galland translated into French large segments of his manuscripts and published them between 1704 and 1717, calling his collection *Mille et une nuits, Comptes Arabs*. They were purchased by the scores in France, and immediately translated into English by anonymous agents.[11] The *Nights* was wildly popular. Over the next century Scheherazade was introduced to three generations of readers.

In some ways, Scheherazade's success in the British Isles is puzzling. Lane's translation is replete with scholarly annotations, as would be Burton's later. This time-consuming and energetic work on the parts of the translators presupposed a readership of "rapt listener[s], intimately connected with folklore, Islam, social convention and anecdote, and with a proper sense of the stories' historical provenance," as Eva Sallis points out. According to Sallis, such readers were "nowhere to be found in Victorian England."[12] Rather, the translations of *Arabian Nights* were attractive because they seemed to promise familiarity with the exotic. But this is impossible, according to Sallis's insightful argument, because precisely what the exotic precludes is familiarity. "The exotic," she says, is "dependent on unfamiliarity" (16). Therefore, this quest for the elusive exotic must "fictionalise the reader as well as the text" (17). According to Sallis, "The text, . . . recreated, [is] shorn of its . . . cultural and historical reality, while the reader in this relation is creator of self and world" (17). Sallis's thesis here is tantamount to my argument that the consequence of the British encounter with the *Nights* was to revamp Victorian subjectivities. It will be this new mentality that initiates the orientalization of the conceptions of both desire and secrecy.

Rana Kabbani reminds us that the tales of the *Arabian Nights* "were originally recounted to an all-male audience desiring bawdy entertainment. They were purposely crude, and pandered to the prejudices of the uneducated men who listened to them being narrated" (48). Antoine Galland's translation had already expunged blatant sexual aspects of the tales, including those dealing with active and aggressive female sexuality,[13] and Edward Lane's English translation made an even more thorough housecleaning, removing suspicious items that Galland had missed. Nevertheless, the Victorian readers, who were familiar with the carefully mannered techniques of suggestion employed by their own favorite authors, were often able to read back into the empty or artificially reworked spaces the erotic possibilities whose faint traces remained. As Billie Melman says, even the expurgated versions "conjured up female stereotypes and stereotypes of female sexuality which had a tremendous effect on Victorian readers and writers" (64–65). And when the seventeen volumes of Burton's *Complete and Literal Translation* began to appear in 1882, the bawdy tales were made whole again. Even though at first Burton's editions reached only a private audience – one that was willing to pay well – the word spread confirming the true nature of Scheherazade's tales. As Kabbani says, speaking of Lane and his censoring eye, "His prudery ended by complementing Burton's pruriency: each man used the *Arabian Nights* to express his personality and his preoccupations, and both of their texts taken together illustrated the contradictory penchants of the Victorian age" (45).

Scheherazade captivated not only the minds of the general reading public but of the intelligentsia. She provided a common vocabulary for writers and readers alike. Muhsin Jassim Ali assures us that when

> Leigh Hunt, Dickens, or Morris, for instance, used to draw upon Scheherazade's mine of allusion and anecdote, they felt sure that their readers were so familiar with the tales that they had no need to check a "scholarly companion to the *Arabian Nights*."[14]

These tales "had penetrated into the very core of English culture" (38), yet this penetration was only one very dramatic example of "how the Orient served as '*alter ego*' to the West, evoking dread as well as fascination," according to Peter Caracciolo (xvi).

It was not only adult readers and writers who were captivated by Scheherazade. It was as common to find *Arabian Nights* in the libraries of the small inmates of middle-class nurseries as to find allusions to it in adult conversation; indeed, in the previous generation, Alexander Pope had asserted that *Arabian Nights* was "proper enough for the Nursery."[15] In curious ways, the *Nights* seemed to break down the strongly erected barriers between childhood and adulthood in Victorian England; therefore, Pope's recommendation concerning the inclusion of *Arabian Nights* in the nursery is perhaps not as startling as it appears. (Other books that were also read by both adults and children were the Bible – another introduction to orientalism – and Alice's adventures in Wonderland and Looking-Glass Land.)[16] At a time when "'official' children's books had few delights to offer" (Caracciolo, 82), the *Nights* provided exciting entertainment. When versions that were clearly meant for children became available they were rendered didactic. For example, what is apparently the first such book is from 1791, with the title *The Oriental Moralist; or, the Beauties of the Arabian Nights Entertainments. Translated from the Original and Accompanied with Suitable Reflection Adapted to Each Story*. This edition was prepared by "the Rev'd Mr Cooper." Another edition from 1829 was called *Oriental Tales: Being Moral Selections from the Arabian Nights Entertainments; Calculated Both to Amuse and Improve the Minds of Youth*[17] (Caracciolo, 83–84, 86). Burtons's translation was not allowed in the nursery, and with good reason. The evidence against that possibility is present from the first pages, where "The Lady of the Glass Case" appears before Scheherazade comes on the scene. Prince Shah Zaman and his brother King Shahryar – who will later marry Scheherazade – are traveling together in the country, bemoaning their discovery that their wives have made them cuckolds in their absence. They find a beautiful lady sitting under a tree next to a sleeping giant, with the ogre's head resting in her lap. The lady brags to the brothers about her former lovers – 570 in Burton's version, 98 in both Lane's and Forster's translations – each of which she has bedded while her master was napping every afternoon. She has required each lover to give her a ring as a souvenir, which she has placed in her glass case. She then forces the two brothers to lay with her, threatening to awaken the ogre if they refuse. ("I want you to mount me and show me how nicely you can sit on my saddle, or else I'll set this ifrit [evil genie] upon you, and he'll slay you in the wink of an eye!" [Burton 10]). They submit, to her satisfaction ("one after the other, after they had dismounted, she said, 'Well done!'" [Burton 10]. In Lang this is handled curtly: "they remained with her as long as she required" [Lang 6]), and each is forced to give her a ring, which she proudly adds to her collection. It is this experience, along with the infidelity of his wife (whom he executes), that makes King Shahryar hate the treachery of all women, and he vows to marry a new wife each evening and have her strangled or beheaded the next morning.

Apparently the indelible impressions left upon the minds of young readers of both adult's and children's versions of the *Nights* were in large part visual memories, as Brian Alderson observes.[18] This is especially true concerning the orientalist fantasies of these readers. Sometimes the illustrations were created by eminent artists, such as Gustave Doré, John Tenniel, and the pre-Raphaelite J. E. Millais:

- Doré does a close-up of the gaping mouth of a grinning giant about to swallow one of Sinbad's companions (1863–65).
- William Miller illustrates the first chapter of the *Nights* showing the beautiful semi-nude "Lady of the Glass Case" in Edward Forster's edition of 1802 and 1810.
- A. B. Houghten shows Prince Firouz Shah and the Princess of Bengal riding a magic horse flying high above snow-covered mountains (1863–65).
- Tenniel shows a beautiful, buxom sorceress wearing a low-cut blouse as she leans forward, angrily casting a spell on Sidi Nouman, turning him into a dog (1863–65).
- J. D. Batten draws a winged, horned, hairy Genie of the Ring making an angry explosive appearance before a startled Aladdin (1895).
- H. J. Ford reveals a horrible one-eyed giant, hairy, thirty feet tall, with fangs and elephantine ears opening his larder to select another of Sinbad's shipmates for a meal (1898). Aubrey Beardsley draws a nearly naked, fat,

bejeweled Ali Baba with a sensuous smile in a black mantel that fails to cover his large body (1900).[19]

The influence of the images in the various editions perused by young readers was profound. According to Alderson, "hardly a writer of note, from Johnson to Dickens, does not hint at, or mention, somewhere or other the recollected pleasure of reading the *Nights* in childhood" (82). The metonymical association between secrecy and things Oriental is established in the child's mind. Recall Simmel's assertion that the secret "produces an immense enlargement of life. . . . [It] offers the possibility of a second world alongside the manifest world; and the latter is deeply influenced by the former" (330). If we apply this insight to what I have been calling orientalized secrecy, we can see how this historicized form of "the secret" participates in the generation of that unique psychological phenomenon, Victorian inwardness. Simmel's notion of a "second world" alongside both the revelations made by characters in Victorian novels and those authors' comments about their childhood memories of encounters with the stories of *Arabian Nights* is reminiscent of Gustave Klimt's claim about the power of art, which for him, "nous conduit dans le rouyaume ideal, le seul andoit ou nous pouvons trouver la pure joie, le pur bonheur, le pur amour."[20] For the Victorian child, the art that created these never-to-be-forgotten experiences was that produced by Scheherazade.

There are indeed secrets galore in the *Nights*, but the version of them that children heard in the nursery were not the same as those read in the adult editions, especially in the Burton translation. Yet, even from the perspective of those little listeners and readers, the secrets that survived the censoring process were exciting and unusual, especially those that were illustrated. In most of the stories there are wealthy characters that surround themselves with a great bounty of exotic food and objects of gold and gems, and often they are served by beautiful female slaves and eunuchs. These wealthy sultans, traders, or magicians are encircled by less esteemed individuals in abject poverty, and the rich praise Allah for their abundance, and give alms to the poor. The stories abound with *jinn* (or genies), supernatural demon-like beings who intervene in human affairs as wondrous aids or devastating enemies. There are almost no stories in *A Thousand and One Nights* without strange forms of magic and unheard-of beasts, giants, or ogres, interrupting everyday life. Life seems very cheap, and Fate, Destiny, and the mysterious will of Allah appear all-powerful. The important figures in the stories have secrets. Both the plot-driving secrets and the more structural secrets that are presupposed by those plot-driving secrets are likely to be orientalized by Western readers, swathed in layers of exoticism that provided a deeper *frisson* than would the Western fairy tales with which these European readers were already acquainted.

It seems nearly impossible to say anything helpful about the narratology of the stories in their earlier forms; nobody knows when they achieved their current unity nor how the various sections differed from one another in the disparate geographies of their origin.[21] It has been suggested by Eva Sallis and a number of other commentators that the stories' origins can be understood along Bakhtinian lines as popular culture's carnivalesque response to strictly controlled political and religious requirements,²² but, as Sallis observes, "all of this is what was, once. What it is now is infinitely more complex because it was reborn into an alien environment" (1). There is little incitement to speculate on the narrative role of secrecy in the "original" text; indeed, its carnivalesque enthusiasm threatens to reveal everything that was supposed to be veiled, even if this revelation is under the aegis of Allah's omniscience. This condition does not necessarily hold in the case of Galland's translation of the documents he purchased, nor of the translations into various European languages during the next 200 years. Concerning the Western rebirth for which Galland acts as wet-nurse, we can at least say that the documents in Arabic that ended up in Galland's possession had more or less the form in which they would appear in nineteenth-century England, and we can make some narrative sense out of those documents while their "orientalization" begins to take place as they are illustrated and translated into French and English.

The book has a prologue, which, while praising Allah, contains these words in Edward Lane's translation of 1839–41: "In the name of God, the Compassionate, the Merciful. . . . Extolled be the perfection of Him who hath thus ordained the history of former generations to be a lesson to those which follow."²³ This prologue, then, stages the narrative strategy as the presentation of cautionary moral tales with religious implications (much as they were to be presented in the English versions for children), but these moral tales become a pretext for eroticism and sometimes for pornography. Indeed, greedy, deceitful, unjust, and criminal behavior is usually punished in the stories – but not always – and the prologue makes no attempt to explain the relation between these moral tales and their often erotic or even pornographic content.

In the manuscripts that came to Galland and later to Burton (but not to Lane), the prologue seems to end in the middle of a sentence that will have religious and hence moral implications. The passage is purposely placed at the bottom of the first page, saying: "And among these tales, thanks to the Omniscient and Almighty Allah, we have been given . . ." at which point the page ends. Then, when the reader turns the page, this incomplete sentence leads into the first adventure, called "The Story of King Shahryar and His Brother" (1–2). It is recounted by an anonymous narrator who opens with a formula easily recognized both by those in the East and the West:²⁴ "A long time ago there was a mighty king. . . ." We are told that this powerful king had two sons, each of which becomes a king himself. However, what starts out appearing to be a fairy tale turns immediately into a frightening story of betrayal and lewdness, as the younger king finds his queen in the arms of a slave from the king's kitchen. As was mentioned above, the king's response is harsh but not unsurprising: "So he drew his scimitar, cut the two in four pieces, and left them on the couch" (4).²⁵ The young king flees in a state of great agitation to his brother's kingdom, where he attempts to recover from the anguish of betrayal he has experienced. One night he peeks out the window of his guest room at his brother's palace and sees his brother's wife engaged in a great orgy involving ten male slaves and ten of the king's concubines, the queen and her slave lover, all of which described is in pornographic detail in the Arabic version received by Galland, bowdlerized by Lane, and restored by Burton. Burton's translation reads: "Then he mounted her, and winding his legs around hers, as a button loop clasps a button, he tossed her to the ground and enjoyed her" (6). Lane renders this as: "and immediately a black slave came to her, and embraced her; she doing the like" (5). We see that the narrative strategy on the part of earlier translators is to disguise the bawdiness and explicit violence of key passages, keeping the exact content of those passages secret without preventing imaginative readers from filling in the gaps that the translator has left open – a slightly different version of the secret in broad daylight.

Shah Zaman tells his brother, King Shahryar, what he has observed. On the next night they both hide in the guest room and witness a repeat performance of the orgy in the courtyard. After ordering the execution of the queen,

> King Shahryar took his sword in hand and went to the seraglio, where he slew all the concubines and their mamelukes. He also swore a binding oath that whenever he married, he would take his new wife's maidenhead at night and slay her the next morning to make sure of his honor, for he was convinced that there never was or could be one chaste woman upon the face of this earth.
> (Burton 12)

At the beginning, the principal narrative strategy seems to be the implementation of a serial repetition of rape and murder provoked by a thirst to avenge masculine honor lost to the sexual conspiracies of women. But it soon becomes apparent that this pursuit of revenge for lost patriarchal honor is displaced when yet another sexual deception by a wily woman undermines the original masculine revenge plot. This new deception will restore and normalize marital sexuality (or premarital sexuality: for some reason King Shahryar does not marry Scheherazade until the end of the one thousand and one nights), as Scheherazade bears three children during the two years and nine months it takes her to complete her tales. So, rather than an infinite repetition of *coitus interruptus* we have *trucidatio* [massacre] *interruptus* in the name of sex, marriage, procreation, happiness, and repentance.

But before Scheherazade intervenes with her brazen plan, nearly all of the virgins in the kingdom are dead. Scheherazade presents herself to the king, who ushers her into his bedchamber, and on the first night she tells him a story, "The Tale of the Merchant and the Jinnee." The original narrator hands over the job to Scheherazade, writing, in a self-referential loop: "So Scheherazade rejoiced, and on the first night of many nights to come, she began telling the tales that were to fill the volumes of *The Arabian Nights*" (22). These sexualized secrets are revealed in the earlier translations in a less direct manner, but they were still easily orientalized in their less pornographic versions.

Of course, real secrets did exist in the geographical area that lay southeast of Europe – the undefined great mass of land that Europeans called the Orient. And the stories those individuals told or listened to were also about secrets – fictive secrets, as are all stories. But these "Oriental" secrets were not *orientalized* until they were viewed by occidental eyes seeking the exotic titillation through a glass warped by fantasy, fear, excitement, disdain, lust, and expectation, among other emotions and predispositions. Through that glass they saw characters who worship a false god, believe in black magic, profit from or are victimized by occult knowledge, and attribute all achievements and failures to Fate (Scheherazade: "But whatever fate ordains for a man, he cannot resist" [541]). In the tales told by these Easterners, life is easily lost, the plots are tainted with cruelty, tyranny, lust, and arbitrariness, and all of this is wrapped in a mysterious sensuality. The women themselves are made more sensual by being gathered into seraglios, from which they can wander only if veiled.

I will select and list shortly several important plot-driving secrets and their resolutions in a pair of well-known stories from the *Nights* that easily lend themselves to such orientalizing. These secrets are known by the narrator Scheherazade, but not by her audience (the king, Scheherazade's sister Dunazade, and, eventually, us) until she deigns to reveal them. First, let us look at a few examples of such secrets in "Ali Baba and the Forty Thieves": Will Ali-Baba's brother's discovery of the magic cave result in tragedy? (Yes. The brother will be drawn and quartered by the captain of the thieves and the four parts of his body hung above the outside of the cave as a warning to others.) Will his brother's body remain there to rot, thereby flouting Muslim law? (No. It will be sewn together, washed, shrouded and buried.) Will the forty thieves manage to penetrate Ali Baba's garden in their quest for revenge? (Yes, they will each hide in forty large clay vessels made to contain olive oil.) Will Ali Baba's beautiful dancing slave manage to kill the thieves and their captain? (Yes. She will stew them all in boiling olive oil.) Will the slave be well rewarded for her loyalty, cleverness, and courage? (Yes. Ali Baba will grant her freedom and marry her to his nephew "in great pomp and [hold] a sumptuous wedding feast for his friends and neighbors" [135].) In addition to these secrets that, in a different cultural context, I would call MacGuffins, we notice that the secret of the source of the cave and the magic spell that allows it to respond to the commands, "Open Sesame!" and "Close Sesame!" is never revealed. It is a *structural* secret in that its truth is presupposed by everything else in the story, and one that is never resolved or even addressed, and it certainly lends itself to orientalizing.

Questions about the plot-driving secrets in "The Seven Voyages of Sinbad the Sailor" include these: Will Sinbad escape with his life from the back of the whale? (Yes.) Will Sinbad survive his flight over the mountains in the claws of the Roc? (Yes.) Will Sinbad escape from the giant, hairy, cannibalistic ogre? (Yes, but his companions will not.) Will Sinbad escape the giant man-eating serpent? (Barely, but his companions will not.) Will Sinbad survive his captivity among the naked cannibals? (Yes.) When Sinbad is buried alive with the body of his dead wife, will he die too (as is the custom of the island on which he has landed)? (No.) Will Sinbad be eaten by the furious Roc after the sailors have broken its giant egg? (No, but all of his fellow sailors will die.) Will Sinbad escape the entrapment by the crazy cannibalistic Old Man of the Sea? (Yes, but only by getting him drunk and then smashing his head with a heavy stone.) On his last voyage, will Sinbad be devoured by the three giant whales? (No.) Will the now wealthy Sinbad – having filled his pockets and sacks with gems from the Valley of Diamonds – live happily ever after? (No. He "enjoyed all the comforts of life until there came to [him] the Destroyer of Delight and the Sunderer of friendship and Caterer for cemeteries" [576].)

Western readers of *Arabian Nights*, both young and old, must have been disoriented (so to speak) by the somber endings of these tales, which are so unlike the Freudian fate of Jack (of "Jack and the Beanstalk"): "Jack and his mother lived happily ever after." Does Aladdin, who owns the magic lamp and who controls the jinni of the ring and of the lamp, fare any better at the end? Will Aladdin and the beautiful Princess, daughter of the Sultan, live happily ever after? Well, they don't do so badly, relatively speaking: "And he lived with his wife in bliss and serenity until the Destroyer of Delights . . . came and visited him" (222). Most of the stories in *Arabian Nights* end with this sobering formula about death, sometimes superseded by a last line praising God, such as "And glory be to the Living One who does not die!" (576), and "This is the end of their story, and may Allah have mercy on them all!" (263). In the Lane translation, nineteen of the thirty-one tales end with one version or other of a *memento mori* – some more startling than others, as in the case of "Abu-L-Hasan the Wag": "until they were visited by the terminator of delights, and the separator of companions, the devastator of palaces and houses, and the replenisher of the graves" (Lang 461). These endings awaken concern about those existential secrets that most of us do not want revealed: When and how will I die? What will become of me after I die? For the moment, even these fears have an orientalist tinge to them; their only solution is Oriental Fatalism.

Again, the structural secret that is never revealed in the story is the secret of Fate and Destiny that guides the narrative ("Only Allah can save us now, and nobody can prevent what fate has ordained!" cries Sinbad [560]). Similarly, the secret of the source of the magic powers that are sometimes so destructive and other times so helpful in almost all the stories of *A Thousand and One Nights* is never addressed: the power of the evil Moroccan sorcerer and his malevolent brother in the story of Aladdin, the power of the genie of the ring and the genie of the lamp – secrets without which the plot-driving secrets would not exist. Both the plot-driving secrets and the structural secrets are orientalist secrets from the point of view of nineteenth-century readers in the British Isles. Of course, the most immediate reason for the projection of orientalist features onto these stories is that they were known to have arrived from the East, but the content of the stories – and all the plot-driving secrets that move the stories along – seem foreign and exotic. Yet, we can ask, what would Victorian children and adults have made of the man-eating giant that Jack the Giant Killer dispatches if the giant had worn a turban; or the murderous giant slain by Jack, of beanstalk fame, if the giant were bearded and wore turned-up silk slippers; or of Little Red Riding Hood's wolf, if he had spoken Arabic; or of the Little Mermaid had she been veiled; or of Rumpelstiltskin if he had a less Germanic name, wore a fez, and cursed Allah while stamping his feet?

In the spirit of D.A. Miller's *Narrative and Its Discontents*, we can think of the narrative of the *Nights* as having denormalized the normal: it has broken with the *status quo ante*, a peace or a quietude, that can only be restored with a kind of closure that ends the narrative, shutting it down. As we saw at the end of chapter 1, Miller argues that such a closure always fails, leaving in its wake unresolved secrets that are the aftermath of a novel's attempt at resolution. If we apply this model to *Arabian Nights*, some interesting features of the stories emerge. We could say that the narration breaks the peace of the happy kingdom of King Shahryar, who "ruled the kingdom with such justice that he was beloved by all the people of his realm" (2). His rage over the deceitful and treacherous women in his life turns him into the most unjust ruler in history, and makes him the terror of the land while the daughters of the kingdom are sacrificed to that rage (and to his lust) until there are few remaining. Shahryar's rage and his depravations are postponed during Scheherazade's narration. At the conclusion of her narrative, Scheherazade asks a favor of the king. Pointing out that during the nearly three years of her storytelling she has borne him three children who, if he kills her, will be motherless, she says to him, "I request that you release me from the doom of death as a dole to these infants" (577). The king promises to marry Scheherazade, and abjures his murderous plan (as does his brother, King Shah Zaman, who admits at the last moment, "Like you I lay with a woman every night during the past three years and put her to death the next morning. But now I desire to marry your wife's sister, Dunazade" [57]). The king prepares a seven-day feast to which all in the kingdom are invited to celebrate his marriage to the mother of his three children. We are told that "the hearts of the people were comforted," and "the people and the provinces remained peaceful" (582–83). The last bit of information that we receive is that after the death of the king many happy years later, the next king – who "loved tales and legends" – found in the royal treasury the thirty volumes of Scheherazade's tales.

> [H]e ordered his clerks to copy them and spread them throughout the world. As a consequence the tales became famous, and the people called them *The Marvels and Wonders of the Thousand and One Nights*. This is all that we know about the origins of this book, and Allah is omniscient.
> (583)

Then, does the termination of the narrative on the last of the thousand and one nights achieve closure, or, as D.A. Miller insists, are there unresolved issues and undiscovered secrets that remain in the wake of the closure? Well, it seems to be a happy ending. We are informed by the original narrator (he who narrated Scheherazade's tales):

> The two brothers continued to live with their wives in great pleasure and solace, especially since Almighty Allah had changed their grief into joy. Indeed, they continued enjoying life until the Destroyer of delights and Severer of societies and Desolator of dwelling places came upon them.
> (583)

The logic of this announcement and its unsettling *FINIS* implies that the words "their," "they," and "them" refer to the two kings. The secret of the narrative is this: the King is dead; long live the Queen! It is difficult to believe that the millions of readers of this story or listeners to this tale, then or now, hold these two murdering brothers in high esteem. We do not know how many virgins King Shahryar deflowered and strangled or beheaded, but his brother admitted to having done this to at least 1,095 of them. The older brother, Shahryar, whose name is rarely remembered, admits to having "slain the daughters of my folk," and credits Scheherazade for stopping these record-breaking serial murders. He also acknowledges Allah for having "appointed her as the means for saving His creatures from oppression and slaughter" (578). Does Allah have another eighty virgins awaiting Shahryar in paradise? Dare we say that this is not likely? Despite this story's genesis in a cruel and powerfully patriarchal society, the secret of this narrative is that the story is not about a man, nor about men. It is about the intelligence, knowledge, creativity, competence, strength, courage, and – yes – beauty of a woman, who conquered an evil patriarchy. It is she who abides with us forever. This is a secret we may not have expected either from "the Orient" or from orientalism.[26]

Veiled secrets

Perhaps partly as a result of the orientalism inspired by *Arabian Nights*, in nineteenth-century Britain the veil became a conspicuous site of secrecy, or perhaps of false secrecy. In British fiction, women typically donned a veil to hide something: their identity, their beauty, or, more rarely, their disfigurement (Esther in *Bleak House*, or Isabel Vane in *East Lynne*). Of course, sometimes in society real women did veil themselves to hide something, but surely often women appeared veiled as a fashion statement, and in that case it was not often assumed by others that these women were in fact hiding anything, but that they were veiling *as if* to hide something – a perfectly acceptable practice. Because the veil was associated with secrecy, and provoked the interest of others precisely because of this association, a woman might make herself more interesting if it was believed she had a secret, or even pretended to have one. In any case, the veil in British culture – both in fiction and in real life – was often associated metonymically with veiling as it took place in non-Western culture. I hypothesize that Western interest in the veil as a fashion statement was probably motivated by a Western interest in the veil worn by Eastern women. In this section I will dwell on the meaning of the "Oriental veil," not from the perspective of non-European women who in fact did don veils but from the perspective of nineteenth-century European observers of this foreign habit who usually made this observation from afar.[27] From this social and historical perspective Oriental veiling was seen, correctly or incorrectly, as an effort to keep something secret (the Western fashion of veiling was a false imitation of this effort), and this "something" often had to do with sex. I will make the Simmelian assumption that when individuals believe that a secret is being withheld from them, they either want to know what that secret is[28] or strive to debunk the secret. Ruth Bernard Yeazell reports a similar dichotomy in nineteenth-century orientalism. She points out that many Western travelers to the East were caught between, on the one hand, their desire to discover the true difference between East and West and to emphasize it, and on the other hand, to unveil the secrets of the East and thereby demystify them, which was tantamount to denying the existence of a real difference between East and West.[29] Indeed, those demystifiers were in fact attacking orientalism itself, not by penetrating the secrets of the Orient but by demonstrating that those "secrets" were invented by Western fantasy.

Mary Anne Doane makes use of an idea she attributes to Nietzsche in her treatment of the veil in Western cinema, saying "the function of the veil is to make truth profound, to ensure that there is a depth that lurks behind the surface of things" (118–19). Eve Sedgwick makes a similar observation in her treatment of veils in the Gothic novel. She writes,

> The veil is ... suffused with sexuality[;] ... the veil that conceals and inhibits sexuality comes by the same gesture to represent it, both as a metonym of the thing covered and as a metaphor for the system of prohibitions by which sexual desire is enhanced and specified.
>
> (143)

Neither Doane nor Sedgwick means for her analysis to be applied to the use of the veil by Muslim women. Their reticence seems justifiable, but it appears to me that their ideas are helpful in conceptualizing the Western imagination's fascination with the "oriental" veil. In the same way that British readers of *Arabian Nights* were able to detect the bawdiness of the tales even in their bowdlerized editions, they were able to imagine the deep secrets that they believed the veil was meant to keep from them.

A related recent theoretical contribution to the theory of the veil is found in John Vignaux Smyth's *The Habit of Lying*.[30] Smyth is interested in the ideas of concealment and revelation as they appear in the history of literature, morality, and fashion. Smyth shows that in the early theories of fashion, influenced by Genesis, clothes were usually assumed to be primarily motivated by modesty, but he claims that most modern theorists have agreed more with Thomas Carlyle "that the origin of dress is not to be located in either modesty or utility, but in 'display'" (161). Smyth develops what John Carl Flugel called "the neurotic paradox of clothes,"[31] perhaps most clearly illustrated in the case of the Renaissance codpiece, in which "'modest' concealment of the penis here frankly coincides with symbolic display" (158). The "neurotic paradox" trades on the logically invalid but psychologically compelling suggestion that "if attractive bodies are concealed, then concealed bodies must be attractive" (164). Smyth relates this theory directly to the veil, quoting approvingly Alan Hunt's observation that the veil is able, on the one hand, to "exhibit piety and modesty, but on the other ... to signify allure by facilitating concealment of identity" (Smyth 226n26).[32] Again, where there is fascination with the veil – as in nineteenth-century Britain – there is fascination with secrets, secrets that are exotic and erotic, but secrets in which the signifier itself becomes the signified; or, to readapt the phrase that has become almost a mantra in my discussion, the signifier denotes secrets whose secret is that there is no secret. But even such secrets as these are more tantalizing if they are orientalized.

The scholars who have catalogued the characteristics projected onto the Muslim woman by the orientalist imagination tend to agree roughly on the appropriate list. If the Victorians knew as much about the Orient as this list implies they believed they knew, then their knowledge of the secrets of the Orient was deep indeed. The list includes the *inaccessibility* of the Oriental female behind her veil in the forbidden harem;[33] the *seclusion* of the Oriental woman, who was "locked away from society and . . . had no significant relationships except with their male sexual partners and/or oppressors";[34] the women of the harem as *"promiscuous, duplicitous, and often as lesbians"*[35] (never mind that some of these attributions contradict each other); the harem as a site of *sexual obsession* – a sexual obsession that is not one of consummation but of deferral. As Malek Alloula observes, speaking of early postcards of Algerian women, the obsession requires that something remain hidden, secret: even if the woman is unveiled and her bare bosom depicted, "the photographer's background must suggest an inaccessible depth, a mystery beyond what is represented" (3). Alloula says of Ingres's odalisque that she is "the very symbol of the harem. . . . [S]he fills it with a presence that is at once mysterious and luminous. She is its hidden, yet available, core, always throbbing with restrained sexuality" (3). Despite the Jungian overtones of her account, Alev Lytle Croutier has captured some of the fascination of all this:

> Harem is a unique archetype of the collective unconscious – matriarchy incubating in the cradle of patriarchy. It is an unsolved enigma, a haunting mystery. . . . It is a shadow world – full of halftones, large areas obscured or lost forever – which we are reluctant to own as our own creation. It belongs in the realm of dark secrets and fears we prefer not to remember. It is about forgetfulness.[36]

The imagined propensity of the inmates of the harem toward hidden, lesbian sex is called by Emily Apter a "transgressive female socius, sequestered and colonized, but capable of sheltering its secrets . . . , the dream of a feminocentric eroticism as yet unconquered."[37] Indeed, the theme of *the Orient as woman* emerges throughout the scholarship, perhaps first designated as such by Edward Said.[38] Joanna da Groot supports Said's observation, writing:

> Since European commentators endowed the Orient they had created with qualities with which men of the period also endowed females, they came on occasion to characterize the Orient as essentially or generally "feminine." The use of the phrase "mysterious Orient," like "mysterious female," indicated that both were seen as hard for western men to understand; references to the irrationality and emotional extremes to which "Orientals" were inclined carried the implied comparison with similar tendencies attributed to women.
> (105)

Da Groot recognizes, in ways that some have not seen, that the sexual characteristics projected upon Oriental women by the Western imagination do not make these imagined females merely receptacles of Western desire; rather, they are actively involved in the makeover of that desire. That is, according to Da Groot, Victorians projected sexuality onto the East, but the reflected image of exoticized sexuality returned to Europe in a creative fashion to transform Victorian sexuality. Here, I am arguing that something similar happened to the Victorian idea of secrecy, which, having been bound up with the idea of sexuality, suffered many of the vicissitudes of its exotic shadow concept. Similarly, according to Yeazell, the exotic eroticism that Westerners projected upon the East came back and haunted their fiction with its veils and secrets. Just as there is "no end to the possibility of inside knowledge about the harem," writes Yeazell, there is also "no end to . . . the lure of a 'SECRET' not yet articulated" (15, emphasis original). In the Victorian imagination, the veil and the harem became metonymically linked with the very idea of a secret not yet articulated.

Men in veils?

Yet another attempt to theorize the veil from the standpoint of the West comes from the perspective of the social sciences. It is unusual in that it deals with the case of a Muslim society in which men rather than women don the veil. I have included it here because it provides a Simmelian theory of the function of veiling in general, and therefore is pertinent to my project. Like orientalism, this approach sees the veil through Western categories – categories that might well be rejected by the Muslim who actually wears the veil – but unlike orientalism it does not find the secret of the veil to be erotic nor exotic.

In 1959 and 1960 anthropologist Robert F. Murphy dwelt among the Tuareg of North Africa, and his much-lauded article, "Social Distance and the Veil," is a theoretical piece attempting to explain the curiosity that in Tuareg communities the men but not the women are veiled.[39] "Tuareg males not only wear their veils during sand storms and blistering heat, but also during the rainy season, and indoors. Furthermore, they are not worn until manhood. Slaves wear them less, and women and children not at all."[40] Murphy asks:

> Why do Tuareg males cover their faces so completely that only areas around the eyes and nose may be seen? Short answer: by doing so, they are symbolically introducing a form of distance between their selves and their social others. The veil, though providing neither isolation nor anonymity, bestows facelessness and the idiom of privacy upon its wearer and allows him to stand somewhat aloof from the perils of social interaction while remaining a part of it.
> (1257)

This is a decidedly Simmelian answer to the question Murphy has posed. Indeed, Murphy begins his article by acknowledging that his study relies heavily on Simmel, "especially [Simmel's] delineation of self-revelation and self-restraint as necessary qualities of all social relationships" (1257). Murphy adds: "Interaction is threatening by definition, and reserve, here seen as an aspect of distance, serves to provide partial and temporary protection to the self" (1259). Murphy supports this view by appealing to Goffman, who "argues that the individual's sense of worth and significance is threatened by his vulnerability and penetrability" (1258). The veil among Tuareg men is a protection against this vulnerability.

Murphy's idea, then, is that not only Tuareg men and non-Tuareg Muslim women veil themselves, but that we *all* veil ourselves. This is because we all need what Tuareg men require – the capacity to withhold knowledge about ourselves from the scrutiny of others. Ironically, this ability promotes not only a certain kind of individuality but also a certain kind of sociality. Ultimately, then, secrets, evasions, lies, and deceptions serve the same purpose as veils. But why do we (Westerners) wear metaphorical veils, while "these people *really* wear veils"? (1269). Murphy tries to answer this question by presenting a detailed analysis of the Tuareg's unusual social organization. Among the Tuareg, there are no laws, rules, customs, or mores that ameliorate the uncertainty and ambiguities of close-quarter, face-to-face relationships. Murphy concludes:

> My thesis, then, is that given this ambiguity and ambivalence of relationships, this immanence of role conflict, the Tuareg veil functions to maintain a diffuse and generalized kind of distance between the actor and those who surround him socially and physically. By the symbolic removal of a portion of his identity from the interactive situation, the Tuareg is allowed to act in the presence of conflicting interests and uncertainty. . . . In a very real sense, he is in hiding.
> (1270, 1272)

In fact, Robert Murphy might have been studying Lucy Snowe. Her strategic reticence, her "staid manner," her "cloak and "hood of hodden gray," these protective performances and devices in Lucy's strategic armamentarium have the same function as the Tuareg veil. They are a protection against vulnerability, they allow her to remove herself symbolically from close-quarter, face-to-face relationships, they give her the ability to withhold knowledge about herself from the aggressive scrutiny of others. Like the Tuareg, and like us, Lucy Snowe is in hiding.

However, from the perspective of orientalism, Murphy's analysis desexualizes the veil and would therefore in some ways put a damper on Victorian fantasies. On the other hand, if we take Murphy's central notion – that the function of the veil is to "withhold knowledge about ourselves from the scrutiny of others" – as indicating that the function of the veil is to demand a right to secrecy, and add the Simmelian idea that wherever there is a secret there is the desire to penetrate the secret, then the orientalist fascination with the veil is the fascination with secrecy.

Unveiling Bulwer-Lytton's Leila

In the final section of this chapter, I will present a brief commentary on Edward Bulwer-Lytton's short novel of 1838, *Leila: or, The Siege of Granada*, in order to show an instance of the conceptual osmosis that takes place between the ideas of secrecy and exoticism in a Victorian novel that is intentionally orientalist. I have not chosen this novel for its excellence – there are good reasons, after all, why Bulwer-Lytton's name was given to the mock prize that many compete for each year by writing the most bombastic, hackneyed, and poorly written paragraph they can invent – indeed, we even find a version of Lord Lytton's most infamous phrase in this novel: "It was a wild and stormy night" (165).[41] Nor have I chosen *Leila* for its fame (although Bulwer-Lytton, close friend of Charles Dickens, was very well known and enormously popular in his day), but precisely because I wanted to include a novel by a writer who chose to demonstrate his mastery of orientalist semiology and who consciously participated in the conflation of Victorian secrecy in general with the "secrets of the Orient." As Andrew Sanders says, "perhaps no English novelist of the 1830s and 1840s more pointedly reflects the intellectual mood of the times than Edward Bulwer-Lytton."[42] Despite Lord Lytton's popularity in his own day, it is difficult to find kind words for him on the part of more recent specialists on the historical novel – Bulwer's forte. Sanders is especially harsh, describing Bulwer as "Scott's dourest Victorian successor" (x). Sanders refers to Lord Lytton's "drab, learned, and aristocratic historical novels" (17), and he contrasts Bulwer's aspirations with his actual achievement: "Perverse as it might seem to any reader familiar with the drudgery of Bulwer's own historical fiction, [Bulwer insists] that the novelist should 'avoid all antiquarian dissertations not essentially necessary to the conduct of his tale'" (12). Bulwer, Sanders asserts, "had little talent as a story-teller, and scarcely any at all as a writer of English" (17–18). His "rhetoric is too thin for a novel which purports to be offering us a psychological insight into historical characters and developing complex private lives beside the public ones" (61–62). What he *did* have was a recognition that "the nineteenth century demanded a truly national art which blended aesthetic, political, social and patriotic considerations" (49). *Leila: or, The Siege of Granada* is particularly pertinent to Victorian studies because it was written at a time when the nineteenth century was trying to reconceptualize the racial and religious historical currents that went into the process of nation building. As Michael Ragussis points out, "nineteenth-century historians and novelists alike began to use fifteenth-century Spain as a paradigm for the birth of a nation based on racial and religious homogeneity."[43] Ragussis sees *Leila* as "a direct response, or even a sequel, to *Ivanhoe*" (479). He notes the "extraordinary anachronism" (479) of Sir Walter Scott's Rebecca, who in the twelfth century plans to flee to Spain for protection under the Moorish King Boabdil, who in fact will not rule Granada until 300 years later – the same king who plays such a major role in *Leila*.

Ragussis astutely notes that the two-tiered title of Bulwer-Lytton's novel parallels the two plotlines in the tale. The main title, *Leila*, relates the story of the Jewish daughter whose father tries to protect her Jewishness in a Muslim world, and whose female protectors in the Christian court of Ferdinand and Isabel try to convert her – all of this is essentially a domestic plot – while the subtitle, *The Siege of Granada*, is the public plot, the story of the last act of the Reconquest of Spain – a military action that had been carried out in fits and starts over a period of more than 700 years by the Christian armies of various Spanish kingdoms. The union of King Ferdinand of Aragon and Queen Isabel of Castile produced a mighty military force that in 1491 laid siege to Granada, whose king, Boabdil (or Muhammad XII), ruled over the last Muslim city-state in Spain. In Bulwer-Lytton's story, Boabdil has fallen under the influence of a wicked sorcerer, Almamen, a crypto-Jew who seeks revenge for the outrages that his people have suffered under various Muslim governments in Spain. (Bulwer-Lytton seems unaware that, in 1491, the Jews living under Muslim governance were generally much better off than those living under Christian governance. This is a secret that we contemporary readers may know, but Bulwer-Lytton did not.)[44] While counseling King Boabdil, Almamen is secretly negotiating with Ferdinand to betray Boabdil to the Christians, under whose rule Almamen incorrectly believes the Jews will be treated more equitably.[45] Almamen's beautiful, sweet-tempered, and rather vacuous daughter, the eponymous Leila, has been raised behind a veil of ignorance, knowing nothing of her father's activities, nothing of her rank, and nothing of her past except shards of mysterious childhood memories from a distant desert land. She apparently knows that she is the "daughter of the great Hebrew race" (20), but she seems to know little of that "race's" religious lore. She has fallen in love with a secret suitor, Muza Ben Abil Gazan, one of Boabdil's best and most trusted young generals, but a fictional warrior rather than an historical one. Bulwer-Lytton's story will be that of an Oriental Romeo and Juliet, where race and religion rather than family feuding will generate the hatred that will separate the heroine from her lover and bring about her tragic end. But this *Romeo and Juliet* will be more baroque than Shakespeare's because of the Eastern fanaticism that fuels its motives.

Almamen betrays Boabdil to Ferdinand, extracting from the Catholic king an agreement about treatment of the Jews under the future Christian governance; in turn, Ferdinand betrays Almamen. Leila, whose past has now been revealed to her, is held hostage by Ferdinand, whose son, Prince don Juan, falls in love with her. Under the influence of Queen Isabel and her handmaidens, Leila is saved from the Inquisition, denounces Judaism, converts to Christianity, and decides to "take the veil" (her second veil) and enter a convent.

Anti-Semitism is a central undercurrent of this novel, sometimes intentionally and sometimes unintentionally. To analyze it adequately would take a number of pages, and would not be directly related to the topic of the present study. Briefly, Bulwer-Lytton tries to represent the Christian anti-Semitism of the late medieval world, and the Muslim anti-Semitism that competes with it in scope and viciousness, but he gives away his own bigotry as well – a bigotry that may have been a secret even to himself. His narrator makes even the novel's most important character – Almamen, the Jew – into an anti-Semite, and his innocent daughter Leila as well. Bulwer-Lytton's own views are decidedly bigoted according to today's standards. For example, many of the stereotypes of anti-Semitic discourse are allowed (Jews are avaricious, usurious, greedy, and cringingly servile), but these characteristics are explained by Bulwer's narrator as functions of the oppression Jews have suffered. And when Leila is converted to Christianity, she tries to illuminate Almamen, saying:

> Father, by that dread anathema which is on our race, which has made us homeless and powerless, outcasts and strangers in the land – by the persecution and anguish we have known, teach thy lordly heart that we are doomed to Him whose footstep hallowed our native earth! FIRST, IN THE HISTORY OF THE WORLD, DID THE STERN HEBREWS INFLICT UPON MANKIND THE AWFUL CRIME OF PERSECUTION FOR OPINION'S SAKE.
> (111, emphasis original)

The narrator tells us that Leila held "the sublime, though fallacious, notion that in her conversion, her sacrifice, the crimes of her race might be expiated in the eyes of Him whose death had been the great atonement of the world" (112). Bulwer-Lytton's novel was published a year after the election of Benjamin Disraeli, the Sephardic "secret Jew," to his first term in Parliament, two years after Victoria ascended the throne. Bulwer-Lytton's unconscious anti-Semitism is typical of the times. Speaking of self-deception, evolutionary anthropologist and biologist Robert Trivers says, "Inevitably, false historical narratives will have their deepest connection with religion." He continues, "Most people are unconscious of the deception that went into constructing the narrative they take to be true."[46] This judgment is pertinent to the case of Edward Bulwer-Lytton. Anthony Julius, in a chapter on English literary anti-Semitism, seems to find *Leila: or, The Siege of Granada* perhaps more trivial than offensive.[47]

After Leila converts to Christianity, Don Juan pleads with her to marry him instead of wasting away behind the convent walls, and when he fails to persuade her turns against her in an anti-Semitic rage. On the day of Leila's investiture, Almamen appears in a fury and stabs his daughter through the heart rather than allow her to betray her ancestry. She dies in Muza's arms just after he has arrived on the scene at the last moment, secretly disguised as a Christian knight. Almamen receives his just deserts; Granada falls; Boabdil takes comfort in the arms of his favorite harem slave. Ferdinand unleashes the Grand Inquisitor Torquemada upon the world, and the Jews and Muslims are expelled from Spain.

The narrative strategy of Bulwer-Lytton's *Leila* is to activate all possible orientalist concepts, images, associations, fears, and attractions in one document, to localize them in one small geographic space, to remind readers that in that beautiful city, in 1491, the Islamic penetration of Western Europe was making its last stand, and to provoke in readers of the novel deeply mixed emotions about this final twilight of Eastern glory. Not only was there the nostalgia over loss of the exotic presence of the Orient in Spain, leaving only the impressive architectural reminder in the magnificent form of the Alhambra (about which the American, Washington Irving, had written four years earlier in his *Tales of the Alhambra*), but there was also the embarrassment at the Christian monarchs' treachery against those who surrendered: first, revoking the promise that they could keep their religion, then exiling even those Muslims and Jews who had converted to Christianity.

However, the story may well have served as a reminder that there was still something of a Muslim threat to Europe, despite the fall of Granada at the end of the fifteenth century. The Turkish Wars, which had begun when Granada was still a Muslim kingdom, penetrated into Europe, resulting in the siege of Vienna in 1529. These wars had ended only in 1791, still remembered by some of Bulwer-Lytton's readers, and freshly recalled from the Greek War of Independence (1820–22), where Christians again fought Muslims to reclaim conquered territory. In fact, the threat of the expansionism of the Ottoman Empire was not eliminated until the end of World War I, when the Turkish Empire collapsed.

Therefore, *Leila: or, The Siege of Granada* is replete with the orientalist stereotypes that would be expected in such a novel. On the first page we are told that, despite the war beyond the walls of the city, there are people within "listening in quiet indolence to the strings of the Moorish lute . . . [in] the stately calm habitual to every Oriental people" (1).[48] The narrator makes numerous references to *Arabian Nights*, thereby evoking an Oriental context that readers would readily recognize. The Muslim king has "Ethiopian guards" who appear "gigantic, – stolid and passionless, machines, to execute, without thought the bloodiest or the slightest caprice of despotism" (54). There are references throughout to the exotic luxury associated with Eastern decadence, as in the description of Boabdil's quarters:

> The ceiling of cedar-wood, glowing with gold and azure, was supported by slender shafts of the whitest alabaster . . . and wrought in that delicate filigree-work common to the Arabian architecture. . . . The pavement was spread with ottomans and couches of the richest azure, . . . broideries of gold and silver. . . . and the curving cimeter of Moorish warfare . . . studded . . . with jewels of rare cost.
>
> (5)

Early on, among the usual orientalist suspects are veiled women and women of the harem, or sometimes, veiled women of the harem. For example, the ambassador of Egypt presents to Boabdil the gift of "four veiled slaves, whose beauty had been the boast of the ancient valley of the Nile" (148). The Christian queen mother veils herself to conceal her emotions (57), and Leila herself is often veiled. She is brought before King Ferdinand veiled, but if the veil was meant to conceal, it fails: "a female figure, whose long veil, extending from head to foot, could conceal neither the beautiful proportions nor the trembling agitation of her frame" (34). When Queen Isabel requests Leila's presence in her pavilion, Leila arrives veiled, and is ordered to unveil. "Leila, in obedience to the queen's request, threw up her veil" (81). The queen, seeing "the paleness of her cheek and the traces of recent tears" (81), decides to intervene on Leila's behalf to protect her from "the licentious gaze" of her son, Don Juan, and from "the iron zeal of the Inquisitor" by sending her to a convent. There, Leila is described as "fated to the veil" (159), and, indeed, she is a woman between two veils, as she will lose one to gain another. But she never makes such a transition, because it is at that moment that her father stabs her, saying, as he commits his murderous act, "the veil is rent" (160), perhaps a symbolic displacement that forecloses the rending of the hymen.

Women of the harem make an early appearance: "through the fairy pillars and by the glittering waterfalls, came the small and twinkling feet of the maids of Araby. As with their transparent tunics and white arms they gleamed, without an echo, through that cool and voluptuous chamber" (6). We are invited to consider the "voluptuousness and dreamy languor of Moorish maidens" (18), and are told by Almamen that he does not trust "the lascivious arts of the Moorish maidens; . . . their harlot songs, their dances of lewd delight" (19).

Bulwer-Lytton's narrator appears to be fascinated by what he takes to be the fatalism of the Moors.[49] "Allah Akbar! What is, is; what shall be, shall be!" cries an old man in the streets of Granada "with all the solemn sagacity of a prophet" (2). Almamen says: "But fate, or Allah, hath placed on the throne . . . a dreamer" (4). Indeed, the narrator calls "the Mohammaden creed" the "doctrine of inevitable predestination" (61). Boabdil's counselors consult "the Books of Fate," imploring "a sign from the Prophet." Their conclusion: "The fall of Granada is predestined. God is great!" (147). They implore Boabdil, "O king, fight not against the will of fate; God is great!" (151). According to this line of thought, there is a future in place already, but that future is to us a *secret*, the most important secret of all – a secret whose hidden information would be the most valuable – yet, at the same time, the most useless – information of all because if it were revealed, nothing could be done about it except descending into a permanent state of resignation. In discussing the powers of Almamen, the narrator says:

> He had not in vain applied himself to such tempting and wild researches, and had acquired many of *those secrets now perhaps lost forever to the world*. We do not mean to intimate that he attained to what legend and superstition impose upon our faith as the art of sorcery. He could neither command the elements nor *pierce the veil of the future*, – scatter armies with a word, nor pass from spot to spot by the utterance of a charmed formula.
>
> (24, emphasis added)

However, he "could not but learn some secrets which all the more sober wisdom of modern times would search ineffectively to solve or to revive" (25). Here, the narrator indulges in the orientalist longing for *secret knowledge* that the East is supposed to possess, a knowledge of secrets from which Western science is hopelessly excluded. This is an example of the Victorian orientalizing of secrecy itself. The secrets to which science can gain access are secrets of the material world, but the secrets of Oriental wisdom are secrets of the soul and of hidden realities that the physical eye cannot see. These are, then, the secrets revealed only by "the arts of the Cabala" (23).

In fact, both Boabdil and Muza seek Almamen's knowledge as an escape from the deadly fatalistic combination of Islam and astrology. The narrator tells us that Boabdil

> sought to contend against the machinations of hostile demons and boding stars, not by human but spiritual agencies. Collecting around him the seers

and magicians of Orient-fanaticism, he lived in the visions of another world; and flattered by the promises of impostors or dreamers, and deceived by his own subtle and brooding tendencies of mind, it was amongst spells and cabala that he thought to draw forth the mighty secret which was to free him from the meshes of preternatural enemies of his fortune, and leave him the freedom of other men to wrestle, with equal chances, against peril and adversities.

(61)

In Bulwer-Lytton's story Almamen is believed by most people in Granada, including the king, to be a Muslim. Yet, this "serpent" (27) of a crypto-Jew is dismissive both of Islam and of the Judaism he tries to defend ("He cared little for its precepts, he thought little of its doctrines; but night and day, he revolved his schemes for its earthly restoration and triumph" [26]). He seems to detest most of the Jews in whose name he seeks vengeance. He essays "to preserve Leila as much as possible from contact even with Jews themselves, whose general character (vitiated by the oppression which engendered meanness, and the extortion which fostered avarice) Almamen regarded with lofty though concealed repugnance" (87). Yet, Almamen himself insists on the common identity of Moors and Jews. He talks to Boabdil of "the Hebrews themselves, that ancient and kindred Arabian race" (10). The narrator seems to agree, speaking of "the keen, sharp Arab features of the Jew" (103), and as in so much of Victorian literature, in *Leila* the Old Testament and *Arabian Nights* seem to have similar authority and are sometimes appealed to in the same breath. (Referring to the maids of Boabdil's harem, the narrator says: "they might well have seemed the Peris of Eastern magic, summoned to beguile the sated leisure of a youthful Solomon" [6–7].)

There is a conflation made by Bulwer-Lytton – and, as we saw, by Lucy Snowe – wherein the figure of the Jew and of the Moor become fused as "Oriental" whose very existence and actions hint of hidden danger, secret sexual pleasures, and despotic acts of cruelty. The figure of the Oriental no doubt produced in Bulwer-Lytton's readers sensations of attraction and repulsion, mystery and fear, prurient curiosity and morbid fascination, all in combination with a self-righteous condemnation, mediated in this story by Leila – a beautiful, sexually attractive, vulnerable, virginal Jewish convert to a new religion. Her "rescue," deveiling, and reveiling will foil the secret cabbalistic powers of her dangerous, powerful, and sinister father. His secret strengths cannot win his daughter back from Christendom, but they have enough depth, blackness, and potency to triumph over the secrets of the Inquisition, whose cruelty has its own fascination for Bulwer-Lytton's readers.[50]

Of all the characters in the novel, it is Almamen, as detestable and fanatical as he is, who is most associated with secrecy – and a very Oriental secrecy at that. Early on he is addressed by Muza as "Pretender to the Dark Secrets" (3). He sneaks through "dark and subterranean passages known only to himself" (104). He studies not astrology but magic, "the true science of enchantment." He explains to Boabdil, "We may thrall and command the subtler beings of realms and elements which our material bodies cannot enter, our gross senses cannot survey. This, then, is my lore" (12). There is a *secret world* of magic, from which, with enough "science," beings can be summoned. And yet, as has been mentioned, this student of the secrets of the Cabala hides the simplest facts from his daughter. Prince Muza, frustrated by Leila's inability to confide in him, cries out:

> "Holy Prophet! . . . why this mystery? Why can I not learn thy origin, thy rank, thy parents?" . . . "Alas!" answered Leila, weeping, "the mystery thou complainest of is as dark to myself as thee. How often have I told you that I know nothing of my birth or childish fortunes, save a dim memory of a more distant and burning clime."[51]

(15)

The most dramatic exhibition of Almamen's exercise of his art takes place in the tribunal room of the Dominican priest, Tomás de Torquemada, the Grand Inquisitor whose function is to tease out the most subtle secrets. Torquemada has threatened Almamen with torture and death if he does not confess that his daughter, Leila, is part of a grand conspiracy against the Catholic throne. Almamen raises his cloak, and suddenly he seems to stand before Torquemada and his guards

> literally wrapped in fire; flames burst from his lip and played with his long locks, as, catching the golden hue, they curled over his shoulders like serpents of burning light; blood-red were his breast and limbs, his haughty crest, and his outstretched arm; and as for a single moment he met the shuddering eyes of his judges, he seemed . . . no longer the trembling captive, but the mighty demon or the terrible magician.

(78)

He dashes a phial to the ground, which releases clouds of black smoke, and when, "after some minutes, the darkness gradually dispersed, Almamen was gone" (79). A blood-soaked, mortally wounded guard has slumped to the floor, his long mantle missing – a proof, says the narrator, that Almamen "feared his more secret arts might not suffice to bear him safe through the camp without a worldly stratagem" (79). This last narrative aside seems to imply that Almamen's "cabalism" is really only a well-practiced form of illusionism. If so, and if this observation is meant to be a commentary on the Victorian passion for the exoticization of secrecy, then once again it seems that the deepest secret is that there is no secret.

Secrecy motivates much of the plot of *Leila* in such a way as to be consistent with Simmel's assertion that "The secret offers . . . the possibility of a second world alongside the manifest world" (330), but the depth and character of secrecy in this novel far outstrip Simmelian and Goffmanian theories of the *a priori* need for secrecy for both the individual and the social worlds, and certainly overwhelm Simmel's formulas. Also, *pace* Simmel, the role of secrecy in *Leila* is not in general a creative one but a tragic one, more often than not resulting in violence, death and destruction. These literary facts, however, do not necessarily constitute an attack on Simmel's theory. Bulwer-Lytton is not *describing* a fifteenth-century Spanish social scene so much as inventing one for a nineteenth-century English readership, an audience fascinated by the idea of the secret, and especially, the exotic, orientalized secret. Simmel himself had admitted that the fascination with secrets is not captured by theories of the instrumentality of secrets ("Not quite so evident are the attractions and values of the secret beyond its significance as mere means" [332]). Although this fascination may be universal, it is also historicized. We are looking here at a particularly Victorian form of fascination, one that is woven into a great many manifestations of Victorian imagination. In this novel secrecy and the Oriental exoticism melt together and are experienced by the Victorian reader as a single sensation. I am suggesting that Bulwer-Lytton's novel mirrors a conceptual confusion that was already widespread amongst a great many nineteenth-century authors and readers.

Secrecy and the historical novel

The closest we have come to the Victorian historical novel in my study is *Vanity Fair*, which reached back from the days in which Thackeray wrote his novel (the early 1840s) to a period that included Napoleon's defeat at Waterloo (1815). But that momentous historical event occurred in the lifetime of most of the characters in the novel (indeed, the night before the battle, George Osborne slipped a note to Rebecca Sharp announcing that he would leave his wife Amelie and proposing that Becky run away with him after the battle – a proposal that Becky did not need to reject, as Captain Osborne was killed the next day by the French troops). Thackeray went on to write two historical novels of his own: *Henry Esmond* (1852) and *The Virginians* (1859). The first treated the Jacobite rebellions against the English royalty in the late seventeenth and early eighteenth centuries, and the second explored the aftermath of that rebellion in America. Georg Lukács compared *Henry Esmond* unfavorably to Walter Scott's *Waverley* because, according to Lukács, Thackeray "does not see the people. He reduces his story to the intrigues of the upper classes" (which may be another way of saying that Thackeray's sense of the past is incompatible with Marxian historical theory).[52]

I will address shortly the question of the role that secrecy can play in the nineteenth-century historical novel, but first I must confront a more basic and rather Kantian question: how is the historical novel possible? For years, this genre's legitimacy has been challenged. Writing in 1828 Alessandro Manzoni complained about the historical novel: "In short it is a work impossible to achieve satisfactorily, because its premises are inherently contradictory; . . . here precisely is its critical flaw."[53] This "hybrid" (De Groot 2) that seduces the reader "into being knowingly misinformed, misled and duped" (De Groot 6) was called by Manzoni "a flimsy, corrupt genre that tends toward obfuscation and falsehood."[54] De Groot himself refers to "the innate dishonesty of historical fiction *per se*" (107). The South American literary critic, Noé Jitrik, writes: "The phrase, 'historical novel,' presents itself to us as an oxymoron."[55] Yet, all three of these critics eventually settle their accounts with this Frankenstein's monster. Manzoni wrote his own historical novel in the same year he registered his complaint (*The Betrothed*, 1827). De Groot wrote his book *The Historical Novel* (2010) in which, without withdrawing his complaint about historical fiction, he asserts, following certain postmodern authors who have influenced him, that the writing of history itself suffers from the same dishonesty as the writing of historical novels. He quotes Keith Jenkins approvingly: "For texts are not cognitive, empirical, epistemological entities, but speculative, propositional invitations to *imagine* the past *ad infinitum.*"[56] According to De Groot, "If, as Hayden White suggests, all historians play with rhetoric and metaphor in constructing their narratives, then all historical fiction is predicated upon fictionalized 'versions' of the past." Indeed, De Groot tells us, Michel de Certeau calls historical treatises "the fiction of history" (115). Noé Jitrik solves the problem in a less radical but perhaps equally provocative fashion. Speaking of the oxymoronic nature of so-called historical fiction, he writes:

> the combination of its two apparently conflicting terms is produced by virtue of a certain well-chronicled philosophical authorization, or perhaps by a system of thought that favors – I would say "authorizes" – the unification of these two dissimilar terms in such a way that not only is no scandal produced but there is a perfect understanding of the task that the union can achieve. From this perspective we could define the historical novel as an accord – perhaps always violated – between "truth," which would be on the side of history, and "lie," which would be on the side of fiction, but thereby the truth can be made more full, more dense, by the intervention of the lie.
>
> (11)

This solution is less postmodern than Platonic: we have here another case of "the noble lie,"[57] and (repeating another of my mantras) wherever there is a lie there is a secret.

Or is there? On the face of it, there would be much less likelihood of secrecy in historical fiction than in other types. An historical novel, especially one written in the Victorian period, is unlikely to shock its readers or challenge established historical fact,[58] and as a recent anonymous reviewer of a new historical novel has suggested, "adopting a character whose fate is sealed reduces the potential for surprise"[59] (i.e., the potential for the revelation of secrets). More importantly, the reader of the historical novel knows things about the future of characters in the novel that the characters themselves do not know. This knowledge gives the reader power over the characters. The reader possesses secrets that are withheld from the characters. Think of another, much more famous historical novel by Edward Bulwer-Lytton, *The Last Days of Pompeii.* We readers, but not the doomed characters, know that these are indeed the last days of Pompeii, that everything will be destroyed and all living things will die together in the twinkling of an eye. It may seem that this knowledge gives us readers the pleasure of a certain incontrovertible power over the novel's personages – historical or fictitious – but in fact it sometimes places us in a perpetual state of dread, like that of the chorus in the ancient Greek dramas. (Oedipus: "I shall go to Thebes." The chorus: "No, no, not to Thebes! To anywhere but Thebes!")

There are ways that authors of historical novels can evade this deadly determinism. Recall that in *Vanity Fair* when Mrs. Rawdon Crawley, née Rebecca Sharp, slips into a boudoir with the Duke of Wales, soon to be the real King of England, the novel's narrator takes great pride in his discretion in not informing his readers of what transpired between Becky and His Majesty in the hidden apartment. This is a titillating version of similar solutions for other authors of historical novels who also place the main actors of the plot adjacent to great historical personages rather than making those great personages themselves the main characters of the plot. Indeed, Edward Waverley, the eponymous hero of Sir Walter Scott's *Waverley* (1814) ("the first commonly defined historical novel" [De Groot 7]), is an everyman, as Andrew Sanders writes,

> a neutral hero, a figure caught up . . . in a political crisis, and coming into immediate contact with men and causes which represent the extremes of political division. The neutral hero stands as the representative of society as a whole, and is able to learn from the extremes he sees and from the humanized historical figures he meets, not as heroes but as men among men. . . . In the great majority of Scott's novels . . . the hero is neutral because he is also fictional and therefore a free agent, able to form decisions which are not necessarily tied by the restrictive need to follow the events of recorded history. The neutral heroes meet, admire, dislike, follow or reject the "great men" of history by first seeing them as fallible and human.[60]

The freedom from historical strictures that Sanders discovers in the neutral hero would be somewhat modified by Noé Jitrik, because, according to him, that freedom is relative to the "heaviness" of the past:

> One could say that the greater the closeness with respect to the temporal location of the referent [the historical period referred to] the more the historical heaviness is alleviated, producing an interaction between the two contexts that lightens the weight of the past. Contrarily, the greater the distance the more the weight of the historical is accentuated, which implies paradoxically fewer possibilities for transformation of the referent.
>
> (68–69)

If Jitrik's formula applies to Bulwer-Lytton's writing, then the heaviness of history must have weighed mightily on his options: 347 years passed between the siege of Granada in 1491 and the publication of Bulwer's *The Siege of Granada* in 1838. However, as we shall see, the recorded accounts of that event that were available to Lord Lytton had provided *una historia falsa*. Significant historical developments had been suppressed by both Christian and Muslim chroniclers: there was a secret that Bulwer-Lytton did not know. We can only imagine the devastation to Bulwer's plot that would have been wreaked by the revelation of that secret.

Although Bulwer-Lytton fashioned his work after Walter Scott's, according to Sanders Bulwer "saw Scott as deficient in accuracy and guilty of distortions of chronology and character, and he attempted instead to restore the academic prestige of the novel, making it worthy of serious study" (17). Bulwer made a great effort to appear objective and scholarly. In *Leila*, as in his other historical novels, he provides scholarly footnotes, clarifying certain historical facts for his readers (though Sanders seems justified in saying that when Bulwer historically annotates his novel "he merely adds to its artificiality and awkwardness" [52]). In *Leila* there are only nine footnotes: giving the meanings of Arabic words or etymologies, an analogy explained, a proverb explained; two of the footnotes name one of Bulwer's authorities, George Sale, while another repeats an anecdote told by Sale without mentioning his name. Other than the attempt to appear scientific, what is the narrative function of these interventions? Who is supposed to have added them, the narrator himself (and if so, does the narrator need to appear to be an historian?) or Bulwer-Lytton (and if so, does that detract from the narrator's authority?). In either case, are we expected to accept the narrator's or Bulwer's historical mentors as authoritative? George Sale (1627–1736) appears in three of Bulwer-Lytton's nine footnotes; his case is instructive.

Sale was an orientalist, a linguist, and a missionary who had spent many years in the Muslim world. In 1734 he published his four-volume annotated translation of the Qurán under the title of *A Comprehensive Commentary on the Qurán: Comprising Sale's Translation and Preliminary Discourse*. It seems to have been directed primarily to other missionaries. He writes in the preface:

> I imagine it almost needless either to make an apology for publishing the following translation, or to go about to prove it a work of use as well as curiosity. They must have a mean opinion of the Christian religion, or be but ill grounded therein, who can apprehend any danger from *so manifest a forgery.* . . . But whatever use an impartial version of the Qurán may be in other respects, it is absolutely necessary to undeceive those who, from the ignorant or unfair translations which have appeared, have entertained too favourable opinion of the original, and also to enable us effectually *to expose the imposture.*
>
> (n.p., emphases added)[61]

Despite Sale's fear that the earlier bad translations of the Qurán disguise its imposture, and his assertion that it is a blatant "forgery," Sale is actually rather sympathetic toward Muhammad:

> He formed a scheme of establishing a new religion, or, as he expressed it, of replanting the only true and ancient one, professed by Adam, Noah, Abraham, Moses, Jesus, and all the prophets, by destroying the gross idolatry into which the generality of his countrymen had fallen, and weeding out the corruptions and superstitions which the latter Jews and Christians had, as he thought, introduced into their religion, and reducing it to its original purity,

which consisted chiefly in the worship of one only God. . . . His original design of bringing the pagan Arabs to the knowledge of the true God was certainly noble, and highly to be commended.

(69)

Sale's ambivalence is commensurate with that of Bulwer-Lytton, who – like so many nineteenth-century orientalists – expresses in equal measure both awe and disdain of the Muslim world about which he writes. In fact, Sale seems much more offended by Roman Catholicism than by Islam. He writes:

> The writers of the Romish communion, in particular, are so far from having done any service in their refutations of Muhammadism, that by endeavouring to defend their idolatry and other superstitions, they have rather contributed to the increase of that aversion which the Muhammadans in general have to the Christian religion, and given them great advantages the dispute. The Protestants alone are able to attack the Qurán with success; and for them, I trust, Providence has reserved the glory of its overthrow. . . . The worshipping of images and the doctrine of substantiation are great stumbling-blocks to the Muhammadans, and the Church which teacheth them is very unfit to bring those people over.
>
> (4)

Sale continues attacking the Catholics with bitter humor. Discussing Arabian idolatry before Muhammad, he writes:

> I shall mention but one idol more of this nation, and that was a lump of dough worshipped by the tribe of Hanifa, who used it with more respect than the papists do theirs, presuming not to eat it till they were compelled to it by famine [presumably, as opposed to the Roman Catholics, who eat their god every week].
>
> (43)

In fact, Bulwer-Lytton turns Sale's anti-Catholic snipe into an anti-Semitic one, having Boabdil, the Muslim king of Granada, characterize the Jews as "Worse than the tribe of Hanifa, who eat their god only in time of famine" (10). Borrowing from Sale without acknowledging him, Bulwer provides a footnote for his readers: "The tribe of Hanifa worshipped a lump of dough" (10).

Lord Lytton's readers probably were not familiar with Georg Sale's translation and commentary on the Qurán published 100 years earlier, so they would not have recognized Bulwer's perversion of Sale's joke. Can we say that Bulwer-Lytton, who purports to be accurate and objective, is keeping this secret from his readers? Perhaps not completely; he does mention Sale in two other footnotes, so his camouflaging of the truth here is more like what Goffman calls a "latent secret," disguised information that could be sought out with an effort.

Let us look more deeply into the role that Bulwer-Lytton bequeaths to his narrator. He (and it certainly is "he") is quite remarkable, and, it seems, keeps a number

170 *Veiled secrets, veiled subjects*

of secrets from his reader. To some extent, he is a "neutral narrator." The book opens with this line:

> It was the summer of the year 1491, and the armies of Ferdinand and Isabel invested the city of Granada. . . . The moon, which broke through the transparent air of Andalusia, shone calmly over the immense and murmuring encampment of the Spanish foe.
>
> (1)

Spain is the foe; therefore the narration begins from the Moorish side. The narrator describes the beautiful view from Boabdil's window in the Alhambra as if from memory, calling our attention to "the woods and orange groves, *which still form the unrivaled landscapes of Granada*" (emphasis added). Then, the narrator is in the present day (1838), describing events in 1491 in the past tense as if he personally remembers them. Here is a narrative secret: the narrator is not only possibly omniscient and omnipresent; apparently he is immortal. He is also multilingual. He reports (and thereby translates into English) conversations that take place in Castilian, Arabic, and Hebrew. As it turns out, the narrator not only describes real historical events and personages (e.g., the fall of Granada to Ferdinand and Isabel – but also fictitious events and personages (Almamen, Leila, and Muza Ben Abil Gazan in battle). Evidently, by virtue of describing fictitious events, the narrator *causes* these events (otherwise this would not be an historical *novel*), but more startlingly, he also seems to cause *historical* events. The narrator partially blames Almamen the wizard for King Ferdinand's "gloomy fanaticism" even though Almamen is the creation of the narrator (and of his co-conspirator, Edward Bulwer-Lytton). In fact, Bulwer and his narrator see to it that one reason for the Christian reprisal against wealthy Jews in Andalusia (which is an historical event) is the fact the Almamen kills a Christian guard while escaping from the military assistants of Torquemada, the Grand Inquisitor (and as such an historical character). Word gets out about Almamen's flamboyant and bloody disappearance from Torquemada's confinement of him, and this story "was distorted and exaggerated by the credulity of the Spaniards into an event of the most terrific character, served to complete the chain of evidence against the wealthy Jews and Jew-descended Spaniards of Andalusia" (92). So, the persecution of the Jews by the Christians at this point (a real event in the history of Spain) is partially attributed to the fictional activity of the fictional character that Bulwer-Lytton had invented. The narrator tells of a rebellion of Jews and *conversos* (former Jews now converted to Christianity) in Cordoba, and "the whole was headed by a man who appeared suddenly amongst them, and whose fiery eloquence and martial spirit produced, at such a season, the most fervent enthusiasm" (105–6). It is clearly implied by the narrator that the leader of this bloody rebellion is Almamen. We find Almamen's name in Bulwer's novel, but we do not find it in the history books of Spain. Bulwer's narrator has an explanation:

> Unhappily, the whole details of this singular outbreak are withheld from us; only by wary hints and guarded allusions do the Spanish chroniclers apprise

us of its existence and its perils. . . . [T]he conspiracy was hushed in the dread silence of the Inquisition, into whose hand the principal conspirators ultimately fell.

(106)

"The dread silence of the Inquisition. . . . " An historical black hole, but a convenient one for Bulwer-Lytton's secret, whose readers are expected to believe that an historical secret that has been suppressed for 347 years has been revealed by Bulwer's novel:

> In this conjunction of hostile planets, Ferdinand had recourse to his favorite policy of wile and strategem. Turning against the Jews the very treaty Almamen had sought to obtain in their favour [a treaty between him and Ferdinand], he caused it to be circulated privately that the Jews, anxious to purchase their peace with him, had promised to betray the Moorish towns and Granada itself into his hands. The paper, which Ferdinand himself had signed with Almamen, and of which, on the capture of the Hebrew, he had taken care to repossess himself, he gave to a spy, whom he sent, disguised as a spy, into one of the revolted cities.

(116)

Once again fictitious events become historical causal agents, along with some astrological forces.

Finally, the narrator describes the ultimate battle between Saracen and Christian knights:

> But still a small and devoted remnant of the Moorish cavaliers remained to shed a last glory over defeat itself. With Muza, their soul and centre, they fought every atom of ground; it was, as the chronicler expresses it, as if they grasped the soil with their arms.

(137)

Who is this chronicler? Is he the narrator's historical authority? Why did Bulwer-Lytton provide no footnote to identify him? These questions probably reveal narrative secrets of which Edward Bulwer-Lytton would prefer that his readers remain ignorant.

As an historian Bulwer-Lytton makes a few errors that may well have been shared by Spanish historians and British students of Spanish history during his time: I have already mentioned the narrator's claim that in 1491 Jews suffered more restrictions and depredations under Muslim rule than under Christian domination, a claim challenged by a number of historians today. A small error occurs when Bulwer writes: "the king of Granada abruptly summoned to his council Jusef, his vizier" (27). According to historian Leonard P. Harvey, in 1490 and 1491 Boabdil's *wazîr* was Abû'l-Qâsim al Mulîh. Yúsuf bin Kumásha had been his *wazîr* in the 1480s.[62] Yet another error occurs when Bulwer's narrator, speaking of Boabdil and Ferdinand, says: "both kings met in the same *mêlée*" (135). In fact, such a *mélée* never happened. This is akin to the meeting between Richard Lionheart and Suleiman the Magnificent that Walter Scott invented in *Ivanhoe*.

There is one other historical mistake in *Leila: or, The Siege of Granada* – and a major one at that – but one that cannot be blamed on Bulwer-Lytton. Had he known about it, he would have to write quite differently about "the siege of Granada" itself, and perhaps would have been discouraged from writing the novel at all. First, some background history provided by L. P. Harvey – history that we do not find in *Leila*. In 1483, after several victories against the Castilian forces, Boabdil's army had been defeated in a sneak attack on the Christian city of Lucena, and Boabdil was captured. There was a debate among the leaders of King Ferdinand's army about what to do with Boabdil. Some thought he should be ransomed, others thought that he should be executed, others that he should be returned to Granada to prevent the success of those who preferred Boabdil's father (Abu l-Hasan) or his uncle (Muhammad al-Zagal) from taking over Granada, thinking that Boabdil would be easier to deal with. In 1485 Boabdil was returned to Muslim lands. In 1486 he was once more captured at the battle of Loja, and once again released. Harvey reports that some historians (including some Muslim historians) correctly see all this as evidence that Boabdil was conspiring with Ferdinand. Harvey writes:

> Many Christians must have been privy to the negotiations, but it did not fit in with the powerful myth of the Reconquest for the truth to be known. Nobody wished it to be public knowledge that the gates of the city were waiting to be opened, with the only outstanding obstacle a problem of public relations and of news management.
>
> (313)

Here is a secret from the past that some historians in the know withheld from the records. Harvey writes:

> It has really only been in modern times, and thanks to such studies as María del Carmen Pescador del Hoyo's "Como fue de verdad la toma de Granada a la luz de un documento inédito" (1955) that the inner truth of what was going on in those days has been understood.
>
> (313–14)[63]

Apparently the *documento inédito* (unpublished document) found by Pescador del Hoyo proved the conspiracy between Ferdinand and Boabdil. Harvey goes so far as to say about the year 1487, "At this stage we can have no reasonable doubt that Boabdil was acting in close collaboration with Ferdinand and Isabella" (294).

If these negotiations had been made public in 1491, Boabdil may well have been beheaded for treason,[64] and the glorious myth of the Reconquest, carried on in the spirit of Saint James ("*¡Santiago, y cierra, España!*" [Bulwer-Lytton, 43]), would have been tarnished – Saint James, whose headless body was directed in a stone boat to northeastern Spain by an angel as a sign that the *Reconquista* was part of a divine plan, according to legend. (It was the discovery of his body in Santiago that forged the *Reconquista*.) If Michael Ragussis is correct in his claim that early Victorian readers, following Scott, looked to fifteenth-century Spain for inspiration for their own acts of nation-building, I believe we can say that Bulwer-Lytton unwittingly played a part in a secret conspiracy that was also supposed to motivate British patriotism. It was indeed a dark and stormy night.

Notes

1 Michel Foucault, *The History of Sexuality*, vol. 1 (New York: Vintage Books/Random House, 1980), 10. Future references to this work will be included parenthetically in the body of the text.
2 As mentioned earlier, I do not find strong support for Foucault's thesis in the novels I investigate in this study, with the possible exception of *Vanity Fair*. Even there, sex and sexual discourse – covert or overt – is simply a strategic tool of the more deeply motivated egoistic power mongering, what Thackeray's narrator calls the cat that escaped the "bag of secrecy" (222). However, most of Foucault's evidence for his thesis is found in documents whose provenance is not fictional but, rather, institutional: medical, psychiatric, educational, and police based. The fiction that Foucault mentions in his refutation of the "repressive hypothesis" is literally pornographic (works of the Marquis de Sade, and *My Secret Life*). Foucault did promise to discuss the rules for transforming sex into public discourse in "the reformed pastoral" in volume 2 of *The History of Sexuality*.
3 Originally, the term "orientalism" referred to the professional study of the Orient, but since the publication of Edward W. Said's *Orientalism* in 1978 it refers to the attitude in Western readers that those studies provoked, a particular form of "the Imaginary."
4 Apparently the fascination was not mutual. Robert Irwin points out that Antoine Galland, the translator of *Arabian Nights* into French, was puzzled by the fact that "Europeans [were] so interested in the Islamic world, while there [was] so little reciprocal interest on the part of Muslims in Christian Europe's civilization and society" (*The Arabian Nights: A Companion* [London: Penguin, 1994], 15). Future references to this work will be included parenthetically in the body of the text.
5 This is, after all, the age of the discovery of alienation, primarily theorized by Hegel in Jena (as Napoleon's bombs fall around him), and Marx in London (to which he had to repair to escape the German courts), and Kierkegaard at his solitary writing desk in Copenhagen (to which he attached himself to escape the grip of Regine Olsen).
6 Joanna da Groot, "'Sex' and 'Race': The Construction of Language and Image in the Nineteenth Century," in *Sexuality and Subordination: Interdisciplinary Studies of Gender in the Nineteenth Century*, ed. Susan Mendus and Jane Rendall (London and New York: Routledge, 1989), 89–128, 108. Future references to this work will be included parenthetically in the body of the text.
7 Rana Kabbani, *Europe's Myths of the Orient* (Bloomington: Indiana University Press, 1986), 22. Future references to this work will be cited parenthetically in the body of the text.
8 "Scheherazade" is the common English spelling today. Lane spelled her name "Sharazád," and Burton spelled it "Sharazâd." In Zipes's edition of Burton's translation, the name has been updated to "Scheherazad." The alternative spelling of "Sheherazade" can also frequently be found.
9 "The Marriage of King Shahryar and Scheherazade," *Arabian Nights: The Marvels and Wonders of the Thousand and One Nights*, ed. Jack Zipes, trans. Richard F. Burton (New York: Dutton Signet, 1991), 577–83, 581. Future references to the *Arabian*

174 *Veiled secrets, veiled subjects*

Nights will be to Burton's translation unless otherwise indicated, and will be included parenthetically in the body of the text.

10 Billie Melman, *Women's Orients: English Women and the Middle East, 1718–1918* (Ann Arbor: University of Michigan Press, 1992), 192. Future references to this work will be included parenthetically in the body of the text.

11 Peter L. Caracciolo tells us that the first pirated edition came to be known as the Grub Street edition, and by 1715 was already into its third printing. By 1793 Galland's French edition had been through eighteen printings. During the next forty years the rate of publication in France and England doubled. Edward Lane's translation of 1839–41 became extremely popular in England, beating out its many competitors for twenty-five years (Peter Caracciolo, "Introduction," in *The "Arabian Nights" in English Literature: Studies in the Reception of "The One Thousand and One Nights" into British Culture* [Houndmills: Macmillan, 1988]), 1–80, 2, 6, 20. Future references to this work will be included parenthetically in the body of the text. Yet there was a large enough audience for all comers. There were more than thirty different English editions of *Arabian Nights* published between 1850 and 1890 (Robert G. Hampson, "The Genie Out of the Bottle: Conrad, Wells, and Joyce," in Caracciolo, *The "Arabian Nights" in English Literature*, 218–43, 218).

12 Eva Sallis, *Scheherazade through the Looking Glass: The Metamorphosis of the "Thousand and One Nights"* (Richmond: Curzon Press, 1999), 16. Future references to this work will be included parenthetically in the body of the text.

13 Mohja Kahf, *Western Representations of the Muslim Woman: From Termagant to Odalisque* (Austin: University of Texas Press, 1999), 112.

14 Muhsin Jassim Ali, *Scheherazade in England: A Study of Nineteenth-Century English Criticism of the "Arabian Nights"* (Washington, DC: Three Continents Press, 1981), 3. Future references to this work will be included parenthetically in the body of the text. According to Muhsin Jassim Ali, the tales Scheherazade spun were

> read and enjoyed by people as diverse in interest as the Methodist Benjamin Gregory, the Christian poet Thomas Cooper, the Utilitarian Charles Knight, the Biblical scholar John Kitto, the Brownings, the Carlyles, the Ruskins, not to mention such devoted readers as the Brontës, Coleridge, Dickens, Hunt, Newman, Tennyson and hundreds of others. (42)

In that list of "hundreds of others" are Burne-Jones, William Morris, Walter Scott, Wilkie Collins, Sheridan Le Fanu, Robert Louis Stevenson, William Thackeray, R. S. Hawker, J. S. Mill, Matthew Arnold, Alexander Pope, and T. H. Huxley (Peter Caracciolo provides these additional names in his introduction to *The "Arabian Nights" in English Literature*, 30–31.)

15 Quoted by Caracciolo in *The "Arabian Nights" in English Literature*, 82.

16 The "Alice" books were read by adults, but often by adults who were worried that the events and characters in Wonderland and Looking-Glass Land might provoke nightmares in their children. *Robinson Crusoe*, published in 1719, was read primarily by adults, but bowdlerized versions were soon read by children, continuing into the twentieth century. (In *Émile*, Rousseau allows that the only novel children are permitted to read is Defoe's.) Later, *Treasure Island* was read by both adults and older children.

17 Caracciolo, *The "Arabian Nights" in English Literature*, 83–84, 86. "The Rev'd Mr. Cooper," by the way, proved to be neither reverent nor Mr. Cooper. His name was Richard Johnson, and he had pirated rather than translated the stories (ibid., 84).

18 Brian Alderson, "Scheherazade in the Nursery," in Caracciolo, *The "Arabian Nights" in English Literature*, 81–94, 87.

19 See the illustration in Caracciolo, *The "Arabian Nights" in English Literature*, 93, and illustrations #1, 5(b), 8, 11, 12, and 13.

20 "[Art] conducts us into an ideal kingdom, the only place where we can find pure joy, pure happiness, pure love" (posted by the curator of the exhibition *Au Temps de Klimt*, Pinacothèque de Paris, February 12–June 21, 2015).
21 Robert Irwin, in *The Arabian Nights: A Companion*, says that discussions of the "narrative techniques" of the *Nights* would be "arguments conducted in a vacuum unless one has some notion of what early versions . . . may have looked like and some notion too of how this corpus of tales came together in an Arab compilation" (42). According to Irwin, at this point current ideas about this problem are merely speculative.
22 Eva Sallis credits Farial Jabouri Ghazoul (*The Arabian Nights: A Structural Analysis*, [Cairo: Cairo Associated Institution, 1980]) and Azma Agzenay ("Theoretical Approach to the 'Other' of Europe: Between Fact and Fiction" [dissertation, University of Nottingham, 1989]) with this Bakhtinian idea (Sallis, *Scheherazade through the Looking Glass*, 1).
23 *The Arabian Nights' Entertainments: Or the Thousand and One Nights*, trans. Edward William Lane [1839–41] (New York: Tudor, 1927), xv. Future references to this translation will be included parenthetically in the body of the text, designated as "Lane." In this Prologue, Lane replaces the word "Allah" with "God." Burton restores "Allah" (Burton 1).
24 Eva Sallis astutely observes: "East and West are designations useful now because of their inaccuracy. They signify imaginary boundaries of identity rather than any real geography. . . . East and West are terms of arbitrary division, and signify attitudes rather than realities" (5n12).
25 Lane's translation reads: "He then drew his sword, and slew them both in bed" (Lane 4).
26 See Susanne Enderwitz, "Shahrazâd Is One of Us: Practical Narrative, Theoretical Discussion, and Feminist Discourse," in *The "Arabian Nights" in Transnational Perspective*, ed. Ulrich Marzolph (Detroit: Wayne State University Press, 2007), 261–75.
27 I have mentioned that in most respects my argument engages only the function of veiling from the point of view of outsiders to that practice; that is, I do not try to determine the semiology and phenomenology of the veil from the perspective of Muslim women who have chosen to don the veil. Still, much work has been done attempting to describe and theorize the experience from "inside to out," a few examples of which I will summarize here: *The veil as sign of the separation of women from men* (Leila Ahmed, "Western Ethnocentrism and Perceptions of the Harem," *Feminist Studies* 8.3 [Fall 1982]: 521–34, 523); *Sign of respectability* – "to differentiate between 'respectable' women and those who are publicly available" (Leila Ahmed, *Women and Gender in Islam: Historical Roots of a Modern Debate* [New Haven: Yale University Press, 1992, 15]); *Sign of upper-class membership* – "veiling was commonplace among the upper classes" (Ahmed, *Women and Gender in Islam*, 55); *Sign of dedication to Muhammad* – "Muhammad's wives being taken as models" (Ahmed, *Women and Gender in Islam*, 56). Similarly, in Christianity, to be married to Christ – To 'take the veil' is to become a nun" (Elizabeth Broadwell, "The Veil Image in Ann Radcliffe's *The Italian*," *South Atlantic Bulletin* 40.4 [1975]: 77); *Sign of modesty* – Following the Qurán's injunction to "guard their private parts" (Ahmed, *Women and Gender in Islam*, 55); *Sign of social status* – "a sign that husband or father was able to maintain the family in respectability" (Sarah Graham-Brown, *Images of Women: The Portrayal of Women in Photography of the Middle East 1860–1950* [London: Quartet, 1988], 83); *Sign of the sacred* – "The veil, veiling patterns and veiling behavior are . . . about . . . the realm of the sacred in this world" (Fadwa El Guindi, *Veil: Modesty, Privacy and Resistance* [Oxford and New York: Berg, 1999], 96); *Sign of Muslim identity and pride* – in the context of a discussion of the rise of the Islamic Group in Egypt in the 1970s, who radicalized most of Egypt's universities: "Soon it became fashionable for male students to grow beards and for female students to wear the veil" (Lawrence Wright, "Profiles: The Man behind

Bin Laden," *New Yorker* [September 16, 2002]: 56–85, 63–64); *Sign of a rejection of the West* – "a symbol of resistance" (Ahmed, *Women and Gender in Islam*, 235).

28 "Most prominently, perhaps, the veil's work would seem to be that of concealing, of hiding a secret" (Mary Anne Doane, "Veiling Over Desire: Close-ups of the Woman," in *Feminism and Psychoanalysis*, ed. Richard Feldstein and Judith Roof [Ithaca and London: Cornell University Press, 1989], 105–41, 110). Future references to this work will be included parenthetically in the body of the text.

29 Ruth Bernard Yeazell, *Harems of the Mind: Passages of Western Art and Literature* (New Haven: Yale University Press, 2000), 211n28. Yeazell attributes this observation to Mary J. Harper, "Recovering the Other: Women and the Orient in Writings of Early Nineteenth-Century France," *Critical Matrix: The Princeton Journal of Women, Gender, and Culture* 1.3 (1985): 10–11. Future references to Yeazell's work will be included parenthetically in the body of the text.

30 John Vignaux Smyth, *The Habit of Lying: Sacrificial Studies in Literature, Philosophy, and Fashion Theory* (Durham and London: Duke University Press, 2002). Future references to this work will be included parenthetically in the body of the text.

31 John Carl Flugel, *The Psychology of Clothes* (London: Hogarth Press, 1930).

32 Alan Hunt, *Governance of the Consuming Passions: A History of Sumptuary Law* (New York: St. Martin's Press, 1996), 55.

33 See, for example, Malek Alloula, *The Colonial Harem*, trans. Myrna Godzich and Wlad Godzich (Minneapolis and London: University of Minnesota Press, 1986), 3.

34 Graham-Brown, *Images of Women*, 74.

35 Inderpal Grewal, *Home and Harem: Nation, Gender, Empire, and the Cultures of Travel* (Durham: Duke University Press, 1996), 50–51. Future references to this work will be included parenthetically in the body of the text.

36 Alev Lytle Croutier, *Harem: The World behind the Veil* (New York: Abbeville Press, 1989), 206.

37 Emily Apter, "Female Trouble in the Colonial Harem," *Differences: A Journal of Feminist Cultural Studies* 4.1 (1992): 205–24, 208–9, 219.

38 Edward W. Said, *Orientalism* (New York: Random House, 1978), 206.

39 In *Veil: Modesty, Privacy and Resistance*, Fadwa El Guindi comments positively on Murphy's essay. She uses Murphy's data in her attack against the "Women's Studies approach" (her favorite *bête noire*) to the study of the veil. According to El Guindi, in the Western feminist approach the veil is invariably presented as reflecting women's invisibility, women's anonymity, female subordination, women's oppression in "patriarchal" societies, or a function of Islam. El Guindi points out that these gender-specific explanations for veiling, cannot account for veiling by men. Men's veiling, an ethnographic fact, becomes an anomaly, particularly against the common misunderstanding that only women veil, and that they veil as a form of submission (117–18).

40 Robert F. Murphy, "Social Distance and the Veil," *American Anthropologist* 66.b (December 1964): 1257–72, 1264. Murphy does not claim that the Tuareg represent the only case of men's veiling, but he clearly holds that the fact that among the Tuareg men veil and women do not is an anomaly, and one that needs an explanation. Future references to Murphy's article will be cited parenthetically in the body of the text.

41 The more well-known version is, of course, "It was a dark and stormy night . . ." – the opening words of Bulwer-Lytton's *Paul Clifford* (London: H. Colburn and R. Bentley, 1830).

42 Andrew Sanders, *The Victorian Historical Novel, 1840–1880* (London and Basingstoke: Macmillan Press, 1978), 48. Future references to this essay will be cited parenthetically in the body of the text.

43 Michael Ragussis, "The Birth of a Nation in Victorian Culture: The Spanish Inquisition, the Converted Daughter, and the 'Secret Race,'" *Critical Inquiry* 20 (Spring 1994): 477. Future references to this essay will be included parenthetically in the body of the text.

44 The end of the long period of prosperous Jewish life in old Spain began in the *annus terribilis* of 1391: widespread anti-Jewish rioting throughout Iberia, and especially in Castile, decimated the Jewish communities. Those who were not killed (and it is estimated that some 100,000 may have perished) either converted or fled to Muslim lands. (María Rosa Menocal, *The Ornament of the World: How Muslims, Jews, and Christians Created a Culture of Tolerance in Medieval Spain* [Boston, New York, and London: Little, Brown, 2002], 269)

45 The capture of Granada gave Isabel the excuse she needed to impose a single religion in Castile. In 1492 all Jews were required to be baptized or be expelled, and within 10 years the same requirement was made of the Muslims ... but ethnic cleansing of the kind which took place in the former Yugoslavia in the 1990s was not to become policy until 1609, when Philip III decreed the expulsion of all descendents of former Muslims (*moriscos*). (B. W. Ife, "The Historical and Social Context," in *Cambridge Companion to Cervantes*, ed. Anthony J. Cascardi [Cambridge and New York: Cambridge University Press, 2002], 11–31, 15–16)

46 Robert Trivers, *The Folly of Fools: The Logic of Deceit and Self-Deception in Human Life* (New York: Basic Books, 2011), 246.

47 Anthony Julius, *Trials of the Diaspora: A History of Anti-Semitism in England* (Oxford and New York: Oxford University Press, 2010), 226–27.

48 Edward Bulwer-Lytton, *Leila: or, The Siege of Granada* [1838] (Boston: Estes and Lauriat, 1892), 1. Future references to this work will be included parenthetically in the body of the text.

49 Certainly the problem of predestination has crept up from time to time in Islamic theology, and at some moments and places stronger than others – and not only in the semi-heretical *Rubáiyát*. The narrator of *Leila* does not acknowledge that the same is true of Christianity – most notably, perhaps, in Saint Augustine, John Calvin, and Martin Luther.

50 Michael Ragussis cites a book published in London in 1810 by the English author J. J. Stockdale, named *The History of the Inquisitions, Including the Secret Transactions of Those Horrific Tribunals* (481).

51 Improbably, Bulwer has created Leila Bat Almamen to be what in John Rawls's theory of justice would be an almost perfect moral agent. According to Rawls, the individual most likely to choose justly on almost all issues would be one behind a "veil of ignorance," operating from rational self-interest, but ignorant of her social background, inheritances, financial status, mental or physical abilities, and racial and religious proclivities. Such an individual would be unable to base moral or political choices on any of these motivations, and would be most likely to choose in ways that benefited the many rather than the individual (John Rawls, *A Theory of Justice* [Cambridge, MA: Harvard University Press, 1971]).

52 Georg Lukács, *The Historical Novel* [1937], trans. Hannah and Stanley Mitchell (Harmondsworth: Penguin, 1969), 242. Future references to this work will be cited parenthetically in the body of the text.

53 Alessandro Manzoni, *On the Historical Novel* [1850], trans. Sandra Berman (Lincoln: University of Nebraska Press, 1984), 72. Cited by Jerome de Groot, *The Historical Novel* (London and New York: Routledge, 2010), 31. Future references to this work will be cited parenthetically in the body of the text.

54 Manzoni, *On the Historical Novel*, 76, quoted by De Groot in *The Historical Novel*, 32.

55 Noé Jitrik, *Historia e imaginación literaria: Las posibilidades de un género* (Buenos Aires: Editorial Biblos, 1995), 10. Future references to the Spanish text will be cited parenthetically in the body of the text. The translations here are my own. (Jitrik is well known in Argentina, but not widely read here. An earlier essay on historical novels by Jitrik, translated into English, called "From History to Writing: Symmetrical and Asymmetrical Tendencies in the Latin American Historical Novel," is in *The Noé Jitrik Reader: Selected Essays on Latin American Literature* (Durham and London: Duke University Press, 2005), 79–95.

56 Keith Jenkins, *Rethinking History* (London and New York: Routledge, 2003), 49. Quoted by De Groot in *The Historical Novel*, 111.
57 In Book III of *The Republic*, Socrates decides to convince the three castes in his ideal city (philosopher rulers, soldiers, workers) to accept the class divisions he will impose upon them by telling them that they all were

> moulded and trained down inside the earth. ... While god moulded you he mingled gold in the generation of some, and those are the ones fit to rule, ... he mingled silver in the assistants; and iron and brass in farmers and the other craftsmen.

Socrates then asks Glaucon, "Now have you any device to make them believe this fable?" "No, ... " says Glaucon" (Plato, *Republic*, in *Great Dialogues of Plato*, trans. W.H.D. Rouse [New York: New American Library, 1956], 214–15).
58 A point made by De Groot, *The Historical Novel*, 8.
59 "Anonymous review of Ronald Frame's *Havisham*," *New Yorker* (January 6, 2014): 67.
60 Sanders, *The Victorian Historical Novel 1840–1880*, 9, 16. Future references to this work will be cited parenthetically in the body of the text.
61 George Sale, *The Qurán with Preliminary Discourse and Notes on the Authority of Baidháwi, Jaláluddin, Al Zamakhshari, &c.* [1732], republished in 1896 in four volumes by the Rev. E. M. Wherry under Wherry's own name as *A Comprehensive Commentary on the Qurán: Comprising Sale's Translation and Preliminary Discourse* (London: Kegan Paul, Trench, Trübner, 1896). My quotations are from Wherry's edition. Future references to this work will be cited parenthetically in the body of the text.
62 L. P. Harvey, *Islamic Spain: 1250–1500* (Chicago and London: University of Chicago Press, 1992), 275. Future references to this work will be cited parenthetically in the body of the text.
63 María del Carmen Pescador del Hoyo, "Como fue de verdad la toma de Granada a la luz de un documento inédito" [How the Fall of Granada Really Happened in the Light of an Unpublished Document], *Al-Andaluz* 20 (1955): 283–344.
64 Boabdil had many enemies in Granada. In 1482 he had usurped the throne from his father, Abu-l-Hasan, who still had followers in the city. Popular uprising forced Boabdil "to take refuge in Christian territory – he was too much hated in Granada." In 1485 there was "street warfare in the capital for two months" when followers of Abu-l-Hasan's brother, Al-Zagal, tried to overthrow Boabdil (J. N. Hillgarth, *The Spanish Kingdoms 1250–1516*, vol. 2 [Oxford: Clarendon Press, 1978], 381–82).

6 The end of secrecy?

The Adventures of Sherlock Holmes

> He that has eyes to see and ears to hear may convince himself that no mortal can keep a secret. If his lips are silent, he chatters with his finger-tips; betrayal oozes out of him at every pore.
> —Sigmund Freud, *Dora: Fragment of an Analysis of a Case of Hysteria*

In 1908, Georg Simmel argued that without secrecy a social world for human individuals would be unthinkable. As we have seen, his view was reaffirmed fifty years later by another sociologist, Erving Goffman, who demonstrated that every "presentation of the self" requires the suppression of certain information. In some of the novels studied in this book we find an exaggerated embrace of this Simmelian-Goffmanian axiom. In Charlotte Brontë's *Villette*, Lucy Snowe's defense of her privacy is so extreme that there are secrets of her soul that are inaccessible even to her conscious self. The narrator of Bulwer-Lytton's *Leila* hints that there are secret worlds below our own world of whose knowledge there remain no traces for members of contemporary society. They could have been unearthed only through the study of the dark arts of the ancient Orient, now lost to us. In Braddon's *Lady Audley's Secret*, the exact nature of the eponymous secret seems still to remain unresolved. Yet, on another register we have seen suggestions of a contrary view in mid- and late-Victorian fiction – a narrative movement whose end point is the disappearance of secrecy itself. Such a conclusion is hinted at by the powerful detective skills that Charlotte Brontë bestowed upon the main characters of her novel; by the triumph of Robert Audley over the subversive cunning of "Lady Audley's" secret – regardless of the nature of that secret (if there is a secret); and by the unmasking of the cynical motives of Thackeray's characters in *Vanity Fair* by the novel's narrator. Each of these episodes suggests the advent of a purely transparent world and the end of secrecy. At the *fin de siècle* we encounter one of the most famous characters in world literature, Sherlock Holmes, who will proclaim to his audience – late nineteenth-century readers inflamed simultaneously with enthusiasm and misgivings over the rapid advances of science – that he has developed an epistemology from which he derives methods of investigation that will make secrecy not only redundant but impossible. In this chapter I will examine this extraordinary theoretical claim by Holmes and ask how seriously we should take it. But before doing so I will address the apparently less metaphysical question of whether there are secrets other than MacGuffins – Hitchcock's term for plot-driving secrets – in the Holmes stories (and in detective fiction in general), and will argue that indeed there are, but that, in the quest for the structure of Victorian secrecy, even MacGuffins matter, showing that many of them are derived from the hushed-up secret anxieties of the age, anxieties that themselves go beyond mere plot-driving secrets that will be revealed by strategies of narratological closure.

At least two critics interested in Sir Arthur Conan Doyle's work point out that there are three fictional individuals who pass as Sherlock Holmes: a Victorian Holmes, an Edwardian Holmes, and a Georgian Holmes.[1] Because this study covers almost exclusively the Victorian period, I will focus here largely on the Victorian Holmes. This brings him to his "first death" at Reichenbach Falls, where he and Moriarty apparently battle to the end.[2] After Sherlock's first demise, Colliers Publishing House in America in 1903 made Conan Doyle a financial offer he couldn't refuse, prompting him to resurrect Holmes while admitting to his friends that he had resisted doing so because he believed he was capable of a higher level of literature. Conveniently for my decision to exclude almost everything written by Conan Doyle after 1901, it seems that several critics find the later work inferior to the earlier stories.[3] The general exception to this judgment is the novella *The Hound of the Baskervilles*, considered by most to be Conan Doyle's greatest work, the first installation of which appeared in August 1901, seven months after Queen Victoria's death (but written during the last months of her life). I will have a few words to say about this work as the chapter progresses.

Plot-driving and structural secrets

Dr. John Watson, Sherlock Holmes's companion, assistant, and the chronicler of his feats, commences "The Adventure of the Engineer's Thumb" (1892) thus:

> The story has, I believe, been told more than once in the newspapers, but, like all such narratives, its effect is much less striking when set forth en bloc in a single half-column of print than when the facts slowly evolve before your own eyes and the mystery clears gradually away as each new discovery furnishes a step which leads on to the complete truth.[4]

This is a perspicacious summary of the narratological structure of detective literature. A detective story presents a set of MacGuffins that are interrogated by specific questions posed by the detectives or the readers, appearing in a consequential series as the story develops. These questions are eventually answered and the secrets are unveiled by a detective, and their revelation amounts to the solving of a mystery – usually but not always a criminal mystery. In Wonderland, Humpty Dumpty informs Alice: "The question is, 'Who is to be master?'" Clearly in the case of detective fiction "the narrator" is to be master because he controls the secrets and their disclosure. As Watson suggests, if the newly revealed information is simply presented as journalistic fact, a story has perhaps been provided, but the art of detection has been eliminated. A detective story requires mysteries,[5] and further, requires clues to the resolution of these mysteries. Finally, it requires the unveiling of secrets by an astute reader of clues. Indeed, *prima facie*, the genre we normally call detective fiction seems to be composed almost exclusively of MacGuffins, and this is one of the reasons that some readers relegate such fiction to an inferior status (as did Conan Doyle himself).

Without ignoring MacGuffins, the current study is an examination of the function of secrecy in nineteenth-century British fiction in terms of secrecy's conceptual aspects (asking, for example, what exactly is the logic of secrecy?), literary aspects (what aesthetic roles do secrets play?), sociological aspects (how does secrecy fit into the structure of the social world?), and historical and cultural aspects (how does secrecy in the Victorian world differ from that of other periods and other cultures?). I mentioned at the outset of my argument that MacGuffins would perhaps be of less interest to my theories of secrecy than other forms of concealment and revelation (the other forms being the overlapping concepts of foundational, structural, and narratological secrecy). Therefore, my decision to end this book with a chapter on the Sherlock Holmes stories of Arthur Conan Doyle may seem to go against my own priorities. I have done so for three reasons. First, in the case of Conan Doyle's serialized stories, the plot-driving secrets are not exclusively "whodunits"; rather, they are often about the use of secrecy by Victorian citizens. In the series as a whole, including those stories written after the turn of the twentieth century, at least a third of the tales involve an attempt to cover up or conceal a past action, and another third involve disguised attempts to avenge a past injury or insult.[6] Second, a study of Conan Doyle's stories leads to the discovery that mere plot-driving secrets, despite their arbitrary and formulaic nature, are culturally and historically anchored, hence theoretically interesting because their revelation, in addition to solving a mystery, exposes the kind of socio-historical conditions in which mystery existed. Here, MacGuffins often lead us beyond their own immediate secrets (how, why, and by whom were these acts of fraud, theft, murder, and revenge committed, and so forth) to deeper structural secrets in the form of cultural anxieties shared by many late-Victorian readers. These are not secrets in the sense of inaccessible hidden truths but secrets in broad daylight. They were known by most adults who, as solitary individuals, worried about them in private, or who, in small clusters of gossipers, talked about them in hushed tones, away from the children and servants. Finally, I will try to show that Conan Doyle's short stories and novels written up to the point when Sherlock Holmes appears to die in "The Adventure of the Final Problem" (1893) – even if they are composed mostly of MacGuffins – represent a "final stage" in the nineteenth-century resolution of the question about whether an interior secret self exists as the most precious and impenetrable possession of an individual human being.

With Georg Simmel and Erving Goffman, we could say that certain kinds of secrets have a structural function because they comprise information presupposed by all successful large-scale social arrangements but normally withheld from public discourse. Yet these semi-secrets determine the nature of both individual subjectivity and social relations. This type of secrecy includes withholding information whose release might block success in everyday practical engagements (secrets about private activities and their relation to selfhood, about one's social position and its relation to finances, about plans for the future that, if made known, might be thwarted by competitors, about problematic relationships among family members), or simply data withheld to avoid overloading the information system: Simmel's assertion that knowing too much "would drive everybody into the insane asylum" (311). In addition, there are also deeper and darker family secrets to be protected whose dissemination would be instantly devastating not to society itself but to an individual or to a small group of individuals (e.g., those small secret societies called families). Both kinds of secrets, "structural" and "dark," are, as Simmel says, historicized in content as well as form. Wealth and power in Victorian Britain were strictly organized along class, familial, and gender lines. Authority, prestige, and respect were functions of the rules governing this specific form of organization, and sometimes there were ruptures of these rules that were so egregious that their revelation would result in some form of excommunication: one could become the object of gossip, be shamed, snubbed, ostracized, or even incarcerated or hanged. As both Simmel and Goffman point out, in all cultures one can find both an anxiety about protecting one's own such secrets and a great curiosity to discover the secrets of others.

A perusal of the plot-driving secrets in the Sherlock Holmes stories reveals a variety of social anxieties beneath the surface of the narrative. To the extent that these anxieties are secret, perhaps they represent the darker side of what Simmel called the secret "second world" alongside the public world (330). For Simmel, this second world was often one that had the potential to provoke creativity in the "first world" (the public world). One way it influenced the agent's participation in the public sphere was to generate novel forms of thought and action. But logic would seem to dictate the opposite possibility as well, that aspects of the parallel secret world could provoke fear and anguish in the thought and behavior of the agent in the public sphere, and make that sphere seem more forbidding. One such secret concern would be the issue of *blackmail*, the fear of which was always paramount in the minds of those who hid devastating secrets ("The Adventure of the Yellow Face" [1893]; "A Scandal in Bohemia" [1891]). In "The Yellow Face" the fear of blackmail shares the foreground with a concern about *miscegenation*, a worry on the part of families who were not sure that their "Englishness" had the pedigrees they claimed for it.

The main MacGuffin in "The Adventure of the *Gloria Scott*" (1893) is the criminal past of a family patriarch, who in his youth was involved in a bloody mutiny on his way to serve a criminal sentence in Australia. This entails another secret, the family's *ill-begotten wealth*, built up as it was from the consequences of the mutiny. The possibility that one's financial history was tainted was an actual fear in the nineteenth century on the part of some younger members of the middle classes whose families had been particularly close-mouthed about their past, and certainly there was a bitter suspicion by some less well-off families about the source of the bounty of those who were better-off. "The 'Gloria Scott'" invites readers to be suspicious of the source of wealth among the upper classes in general.

Another concern of the Victorian bourgeoisie – one explored also by Mary Elizabeth Braddon – is that of *bigamy*, a secret that, unless exposed and punished, undermines both the purported "naturalness" of the nuclear family, and the family's ideological function as the foundation of the British nation. The issue of bigamy appears in "The Adventure of the Noble Bachelor" (1892), and in "The Boscombe Valley Mystery" (1891). In the latter story Holmes decides not to tell a bride that her father is the murderer of her new husband's father, nor to tell her that her marriage may be bigamous. Watson concludes the story, saying, "there is every prospect that the [two] may come to live happily together, in ignorance of the black cloud which rests upon their past" (BOSC I, 132). (Many commentators have pointed out that this hope is highly unlikely now that Watson has made public their dark secret.)

In "The Adventure of the Speckled Band" (1892), the plot-driving secret is the answer to the question, How did the Colonel's stepdaughter die?[7] Conan Doyle also taps into mid- and late-Victorian anxieties about *conspiracies* hatched by *secret societies*, usually foreign in origin, with either criminal goals ("The Red-Headed League" [1891]), or politically subversive goals ("The Five Orange Pips" [1891], *The Sign of the Four* [1890], *A Study in Scarlet* [1887]). There are moments, nevertheless, when it seems that Conan Doyle scoffs at the tendency of the British reading public to wallow in conspiracy theories about secret societies. In *A Study in Scarlet*, two Americans are found murdered. The police have trouble solving the crime. In a mocking tone, Watson reads aloud to Holmes all of the possible culprits to which one of the main London newspapers points:

> The *Daily Telegraph* remarked that in the history of crime there had seldom been a tragedy which presented stranger features. The German name of the victims, the absence of all other motive, and the sinister inscription on the wall, all pointed to its perpetration by political refugees and revolutionists. The Socialists had many branches in America, and the deceased had, no doubt, infringed their unwritten laws, and had been tracked down by them. After alluding airily to the *Vehmgericht* [a medieval German vigilante tribunal whose members were sworn to secrecy and often put their victims to death], aqua tofana [a poison clandestinely brewed by members of secret groups who anonymously applied it to their perhaps 600 victims], Carbonari [secret revolutionary clubs organized into small cells in Italy and France], and the Marchioness de Brinvilliers [who poisoned her father, daughter, two brothers, two sisters, and lover, probably with aqua tofana], the Darwinian theory, the principles of Malthus, and the Ratcliffe Highway murders [serial killings committed over twelve days in Wapping, England, in 1811], the article concluded by admonishing the Government and advocating a closer watch over foreigners in England.
>
> (STUD III, 92)

Conan Doyle's writing here is satirical and does not pander to fears of foreign conspiracies in the way that the work of his contemporary, Bram Stoker, managed to do; on the contrary, it mocks these imagined conspiracies.

Another concern was the fear of *imposture* in plots in which a member of one social class takes pecuniary advantage of claiming to be a member of another social class ("The Man with the Twisted Lip" [1891]). If a gentleman can pass as a beggar, how do we know that a beggar cannot pass as a gentleman? Commenting on this story, Nancy Ann Marck asserts, "imposture is an inherently subversive and criminal tendency."[8] Not only does "Twisted Lip" raise concerns about *identity* and *class*, but about the *theatricality of the social world*. It is as if the late-Victorians anticipated with dread Goffman's argument that there are no honest "presentations of the self."

Many critics who offer "symptomatic readings" of the MacGuffins in the Holmes stories are able to produce convincing evidence that Conan Doyle's work serves the cause of conservatism. For example, Rosemary Jann attributes to Conan Doyle the assumption that class distinctions have a natural foundation. Conan Doyle's stories presupposed "that class superiority had a biological basis, that social identity was transparent to the trained viewer, that the higher classes could be counted upon to police themselves" (Jann 1990, 705). Jann may be right, but she fails to point out that Conan Doyle has given the general public reason to suspect the very assumptions she claims are implicit in Holmes's activities, and, to that extent, Conan Doyle's work – as opposed to Holmes's – cannot be considered wholly conservative. Conan Doyle provokes in his readers suspicions about wealth, aristocracy, class boundaries, police competence, morality among certain members of the royal family, and the character of military officers – mainly colonels. He also allows Holmes to question the very nature of British justice: "many men have been wrongfully hanged" (BOSC I, 109).

Another worry in mid- and late-Victorian society that did not generate much open discussion was the ill-kept secret of the *atrocities committed by British troops* during the Indian Mutiny of 1857–58, and one that serves as the context for several of the MacGuffins that Holmes is called upon to resolve. This slaughter on the part of British troops was in response to Indian violence committed against both British combatants and civilians, including women and children. Many British troopers responded in kind. Klinger notes:

> There were reports . . . of Muslims smeared with pork fat before they were killed; Indians lashed to mouths of cannons and blown to pieces by grapeshot; women and children raped and then burnt alive; a bayoneted sepoy [native soldier] being roasted over a fire. Hundreds of Indians were executed by being shot from cannons.
>
> (Klinger's note 234, SIGN III, 350)

Discussing the British invasion and occupation of the Andaman Islands off the coast of India, Klinger writes: "The British who arrived in 1859 decimated the Andamanese not only with guns and artillery but by introducing bronchitis, syphilis, measles, and smallpox. A pre-1859 population of 3,000 to 3,500 was reduced, by 1895, to approximately 400" (Klinger's note 265, SIGN III, 366). These facts were all official secrets, but rumors flourished. In *The Sign of the Four* (1890), Conan Doyle stirs these harsh memories painfully, situating much of the criminal action that Holmes must punish in the time of the Indian Mutiny.

Yet another "not-so-secret" secret is the pervasive late-Victorian anxiety about the *problem of atavism*. This kind of secret does not involve the withholding of information in the fear that its disclosure would be damaging; rather, it is a recurring worry that, for any number of reasons, some people preferred not to discuss in any detail. (The fear of venereal disease occupied a similar status, as did the suspicion of alcoholism – especially in one's own case.) The concern about atavism is peculiarly Victorian, engendered and reinforced by the publication of *The Origin of Species* in 1859. Although today we would say that this apprehension is based on a misunderstanding of the theory of evolution, there are indications that Darwin himself worried about atavism.[9] Recall that when Conan Doyle mocks the paranoid excesses of the popular press, represented by *The Daily Telegraph*, he claims that they include "the Darwinian theory" among the dangerous sources of crime. If human beings descend from a primitive simian species – a species that might have exhibited more violent propensities and fewer moral compunctions than we – what is to prevent the appearance of an occasional reversion among us? Or what if we all harbor the violent and irrational propensities of our forbears – propensities that have been repressed by civilization's demands, but that might be brought back to the surface under the very kind of stress that civilization causes in us? (Think Sigmund Freud.) Certainly such concerns were expressed in novels such as *Dr. Jekyll and Mr. Hyde*, *The Island of Dr. Moreau*, *Dracula*, and *She*. In *A Study in Scarlet*, Watson describes the distorted face of a murdered man, killed in revenge for the heinous crimes he had committed:

> Every time I closed my eyes I saw before me the distorted, baboon-like countenance of that murdered man. So sinister was the impression which that face had produced upon me that I found it difficult to feel anything but gratitude from him who had removed its owner from the world. If ever human features bespoke vice of the most malignant type, they were certainly those of Enoch J. Drebber, of Cleveland.
>
> (STUD III, 79)

When Dr. Watson, out on the moor, first sees Selden, the escaped criminal in *The Hound of the Baskervilles*, he associates him immediately with ancient primitives who long ago inhabited the moors:

> there was thrust out his evil yellow face, a terrible animal face, all seamed and scored with vile passions. Foul with mire, with a bristling beard, and hung with matted hair, it might well have belonged to one of those old savages who dwelt in the burrows on the hillsides.
>
> (HOUN III, 515)

Lawrence Frank notes, "Watson apparently sees in Selden proof that atavism occurs, that it is organic in its causes and can produce a freak like the Notting Hill murderer, a physiological and moral reversion to a past type."[10] The concern about atavism had been solidified by the theories of criminality of the Italian physician turned criminologist, Cesare Lombroso (1835–1909), whose work, we are told, had influenced Conan Doyle. Lombroso used statistics, cranial measurements, a form of physiognomy, and what he called "forensic phrenology" to conclude that criminals exhibited physiognomic characteristics and deformities, as well as atavistic propensities, such as long, ape-like arms. Although Dr. Lombroso advocated the humane treatment of criminals and argued against capital punishment, his theories have since been debunked as sexist, racist, and unscientific.[11] Like many evolutionists working before the development of the science of genetics, he was hindered by the assumption that evolution was a progression from lower forms of life to higher forms, and that there was an active force that could pull us back into the past. In *The Hound of the Baskervilles* especially we see, according to John and James Kissane, the fear that "civilization itself has at best a precarious hold on its hard-won position,"[12] an idea that fed the ill-disguised uneasiness provoked by Darwinian theories in the late-Victorian world. The Kissanes remind us that the detective story can be viewed as "having been born of nineteenth-century 'scientism'" (355). That is, many of the mysteries these stories solve are similar to the kinds of "mysteries" solved by the pseudo-sciences, mysteries that don't in fact exist, and to that extent the "scientific" solutions offered by the theories are extensions of irrationality rather than battles against it. My specific claim here is that the solution to a number of the MacGuffins in *A Study in Scarlet* and *The Hound of the Baskervilles* are embedded in the semi-secret anxiety at the end of the Victorian period about the possibility of atavism.

There was another secret fear in the Victorian *fin de siècle* that would not dare to appear overtly as the theme of a MacGuffin in Conan Doyle's fiction, and that is the *fear of homosexuality* – sometimes a secret fear about oneself, or sometimes about others, if they were family members or objects of romantic affection. Homosexuality was deemed a criminal activity, but it is difficult to imagine a Sherlock Holmes adventure that would end with Holmes's revelation that one of the characters is in fact gay – and therefore a criminal. This is not the kind of criminal mystery that Sherlock Holmes solved. It is likely that private detectives were occasionally hired in order to "out" closeted homosexuals in Holmes's London, but no such quest in the Holmes canon would deal with what Lord Alfred Douglas famously dubbed "the love that dare not speak its name." Conan Doyle's audience would not have received such a story happily; indeed, it is unlikely that the *Strand* magazine would have published one in the first place. Conan Doyle was an acquaintance of Oscar Wilde's, and in his autobiography he wrote of Wilde's trial: "I thought at the time, and still think, that the monstrous development which ruined him was pathological, and that a hospital rather than a police court was the place for its consideration."[13]

Although it is difficult to believe that Conan Doyle *meant* for his readers to speculate about Holmes's sexual orientation, it is nonetheless the case that many do. As Klinger states, Holmes's "sexuality is virtually unmentioned in the Canon" (note 33 to BLUE, I, 210). Holmes and Watson live in adjacent rented rooms with a separate entrance above the larger common room that serves as their living and dining space and as Holmes's workplace. Watson marries Mary Morstan, a client of Holmes's in "*The Sign of the Four*" (1890), and moves out from 221B Baker Street to live with her. In the opening story of the collection published after Holmes returns from his first "death," Watson tells him of his own recent bereavement and Holmes displays his sympathy ("The Adventure of the Empty House" [published in 1903; set in 1894]). All readers assume that Conan Doyle is announcing the death of Mary Morstan as Watson moves back into the Baker Street apartment with Holmes. In two later stories ("The Adventure of the Illustrious Client" [published in 1924; set in 1902] and "The Adventure of the Blanched Soldier," [published in 1926; set in 1903]), a second wife is rather mysteriously mentioned, but she has no obvious effect on the relations between detective and physician – nor, apparently, on their living arrangement. The Holmes adventures are certainly stories "between men," and there is a distinctively homosocial relation between them, though arguably no more than that between other fictional avengers and their sidekicks (the Lone Ranger and Tonto, Batman and Robin, Don Quixote and Sancho Panza, et al.). Nevertheless, Graham Robb, in *Strangers: Homosexual Love in the Nineteenth Century*, decisively declares: "Everyone already knows, instinctively, that Holmes is homosexual."[14] Well, if we had read the pornographic gay novel, *The Sexual Adventures of Sherlock Holmes*,[15] whose jacket cover claims it to be a recently discovered manuscript found in a secret drawer of Dr. Watson's cabinet, without our realizing that it was *not* written by either Watson or Conan Doyle, we would have no doubt about Holmes's sexuality. Even if we had other reasons to believe that Sherlock and Watson were occasionally intimate, most of us today would not be shocked by that discovery. We must remember, however, that in Conan Doyle's day, keeping that knowledge to ourselves in the case of a real-life detective and his companion would involve us in a conspiracy of silence: that of concealing knowledge of criminal activity.[16]

Finally, on this topic of ill-kept secret anxieties motivating the Holmes stories, which in turn fueled those very anxieties, I will discuss a story written by Conan Doyle about which he had immediate regrets, apparently feeling that he had crossed a forbidden line. "The Adventure of the Cardboard Box," published in the *Strand* magazine in January 1893, has been called "[e]asily the darkest tale in the entire Canon" (Klinger's preface, CARD I, 422). In it, a young woman receives a packet containing two severed ears. The horrified recipient informs the police, who can make no sense of this grotesque joke. Inspector Lestrade of Scotland Yard asks Sherlock Holmes to help him discover to whom these body parts belonged, how and why they had been removed, and why this young woman had been chosen to receive them. These are the story's MacGuffins, but apparently Conan Doyle himself came to realize that their resolution revealed information concerning late-Victorian society that his audience would find disturbing. Many of the Holmes stories involve murder, but this one in addition involves alcoholism, betrayal of one sister by another, and adultery that provokes a murder of revenge by the offended husband. The husband catches his wife and her lover in a rowboat, smashes an oar into the head of the lover ("crushed his head like an egg" [CARD I, 447]), and stabs his wife with a knife as she clings, sobbing, to the body of her lover. The enraged murderer cuts an ear from each of his victims before tying their bodies to their boat and sinking it. He correctly blames his dead wife's older sister for turning his wife against him after he has rejected the sister's sexual advances, and, after the murders, he retaliates against that sister by sending the gory souvenir to her. However, the packet is mistakenly opened by a third sister who knows nothing about these ghastly events. Having admitted his guilt, the husband will surely be hanged, but Watson withholds from his readers the murderer's fate, perhaps knowing that some of his readers will react to such an ending to the story feeling that another injustice has been committed. The final lines are spoken by Holmes:

> "What is the meaning of it, Watson?" said Holmes, solemnly, as he laid down the paper. "What object is served by this circle of misery and violence and fear? It must tend to some end, or else our universe is ruled by chance, which is unthinkable. But what end? There is a great standing perennial problem to which human reason is as far from an answer as ever."
>
> (CARD I, 448)

If the goal of the Holmes stories is to convince his readers that reason can grasp all mysteries and that therefore the world is controllable, as many critics assert, then, according to Christopher Metress, "The Adventure of the Cardboard Box" subverts "everything . . . Conan Doyle was trying to achieve in the Holmes tales."[17] Holmes might well have agreed with the rationalist's dictum, "The real is the rational and the rational is the real."[18] If so, then the horror of the opposite – "our universe is ruled by chance" – would have eradicated any optimism about reason's ability to fathom everything. Many of Conan Doyle's readers had hoped that this metaphysical problem had been resolved and were not happy to hear that it had not – that even their great hero feared the answer. If this was so, it was information that they would have preferred not to know. Its deep pessimism was more than they had bargained for. The solving of the mystery in "The Cardboard Box" (that is, the elimination of its key MacGuffins) seemed to have torn the veil from structural secrets that were best left concealed: wife-murder was a reality but one not one extensively discussed;[19] sisterhood was not pure and sacred, as the Victorian myth assured them it was;[20] alcoholism was endemic, as was adultery; good intentions could lead to unhappiness, murder and misery; families could be destroyed by hatreds generated by family dynamics; horrible violence could seem morally justified; vicious chance could trump reason.

The Memoirs of Sherlock Holmes (1894), comprising his stories to date in book form, was to come out the year following the publication of "The Cardboard Box." Conan Doyle saw to it that this story was not included in *The Memoirs*, but the American edition did come out with all twelve stories, including "The Cardboard Box." Klinger observes: "almost immediately afterward, however, a 'new and revised' Harper edition appeared that, like the British edition, omitted 'The Cardboard Box'" (Klinger, note 1, CARD I, 422). It seems that Conan Doyle decided to keep secret the existence of this distressing story; its own internal disturbing revelations prompted Conan Doyle to suppress its subsequent publication. If there was ever a Victorian story whose secret needed to be hidden, this is it.

In chapter 2 I referred to Foucault's theory in *The History of Sexuality* that, in the nineteenth century, rather than repression of sexuality there was a "veritable discursive explosion" (17) about sex. I evinced some doubts about the applicability of that theory to Charlotte Brontë's *Villette*. Foucault develops this claim in such a way that the "discursive explosion" is allowed to include "silences" that are "an integral part of the strategies that underlie and permeate discourses" about sex (27). Perhaps Foucault's claim can be more successfully employed in reading some of the Holmes stories. I will follow Catherine Belsey's discussion of Conan Doyle's "The Adventure of Charles Augustus Milverton,"[21] in *The Return of Sherlock Holmes*, a story published in 1904, hence slightly outside the strict parameters of the Victorian era, but also slightly inside it, as the episode described takes place sometime before the *fin de siècle*. Here we have another tale of attempted blackmail. Belsey points out that Watson opens his history apologizing for the "reticence" of the narrative, claiming that it is possible to publish this story only at the current moment because "the principal person concerned is beyond the reach of human law" (MILV II, 1006), so that finally "and with due suppression the story may be told in such a fashion as to injure no one."[22] Watson continues: "The reader will excuse me if I conceal the date or any other fact by which he might trace the actual occurrence" (MILV II, 1006). Belsey asks, "Besides the date, what has been suppressed in the story? What secrets withheld?" (102). We know the name of the blackmailer (in fact, the *eponymous* blackmailer, as his name titles the story); we know the name of the blackmailed, Lady Eva Blackwell; and the identity of the nobleman, the Earl of Dovercourt, who will certainly not marry Lady Eva if he ever sees the contents of the purloined letter that will damage her reputation. Belsey writes:

> Indeed, Watson apparently publishes these names and that fact without hesitation of compunction. What, then, has Watson refused to tell us? Apparently, what he "withholds" is something he does not know himself, namely, the sexual content of the letters that Lady Eva wrote to "an impecunious young squire in the country."
>
> (Belsey, 104)

Holmes has chosen not to reveal this content, though he does say that the letters are "imprudent, . . . nothing worse" (MILV II, 1010). In a deft move, Belsey associates this suppression of the sexual message with the more general suppression of the nature of female sexuality itself – of "shadowy, mysterious, and often silent women [whose] silence repeatedly conceals their sexuality, investing it with a dark and magical quality which is beyond the reach of knowledge" (Belsey 104). Indeed, there are six women mentioned in the story: Lady Eva, whom Milverton tries to blackmail; Agatha, Milverton's servant, whom Holmes, disguised as a plumber, rapidly courts and betroths in order to find where in his mansion Milverton has hidden the purloined letters; a certain Miss Miles, whose wedding was suspended after she refused to pay Milverton – a refusal that provokes him to make incriminating love letters available to her fiancé. There is a Countess d'Albert, who abuses her unnamed maid, a maid who, motivated by a desire for revenge, agrees to meet Milverton to sell him compromising letters in the possession of the Countess. There is a mysterious woman dressed as if she is Countess d'Albert's servant, but who in fact has been a victim of Milverton's blackmail schemes, and has come to kill him, which she does, unloading all the cartridges of her revolver into his body – an act to which suddenly Holmes and Watson are made unwilling witnesses, hiding as they are behind a heavy curtain in the murdered man's house, after having broken in to steal the purloined letters.

Belsey has indeed located another Victorian secret in the stories of Conan Doyle, a secret of the type that I am calling structural. In this story, and in others, according to Belsey, hidden behind the plot-driving secrets is often the secret of female sexuality. There is even a hint in "Milverton" that Sherlock-the-plumber has more knowledge of Agatha than he has told to Watson. He says, "I have walked with her each evening, and have talked with her. Good heavens, those talks!" (MILV II, 1016). Here, the innuendos and "strategic silences" could well be interpreted as evidence of the aptness of the Foucauldian formula. Female sexuality is a secret in the Victorian world only because it had been deemed a secret – another mystery in broad daylight (Sartre) – a secret whose secret is that there is no secret (Goffman).

With her symptomatic reading of the Sherlock Holmes stories, Belsey believes she has ferreted out another component of late-Victorian ideology in the Holmes stories, the promotion of positivism, and its own deconstruction. However, it was Conan Doyle himself (or Watson, the "presumed author") who let the cat out of the bag concerning the vulnerability of positivistic science long before Belsey did so. Belsey herself quotes one such moment. Holmes berates Watson concerning that which he "deplores" in Watson's "narratives": "Your fatal habit of looking at everything from the point of view of a story instead of as a scientific exercise has ruined what might have been an instructive . . . series of demonstrations" (GRAN II, 1160). Therefore, by insisting on narrative concerns rather than the scientific ones, it was Watson's deconstructive project and not Belsey's that demoted positivistic science. No "new meanings" need to be produced (Belsey's stated goal of good literary criticism) to understand what is happening here. Belsey's conception of ideology requires that its mechanism function unconsciously, and not as an intentional part of writing, yet Conan Doyle clearly is in control of his narrative strategy in this case (or he puts Watson in control of it). This is not to say that it never escapes his control. As I mentioned earlier, such a breakdown may have taken place at the ending of "The Cardboard Box," where Holmes's methods, science itself, and ideology all fail to prevent despair, defeat, and moral horror. As we saw, Conan Doyle's only remedy in that case was to try to withdraw the story from circulation.

Another narrative secret over which Watson (and perhaps Conan Doyle) loses control is one of the foremost secrets of the canon, the "secret" of Holmes himself. Who is this misogynistic individual who is shattered when a female felon outsmarts him, who plays the violin symptomatically, lapses into mind-numbing drug use, stays awake many a night, leads a young woman to believe he is about to propose – all the while milking her for information, and perhaps more – performs scientific experiments with corpses, and seems to have almost supernatural powers? These are habits that don't add up. It is as if the entire Holmes canon is about Watson's trying (unsuccessfully) to penetrate his partner's secret. Would Watson tell us if he figured it out? In the final analysis, Holmes is more like Lucy Snowe than is any other fictional character dealt with in this study. In both cases we feel that there are genuine depths that remain unplumbed and cannot be reduced to Goffmanian performance. Is it possible to admire a pathological condition? In Holmes's case the secret in question is not a MacGuffin: it is a structural feature of the entire canon.

Nevertheless, the earlier examples of MacGuffins in the Sherlock Holmes stories demonstrate, I hope, that these plot-driving secrets are frequently couched in contexts that reveal certain typical Victorian anxieties, some of which were rarely discussed in public forums but all of which were well-known types of secrets – secrets in broad daylight (Goffman's "latent secrets" [144]). Even though the plot-driving secrets in the Holmes stories derive from these latent secrets, the resolution of the questions posed in the MacGuffins usually does not go far toward dealing with these anxieties. Therefore, the very existence of these anxieties seems to test Holmes's assertion that a thorough application of his method will eliminate secrecy from human interaction. I will now turn to the question of whether Sherlock Holmes believed that his methods did indeed spell the end of secrecy – including, apparently, the type of semi-secret we have just inspected.[23]

"You know my methods":[24] the omniscience of rationalism

Has Arthur Conan Doyle imagined an epistemological method for Holmes that, if correctly applied, would represent the end of secrecy? For those who have mastered these methods, would no secret interior world exist, hence no logical possibility of successful lies, deceit, pretense, or dissimulation? Is the outer, correctly read, the expression of the inner? To answer these questions, I must involve us in what may initially appear to be a rather extraneous side-trip into aspects of the history of philosophy, but I believe such an excursion has the benefit of establishing the kind of theory of knowledge that Conan Doyle has developed for his main character. By probing Sherlock Holmes's epistemological commitment we will be able to see why he claims that his theory spells the veritable end of secrecy – a thesis that, if true, either means that individuality and society themselves come to an end, according to the theories of Georg Simmel and Erving Goffman, or it refutes the sociology of secrecy found in the works of these sociologists, and therefore also refutes the thesis of my own book. Either way, we will be left with another question: Does a large segment of the late-Victorian reading public approve of

Holmes's project of ushering in an age of total transparency? Does it want a real Sherlock Holmes?

Though there may be "no systematic statement of [Holmes's method] in the canon,"[25] the epistemological theory – and its implied metaphysical theory (as opposed to a merely practical one) that justifies Holmes's method – is presented in a robust manner to Dr. Watson and his readers. Watson, in a state of irritable boredom as he awaits his breakfast, picks up a magazine and commences to read an article that catches his eye because someone had underlined certain passages with a pencil. Watson tells us, "The reasoning was close and intense, but the deductions appeared to me to be far-fetched and exaggerated" (STUD III, 39). Its apparently pseudonymous author claimed to be able,

> by a momentary expression, a twitch of a muscle or a glance of an eye, to fathom a man's inmost thoughts. *Deceit, according to him, was an impossibility in the case of one trained to observation.* . . . "From a drop of water," said the author, "a logician could infer the possibility of an Atlantic or a Niagara without having seen or heard of one or the other. So all life is a great chain, the nature of which is known whenever we are shown a single link of it. Like all other arts, the Science of Deduction and Analysis is one which can only be acquired by long and patient study, nor is life long enough to allow any mortal to attain the highest possible perfection in it."
>
> (STUD III, 39, emphasis added)

Watson, who takes umbrage at the pretentiousness of the magazine article – "What ineffable twaddle!" he cries – is surprised to learn its provenance. Holmes laconically reveals, "As for the article, I wrote it myself" (STUD III, 41).

The practical claims Holmes makes remind us of those boasted of by Monsieur Paul Emanuel in *Villette*, but philosophically they run much deeper than M. Paul's Jesuitical strategies. They are more metaphysical in nature and find their closest analogy in the great rationalistic philosopher, mathematician, and logician Gottfried Leibniz (1646–1716). The features of Leibniz's theories that are pertinent here are roughly these: All true propositions are linked logically to one another. A Perfect Logician (that is, God) would be able to deduce any proposition from any other. So, *sub specie aeternitatis* – from the perspective of eternity, namely, God's point of view – the proposition, "It rained in Paris at noon, June 4, 1700," could be deduced from the proposition, "The sun shone brightly in Berlin at noon, June 3, 1700." In real life, human science must trace these kinds of connections causally: in this case, talking about prevailing winds, high and low barometric pressure zones, and concentrations of humidity. However, according to Leibniz, *sub specie aeternitatis*, the two propositions stand in the same relationship as the mathematical fact that from the proposition, "$2 \times 3 = 6$," it can be deduced that "$2 \times 6 = 12$." Thus akin to Holmes's assertion:

> The ideal reasoner would, when he has once been shown a single fact in all its bearings, deduce from it not only all the chain of events which led up to

it, but also all the results that would follow from it. . . . Problems may be solved in the study which have baffled all those who sought a solution by aid of their senses.

(FIVE I, 150)[26]

It is here that we find deduction in its strictest form. Leibniz realized that his theory was not self-evidently true to human logicians in the case of propositions he called "contingent" (and contemporary philosophers call "synthetic propositions": those propositions that scientists and laypersons can prove only by empirical observation.) He did not claim that scientists would someday be able to occupy the perspective *sub specie aeternitatis*; nevertheless, he did support his theory that ultimately all truths are necessary truths by developing a metaphysics showing what the ultimate nature of reality must be if every fact is logically linked to every other fact.[27]

Because this schema results in a thoroughly determined universe, it left Leibniz, a Christian, struggling to prove that the concept of free will could have any meaning in his system.[28] It should have provoked a comparable concern in the mind of Sherlock Holmes as well. Holmes's analogous theory does not involve a deity, and so is completely human, though, as we saw in the passage cited earlier from *A Study in Scarlet*, Holmes admits that a single life is not long enough "to allow any mortal to attain the highest possible perfection" in the mastery of the techniques that follow from this theory. As noted earlier, the human being who replaces Leibniz's God in Holmes's metaphysics is called by Holmes "the ideal reasoner." Notice the contrast Holmes makes here between knowledge acquired "by the aid of the senses" (*a posteriori* knowledge) and knowledge acquired by logical deduction (*a priori* knowledge), and the priority given to the latter category, as in Leibniz.

In the history of Western philosophy, the orientation that favors *a priori* reasoning over *a posteriori* reasoning (i.e., logic and mathematics over the data of the five senses) has been called rationalism. Based on these philosophical definitions, the prioritizing of logic over sense impressions in Holmes's article would definitely place Holmes in the rationalist camp, with Leibniz. The orientation that favors *a posteriori* reasoning (i.e., knowledge derived from observation) has been called empiricism.[29] Holmes seems to be aligning himself with rationalism when in "The Adventure of the Copper Beeches" (1892) he speaks of "those faculties of deduction and of logical synthesis which I have made my special province" (COPP I, 351). In the same story, he maligns his reading public for not caring about "the finer shades of analysis and deduction" (COPP I, 353). This tendency is supported in *A Study in Scarlet* when he describes the process of his reasoning, saying, "the whole thing is a chain of logical sequences without a break or flaw" (STUD III, 200). Therefore, when in "A Scandal in Bohemia" Holmes chides Watson by saying, "You see, but you do not observe" (SCAN I, 10), he gives the word "observation" a special meaning, contrasting it with the empiricist's idea of observation as the reception of sensorial data.

Outside of philosophy, the terms "rationalism" and "empiricism" have been used to evoke broader contexts. Some critics call Sherlock Holmes an empiricist and others call him a rationalist, and sometimes he is called both at once.[30] Probably the truth is that Holmes is a rationalist in the strict sense of the word, but also has great respect for a certain kind of observation. Ronald R. Thomas credits Holmes (Conan Doyle) with what in my mind amounts to a rationalist insight concerning observation. There is no innocent eye to which epistemologists should return, as in the empirical tradition; rather, there are "ways of seeing," to borrow the title of the well-known book by John Berger.[31] Thomas himself attributes this epistemological breakthrough to the invention of the camera. According to Thomas, Holmes's vision (supported by the methods used with the new invention) "is not innocent or objective, but is 'deduced,' reasoned out, rationalized, managed. It is the product of a certain way of knowing" (134–35). This is, of course, a way of making known what was secret before. Rather than making sense data the foundation of his knowledge, as empiricists do, Holmes realizes that there are *a priori* decisions that can be made in advance of "seeing," and, with practice and skillful application, these decisions actually change the observed data, just as, when he assumes his slightly paranoid perspective, he can read the private thoughts of others, thereby "drawing the veil from men's motives and actions" (SCAN I, 5). Much to Watson's amazement, Holmes deduces from his inspection of a lost hat that its owner is highly intellectual, has fallen on evil days, has succumbed to some bad influence – probably drink – his wife has ceased to love him, but he has nevertheless retained some degree of self-respect. The hat's owner goes out little, is out of training entirely, has grizzled hair that he has cut in the last few days, and that he anoints with lime-cream, it is extremely improbable that his home has gas lighting, and, when he lost his hat, he was bringing home a goose "as a peace offering to his wife" (BLUE I, 201–3). Watson examines the hat and sees nothing but an old hat. But, to Holmes, the deduction is elementary.

I do not want to overdevelop the image of Sherlock Holmes as a philosophical rationalist. It is clear that there is a kind of eclecticism in Holmes's methods and, as a detective if not as a philosopher, he dips often into a bag of tricks that can hardly be limited to the tools of rationalism. He is prepared to enlist the insights not only of Lombroso and Bertillon[32] but of phrenology (Holmes says to Watson that Dr. Mortimer, whose specialty is "knowledge of human skulls" – i.e., phrenology – is "a colleague after our own heart" [HOUN III, 417]),[33] as well as physiognomy and pathognomy ("the reading of emotions from facial expressions")[34] into his procedures. He resorts to imagination ("'See the value of imagination,' said Holmes" [SILV I, 405]), and to intuition ("I have a kind of intuition that way" [STUD III, 42]). Perhaps more shocking to a rationalist such as Kant, whose categorical imperative condemns all lying, Holmes has few qualms about prevaricating in order to extract hidden information,[35] engaging in "fraudulent imitation" [RESI I, 622], or hiring "six dirty scoundrels" – the famous "Baker Street boys" or "Baker Street Irregulars" – to follow people, intimidate them, and obtain information about them (STUD III, 97). He also disguises himself, impersonates others (as in "A Scandal in Bohemia" and "The

Man with the Twisted Lip"), or even commits crimes, as we saw in "Charles Augustus Milverton."³⁶

In addition to these tricks that would never be found in a rationalist's handbook, I have, I must admit, found no biographical hints that Conan Doyle was impressed by Leibniz's metaphysics, nor even that he had ever read Leibniz's philosophy. Leibniz's name appears in none of the indexes of the fifteen biographies of Conan Doyle I have inspected (and in neither of the "biographies" of Sherlock Holmes himself).³⁷ I suspect that the distinct similarity between Leibniz's theory of analyticity and that of Sherlock Holmes is a coincidence but, I want to claim, an instructive one. Nevertheless, because Conan Doyle wrote so fast and furiously, it appears to me that there are enough contradictions in Holmes's dicta that no single completely consistent theoretical position can be attributed to him. For example, despite his derogation of investigators who depend too much on the senses (see earlier), Holmes advocates approaching each case with "an absolutely blank mind" (CARD I, 439), which sounds very much like the theory of the mind as a *tabula rasa*, advocated by John Locke, the foundation of early modern empiricism. Again, he seems close to that Lockean view when he tells Watson, "It is a capital mistake to theorize before one has data" (SCAN I, 11). Perhaps he presents this idea in a more justifiable – though also more trivial – manner when he later explains to Watson "how dangerous it is to reason from insufficient data" (SPEC I, 257). (What empiricist *or* rationalist could disagree with this?)

Holmes's rationalism is revealed in his more thoughtful theoretical considerations when he recognizes that so-called data are often context-laden and must be viewed as possibilities and not certain truths; exactly which context is the correct one to provide a perspicacious view is determined by reason rather than by the psychopathology of everyday life (common sense). Indeed, he tells Watson, "There is nothing more deceptive than an obvious fact" (BOSC I, 108). Similarly, he informs Watson:

> Circumstantial evidence is a very tricky thing. It may seem to point to one thing, but if you shift your own point of view a little, you may find it pointing in an equally uncompromising manner to something entirely different.
> (BOSC I, 107–8)

Holmes appears to maintain an *a priori* wariness about the significance of any material fact. We can get at this wariness by asking, what is the difference between a fact and a clue? Usually, I think, we would say a fact – something that is the case – can become a clue only in an environment of suspicion, or at least, of investigation. (Noticing that there is peanut butter in a jar is not the same as having detected a clue; noticing peanut butter on a dead man's fingers may be the discovery of a clue.) By adopting a nearly paranoid perspective, Holmes has learned to see almost all facts as clues. His suspicions concerning sensorial data seem to bring him back toward rationalism. For Holmes, the fact that a dog does not bark in the night is a clue to the fact that the dog's owner is the murderer,³⁸ as is the fact that a man's hat is unbrushed is a clue that his wife no longer loves him (BLUE I, 201).

We see what may be an example of this phenomenon in an exchange between Watson and Holmes:

WATSON: You speak of danger. You have evidently seen more in these rooms than was visible to me.
HOLMES: No, but I fancy that I may have deduced a little more. I imagine that you saw all that I did.
(SPEC I, 252)

Holmes's slightly paranoid sensitivity allows him to see important signs in what others would think of as useless detail, such as his ability to distinguish "the ashes of 140 different varieties of pipe, cigar, and cigarette tobacco" (BOSC I, 126).

The critical concern about the relation between theory and observed fact in Holmes's investigative approach was intensified with the publication in 1983 of a book edited and contributed to by Umberto Eco and Thomas A. Seboek, *The Sign of Three: Dupin, Holmes, Peirce*, mentioned earlier. Almost every discussion of Holmes's methods since that time alludes to material from the Eco-Seboek book. Most of the essays in the anthology discuss Holmes's method in terms of the concept of "abduction," a term coined by the American philosophical logician Charles S. Peirce, a category that the contributors to *The Sign of Three* append to Holmes's usual categories of deduction, induction, and analysis. Despite the patently false asseveration of Sherlock Holmes, "I never guess. It is a shocking habit" (SIGN III, 224),[39] abduction is a kind of scientific guessing in which some important historical scientists have excelled. Massimo Bonfantini and Giampaolo Prioni, two Italian critics who appear in *The Sign of Three* and equate abduction with hypothesis, have this to say about the process of abduction: "A detective is a riddle-solver, not an interpreter of 'opaque' facts. His art of abduction must thus belong to puzzle-solving and not to hermeneutics."[40]

If Bonfantini and Prioni are right concerning Holmes's technique as puzzle-solving – as they seem to me to be – then we have by implication another indication that, ultimately, *in Holmes's model there are no secrets*. If we are presented with the problem: "$3 + 2 = X$; solve for X," X is not a secret but rather simply a problem to be solved. It is true that in order to solve his puzzles, Holmes must force secrets out of both his clients and criminals who have victimized his clients, but his job is not to reveal secrets but to establish logical and causal chains of events – to show that, in theory at least, secrecy is impossible. Deceit is a logical impossibility; nothing can be hidden from reason and (the right kind of) observation. Of course, deceit can be attempted, and may well work on some people, but it cannot work in the world of Sherlock Holmes.

Holmes's (mostly male) readers may have been fascinated by the logical possibility of a world transparent to reason. They may have believed that the Holmes stories, with their glorification of both science and individuality, had finally demonstrated that the religiously begotten secret inner self that had been so important to an older generation of Victorians could now be jettisoned. If so, they must have forgotten that, although Holmes's Leibnizian-like *theory* of logical connections among all facts had finally revealed the secret that there are no secrets, Holmes himself had used the *practice* based on that theory to protect the secrets of his clients. Also, many readers may not have realized that, personally, Conan Doyle was moving ever closer to a belief in a secret realm of spiritualism. Among other things, he supported the claims of two English girls who produced what they claimed to be real photographs they had taken of fairies in their garden.[41]

Another blow to Holmes's apparent omniscience is the easy detection of serious flaws in Holmes's methods and their results; indeed, a number of critics did call attention to mistakes in Conan Doyle's own time.[42] Holmes himself admits to a number of major errors. In "The Adventure of Silver Blaze," Holmes says to Watson, "I made a blunder, my dear Watson – which is, I am afraid, a more common occurrence than anyone would think who only knew me through your memoirs" (SILV I, 389). Holmes had earlier accused Watson of sensationalizing his accounts of Holmes's detective activities (COPP I, 352), and Watson has admitted to being selective, usually picking among Holmes's many cases those of most interest and in which Holmes has had the most success (FIVE I, 133). As Watson says elsewhere, "it is only natural that I should dwell rather upon his successes than upon his failures" (YELL I, 445).

Secrets from Afghanistan and points east

I have argued throughout this book, and especially in the preceding chapter, that in the fiction of the mid-Victorian period there was a tendency to orientalize the very concept of secrecy, a tendency that made secrecy in general more exotic, more erotic, and hence more disturbing in this historical moment. One finds in the Sherlock Holmes stories that this propensity has been carried over into the late-Victorian period. If one chooses to write in a fictional genre that depends heavily on the revelation of secrets – even if these secrets are only MacGuffins (that is, if one chooses to write detective fiction) – then the orientalizing of secrecy adds more excitement to the process of unveiling hidden information.[43]

In "The Man with the Twisted Lip," a major scene occurs in an opium den, and the action of the plot takes place within a stone's throw of that den. In fact this story and the resolution of its mystery have nothing to do with opium and its use. Conan Doyle seems to know perfectly well that he is taking advantage of his readers' fascination with what they take to be Eastern licentiousness and corruption, particularly as represented by the use of opium. He understands that his audience likes secrets (even if only MacGuffins) to have the scent of the Orient in them. In addition to the opium smoke that wafts through a number of stories, we also find in one case a "strangely incongruous" Hindoo servant wearing "a yellow turban, white loose-fitting clothes, and a yellow sash" (SIGN III, 245), who is butler to a man who will soon be murdered – though not before the victim experiences an Oriental "ecstasy of fear" (SIGN III, 248). In his house the "[t]wo great tiger-skins thrown athwart [the carpet] increased the suggestion of Eastern luxury, as did a huge hookah which stood upon a mat in the corner" (SIGN III, 247).

Three adventures commence with crimes that have been committed in India and imported to Britain for Holmes's solution: "The Crooked Man," involving another dastardly British colonel who has served in India; the novel-length adventure *The Sign of the Four*, in which Holmes is almost killed by a poison dart from a blowgun used by an avenging native whom Holmes is then forced to dispatch for his own survival; and "The Adventure of the Speckled Band," in which the evil Dr. Roylott, who practiced medicine in Calcutta before being imprisoned for beating his native butler to death, leaves India and returns to England with a plot to obtain his stepdaughters' money. He kills one of them and tries to kill the other; his "violence of temper approaching to mania . . . had been intensified by his long residence in the tropics" (SPEC I, 234). An Indian swamp adder becomes his murder weapon but, due to Sherlock's intervention, the schemer's plot backfires and he is killed by the snake with which he murdered his one stepdaughter while trying to murder the other. Holmes says of this plot, "The idea of using a poison which could not possibly be discovered by any chemical test was just such a one as would occur to a clever and ruthless man who had had an Eastern training" (SPEC I, 258). This Oriental cunning is reminiscent of that of the evil Almamen in Bulwer-Lytton's *Leila*, and the secrets of Dr. Roylott that Holmes must uncover are orientalized in myriad ways, provoked by the murderer's "long residence in the tropics," and surrounded by Oriental signifiers, including exotic animals from India and a mania developed in the East. Conan Doyle orientalizes secrets in the Holmes stories by placing the mysteries in East Indian contexts, and giving his criminals motives deriving from the East, rendering them at times sensual, and sometimes sinister, but always sensational.

Sherlock Holmes: a loose canon?

Finally, let us take a deeper look into the question of whether the Sherlock Holmes stories work primarily in the service of conservative causes. If so, in what way would "the end of secrecy" support those causes, and how would Holmes's theory of secrecy relate to Simmel's theory? According to Rosemary Jann, "Holmes allows genteel or aristocratic people to escape scandal or the legal repercussions of their wrong-doing, so long as chivalric codes of justice . . . have been served" (Jann 1990, 704).[44] Moreover, it is not simply the "genteel or aristocratic" classes that Holmes succors: he "helps to preserve the security of the middle-class family by protecting its secrets and, in the process, guaranteeing that its wealth will stay within the family" (Jann 1990, 88). Jann summarizes her argument by calling attention to "Holmes's essentially conservative role in maintaining the status quo" (Jann 1990, 74). And it is not only Holmes who plays this role but Watson also: "Like Holmes, Watson can always be counted on to protect family honor and reputation by concealing identity" (Jann 1990, 474).

It is difficult to deny Jann's evidence and the conclusion she draws from it concerning the manner in which the Holmes stories express and perpetuate conservative ideology. However, there is a fly in her ointment. She is misguided in saying that Watson can always be counted on to protect family honor and reputation by concealing identity. By publishing Holmes's adventures, Watson gives everything away: he blows everybody's cover. Watson's publication of Holmes's adventures is as much a part of Conan Doyle's fiction as are the adventures themselves, so when we estimate the political impact of Conan Doyle's fiction, the "fact" that Watson "publishes" these adventures must be taken into consideration. Therefore, if sustaining the privileges of the upper classes requires keeping its secrets, Conan Doyle gives away the store. He reveals to his readers all of the secrets that, according to Jann, sustain the privileges of the "superior" classes. Watson's project of revelation undermines Jann's thesis. The Holmes stories cast doubt on the claim that the superiority of the genteel classes is innate and universal, that their secrets are immune to discovery, that their social identity cannot be successfully simulated, and that they can be counted upon to police themselves. According to Jann, by assuring that Holmes does not reveal these secrets, Conan Doyle's art is in the service of conservative forces (Jann 1990, 704–5). But Conan Doyle *does* allow these secrets to be revealed.[45]

As is usual in these kinds of debates, the story is not quite so simple as to allow an unqualified generalization. We have already inspected Watson's mocking of the xenophobia of the *Daily Telegraph*, whose editorial policy seeks to blame all unsolved crime on outside agitators, foreign criminal gangs, or on Darwin's theory of evolution (STUD III, 92). We have seen that some of the stories leave readers with suspicions about the source of wealth among the moneyed classes (e.g., GLOR I, 187), as they discover that even socially important gentlemen ("these country magnates") can be hiding criminal pasts (REIG I, 575). The military history of Britain sometimes appears tainted, not only in *The Sign of the Four* but elsewhere, as when, in "The Reigate Puzzle," a certain Col. Hayter is introduced, provoking Klinger to identify him in a note as "[p]erhaps the only reputable colonel in the entire Canon" (REIG I, 557). And, a question that persistently resurfaces: if Sherlock Holmes represents the forces of conservatism, why does he defend his addiction to cocaine, opium and morphine? (SIGN III, 214, 224).

The debate over the political implications of the Holmes stories has relevance for the question of the significance of secrecy in Victorian literature. If secrecy's role in Conan Doyle's stories is primarily the protection of the vested interests of the ruling classes, then Simmel's thesis concerning the function of secrecy in the production of individuality and sociality would be seen in a different light in terms of that theory's application to *The Adventures of Sherlock Holmes*, and maybe its application to most detective literature in general. Does the application of Simmel's theories of secrecy to the Holmes stories provide evidence that Simmel's theory is itself conservative? By claiming that secrecy and even deception has social functions, is Simmel justifying the kinds of secrecy that benefit those whose privileges are acquired and maintained at the expense of the unprivileged? Detective fiction appears to be a genre whose narratives require as closure the revelation of criminal secrecy. However, as many critics have pointed out, while Sherlock Holmes makes such discoveries and reveals them, he often guards the secrets of the victims of criminality, that is, guards the secrets of the privileged individuals who were the object of the fictional criminal intent. A Simmelian analysis of such secrecy might necessarily conclude that the social "creativity" of secrets in these cases is that of sustaining an unjust *status quo ante*. Let us consider this challenge.

Conan Doyle's narrator, Dr. Watson, writes stories about the adventures of Sherlock Holmes, his colleague and friend. Holmes and Watson are, of course, fictional personages; the stories that Watson writes are fiction, and the "fact" that Watson writes them and publishes them is also fiction. By extension, the readers to whom Watson directs these stories when he has them "published" are also fictional. Real readers (in Conan Doyle's day and ours) are reading the same stories that Watson's fictional audience reads, but the logic of the narrative strategy dictates that these stories are directed by Watson to his fictional audience, not to us (although the same stories published by Conan Doyle *are* directed to us). None of the secrets that Holmes protects and none that Watson reveals is a secret in the real world. (The King of Bohemia is not in danger of being blackmailed [SCAN]; there never was a Dr. Roylott who killed his stepdaughter with a swamp adder [BLUE]; there never was such a serpent as a "swamp adder," etc.) Holmes himself is only in indirect contact with a reading public, fictional or otherwise. The fictional secrets that Holmes reveals to the fictional authorities, and those that he hides from those authorities, are revealed to Watson's fictional readership through Watson's fictional publication of them, and are revealed to us real readers by Conan Doyle's "usurpation" of those stories. Intentionally or not, Conan Doyle as author places himself in a position twice removed from the secrets his stories reveal: Holmes uncovers the secrets, Watson records them and communicates them to a fictional readership through his fictional publications, and Conan Doyle expropriates those fictional secrets and reveals them to an audience of Victorian and Edwardian readers. If such a reader tries to determine the ideological function of those secrets, Conan Doyle's maneuver forces the reader (and us) to realize that there is no certain answer to the question.

The role of secrecy in Conan Doyle's stories seems to support political conservatism in that many of the secrets of his fictional wealthy clients that Holmes protects are secrets whose revelation would damage the interests of the social classes of which those fictional clients are members. But these clients are after all fictional, so it can't be *their* interests that concern us. The sense in which the role of secrecy in these stories is *not* conservative is that Holmes reveals to Dr. Watson many of these secrets (either by telling them to him or by allowing Watson to participate in the investigations that unveil these secrets), and Watson in turn publishes these secrets to his fictional audience of working members of the middle classes. At the same time, *Conan Doyle* publishes them in the *Strand* magazine to *real* members of the real middle class. Therefore, I think it can be said that the revelation of the fictional secrets in the *Strand* magazine does indeed damage the interests of real members of the wealthy classes, because the readers of the magazine learn the ways in which certain kinds of secrets of the wealthy and the protection of those secrets by paid agents or the authorities creates injustices that go against the interests of the society at large, and, particularly, to the interests of those middle-class readers themselves. If in Conan Doyle's stories Sherlock Holmes often caters to a conservative cause by protecting secrets of the privileged classes who are his usual clients, Dr. Watson undermines those conservative causes by revealing almost all the secrets that Holmes himself tries to protect. Therefore, Conan Doyle has chosen an anti-Simmelian narrative strategy that supports Holmes's fictional attack on all secrecy. Ironically, this attack is not made through Holmes himself, who proves by his actions if not his theory that he does in fact respect secrecy, but through Watson, who proves through his actions that he does not. However, if for internal reasons Conan Doyle's attack on secrecy fails logically, it succeeds aesthetically. Therefore, I conclude that the application of Simmelian sociology to the detective stories of Sir Arthur Conan Doyle does not provide an ideological support for privilege.

Conclusion

I noted earlier some of the similarities between Conan Doyle's fiction and that of Mary Elizabeth Braddon. Still more vital to my general thesis are the commonalities between the Holmes stories and Charlotte Brontë's *Villette* because here, if I am right, we find an ironic philosophical agreement concerning the roles of privacy, secrecy, and their penetration and dissolution. In chapter 2 I argued that, in *Villette*, Brontë had – probably unconsciously – created a dialectic between secrecy and ontological privacy on the one hand, and penetration, discovery, and transparency on the other. Brontë's decidedly dualistic theory of selfhood clearly favors the former, while her privileging the detective skills of her three principal characters – Monsieur Paul, Madame Beck, and Miss Snowe – favors the latter. In the Sherlock Holmes adventures we find a continuation and updating of this same dialectic. With the exception of the Leibnizian epistemology that Conan Doyle bestows on Holmes, the detective's staging of the problem is considerably less metaphysical than Brontë's, more sociological than philosophical, and it certainly is not committed to a profoundly private interiority, but his practice if not his theory does contain a psychology and a defense of a certain kind of secrecy and privacy. In this respect, such a defense brings Conan Doyle close to Simmel and Goffman. However, I think the question to be answered is whether Conan Doyle's defense of privacy and secrecy exhibits a kind of Simmelian sociological theory (according to which secrecy generates individuality and sociation), or whether the skillful and aggressive deployment of the art of detection undermines the defense of privacy and secrecy that both Brontë and Conan Doyle would like to defend. Does Sherlock Holmes after all represent the end of secrecy, and with it, the end of privacy and selfhood?

My discussion of *Villette* concluded that the novel's main character, Miss Lucy Snowe (and perhaps her creator, Miss Charlotte Brontë), held fast to the idea that the distinction between the inner and the outer should be protected at almost any cost (a posture constituting an exaggerated form of Simmelianism). The inner self would remain a private sphere where secrets of the soul would be guarded from penetration by others, and the outer self would consist of layers of armor in the form of strategic reticence, withdrawal, and studied performance, all of which serve to protect the privacy of the inner self. I also concluded that the dualistic metaphysics presupposed by this stance was finally overridden by the powerful detective skills that Brontë bestowed upon Lucy Snowe and the other principal characters of the tale, Monsieur Paul Emanuel and Madame Modeste Beck. The present chapter moves ahead some forty-five years to approach the end of Victoria's reign. My conclusion about the Sherlock Holmes stories of Arthur Conan Doyle is *structurally* similar to that of chapter 2 (that is, its main thesis is undermined by a competing secondary thesis), but that thesis in Dr. Watson's case is inverted. In *Villette*, the promotion of the priority of a secret, private self is defeated by the detective skills of the protagonists; in *The Adventures of Sherlock Holmes* the promotion of detective skills that no secret can withstand is defeated by the privacy and secrecy that the practice of these skills requires.

The eponymous hero in the short stories and novellas of Conan Doyle is an excellent detective – perhaps the best ever. Sherlock Holmes articulates a theory of logical interconnectedness of facts that, in principle, spells the end of secrecy and of all forms of deception, collapses the distinction between inner and outer, and ends the storied metaphysics of the true self as a deep, impenetrable secret place. Holmes develops this theory to explain his extraordinary ability to solve crimes and bring criminals to justice. However, at the same time, Holmes undermines his metaphysics of transparency. He does so, first, because he can only put his theory into practice by stealth, deception, and secrecy. Second, he does so by using that same theory-laden practice to protect the secrets of his clients or others whom he investigates. Third, he sometimes fails to apply his theory to his own practice in ways that produce basic contradictions between the two. Fourth, Sherlock Holmes, like Lucy Snowe, keeps readers of his stories in the dark about his own personal history (perhaps in collusion with John Watson, who admits that he has cherry-picked information that will concentrate on Holmes's successes rather than his failures).

Simmel says that in different societies the content of secrecy changes, but the amount of secrecy remains roughly the same. If this is so, the Holmes stories give us a good idea of the kinds of secrecy that were found to be necessary in late nineteenth century Britain. A study of the dialectics of secrecy in Conan Doyle's stories reveals that the real secrets in the stories are not the MacGuffins – mysteries whose secrets only criminals and subjects of blackmail know and that Holmes must uncover – but the detective's revelations consistently lead to what I have been calling structural secrets, "secrets in broad daylight," and these latter ill-kept secrets often protect privileges of the established powers. In chapter 4, I came to a similar conclusion about *Lady Audley's Secret*, which is also a detective novel of sorts. However, in the case of Conan Doyle's stories, I have argued that it is through the plot-driving secrets that the detective reveals that the semi-secret anxieties of real citizens of late nineteenth-century London are exposed.

Can we apply in good faith Simmel's theory of secrecy to Conan Doyle's project? First, we have seen that if Holmes's "Leibnizian" epistemology is true, then Simmel has been refuted. If the advent of Sherlock Holmes heralds the end of secrecy, then Simmel's thesis about the necessity of secrecy for the development of both individual and social life is false. However, we have seen that Holmes's audacious claim is unsustainable: without the use of secrecy, he is unable to achieve his immediate goal – that of solving the mystery of the MacGuffins in each of his cases; indeed, he not only employs secrecy himself but he strives to *guard* the secrets of his clients. Furthermore, when he does unveil the plot-driving secrets in a particular story, that revelation leaves mostly untouched the structural secret on which the MacGuffins are based. Therefore, Holmes is also unable to realize the implied conclusion of his epistemological theory, that of ending secrecy. In addition, there is no good reason to accept as true Holmes's doctrine of logical determinism (i.e., the doctrine that every proposition is logically related to every other proposition, and that therefore any true proposition could be deduced from any other true proposition). With the exception of Leibniz and possibly Plato,[46] virtually every logician in the history of philosophy and on the contemporary scene rejects this theory. Apparently, even the idea of a universal *causal* determinism has been dealt a serious blow with the development of quantum mechanics. So I think it is safe to say that Conan Doyle has not refuted the theory of secrecy put forth by his contemporary, Georg Simmel.

If Holmes/Conan Doyle has not refuted Simmel's theory, then the application of that theory to Holmes's adventures may prove to be warranted. However, the fact that the Holmes stories are driven primarily by MacGuffins means that the aspect of Simmel's theory that stresses the social creativity of secrecy will be somewhat eclipsed. This is because many of the secrets involved in *The Adventures of Sherlock Holmes* are criminal in nature, and therefore they hide information or activities that are socially disruptive (murder, theft, fraud, bigamy, etc.) in the stories they motivate. Other secrets in these stories have to do with personal or familial embarrassments (false genealogies, latent insanity, illegitimacy, impending bankruptcy, etc.) whose revelation would be destructive to individuals, families, or social units. Neither of these kinds of secrets would normally be designated as *creative*, though there are two important exceptions to this conclusion: (A) First, the revelation of the crimes against members of the middle classes and the nobility helps maintain the *status quo*, as does the guarding of the incriminating, indicting, or humiliating secrets of those same social classes in many of the Holmes stories. The fact that their veiling *perpetuates* an already existing form of social and individual life is constructive in the Simmelian sense. However, the result of this formulation is to make Simmel's theory, as applied to these stories, appear more conservative than he probably meant it to be. (B) The second exception goes against the grain of the first exception. Dr. Watson's revelation to his fictional audience of fictional secrets concerning indictments, embarrassments, and humiliations of members of fictional ruling classes could well provoke real readers (viz., Dr. Conan Doyle's readers) to suspect similar kinds of secrets about the members of the real ruling classes. (After all, Conan Doyle's stories reveal real kinds of class-based secrets to real Victorian readers.) In this sense, the Sherlock Holmes stories can be justifiably called progressive. Despite the tension between (A) and (B), both could be true at the same time. According to specific political and moral standards, the social world that is sustained by the individuals and families that are Holmes's clients may itself merit reformation (or, on at least one Victorian theory, eradication through revolution).

That fact does not challenge the descriptive capability of Simmel's theory. There is another feature of Simmel's theory that sheds more light onto the strange literary figure that Conan Doyle has created, going beyond the eccentricity of Holmes's problem with opium and cocaine, beyond his misogyny, his strange lapses into a near coma as he listens to his clients recount their problems and terrors, and his fear of boredom. We will conclude by looking briefly at that insight.

According to Simmel, social life is based upon "the faith in the honesty of the other" (313). Yet, while we know there is always some information withheld in every interaction with another person, we usually do not know how much deception is involved in any specific encounter. The other person "may intentionally either reveal the truth about himself, or deceive us by lie and concealment" (Simmel 310). Normally sociality can proceed despite this awkwardness. This is part of the precariousness of the social world. The problem is compounded by the fact that moral standards oblige us to maintain a certain amount of discretion when it comes to the quantity of personal information we insist that the other disclose. Discretion obliges us to "stay away from the knowledge of all that the other does not expressly reveal to us" (Simmel 320–21). There is "an ideal sphere [of discretion] around every human being." This sphere cannot be penetrated without challenging the value of the other person. "To penetrate this circle . . . constitutes a violation of . . . personality." It "constitutes a lesion of the ego in its very center" (322).

Now, if we apply these maxims to the case of Sherlock Holmes, we discover that he is a moral outlaw, what Goffman would come to call "a thief of information."[47] In order to do his job Holmes must abandon all discretion. He is professionally obligated to treat everyone with whom he deals as if he were on intimate terms with them, demanding of them total disclosure while at the same time giving away nothing of himself. It is "unbearable" to him if anyone lies or even keeps a secret. To get to the bottom of things he must "insult everyone's honor" and violate everyone's "personality and ego." This makes him an enemy of every person he meets in a professional capacity. Under normal conditions, everyone Holmes encounters withholds some information from him, just as he certainly hides much from them. Everyone must take a stance against Holmes in the form that Simmel calls "aggressive defense" (330), and Holmes must reciprocate. No wonder he is such a strange and almost ghoulish individual. He has this in common with Monsieur Paul Emanuel, and with the sociologists Georg Simmel and Erving Goffman. Therefore, the paradox of Sherlock Holmes's epistemology is an inverted mirror image of Simmel's epistemology: Holmes can end secrecy only by employing methods that are laden with secrecy. Simmel claims that social and individual life are possible only with secrecy, yet, as a sociologist, his methods must violate the very space that, according to his theory, are required for social life to be possible. Similarly, Goffman claims that social interaction can only succeed if falsification is endemic to all social interchange, yet the function of his own work is to expose that falsification.

In sum, despite the theoretical "end of secrecy" achieved in *The Adventures of Sherlock Holmes*, all is well at the end of the century in the world of Victorian fiction from the point of view of a Simmelian-Goffmanian theory: there are still secrets – both socially productive and destructive – there are deceptive performances, and there are strategic points of reticence. Indeed, Conan Doyle's work provides an appropriate framework for analyzing the secrets that his fictions sought to make obsolete. Did Conan Doyle's many readers want "the end of secrecy"? If so, then they did not get their wish. Still, I think it is safe to say that whatever they wanted from Sherlock Holmes, they got.

Notes

1 Joseph A. Kestner, *Sherlock's Sister: The British Female Detective, 1864–1913* (Aldershot: Ashgate, 2003), 13, and Lisa Surridge, "'Are Women Protected?' Sherlock Holmes and the Violent Home," in *Bleak Houses: Marital Violence in Victorian Fiction* (Athens: Ohio University Press, 2005), 216–46, 227.
2 Holmes's second death must have come after Conan Doyle's, as evidently Holmes was still active – or still reactivated – in 1930 at the time of Conan Doyle's death.
3 Rosemary Jann, for example, refers to "the later and less inspired stories" ("Sherlock Holmes Codes the Social Body," *ELH* 57.3 [Autumn 1990]: 685–708, 466). Future references to this article will be cited in the text as "Jann 1990."
4 Arthur Conan Doyle, *The New Annotated Sherlock Holmes*, Volumes 1, 2, and 3, edited with a foreword and notes by Leslie S. Klinger, and with an introduction by John le Carré (New York and London: W.W. Norton, 2005). Hereafter, references to individual stories will be denoted by volume number, using the standardized abbreviations adopted from Jack Tracy, ed., *The Encyclopedia Sherlockiana, or Universal Dictionary of the State of Knowledge of Sherlock Holmes and His Biographer, John H. Watson, M.D.* (Garden City, NY: Doubleday, 1977), xix. (See list of abbreviations at the beginning of this book.) Current reference is to ENGI I, 264.
5 A mystery, as I am using the word here, is a condition that is attributed to a secret or concatenation of secrets when there appears to be no obvious way to reveal these secrets and when attempts to reveal them have failed. This applies to murder-mysteries, and, metaphorically, to "the mysteries of the universe." It also applies to religious mysteries. This is true even if the "secrets" in the religious doctrine turn out to be pseudo-secrets.
6 A point made by Don Richard Cox, *Arthur Conan Doyle* (New York: Ungar, 1985), 81. Roger Anderson makes a similar point: "What Sherlock Holmes Knew and How He Knew It," *Baker Street Journal* 48.2 (June 1998): 9–18, 11. Future references to this work will be cited in the body of the text.
7 Klinger, commenting on this case, writes: "In Victorian England the plight of abused children went largely unaddressed until the late 1880s. The NSPCC (National Society for the Prevention of Cruelty to Children) was established in 1889, with Queen Victoria as its royal patron" (Klinger's n. 26, SPEC I, 240).
8 Nancy Anne Marck, "Drugs, Doubling, and Disguise: Sherlock Holmes and 'The Man with the Twisted Lip,'" in *Unrespectable Recreations*, ed. Martin Hewitt (Leeds: Leeds Centre for Victorian Studies, 2001), 107–16, 111.
9 "With mankind some of the worst dispositions, which occasionally without any assignable cause make their appearance in families, may perhaps be reversions to a savage state, from which we are not removed by very many generations"; "crossed races of man would be eminently liable to revert to the primordial hairy character of their early ape-like progenitors" (Charles Darwin, *The Descent of Man, and Selection in Relation to Sex* [Norwalk, CT: Heritage Press, 1972], 120, 311). For a discussion of Darwin and atavism, see Leila S. May, "'Monkeys, Microcephalous Idiots, and the Barbarous Races of Mankind': Darwin's Dangerous Victorianism," *Victorian Newsletter* 102 (Spring 2003): 20–27.

10 Lawrence Frank, *Victorian Detective Fiction and the Nature of Evidence: The Scientific Investigations of Poe, Dickens, and Doyle* (Basingstoke and New York: Palgrave Macmillan, 2003), 179. Future references to this work will be cited in the body of the text.
11 See Stephen J. Gould's *The Mismeasure of Man* (New York: W. W. Norton, 1996).
12 James Kissane and John M. Kissane, "Sherlock Holmes and the Ritual of Reason," *Nineteenth Century Fiction* 17.4 (March 1963): 353–62, 361. Future references to this work will be cited in the body of the text.
13 Arthur Conan Doyle, *Memories and Adventures* [1924] (London: John Murray, 1930), 95.
14 Graham Robb, *Strangers: Homosexual Love in the Nineteenth Century* (New York and London: W. W. Norton, 2003), 260.
15 Dr. J. Watson, *The Sexual Adventures of Sherlock Holmes* (New York: Traveller's Companion, 1971).
16 Roger Ebert, writing about the 2009 cinematic versions of Holmes (Robert Downey, Jr.) and Watson (Jude Law), says: "Both of them now seem more than a little gay; it's no longer the case of 'Oh, the British all talk like that.'" If Holmes *was* gay, there are still people today who would prefer to keep that fact a secret, including lawyers of the Arthur Conan Doyle estate, who have threatened to revoke Guy Ritchie's rights to a sequel if he "tries any funny business" (Ebert's movie review and the legal warning from the Conan Doyle estate reported by Nikki Gloudeman in *Mother Jones*, "Is Sherlock Holmes Gay?" [posted January 6, 2010, 8:47 pm EST]: http://www.motherjones.com/riff/2010/01/gay-holmes-watson).
17 Christopher Metress, "Thinking the Unthinkable: Reopening Conan Doyle's 'Cardboard Box,'" *Midwest Quarterly: A Journal of Contemporary Thought* 42.2 (Winter 2001): 183–98, 185.
18 G.W.F. Hegel, *Philosophy of Right*, trans. T. M. Knox (Oxford: Clarendon Press, 1949), 10.
19 Lisa Surridge discusses this theme in detail in "'Are Women Protected?,'" 216–47. Surridge argues that the suppression of information about this serious problem allowed the ideology of the husband as protector to flourish. As she points out, "A striking number of Sherlock Holmes stories deal with abuse of women, ranging from coercion and imprisonment to assault and murder" (226).
20 Sisterly love as a key component of Victorian ideology in treated in my *Disorderly Sisters: Sibling Relations and Sororal Resistance in Nineteenth-Century British Literature* (Lewisburg, PA: Bucknell University Press, 2001). See especially chapter 1.
21 Catherine Belsey, *Critical Practice*, 2nd ed. (London and New York: Routledge, 2001), 102. Future references to this work will be cited in the body of the text.
22 Leslie Klinger mentions an issue raised by D. Martin Dakin's *Sherlock Holmes Commentary* (Newton Abbot: David and Charles, 1974), where Dakin points out that Watson is revealing far too many secrets: "Why would Watson risk confessing his and Holmes's illegal activities [breaking and entering, theft] (not to mention their suppression of evidence regarding a murder) at all? Surely he must have realized that legal repercussions were inevitable" (Klinger's note 27 [MILV II, 1032]).
23 If so, then, ironically, Sherlock Holmes should also end detective fiction as a genre.
24 MUSG, I, 549.
25 Marcello Truzzi, "Sherlock Holmes: Applied Social Psychologist," in *The Sign of Three: Dupin, Holmes, Peirce*, ed. Umberto Eco and Thomas A. Seboek (Bloomington: University of Indiana Press, 1983), 55–80, 59. Future references to this work will appear as "Eco 1983" in the body of the text.
26 Leibniz admitted that such logical relationships were self-evident to human logicians only in cases of propositions that he called "necessary" truths, propositions that contemporary philosophers call "analytic truths": definitions or parts of definitions

("squares have four right angles"), arithmetic truths ("2 × 3 = 6"), and logical truths ("if A implies B and B implies C then A implies C").

27 In his ontology, Leibniz posits basic psychic units that he calls "monads" as the foundational forms of reality, and he demonstrates that each monad must contain all of its past and future states (a monad is "pregnant" with its future) (Gottfried Wilhelm von Leibniz, *Monadology and Other Philosophical Essays* [1696], trans. Paul Schrecker and Anne Martin Schrecker [New York: Bobbs-Merrill, 1965], 151).

28 Carlo Ginzburg, in his essay on Sherlock Holmes, also sees a connection between Holmes's form of determinism and Leibniz's, quoting Leibniz's phrase, *"ens omnimodo determinatum"* – "a being is in every way determined" (Carlo Ginzburg, "Clues: Morelli, Freud, and Sherlock Holmes," in Eco and Seboek, *The Sign of Three*, 81–119, 107). Umberto Eco too discusses a connection between Holmes and Leibniz in "Horns, Hooves, Insteps: Some Hypotheses on Three Types of Abduction," in Eco and Seboek, *The Sign of Three*, 198–220, 217–18). Brian Domino discusses Holmes and Leibniz concerning the idea of optimism ("The Thing the Lion Left," in *Sherlock Holmes and Philosophy: The Footprints of a Gigantic Mind*, ed. Josef Steif [Chicago and La Salle, IL: Open Court, 2011], 221–28, 222–25). However, neither Ginzburg, Eco, nor Domino focuses on the connection between Leibniz and Holmes that I develop here, viz., the theory that every true proposition is logically linked to every other true proposition.

29 The primary rationalists in the history of philosophy are Plato in the classical period, and Descartes, Spinoza, Leibniz, and (more or less) Kant in the modern period. In the empiricist camp we find Aristotle (more or less), and Locke, Berkeley and Hume.

30 For example, Rosemary Jann says that "Holmes' rationalism" entails "the strictest empiricism" (Rosemary Jann, *The Adventures of Sherlock Holmes: Detecting Social Order* [New York: Twayne/Macmillan, 1995], 88). Future references to this book will be cited in the body of the text as "Jann, 1995"), and James and John Kissane refer to "Sherlock Holmes in all his rationalism" (Kissane and Kissane, "Sherlock Holmes and the Ritual of Reason," 355), and also to "his rigorous empiricism" (358).

31 John Berger, *Ways of Seeing* (Harmondsworth: Penguin, 1972).

32 In "The Naval Treaty" (1893), Holmes expresses enthusiasm for the work of Alphonse Bertillon (1853–1914), who held criminological views similar in many ways to those of Lombroso – i.e., two pseudo-scientific quacks who impressed Conan Doyle.

33 Theodore Dalrymple denies the phrenological connection, saying:

> Dr. Mortimer's fascination with Holmes's skull is not because of his belief in phrenology – he is not feeling the bumps that supposedly correspond, for example, to fidelity or discretion. . . . On the contrary, Dr. Mortimer is clearly a follower of Cesare Lombroso, the Italian anthropologist and criminologist. . . . Thus Dr. Mortimer is inspecting Holmes to estimate his criminal propensities or otherwise, an irony that would probably have been understood by the story's original readers, for at the time Lombroso was very famous. (Theodore Dalrymple, "Holmes and His Commentators," *New Criterion* 24.3 [November 2005]: 4–8, 8)

34 Jann, "Sherlock Holmes Codes the Social Body," 69.

35 In "The Adventure of the Blue Carbuncle," Holmes lies to the owner of a goose in whose crop a diamond has been found about having eaten the goose himself (I, 208), and he lies to a seller of geese about his reasons for wanting information about the goose's history (I, 214).

36 In SCAN I, 26, Holmes asks Watson, "You don't mind breaking the law?. . . . Nor running the chance of arrest?" Watson does not. In "The Adventure of the Blue Carbuncle," Holmes admits to "commuting a felony" (BLUE I, 224).

37 John T. Irwin, in *The Mystery to a Solution: Poe, Borges, and the Analytic Detective Story* (Baltimore and London: Johns Hopkins University Press, 1994), incorporates Leibniz into his analysis of Poe's "Maelzel's Chess Player," but the issue there is the

mind/body problem and not Leibniz's theory of necessary truth (122–23). Irwin refers to Leibniz again when commenting on Poe's Dupin stories. Here the issue is Poe's and Leibniz's equating mathematical reason with reason itself. Irwin only mentions Sherlock Holmes twice in his book of 464 pages. According to him, Conan Doyle has produced a "caricature" of an analytic detective (1–2). In this respect, Poe's César Auguste Dupin is superior to Conan Doyle's Sherlock Holmes.

38 Police Inspector Gregory: "Is there any other point to which you would wish to draw my attention?"

> Holmes: "To the curious incident of the dog in the night-time."
> Inspector Gregory: "The dog did nothing in the night-time."
> Holmes: "That was the curious incident." (SILV, 411)

39 Michael Chabon, in his review of *The New Annotated Sherlock Holmes*, vols. 1 and 2, refers to Sherlock's "feats of inspired guessing" ("Inventing Sherlock Holmes," *New York Review of Books* 52.2 [February 10, 2005]: 5). In *The Hound of the Baskervilles*, after listening to one of Holmes's labyrinthine deductions, Dr. Mortimer challenges Holmes, saying: We are coming now into the region of guesswork," to which Holmes replies: "Say, rather, into the region where we balance probabilities and choose the most likely. It is the scientific use of imagination, but we always have some material basis on which to start our speculation" (HOUN III, 436).

40 Massimo A. Bonfantini and Giampaolo Proni, "To Guess or Not to Guess?" in Eco and Seboek, *The Sign of Three*, 119–34, 127.

41 Elsie Wright, sixteen, and her younger cousin Frances Griffiths sent a role of film to Kodak that depicted them "frolicking with fairies in front of a waterfall" (Andrew Lycett, *The Man Who Created Sherlock Holmes: The Life and Times of Sir Arthur Conan Doyle* [New York, London, Toronto, and Sydney: Free Press, 2007]), 409. The episode was captured in the delightful film, Charles Sturridge's "Fairy Tale: A True Story" (1997), with Peter O'Toole playing Conan Doyle and Harvey Keitel as Houdini.

42 I will list a few of the most obvious ones (some of which are no doubt Conan Doyle's errors rather than the detective's): Concerning the blue carbuncle that Holmes finds in a goose's crop: "A goose has no crop" (Klinger's note, BLUE I, 224). In one episode, Holmes asks Watson to bring along his gun: "An Elsey's No. 2 is an excellent argument" (SPEC I, 244); however, in note 31, Klinger tells us: "such a make of gun did not in fact exist." In "The Adventure of the Speckled Band," – one of Conan Doyle's most popular stories and his own favorite – Holmes says of a snake who has killed the story's villain, "It is a swamp adder! – the deadliest snake in India. He has died within ten seconds of being bitten" (SPEC I, 256–57). In a note on the same page Klinger points out that there is no such snake, and no snake can kill a human in ten seconds. In this same story Holmes's main hypothesis turns out to be false, and he berates himself for reasoning from insufficient data (SPEC I, 257). In "The Adventure of the Copper Beeches" Holmes's initial hypothesis is also proved false. Klinger writes that the hypothesis "makes no sense in any event" (COPP I, 382). Holmes never seems to get over his main error – being beaten at his own game by Irene Adler in "A Scandal in Bohemia."

43 Rosemary Hennesy and Rajeswari Mohan, writing about "The Speckled Band," say:

> The entangled encoding of the feminine and the Oriental as sexualized other in the Holmes story is an instance of the ways the sexualization of women and Oriental males re-secured patriarchal and imperial interests across a range of class positions. ("'The Speckled Band': The Construction of Woman in a Popular Text of Empire," in *Critical Essays in Sherlock Holmes: The Major Stories with Critical Essays*, ed. John A. Hodgson [Boston and New York: Bedford Books of St. Martin' Press, 1994], 389–401, 400)

44 Two other articulate scholars who view Conan Doyle's work as supporting conservative causes are Jon Thompson, *Fiction, Crime, and Empire: Clues to Modernity and Postmodernism* (Urbana and Chicago: University of Illinois Press, 1993), and Anderson, "What Sherlock Holmes Knew and How He Knew It." For Thompson, Conan Doyle's fiction "ratified the principles and ideologies of an imperial, patriarchal Britain" (75). Anderson insists, "Holmes's conservative task is to guard his culture from splitting off from its idealized roots" (11).
45 Apparently Jann thinks that by protecting the secrets of the middle-class and aristocratic characters in the stories from the knowledge of other characters in the stories, Holmes (and Conan Doyle) are supporting the interests of these classes not only in the stories but in the real world. However, again, precisely what Watson and Conan Doyle have done is to reveal these secrets to individuals in the story (viz., to all those fictitious individuals for whom the fictitious Dr. Watson is supposed to be publishing Holmes's adventures); furthermore, Conan Doyle is revealing to real readers (i.e., the gentlemen reading the *Strand* magazine on the train on their way to work) that the kinds of fictional secrets revealed in his stories may well exist among their social superiors in the real world.
46 I am indebted to Donald D. Palmer for this idea about Plato.
47 Goffman quoted by Malcolm Gladwell in "The Naked Face," *New Yorker* (August 5, 2002): 49.

Afterword

> [N]othing in the world is hidden for ever. . . . the lasting preservation of a secret is a miracle which the world has never yet seen.
> —Wilkie Collins, *No Name*

The sociology of secrecy

The general conclusions that I reached in my investigation have been scattered through the chapters; here, I will summarize some of the more salient points. First, I have determined that in Victorian fiction there is a form of radical dualism that I am calling neo-Cartesian, according to which the mind (or soul) and the body each has a dramatically different ontological status from the other substance, and in which the spiritual component is prioritized over the material. This dualism, as we have seen, is most conspicuous in Charlotte Brontë's *Villette*. It also appears prominently in Dickens's work, especially in *David Copperfield*, which I have briefly discussed. Hints of this radical dualism also appear in Mary Elizabeth Braddon's *Lady Audley's Secret*, and, indeed, throughout the Victorian world. What makes this view more Victorian than Cartesian – and, what makes it an object of interest in this book – is that this true self is deemed to be a secret self, one of deep spirituality, and one that requires vigilant protection against worldly intrusions, and even against access by other individuals. Complete revelation threatens to destroy the very object that was revealed: the self.

However, at the same time as the priority of the secret self is being touted, an opposite tendency develops in Victorian fiction that undermines and devalues the reign of the secret self, or even denies its existence. This secondary tendency is strongly seen in *Vanity Fair*, in *The Adventures of Sherlock Holmes*, and, curiously, in *Villette* itself, where Brontë bestows on Lucy Snowe and her colleagues great powers of observation whose scrutiny dissolves the inner/outer distinction on which Brontë elsewhere insists. This tendency will become more dominant in later nineteenth-century and early twentieth-century fiction than will the spiritual one. Perhaps the idea of a secret spiritual self is in its last throes in the mid-Victorian period.

Lucy Snowe's version of what fifty years later would become a Simmelian axiom about the necessity of secrecy in the creation of both subjectivity and sociality is certainly *in extremis*. Animus against the excessiveness of her view by twenty-first-century critics does not damage Simmel's axiom. In other ways, Simmel supports Brontë's ontological views. Lucy Snowe's case is an excellent example of Simmel's claim that the "parallel world" opened up by secrecy creates a private escape from the constraints and miseries of social life and thereby helps determine subjectivity.

The American philosopher Martha Nussbaum has championed the thesis that fiction is "indispensable to a philosophical inquiry into the ethical sphere," offering as it does "sources of insight without which the inquiry cannot be complete."[1] This is a bold claim, but it is trumped by several Victorian novelists who presume that fiction can reveal not only moral but *metaphysical* secrets about the human condition. In several cases my study reveals a radical metaphysical thesis presented by a narrator who seems to imply that this truth is already known by most readers in some subliminal manner. This knowledge is secret in that people avoid discussing it outright, and often have failed to confront its implications directly (roughly, Goffman's "*latent secrets*"). Apparently novels provide opportunities for bringing this sub-rosa information into the harsh light of midday. We see a dramatic example of this in *Lady Audley's Secret*, when the narrator articulates the secret in broad daylight whose truth she assumes everyone will recognize: namely, that we are all close to madness. The very nature of the human mind in its relation with the world of commonplace material objects results in the descent into lunacy of each of us at one time or another. However, this shocking secret disclosed by Braddon's narrator is upstaged by Thackeray's narrator, who reveals *two* such metaphysical secrets (again, secrets that we may all have suspected). First, there is the bad news that we are all Becky Sharp; that is, we are all "straightforward maximizers," pretending to be "constrained maximizers," in Gauthier's words, and that therefore we all still must struggle in that war of each against all that we hoped had been left behind when our forebears left "the state of nature." However, rather than abandoning this war, we have imported it into the world of sociality – that is, into "Vanity Fair" – in more subtle and sophisticated forms than those crude ones we encountered in the primal state. Those secrets revealed in Thackeray's novel that seem to be strategies of class warfare prove to be merely sublimates of that deeper secret war (secret until it was revealed by the puppet master), the war of each against all. In the final analysis, it would not be accurate to call this a Simmelian revelation, but it is certainly Goffmanian.

As if that secret were not bad enough, Thackeray's narrator then reveals to us that Rebecca Sharp *delights* in the horror of battle. (In the movie "Patton," the eponymous General, walking among the German and American corpses strewn about the field after a particularly vicious battle, mutters to himself, "God help me, I love it!") The narrator describes Rebecca as a siren, "devouring dead human flesh" in the depths of the turbulent brine. This renders the accusation that we are all Becky Sharp still more horrifying. These kinds of secrets find no place in either

Simmel's or Goffman's thinking, but belong more to the world of Hieronymus Bosch.

Thus, we are all motivated exclusively by self-interest, we are all mad, and we are all cannibals devouring the flesh of our victims. I suspect that these incendiary kinds of secrets are not the type one might have expected to encounter when studying the structure and content of nineteenth-century British secrecy. But perhaps this discovery should not be so startling: Dracula, Frankenstein's creature, Mr. Hyde, Freud's id, Darwin's ape-like ancestor, Jack the Ripper, the "specter" that is haunting Europe (a specter conceived in the bowels of the British library), the frumious Bandersnatch, London's opium dens, and the Jabberwock – all emerged out of the same depths that hide these secrets.

It is not surprising to discover on a somewhat less dramatic register the extent to which secrecy's functions in the nineteenth century are so often class based. Here, this phenomenon is most salient in Braddon's *Lady Audley's Secret*, whose very title foreshadows class warfare. The eponymous secret in that novel seems on the surface to be in the service of the ambition of one individual, Helen Talboys, who hides it in order to climb out of poverty and its attendant miseries, but because that poverty and those miseries are class based, the function of secrecy is to serve as a weapon. Robert Audley, in combating "Lady Audley's" invasion and occupation of aristocratic space, must also use secrecy to retake that occupied territory, because a public challenge would prove damaging to the social myths that justify the aristocratic privileges allowing such dominion in the first place. Hence, what we observe here is armed class conflict, but in secret, each side wielding the Simmelian-like creativity of secrecy to perpetuate its own ends, then using Goffmanian-like secrecy to impose its definitions on social reality, to sustain those definitions through the deployment of "the defensive techniques of impression management."[2]

Here, as in the Sherlock Holmes stories, the Simmelian social creativity attributed to secrecy seems more politicized than Simmel intended it to be. It may seem that the management of secrecy by the future Baronet of Audley produces a triumph for the aristocratic cause in the end. "Lady Audley" is disenfranchised of title, name, and personhood, given a tombstone in a foreign land carved with a false name and false story. But at the conclusion of the story Audley Court itself is reduced to a rarely visited museum as it slips into decrepitude, and all of its secrets have been revealed to an awestruck public by Braddon's narrator. Of course, the narrator, the manor, and its secrets are all fictitious, but the public – Braddon's readership – is not fictitious, and the revelation of the fictional secrets becomes part of the revolution that transforms not only Audley Court but deposits the class that occupied the Audley Courts of Britain into "the museum of antiquities, by the side of the spinning wheel and the bronze axe" (Engels).

I have argued that a similar process occurs with the revelation of the secrets of Sherlock Holmes's clientele to Dr. Watson's readership (all fictional, of course: doctor, detective, detective's clients, secrets, and doctor's readers). Though Watson's revelation had no real effect in the world, Arthur Conan Doyle's did have an impact.[3] Despite his own decidedly conservative proclivities, he discloses to his readers police incompetence, military malfeasance, illicitly gained wealth, royal debauchery, abuse of aristocratic privilege, and indeed, the possible collapse of the rule of reason. The latter secret is revealed almost as dramatically as are similar secrets in *Lady Audley's Secret* and *Vanity Fair*. The proof of this unreason is a pair of raggedly cut ears discovered in a simple cardboard box (*the* "Cardboard Box" of the story's title) delivered to the door of one of Holmes's clients. The contents of this box drives Sherlock to admit depression and despair, and leads Conan Doyle to regret revealing the box's grisly contents, and hence to suppress the story.

To us in the twenty-first century, Conan Doyle's plot-driving secrets also reveal many of the anxieties of *fin-de-siècle* Britain, as each MacGuffin seems to touch on one or another of these concerns. These secrets, in their familial configurations, are identifiably Victorian: fear of miscegenation or its discovery, fear of revelation that one's ancestors are not English enough, or that they had been shipped off to Australia, or – in the absence of reasonable divorce laws – fear of bigamy. Also, we sense the fear of repercussions of foul deeds committed in the Indian or Crimean Wars whose consequences have followed their perpetrators back to London, fear of conspiracies hatched by secret foreign societies, fear of atavism, fear that phrenological bumps on one's head might reveal criminal propensities, fear of imposture, fears of the theatricality of the social world. In addition, there was the fear of blackmail, because these secrets could possibly be discovered by any number of nefarious individuals. The family resemblances among these secrets may be more obvious to us today than to Conan Doyle's Victorian readership: as Hegel notes, "The owl of Minerva flies only at dusk."

Finally, I have argued that in the discourse of nineteenth-century Britain the very idea of secrecy became orientalized, sometimes blatantly and sometimes subtly. Secrecy becomes associated with "the mysterious Orient," a "place" that existed nowhere but in European fantasy. I maintained that this association was both the result of certain historical actions and processes involving British contact with Asia and the Middle East (tourism, trade, military intervention, colonialism, and imperialism) and of a specifically literary event: the triumph of Scheherazade over the literary mentality of Britain (indeed, of Europe). I traced the history of the diffusion of *A Thousand and One Nights* into the imagination of British readers, both young and old, and British writers, including the majority of the most influential novelists and poets. I argued that the "secrets" revealed in these ancient Persian, Arabic, and Indian tales – violent, magic-laden, and semi-pornographic – became "orientalized," thereby producing exotic titillation as they were viewed by occidentals through a glass warped by fantasy, fear, excitement, disdain, lust, and expectation, as the plots of Scheherazade's various tales seemed to be tainted with cruelty, tyranny, sexuality, and arbitrariness, and all wrapped in the mystery of foreignness. Through a process of mental capillarity, orientalism transformed the concept of secrecy in the Victorian age into a new kind of excitement, an excitement that fashionable veils in the culture of British haberdashery tried to provoke. These orientalized secrets became memes that overlapped and entwined with other memes, as did secrecy's class-based provenance, creating a "family" (in the Wittgensteinian sense of the term) that I call "Victorian secrets."

The narratology of secrecy

In addition to viewing the idea of secrecy from a sociological standpoint, I have also considered it from a narratological perspective. The key ideas of narratological strategy involve questions such as these: What information is to be communicated? How much of it? When? On what schedule? To whom? By whom? Should misinformation, disinformation, bullshit, or lies be communicated? When should silence be maintained? Each of these questions has to do with the dialectics of withholding and disclosing information. Therefore, narratology is in an important sense the study of secrecy. As we saw, Dr. John Watson implies this when he contrasts the newspaper's story of a particular crime with his own version of the same story.

> The story has, I believe, been told more than once in the newspapers, but, like all such narratives, its effect is much less striking when set forth en bloc in a single half-column of print than when the facts slowly evolve before your own eyes and the mystery clears gradually away as each new discovery furnishes a step which leads on to the complete truth.
>
> (ENGI I, 264)

We know more or less with what authority the newspaper reporter provides his or her version of the facts, just as we know roughly by what authority an historian presents the facts, but a storyteller has much more freedom than the journalist or the historian. We do not demand that the facts presented by the narrator be facts-in-the-world. (Most of them probably are not; these are *tales* that are being told, after all.) Yet we do occasionally accuse narrators of exaggeration, of unreliability, of forgetfulness, or, on rarer occasions, of lying, but that can happen. Such accusations seem to imply a standard of judgment to which we hold narrators. But how is this possible? Other than the etymological connection between "authority" and "author," how can narrators of "lies"[4] have any authority at all? Is this merely the authority of that most unreliable of narrators, Humpty Dumpty, who imposes meaning in arbitrarily ways that are the product of an addled brain (or yolk)? And why should we care about such a narrator's control of "secrecy"? Can there be secrets in nonsense?

The problem is made clear in a passage in a letter from Edgar Allan Poe to Philip Pendleton Cooke in August of 1846, one that has been noted by a number of critics.[5] In that letter, Poe reminds his friend that in fiction it is not the world but the author who is the source of the secret; hence, in detective fiction at least, the secret that the reader confronts is not the one that the sleuth in the story will reveal, but rather it is the secret of the narrative that the author has invented. According to Poe, the author (Poe himself in "The Murders in the Rue Morgue") is "unravelling a web" that he himself has woven "for the express purpose of unraveling."[6] In this dynamic, rather than the detective's being the sleuth, it is as if the reader is the sleuth and the author is the criminal. What is the crime? Apparently it is the very act of fictive narration. In the spirit of D. A. Miller's *Narrative and Its Discontents*, the narrative has de-normalized the normal; it has broken the peace that peace officers are armed to maintain. Only in closure can normality be restored. As we saw, however, according to Miller, in the nineteenth century at least, closure never succeeds. Attempted closures reinstate the problems that the narrative had awakened, or, according to Poe, artificially generated. If the crime is the narration, as it seems to be for Poe and Miller, then it is a crime that, once committed, can never be expiated. Like its ancient ancestor and inspiration, *A Thousand and One Nights*, it will go on and on, becoming a never-ending story.[7]

Is this process of narration a useless redundancy? Is the weaving of fictitious secrets "for the express purpose of unraveling them" a fool's occupation? I have already alluded to Martinich and Stroll's *Much Ado about Nonexistence* in order to resolve a closely related problem, that of how attributions of truth conditions can be allowed to fictitious propositions.[8] Martinich and Stroll appeal to the Wittgensteinian paradigm of "language games." The kinds of facts produced by such games are not like those facts that follow from natural laws ("$f = ma^2$"), but they are facts just the same. ("Susan and Bill are divorced." "You are guilty as charged, and will hang by the neck until dead.") Martinich and Stroll see fiction as yet another kind of language game producing its own species of truths, and, we might add, its own species of secrets. Perhaps no philosophical justification is needed. We could simply say with Wittgenstein, "These language games are played."[9] If it is felt that a further philosophical justification *is* needed, perhaps Martha Nussbaum's will do.[10]

Another kind of challenge to the power of narration and of authorship is expressed in some recent theories that seem to have denied that there can be any control of voice at all, whether authorial or narrative. John Maynard attributes to Foucault the view that "the age rather than the author speaks through the text"[11] (it would follow that author and narrator would be equally restricted), and Roland Barthes has notoriously declared "the death of the author."[12] But Maynard astutely argues that these ideas are too constricting: "Culture and language are not prison houses but huge playgrounds – as Ludwig Wittgenstein realized in his later work on language games – with lots and lots of options" (85). Maynard writes:

> Even if we conjure up the most monologic and totally controlling culture imaginable, . . . an age deader than the Dead Ages, where patriarchal and matriarchal wisdom combine to deaden all possibility of other thinking or acting, still there will be some maverick, with . . . a liking for a brawl, a positive capacity not to fit in and not to please the elders, and this psychological . . . resistance place . . . will open up subversive spaces in the culture.
>
> (86)

I believe that the "resistance place" of which Maynard speaks overlaps (or perhaps is even identical with) the "alternative world" that secrecy provides to the individual, a space that participates in the creation of the individual's subjectivity. Certainly Lucy Snowe, as the narrator of her own life's story, has mastered this creative act, for better or for worse. If most Victorian narrators are not allowed as much control as Humpty Dumpty arrogates to himself ("When *I* use a word, it means just what I choose it to mean – neither more nor less"), some nevertheless do push the envelope. As we have seen, the most prominent case is indeed that of Lucy Snowe in Charlotte Brontë's last novel, who controls the flow of information as if she were a rather capricious supervisor of a system of dams and locks on a river, cutting off the flow for long periods, giving no explanation other than her own pleasure at doing so, sometimes flooding us with the most personal details of her own flaws and fears, and at other moments refusing absolutely to tell us what we most wish to know, leaving us to assume, falsely, that she will inform us in her own good time. In concealing this information, she not only frustrates those of us who read her story today but she intentionally undermines the expectations of her own generation: a domestic story with no domesticity, a smitten heart that completely fails to snare the object of its desire, pursuer of passion who in disappointment abandons her amorous efforts and curtly chooses another lover, a Victorian novel without a happy ending – nor, indeed, without any ending at all.

We have read Georg Simmel's assertion that without secrecy no social or individual world is possible. In addition, we saw D.A. Miller's claim that "the social function of secrecy [is] isomorphic with its novelistic function."[13] If we put these two claims together we see that Lucy Snowe has usurped the powers of God. She has created a world of her choice by manipulating the secrecy that is requisite for any world at all. In addition, it seems that Miss Snowe justifies this Promethean act on religious grounds. She believes that her soul is her true and eternal self, that it has a mysterious connection with its maker, God, and that the self must keep secrets about itself from others: from characters in her story, from her readers, and most certainly from priests. The structure and content of her narrative style testify to these beliefs, according to which the control of information is a part of her protection of her true selfhood.

Most citizens of the mostly Catholic city of Villette would disagree with Lucy's beliefs about the self and its individualized relation to divinity, and many of her readers today would say that she is wrong about all of them, but no one could deny that the secrets she refuses to reveal have powerfully fashioned her subjectivity. We may want to say with Friedrich Engels that as a result of holding these beliefs she is in a state of "false consciousness," or with Sally Shuttleworth that the "inner mental life" of Lucy Snowe (and of everyone else) is revealed to have only a "fictional status" (241), but we cannot deny that Lucy has created her own subjectivity. And many of us like what we see.[14] Brontë's Lucy Snowe is one of the most fascinating characters in the Victorian world, fictitious or not, and her secrecy makes it so. In *Vanity Fair* we find a narrator even stranger than the narrator of *Lady Audley's Secret*. He is a satirist and an ironist who mocks not only all of the characters in the story he tells, but he also mocks us readers, and himself in the role of narrator. He is at different moments introduced as a stage manager, a puppeteer, a puppet, a character in the novel, a gossip, a moralist, a social critic, and a philosopher. He is also certainly a secretary to all the characters in the novel in the term's original meaning: someone who has been entrusted with the secrets of others. If so, he has shamefully betrayed the trust. He has tattled on everyone, revealing all of their most protected secrets, and showing them all to be passengers on the Ship of Fooles. Judith Fisher is correct to call our attention to "a rhetorical intent that ties narrative technique and story together as mirror images of each other." She concludes, "Thackeray deliberately attempted to disrupt the reading process in order to thwart any stable interpretation."[15]

As we open the novel we see a pen and ink drawing (by Thackeray) depicting the narrator lying sadly on an empty stage looking at himself in a cracked mirror while wearing the motley costume of a clown, torn and with patches. His back leans against an open chest, out of which has fallen a puppet of a woman now sprawled on the floor (Rebecca Sharp?). In the book's first sentence the narrator describes himself as "the Manager of the Performance," and as being in a state of "profound melancholy" (xiv). The book closes, 689 pages later in the Norton edition, with the last of Thackeray's illustrations: two children looking into another open chest of puppets, with three puppets strewn on the floor. One of the puppets prone on the stage is a portly man who looks like earlier illustrations of Jos Sedley. If marionettes can die, he is dead, with his legs sticking up in the air. (Did Becky kill Jos?) One of the other two puppets lying on the floor is a young female (Becky?), and on top of her in a suggestive position is puppet clown in motley, with an evil grin on his face. He seems to be holding her down with his arm across her bosom. If this frightening character is the narrator depicted as a clown in the opening illustration, then the drawing shows us that "the Manager of the Performance" has become a puppet himself with malevolent intentions. The scene raises shocking questions about the meaning of the positions of the unseemly puppets on the floor. In fact, as we have seen, the narrator does become a character in the story (i.e., a puppet), but the questions that we pose as we gaze on this final illustration will remain unanswered, secrets that will never be revealed. The situation becomes more complicated when we recall that the narrator once addressed us readers, crying out, "O brother wearers of motley! Are there not moments when one grows sick of grinning and tumbling, and the jingling of cap and bells?" (190). Then perhaps the clown, wearing motley, sprawled out upon the puppet of Becky Sharp represents us readers, and we are complicit in the act of violence that ends the novel. But it is possible that we deserve this condemnation. If, beneath the surface, we, like Rebecca Sharp, are fiendish cannibals, feasting on our wretched pickled victims, this may be the deepest secret revealed by any narrator in Victorian fiction, far outstripping the secret that the narrator of *Lady Audley's Secret* claimed to reveal, that we are all mad, and the revelation by the narrator of *Vanity Fair* himself that we are all egoists.

The narrator and her strategies in *Lady Audley's Secret* are also curious. Despite being able to read the minds of the characters in her narrative, at the beginning of her tale the narrator of *Lady Audley's Secret* talks as though my lady's secret is her guilt, not her madness, and when Lady Audley declares her own madness ("I AM MAD"), the narrator, like us, does not seem to know whether Lady Audley is in fact insane or is acting. The narrator does not connect Lucy's confession of madness to the narrator's own earlier philosophical discourse about the universal propensity to insanity ("Sane today, mad tomorrow"). Nor does she seem to anticipate George Talboys's "return from the dead." In other words, the narrator is not simply exercising her prerogative to choose when to withhold information and when to reveal it; she seems genuinely puzzled by the developments that unfold. The moral of the story appears to be that there are secrets whose sudden revelation surprises even the omniscient. Are there secrets withheld even from God? Is He as surprised as we when they are revealed? Perhaps it is fitting that the last book of the Christian Bible is the Book of Revelation, even if the secret facts revealed in that ghastly book are not facts at all, even if the revelation is that there is nothing to be revealed.

Dr. John Watson, companion to Sherlock Holmes and narrator of his adventures, is a descendent of Scheherazade, though one less physically and mentally attractive and, potentially, more sexually ambiguous. Like her, he has learned the art of differential iteration, taking roughly the same story and retelling it in an apparently infinite series, series that continue to be repeated to our own day, and continue to be reinvented and updated. Like Scheherazade, Watson well understands that narrative skill involves a science, that of controlling secrets and their revelation. As we saw in chapter 6, he even explains some of narration's secrets to his readers. Arthur Conan Doyle understands this science even better, using Watson to mediate between some of the most irritating features of the abuse of narrative strategy. This mediation takes place when Conan Doyle records Holmes as remonstrating with the doctor for cherry-picking facts, exaggerating drama, withholding information, controlling the timetable of revelation, and, occasionally, for uncovering secrets that should remain hidden. On more than one occasion, Holmes refuses to reveal certain secrets to Watson, knowing that Watson will publish them to a wide (fictional) audience. If Georg Simmel knows that without secrecy sociality is impossible, Watson knows that without narrative control of secrecy there is no story. He, Holmes, and Conan Doyle also know, with Erving Goffman, that sleuthing is not the only human activity that requires theatricality.

Notes

1 Martha C. Nussbaum, *Love's Knowledge: Essays on Philosophy and Literature* (New York and Oxford: Oxford University Press, 1990), 23–24.
2 Erving Goffman, *The Presentation of Self in Everyday Life* (New York and London: Anchor Books Doubleday, 1959), 229. Future references to this work will be cited parenthetically in the body of the text.
3 This is why it does not matter that Dr. Watson gives away the secrets of Holmes's clients: those clients and their secrets are fictional, as is the readership for whom Watson claims to be writing. But in publishing these tales to real British readers of the working middle class, Conan Doyle *does* give away whole categories of secrets, kinds of secrets that are damaging to the interests of the classes that do not need to seek gainful employment. Just as the real secrets of members of the moneyed classes were creative in maintaining the interests of those classes, so were the revelations of such categories of secrets destructive to the members of that social elite.
4 Fiction has been accused of lying many times, beginning with Plato. There are no facts in fiction if a "fact" is a condition denoted by a true proposition, because according to Plato, there are no true propositions in fiction. (See introduction, note 14.)

5 See, for example, Shawn Rosenheim, "Detective Fiction, Psychoanalysis, and the Analytic Sublime," *Edgar Allen Poe*, ed. and intro. Harold Bloom (New York: Chelsea House, 2006), 65–88, 86.
6 Letter from Edgar Allan Poe to Philip Pendleton Cooke [August 9, 1846], Publication of the Edgar Allan Poe Society of Baltimore (Ltr240/RCL654).
7 More than being merely the narration of numerous stories, *Arabian Nights* is a narrative about narration.
8 See introduction, note 14.
9 Wittgenstein says, "If I have exhausted the justifications I have reached bedrock, and my spade is turned. Then I am inclined to say: 'This is simply what we do," and "What has to be accepted, the given is – so one could say – *forms of life*" (*Philosophical Investigations*, trans. G.E.M. Anscombe [New York: Macmillan, 1964], 85, 226).
10 See note 3.
11 John Maynard, *Literary Intention, Literary Interpretation, and Readers* (Peterborough, ON: Broadview, 2009), 34. Future references to this work will be cited parenthetically in the body of the text.
12 Roland Barthes, "The Death of the Author," in *Image-Music-Text* (New York: Hill and Wang, 1977), 148.
13 D.A. Miller, *The Novel and the Police* (Berkeley and Los Angeles: University of California Press, 1989), 206.
14 E.g., Joseph Boone, John Kucich, and me.
15 Judith Law Fisher, *Thackeray's Skeptical Narrative and the "Perilous Trade" of Authorship* (Burlington, VT: Ashgate, 2002), 1.

Bibliography

Abbott, H. Porter. *The Cambridge Introduction to Narrative*, 2nd ed. Cambridge and New York: Cambridge University Press, 2008.

Abdullah, A. "The Arabian Nights in English Literature to 1900." Ph.D. dissertation. Cambridge, 1961.

Abu Odeh, Lama. "Post-Colonial Feminism and the Veil: Thinking the Difference." *Feminist Review* 43 (Spring 1993): 26–37.

Adams, James Eli. *Dandies and Desert Saints: Styles of Victorian Masculinity*. Ithaca and London: Cornell University Press, 1995.

Agzenay, Azma. "Theoretical Approach to the 'Other' of Europe: Between Fact and Fiction." Dissertation. University of Nottingham, 1989.

Ahmed, Leila. "Western Ethnocentrism and Perceptions of the Harem." *Feminist Studies* 8.3 (Fall 1982): 521–34.

———. *Women and Gender in Islam: Historical Roots of a Modern Debate*. New Haven: Yale University Press, 1992.

Alderson, Brian. "Scheherazade in the Nursery." In Caracciolo, ed. 81–94.

Ali, Muhsin Jassim. *Scheherazade in England: A Study of Nineteenth-Century English Criticism of the "Arabian Nights."* Washington: Three Continents Press, 1981.

Alloula, Malek. *The Colonial Harem*. Trans. Myrna Godzich and Wlad Godzich. Minneapolis and London: University of Minnesota Press, 1986.

Anderson, Roger. "What Sherlock Holmes Knew and How He Knew It." *Baker Street Journal* 48.2 (June 1998): 9–18.

"Anonymous review of Ronald Frame's *Havisham*." *New Yorker* (January 6, 2014): 67.

Apter, Emily. "Female Trouble in the Colonial Harem." *Differences: A Journal of Feminist Cultural Studies* 4.1 (1992): 206–19.

Asaad, Thomas J. *Three Victorian Travellers*. London: Routledge and Kegan Paul, 1964.

Austin, J.L. *How to Do Things with Words* [1962]. Ed. J.O. Urmson and M. Sbisà, 2nd ed. Cambridge, MA: Harvard University Press, 1975.

Badowska, Eva. "Choseville: Brontë's *Villette* and the Art of Bourgeois Interiority." *PMLA* 120.5 (October 2005): 1509–23.

———. "On the Track of Things: Sensation and Modernity in Mary Elizabeth Braddon's *Lady Audley's Secret*." *Victorian Literature and Culture* 37.1 (March 2009): 157–75.

Barnes, J.A. *A Pack of Lies: Towards a Sociology of Lying*, Cambridge: Cambridge University Press, 1994.

Barthes, Roland. "The Death of the Author." In *Image-Music-Text*. New York: Hill and Wang, 1977.

Behdad, Ali. *Belated Travelers: Orientalism in the Age of Colonial Dissolution.* Durham and London: Duke University Press, 1994.

———. "Visibility, Secrecy, and the Novel: Narrative Power in Brontë and Zola." *LIT* 1 (1999): 253–64,

Belsey, Catherine. *Critical Practice*, 2nd ed. London and New York: Routledge, 2001.

Benjamin, Marina, ed. *A Question of Identity: Women, Science, and Literature.* New Brunswick, NJ: Rutgers University Press, 1993.

Berger, John. *Ways of Seeing.* Harmondsworth: Penguin, 1972.

Berger, Peter and Thomas Luckman. *The Social Construction of Reality.* Garden City, NY: Doubleday, 1967.

Bergner, Gwen. "Who Is That Masked Woman? Or, the Role of Gender in Fanon's *Black Skin, White Masks.*" *PMLA* 110.1 (January 1995): 75–88.

Bidwell, Robin. *Travellers in Arabia.* London: Hamlyn, 1976.

Birkett, Dea. *Spinsters Abroad.* London: Basil Blackwell, 1989.

Boer, Inge E. "Despotism from under the Veil: Masculine and Feminine Readings of the Despot and the Harem." *Cultural Critique* (Winter 1995–96): 43–73.

Bok, Sissela. *Lying: Moral Choice in Public and Private Life.* London, Melbourne, and New York: Quartet Books, 1980.

———. *Secrets: On the Ethics of Concealment and Revelation.* New York: Vintage/Random House Books, 1989.

Bonfantini, Massimo A. and Giampaolo Proni. "To Guess or Not to Guess?" In Eco and Seboek, eds. 119–34.

Boone, Joseph A. "Depolicing *Villette*: Surveillance, Invisibility, and the Female Erotics of 'Heretic Narrative.'" *Novel* 26.1 (Fall 1992): 20–42.

———. *Libidinal Currents: Sexuality and the Shaping of Modernism.* Chicago: Chicago University Press, 1998.

———. "Vacation Cruises: Or, the Homoerotics of Orientalism." *PMLA* 110.1 (January 1995): 89–107.

Booth, Wayne. *The Rhetoric of Fiction.* Chicago: University of Chicago Press, 1983.

Boumelha, Penny. *Charlotte Brontë.* London: Harvester Wheatsheaf, 1990.

Braddon, Mary Elizabeth. *Lady Audley's Secret* [1861–62]. Ed. Lyn Pykett, notes and intro. by Lyn Pykett. Oxford and New York: Oxford University Press, 2012.

Brantlinger, Patrick. "Nations and Novels: Disraeli, George Eliot, and Orientalism." *Victorian Studies* (Spring 1992): 255–75.

———. "What Is 'Sensational' about the 'Sensation Novel'?" *Nineteenth Century Fiction* 37.1 (June 1982): 1–28.

Breen, Margaret Sonser. "Review of *The Power of Lies: Transgression in Victorian Fiction*, by John Kucich." *George Eliot-George Henry Lewes Studies* 30–31 (April 1996): 87–90.

Briganti, Chiara. "Gothic Maidens and Sensation Women: Lady Audley's Journey from the Ruined Mansion to the Madhouse." *Victorian Literature and Culture* 19 (1991): 189–211.

Broadwell, Elizabeth. "The Veil Image in Ann Radcliffe's *The Italian.*" *South Atlantic Bulletin* 40.4 (1975): 76–87.

Brontë, Charlotte. *Villette.* Ed. Mark Lilly, intro. Tony Tanner. Harmondsworth and New York: Penguin Books, 1984.

———. Villette. Ed. and Intro. Helen Cooper. London: Penguin Books, 2004.

Brown, Kate. "Catastrophe and the City: Charlotte Brontë as Urban Novelist." *Nineteenth-Century Literature* 57.3 (December 2002): 350–80.

Bulwer-Lytton, Edward. *Leila: or, The Siege of Granada* [1838]. Boston: Estes and Lauriat, 1892.

Butler, Judith. *Gender Trouble: Feminism and the Subversion of Identity*. New York and London: Routledge, 1990.

———. "Performative Acts and Gender Constitution: An Essay in Phenomenology and Feminist Theory." In Sue Ellen Case, ed. *Performing Feminisms: Feminist Critical Theory and Theatre*. Baltimore: Johns Hopkins University Press, 1990. 270–82.

Button, Marilyn Demarest and Toni Reed, eds. *The Foreign Woman in British Literature: Exotics, Aliens, and Outsiders*. Westport, CT and London: Greenwood Press, 1999.

Bynum, W. F., Roy Porter, and Michael Shepherd. *The Anatomy of Madness: Essays in the History of Psychiatry*, vol. 1. New York: Routledge, 1988.

Capuano, Peter J. "At the Hands of Becky Sharp: (In)Visible Manipulation and *Vanity Fair*." *Victorians Institute Journal* 38.1 (2008): 167–91.

Caracciolo, Peter L., ed. *The "Arabian Nights" in English Literature: Studies in the Reception of "The Thousand and One Nights" into British Culture*. Houndmills: Macmillan, 1988.

Carlisle, Janice. "The Face in the Mirror: *Villette* and the Conventions of Autobiography." *ELH* 46 (1979): 262–89.

Carroll, Lewis. "*Alice's Adventures in Wonderland*." In *The Annotated Alice: Alice's Adventures in Wonderland & Through the Looking-Glass*. Introduction and notes, Martin Gardner. New York: Bramhall House, 1960.

Carson, Cindy L., Robert L. Mazzola, and Susan M. Bernardo, eds. *Gender Reconstructions: Pornography and Perversions in Literature and Culture*. Aldershot and Burlington, VT: Ashgate, 2002.

Casteras, Susan. *Images of Victorian Womanhood in English Art*. London: Associated University Press, 1987.

Cervantes Saavedra, Miguel de. *The Adventures of Don Quixote*. Trans. J. M. Cohen. New York: Penguin, 1983.

Chabon, Michael. "Inventing Sherlock Holmes." *New York Review of Books* 52.2 (February 10, 2005). Web.

Chandhuri, Nupur and Strobel, Margaret, eds. *Western Women and Imperialism: Complicity and Resistance*. Bloomington: Indiana University Press, 1992.

Chase, Karen and Michael Levinson. "Bigamy and Modernity: The Case of Mary Elizabeth Braddon." In *The Spectacle of Intimacy: A Public Life for the Victorian Family*. Princeton: Princeton University Press, 2000.

Chattman, Laura. "Diagnosing the Domestic Woman in *The Woman in White* and *Dora*." In Carol Siegel and Ann Kibbey, eds. *Eroticism and Containment: Notes from the Flood Plain*. New York and London: New York University Press, 1994. 123–53.

Chesterton, G. K. *A Miscellany of Man*. New York: Dodd, Mead, 1912.

Clarke, Micael M. *Thackeray and Women*. DeKalb: Northern Illinois University Press, 1995.

Cohen, Steven and Linda M. Shires. *Telling Stories: A Theoretical Analysis of Narrative Fiction*. New York and London: Routledge, 1988.

Cohen, William A. "Material Interiority in Charlotte Brontë's *The Professor*." *Nineteenth-Century Literature* 57.4 (March 2003): 443–76.

Conan Doyle, Arthur. *Memories and Adventures* [1924]. London: John Murray, 1930.

———. *The New Annotated Sherlock Holmes*. 3 Vols. Edited with a foreword and notes by Leslie S. Klinger. Introduction by John le Carré. New York and London: W. W. Norton, 2005.

Cook, Cornelia. "Elizabeth Gaskell and George Meredith." In Caracciolo, ed. 197–98.
Cox, Don Richard. *Arthur Conan Doyle*. New York: Ungar, 1985.
Crawley, E. *Dress, Drinks, and Drums: Further Studies of Savages and Sex*. Ed. Theodore Besterman. London: Methuen, 1931.
Crosby, Christina. "Charlotte Brontë's Haunted Text." *Studies in English Literature* 24 (1984): 701–15.
Croutier, Alev Lytle. *Harem: The World behind the Veil*. New York: Abbeville Press, 1989.
Cvetkovich, Ann. "Detective in the House: Subversion and Containment in *Lady Audley's Secret*." In *Mixed Feelings: Feminism, Mass Culture, and Victorian Sensationalism*. New Brunswick, NJ: Rutgers University Press, 1992.
Da Groot, Joanna. "'Sex' and 'Race': The Construction of Language and Image in the Nineteenth Century." In Susan Mendus and Jane Rendall, eds. *Sexuality and Subordination: Interdisciplinary Studies of Gender in the Nineteenth Century*. London and New York: Routledge, 1989. 89–128.
Dakin, D. Martin. *Sherlock Holmes Commentary*. Newton Abbot: David and Charles, 1974.
Dalrymple, Theodore. "Holmes and His Commentators." *New Criterion* 24.3 (November 2005): 4–8.
Dames, Nicholas. *Amnesiac Selves: Nostalgia, Forgetting, and British Fiction, 1810–1970*. Oxford: Oxford University Press, 2001.
Darwin, Charles. *The Descent of Man, and Selection in Relation to Sex*. Norwalk, CT: Heritage Press, 1972.
David, Deirdre. *Rule Britannia: Women, Empire, and Victorian Writing*. Ithaca, NY: Cornell University Press, 1995.
Davidoff, Leonore and Catherine Hall. *Family Fortunes: Men and Women of the English Middle Class, 1780–1850*. London: Hutchinson, 1987.
Davidson, Jenny. *Hypocrisy and the Politics of Politeness: Manners and Morals from Locke to Austen*. Cambridge: Cambridge University Press, 2004.
Debenham, Helen. "Rhoda Broughton's *Not Wisely But Too Well* and the Art of Sensation." In Ruth Robbins and Julian Wolfreys, eds. *Victorian Identities: Social and Cultural Formations in Nineteenth-Century Literature*. New York: St. Martin's, 1996. 9–24.
Dee, Phyllis Susan. "Female Sexuality and Triangular Desire in *Vanity Fair* and *The Mill on the Floss*." *Papers on Language and Literature* 35.4 (Fall 1999): 391–416.
De Giustino, David. *Conquest of Mind: Phrenology and Victorian Social Thought*. London: Croom Helm and Totowa, NJ: Rowman and Littlefield, 1975.
De Groot, Jerome. *The Historical Novel*. London and New York: Routledge, 2010.
Delamotte, Eugenia. "*Villette*: Demystifying Women's Gothic." In *Perils of the Night* New York: Oxford University Press, 1990. 229–89.
Delarue-Mardrus, Lucie. *El-Arab: L'Orient tel que je l'ai connu*. Lyons: Editions Lugelunum, 1944.
Dellamora, Richard. "Traversing the Feminine in Oscar Wilde's *Salomé*." In Thaïs E. Morgan, ed. *Victorian Sages and Cultural Discourse: Renegotiating Gender and Power*. New Brunswick, NJ: Rutgers University Press, 1990. 246–64.
Derrida, Jacques. *Limited Inc*. Trans. Samuel Weber and Jeffrey Mehlman. Evanston, IL: Northwestern University Press, 1988.
———. "Otobiographies: The Teaching of Nietzsche and the Politics of the Proper Name." Trans. Avital Ronell. In *The Ear of the Other: Otobiography, Transference, Translation*. Lincoln: University of Nebraska Press, 1988. 1–38.
Descartes, René. *Discourse on Method* and *Meditations* [1637 and 1641]. Trans. Laurence J. Lafleur. New York: Bobbs-Merrill, 1960.

Djebar, Assia. *Women of Algiers in Their Apartment*. Trans. Marjolijn de Jager. Charlottesville: University of Virginia Press, 1992.

Doane, Mary Anne. "Veiling Over Desire: Close-ups of the Woman." In Richard Feldstein and Judith Roof, eds. *Feminism and Psychoanalysis*. Ithaca and London: Cornell University Press, 1989. 105–41.

Dobie, Madeleine. "The Woman as Look and the Woman as Voice: Assia Djebar and Leila Sebar." *Constructions* 9 (1994): 89–105.

Domino, Brian. "The Thing the Lion Left." In *Sherlock Holmes and Philosophy: The Footprints of a Gigantic Mind*. Ed. Josef Steif. Chicago and La Salle, IL: Open Court, 2011. 221–28.

Donaldson, Laura E. "The Miranda Complex: Colonialism and the Question of Feminist Reading." *Diacritics* 18.3 (Fall 1988): 65–77.

Drew, Paul and Anthony Wootton, eds. *Erving Goffman: Exploring the Interaction Order*. Boston: Northeastern University Press, 1988.

Eagleton, Terry. *Myths of Power: A Marxist Study of the Brontës*. London: Macmillan, 1975.

Eco, Umberto. "Horns, Hooves, Insteps: Some Hypotheses on Three Types of Abduction." In Eco and Seboek, eds. 198–220.

Eco, Umberto and Thomas A. Seboek, eds. *The Sign of Three: Dupin, Holmes, Peirce*. Bloomington: University of Indiana Press, 1983.

El Guindi, Fadwa. *Veil: Modesty, Privacy and Resistance*. Oxford and New York: Berg, 1999.

Enderwitz, Susanne. "Shahrazâd Is One of Us: Practical Narrative, Theoretical Discussion, and Feminist Discourse." In Marzolph, ed. 261–75.

Engels, Friedrich. "The Origin of the Family, Private Property and the State" [1884]. In Lewis S. Feuer, ed. and trans. *Basic Writings on Politics and Philosophy: Karl Marx and Friedrich Engels*. Garden City, NY: Doubleday, 1959. 392–94.

Fanon, Frantz. *A Dying Colonialism*. Trans. Haakon Chevalier. New York: Grove Press, 1965.

Faulkner, Rita A. "Assia Djebar, Frantz Fanon, Veils, and Land." *World Literature Today* 70.3–4 (Summer 1996): 847–55.

Feldstein, Richard and Judith Roof, eds. *Feminism and Psychoanalysis*. Ithaca and London: Cornell University Press, 1989.

Felski, Rita. "After Suspicion." *Profession* (January 2009): 28–35.

Fisher, Judith Law. *Thackeray's Skeptical Narrative and the "Perilous Trade" of Authorship*. Burlington, VT: Ashgate, 2002.

Fisk, Nicole P. "Lady Audley as Sacrifice: Curing the Female Disadvantage in *Lady Audley's Secret*." *Victorian Newsletter* 105 (Spring 2004): 24–27.

Flugel, John Carl. *The Psychology of Clothes*. London: Hogarth Press, 1930.

Foucault, Michel. *The History of Sexuality*, vol. 1, *An Introduction*. Trans. Robert Hurley. New York: Vintage Books/Random House, 1980.

———. *Madness and Civilization: A History of Madness in the Age of Reason*. Trans. Richard Howard. New York: Random House Vintage Books, 1973.

Frank, Lawrence. *Victorian Detective Fiction and the Nature of Evidence: The Scientific Investigations of Poe, Dickens, and Doyle*. Basingstoke and New York: Palgrave Macmillan, 2003.

Frankfurt, Harry. *On Bullshit*. Princeton: Princeton University Press, 2005.

Frawley, Maria. *A Wider Range: Travel Writing by Women in Victorian England*. Rutherford, NJ: Fairleigh Dickinson University Press and London: Associated University Presses, 1994.

Freud, Sigmund. *Moses and Monotheism* [1938]. Trans. Katherine Jones. New York: Random House, n.d.

———. "The 'Uncanny.'" In *The Standard Edition of the Complete Psychological Works of Sigmund Freud*, vol. 17. Ed. James Strachey. London: Hogarth Press, 1955.

Friend, Tad. "Letters from California, 'Protest Studies.'" *New Yorker* (January 4, 2010): 22–28.

Galland, Antoine. *The Arabian Nights: A Companion.* London: Penguin, 1994.

Gamman, Lorraine and Margaret Marshment, eds. *The Female Gaze: Women as Viewers of Popular Culture.* Seattle: Real Comet Press, 1989.

Gauthier, David. "Morals by Agreement." In Stephen Darwall, ed. *Contractarianism/Contractualism.* Oxford and Malden, MA: Blackwell, 2003. 108–37.

Gendron, Charisse. "Images of Middle-Eastern Women in Victorian Travel Books." *Victorian Newsletter* (Spring 1991): 18–23.

Gert, Bernard. "Hobbes and Psychological Egoism." In Robert Shaver, ed. *Hobbes.* Brookfield, VT: Dartmouth, 1999. 255–72.

Ghazoul, Farial Jabouri. *The Arabian Nights: A Structural Analysis.* Cairo: Cairo Associated Institution, 1980.

Gibson, Andrew. *Towards a Postmodern Theory of Narrative.* Edinburgh: Edinburgh University Press, 1996.

Gibson, Mary Ellis. "The Seraglio or Suttee: Bronte's *Jane Eyre.*" *Postscript* 4 (1987): 1–8.

Giddens, Anthony. "Goffman as a Systematic Social Theorist." In Drew and Wootton, eds. 250–79.

Gilbert, Pamela K. "Madness and Civilization: Generic Opposition in Mary Elizabeth Braddon's *Lady Audley's Secret.*" *Essays in Literature* 23.2 (Fall 1996): 218–33.

Gillis, Stacy and Philippa Gates, eds. *The Devil Himself: Villainy in Detective Fiction and Film.* Westport, CT and London: Greenwood Press, 2002.

Ginzburg, Carlo. "Clues: Morelli, Freud, and Sherlock Holmes." In Eco and Seboek, eds. 81–119.

Gladwell, Malcolm. "The Naked Face." *New Yorker* (August 5, 2002): 38–49.

Goffman, Erving. *Asylums: Essays on the Social Situation of Mental Patients and Other Inmates.* New York: Anchor Books Doubleday, 1961.

———. *Behavior in Public Places: Notes on the Social Organization of Gatherings.* New York and London: Macmillan, 1963.

———. *Encounters: Two Studies in the Sociology of Interaction.* Indianapolis: Bobbs-Merrill, 1961.

———. *Forms of Talk.* Philadelphia: University of Pennsylvania Press, 1981.

———. *Interaction Ritual: Essays on Face-to-Face Behavior.* New York: Pantheon Books, 1967.

———. *The Presentation of Self in Everyday Life.* New York and London: Anchor Books Doubleday, 1959.

———. *Where the Action Is: Three Essays.* London: Penguin Press, 1969.

Gould, Stephen J. *The Mismeasure of Man.* New York: W. W. Norton, 1996.

Graham-Brown, Sarah. *Images of Women: The Portrayal of Women in Photography of the Middle East 1860–1950.* London: Quartet, 1988.

Gramm, David. *The Devil and Sherlock Holmes: Tales of Murder, Madness, and Obsession.* New York: Vintage, 2011.

———. "A Murder Foretold: Unravelling the Ultimate Political Conspiracy." *New Yorker* (April 4, 2011): 42–61.

Grewal, Inderpal. *Home and Harem: Nation, Gender, Empire and the Cultures of Travel.* Durham: Duke University Press, 1996.

Halperin, John. *Egoism and Self-Discovery in the Victorian Novel: Studies in the Ordeal of Knowledge in the Nineteenth Century*. New York: Burt Franklin, 1974.

Hampson, Robert G. "The Genie Out of the Bottle: Conrad, Wells and Joyce." In Caracciolo, ed. 218–43.

Hanna, Edward B. "'Where Do You Get Your Ideas?'" In Charles R. Putney, Joseph A. Cutshall King and Sally Sugarman, eds. *Sherlock Holmes: Victorian Sleuth to Modern Hero*. Lanham, MD and London: Scarecrow Press, 1996. 10–14.

Harden, Edgar F., ed. *Selected Letters of William Makepeace Thackeray*. New York: New York University Press, 1996.

Hardy, Barbara. *The Exposure of Luxury: Radical Themes in Thackeray*. London: Peter Owen, 1972.

Harper, Mary J. "Recovering the Other: Women and the Orient in Writings of Early Nineteenth-Century France." *Critical Matrix: The Princeton Journal of Women, Gender, and Culture* 1.3 (1985): 1–31.

Harvey, L.P. *Islamic Spain: 1250–1500*. Chicago and London: University of Chicago Press, 1992.

Haynie, Aeron. "An Idle Handle That Was Never Turned, and a Lazy Rope So Rotten: The Decay of the Country Estate in *Lady Audley's Secret*." In Marlene Tromp, Pamela K. Gilbert, and Aeron Haynie, eds. *Beyond Sensation: Mary Elizabeth Braddon in Context*. Albany: State University of New York Press, 2000. 63–74.

Hegel, G.W.F. *Philosophy of Right*. Trans. T.M. Knox. Oxford: Clarendon Press, 1949.

Heinrichs, Rachel. "Critical Masculinities in *Lady Audley's Secret*." *Victorian Review* 33.1 (2007): 103–20.

Hennesy, Rosemary and Rajeswari Mohan. "'The Speckled Band': The Construction of Woman in a Popular Text of Empire." In John A. Hodgson, ed. *Critical Essays in Sherlock Holmes: The Major Stories with Critical Essays*. Boston and New York: Bedford Books of St. Martin's Press, 1994. 389–401.

Herman, David, ed. and intro. *Narratologies: New Perspectives on Narrative Analysis*. Columbus: Ohio State University Press, 1999.

Hiley, David R., James F. Bohman, and Richard Shusterman, eds. *The Interpretive Turn: Philosophy, Science, Culture*. Ithaca and London: Cornell University Press, 1991.

Hillgarth, J.N. *The Spanish Kingdoms 1250–1516*, vol. 2. Oxford: Clarendon Press, 1978.

Hobbes, Thomas. *Leviathan: Or the Matter, Forme and Power of a Commonwealth Ecclesiasticall and Civill* [1651]. Oxford and New York: Oxford University Press, 1988.

Hodgson, John A., ed. *Critical Essays on Sherlock Holmes: The Major Stories with Contemporary Critical Essays*. Boston and New York: Bedford Books of St. Martin's Press, 1994.

Hughes, Winifred. *The Maniac in the Cellar: Sensation Novels of the 1860s*. Princeton: Princeton University Press, 1980.

Hume, David. *A Treatise of Human Nature* [1738]. Oxford: Clarendon Press, 1941.

Hunt, Alan. *Governance of the Consuming Passions: A History of Sumptuary Law*. New York: St. Martin's Press, 1996.

Hunt, Linda. "*Villette*: The Inward and the Outward Life." *Victorians Institute Journal* 11 (1982–83): 23–31.

Hurley, Kelly. "The Inner Chambers of All Nameless Sin: The Beetle, Gothic Female Sexuality, and Oriental Barbarism." In Lloyd Davis, ed. *Virginal Sexuality Textuality in Victorian Literature*. Albany: State University of New York Press, 1993. 193–213.

Hussain, Asaf, Olson, Robert, and Qureshi, Jamil, eds. *Orientalism, Islam, and Islamists*. Brattleboro, VT: Amana Books, 1984.

Ife, B. W. "The Historical and Social Context." In Anthony J. Cascardi, ed. *Cambridge Companion to Cervantes*. Cambridge and New York: Cambridge University Press, 2002. 11–31.
Irwin, John T. *The Mystery to a Solution: Poe, Borges, and the Analytic Detective Story.* Baltimore and London: Johns Hopkins University Press, 1994.
Irwin, Robert. *The Arabian Nights: A Companion*. London: Penguin, 1994.
Iser, Wolfgang. "The Reader in the Realistic Novel: Esthetic Effects in Thackeray's *Vanity Fair*." In Harold Bloom, ed. *William Makepeace Thackeray's "Vanity Fair."* New York, New Haven, and Philadelphia: Chelsea House, 1987. 37–55.
Jacobus, Mary, ed. *Women Writing and Writing about Women*. London: Croom Helm, 1979.
Jadwin. Lisa. "Clytemnestra Rewarded: The Double Conclusion of Vanity Fair." In Alison Booth, ed. *Famous Last Words: Changes in Gender and Narrative Structure*. Charlottesville and London: University of Virginia Press, 1998. 35–61.
———. "The Seductiveness of Female Duplicity in *Vanity Fair*." *Studies in English Literature, 1500–1900* 32.4 (Autumn 1992): 663–87.
Jaffe, Audrey. "Detecting the Beggar: Arthur Conan Doyle, Henry Mayhew, and 'The Man with the Twisted Lip.'" In John A. Hodgson, ed. *Critical Essays on Sherlock Holmes: The Major Stories with Contemporary Critical Essays*. 402–27.
James, Henry. "Miss Braddon," *Nation* (November 1865): 593–95.
James, William. *The Philosophy of William James.* New York: Modern Library/Random House, n.d.
Jameson, Fredric. *The Political Unconscious: Narrative as a Socially Symbolic Act.* Ithaca: Cornell University Press, 1985.
Jann, Rosemary. *The Adventures of Sherlock Holmes: Detecting Social Order*. New York: Twayne/Macmillan, 1995.
———. "Sherlock Holmes Codes the Social Body." *ELH* 57.3 (Autumn 1990): 685–708.
Jassim Ali, Muhsin. *Scheherazade in England: A Study of Nineteenth-Century English Criticism of the "Arabian Nights."* Washington, DC: Three Continents Press, 1981.
Jay, Martin. *Downcast Eyes: The Denigration of Vision in Twentieth-Century French Thought*. Berkeley and Los Angeles: University of California Press, 1993.
Jenkins, Keith. *Rethinking History*. London and New York: Routledge, 2003.
Jitrik, Noé. "From History to Writing: Symmetrical and Asymmetrical Tendencies in the Latin American Historical Novel." In *The Noé Jitrik Reader: Selected Essays on Latin American Literature*. Durham and London: Duke University Press, 2005. 79–95.
———. *Historia e imaginación literaria: Las posibilidades de un género*. Buenos Aires: Editorial Biblos, 1995.
Julius, Anthony. *Trials of the Diaspora: A History of Anti-Semitism in England.* Oxford and New York: Oxford University Press, 2010.
Kabbani, Rana. *Europe's Myths of the Orient*. Bloomington: Indiana University Press, 1986.
Kahf, Mohja. *Western Representations of the Muslim Woman: From Termagant to Odalisque*. Austin: University of Texas Press, 1999.
Kanidis, Rita S. *Imperial Objects: Victorian Women's Experience and the Unauthorized Imperial Expedition*. New York: Twayne/Macmillan, 1998.
Kant, Immanuel. "Anthropology from a Pragmatic Standpoint" [Anthropologie in pragmatischer Hinsicht]. Segments quoted by Wood *Kant's Ethical Thought*. Trans. Allan W. Wood.
———. *Foundations of the Metaphysics of Morals* [1785]. Trans. John Ladd. Indianapolis: Bobbs-Merrill, 1976.
———. "Lectures on the Philosophical Doctrine of Religion" [Vorlesungen über die philosophische Religionslehre]. Segments quoted by Wood *Kant's Ethical Thought*. Trans. Allan W. Wood.

———. "Religion within the Boundaries of Mere Reason" [Religion innerhalb der Grenzen der bloßen Vernunft]. Segments quoted by Wood *Kant's Ethical Thought*. Trans. Allan W. Wood.

Kaplan, Caren. *Questions of Travel: Postmodern Discourses of Displacement*. Durham and London: Duke University Press, 1995.

Kaye, Richard A. *The Flirt's Tragedy: Desire without End in Victorian and Edwardian Fiction*. Charlottesville and London: University of Virginia Press, 2002.

Kermode, Frank. *The Genesis of Secrecy*. Cambridge, MA: Harvard University Press, 1979.

———. "Secrets and Narrative Sequence." *Critical Inquiry* 7.1 (Autumn 1980): 83–101.

Kern, Stephen. *Eyes of Love: The Gaze in English and French Culture*. New York: New York University Press, 1996.

Kestner, Joseph A. *Sherlock's Sister: The British Female Detective, 1864–1913*. Aldershot: Ashgate, 2003.

Kettle, Arnold. *An Introduction to the English Novel*. London: Basil Wiley, 1951.

Kierkegaard, Søren. *The Concept of Dread* [1844]. Trans. Walter Lowrie. Princeton: Princeton University Press, 1957.

———. *Fear and Trembling* [1843]. Trans. Walter Lowrie. Garden City, NY: Doubleday Anchor Books, 1954.

Kissane, James and John M. Kissane. "Sherlock Holmes and the Ritual of Reason." *Nineteenth Century Fiction* 17.4 (March 1963): 353–62.

Knight, Steven. "The Case of the Great Detective." In John A. Hodgson, ed. *Critical Essays in Sherlock Holmes: The Major Stories with Contemporary Critical Essays*. Boston and New York: Bedford Books of St. Martin's Press, 1994. 368–80.

Knoepflmacher, U.C. "*Vanity Fair*: The Bitterness of Retrospection." In *Laughter and Despair: Readings in Ten Novels of the Victorian Era*. Berkeley and Los Angeles: University of California Press, 1971. 50–83.

Koritz, Amy. "Salomé: Exotic Woman and the Transcendent Dance." In Antony H. Harrison and Beverly Taylor, eds. *Gender and Discourse in Victorian Literature and Art*. DeKalb: Northern Illinois University Press, 1992. 251–73.

Kreilkamp, Ivan. "Powerful Lies." *Novel: A Forum on Fiction* 29.2 (Winter 1996): 253.

Kucich, John. "Passionate Reserve and Reserved Passion." *ELH* 52.4 (Winter 1985): 913–37.

———. *The Power of Lies: Transgression in Victorian Fiction*. Ithaca and London: Cornell University Press, 1994.

———. *Repression in Victorian Fiction: Charlotte Brontë, George Eliot, and Charles Dickens*. Berkeley, Los Angeles, and London: University of California Press, 1987.

Leask, Nigel. *British Romantic Writers and the East: Anxieties of Empire*. Cambridge: Cambridge University Press, 1992.

Leibniz, Gottfried Wilhelm von. *Monadology and Other Philosophical Essays* [1696]. Trans. Paul Schrecker and Anne Martin Schrecker. New York: Bobbs-Merrill, 1965.

Lévi-Strauss, Claude. *Structural Anthropology*. Trans. Claire Jacobson and Brooke Grunfest Schoepf. New York: Basic Books, 1963.

Lewis, Reina. *Gendering Orientalism: Race, Ethnicity and Representation*. London and New York: Routledge, 1996.

Loesberg, Jonathan. "The Ideology of Narrative Form in Sensation Fiction." *Representations* 13 (Winter 1986): 115–38.

Lougy, Robert E. "Vision and Satire: The Warped Looking Glass in *Vanity Fair*." *PMLA* 90.2 (March 1975): 256–69.

Love, Heather. *Feeling Backward: Loss and the Politics of Queer Theory*. Cambridge, MA: Harvard University Press, 2007.

Lowe, Lisa. *Critical Terrains: French and British Orientalisms.* Ithaca and London: Cornell University Press, 1991.
Lukács, Georg. *The Historical Novel* [1937]. Trans. Hannah and Stanley Mitchell. Harmondsworth: Penguin, 1969.
Lycett, Andrew. *The Man Who Created Sherlock Holmes: The Life and Times of Sir Arthur Conan Doyle.* New York, London, Toronto, and Sydney: Free Press, 2007.
Makhlouf-Obermeyer, Carla. *Changing Veils: A Study of Women in South Arabia.* Austin: University of Texas Press, 1979.
Malone, Cynthia Norcutt. "'Flight' and 'Pursuit': Fugitive Identity in *Bleak House.*" *Dickens Studies Annual* 19 (1990): 107–24.
Manning, Philip. "Ethnographic Coats and Tents." In Greg Smith, ed. *Goffman and Social Organization: Studies in Sociological Legacy.* 104–18.
Mannsaker, Frances. "Elegancy and Wildness: Reflections of the East in the Eighteenth-Century Imagination." In G. S. Rousseau and Roy Porter, eds. *Exoticism in the Enlightenment.* Manchester: Manchester University Press, 1990. 175–95.
Manzoni, Alessandro. *On the Historical Novel* [1850]. Trans. Sandra Berman. Lincoln: University of Nebraska Press, 1984.
Marck, Nancy Anne. "Drugs, Doubling, and Disguise: Sherlock Holmes and 'The Man with the Twisted Lip.'" In Martin Hewitt, ed. *Unrespectable Recreations.* Leeds: Leeds Center for Victorian Studies, 2001. 107–16.
Marcus, Sharon. *Between Women: Friendship, Desire and Marriage in Victorian England.* Princeton and Oxford: Princeton University Press, 2007.
Martineau, Harriet. "The Hareem." In Gayle Graham Yates, ed. *Harriet Martineau on Women.* New Brunswick, NJ: Rutgers University Press, 1985. 173–84.
Martinich, A. P. and Avrum Stroll. *Much Ado about Nonexistence: Fiction and Reference.* Lanham, MD: Rowman and Littlefield, 2007.
Marx, Karl. "Economic and Philosophical Manuscripts." In Erich Fromm, ed. Trans. T. B. Bottomore. *Marx's Concept of Man.* New York: Frederick Unger, 1966. 85–196.
Marzolph, Ulrich, ed. *The "Arabian Nights" in Transnational Perspective.* Detroit: Wayne State University Press, 2007.
Matus, Jill L. "Disclosure as 'Cover Up': The Discourse of Madness in *Lady Audley's Secret.*" *University of Toronto Quarterly: A Canadian Journal of the Humanities* 62.3 (Spring 1993): 334–55.
———. "Looking at Cleopatra: The Expression and Exhibition of Desire in *Villette.*" *Victorian Literature and Culture* 8 (1993): 345–67.
May, Leila S. *Disorderly Sisters: Sibling Relations and Sororal Resistance in Nineteenth-Century British Literature.* Lewisburg, PA: Bucknell University Press, 2001.
———. "How Lucy Snowe Became an Amnesiac." *Brontë Studies* 34.3 (November 2000): 220–33.
———. "Lucy Snowe, a Material Girl? Phrenology, Surveillance, and the Sociology of Interiority." *Criticism* 25.1 (Winter 2013): 43–68.
———. "'Monkeys, Microcephalous Idiots, and the Barbarous Races of Mankind': Darwin's Dangerous Victorianism." *Victorian Newsletter* 102 (Spring 2003): 20–27.
———. "The Sociology of Thackeray's 'Howling Wilderness': Selfishness, Secrecy and Performance in *Vanity Fair.*" *Modern Language Studies* 37.1 (Summer 2007): 18–41.
———. "Wittgenstein's Reflection in Lewis Carroll's Looking-Glass." *Philosophy and Literature* 31.1 (April 2007): 79–94.
Maynard, John. *Literary Intention, Literary Interpretation, and Readers.* Peterborough, ON: Broadview Press, 2008.

McClintock, Anne. *Imperial Leather: Race, Gender, and Sexuality in the Colonial Conquest*. London: Routledge, 1995.
Meester, Marie de. *Oriental Influences in the English Literature of the Nineteenth Century* [1915]. London: Forgotten Books, 2013.
Melman, Billie. *Women's Orients: English Women and the Middle East: 1718–1918*. Ann Arbor: University of Michigan Press, 1992.
Mendus, Susan and Jane Rendall, eds. *Sexuality and Subordination: Interdisciplinary Studies of Gender in the Nineteenth Century*. London and New York: Routledge, 1989.
Menocal, María Rosa. *The Ornament of the World: How Muslims, Jews, and Christians Created a Culture of Tolerance in Medieval Spain*. Boston, New York, and London: Little, Brown, 2002.
Mernissi, Fatima. *Beyond the Veil: Male-Female Dynamics in a Modern Muslim Society*. Cambridge, MA: Schenkman, 1975.
———, ed. and intro. *Fantasies de l'harem i noves Xahrazads* [book on exposition in Barcelona, spring 2003] Centre de Cultura Contemporània de Barcelona I Institutt d'Edicions de la Diputació de Barcelona, 2003.
———. *The Forgotten Queens of Islam*. Trans. Mary Jo Lakeland (with the assistance of French Ministry of Culture). Cambridge: Polity Press, 1993.
———. *Le harem politique: le prophete et les femmes*. Paris: Albin Michel, 1987.
———. *The Veil and the Male Elite*. New York: Addison Wesley, 1987.
Metress, Christopher. "Thinking the Unthinkable: Reopening Conan Doyle's 'Cardboard Box.'" *Midwest Quarterly: A Journal of Contemporary Thought* 42.2 (Winter 2001): 183–98.
Meyer, Susan. *Imperialism at Home: Race and Victorian Women's Fiction*. Ithaca and London: Cornell University Press, 1996.
Michie, Helena. *Sororophobia: Differences among Women in Literature and Culture*. Oxford and New York: Oxford University Press, 1992.
Miller, Andrew H. *The Burdens of Perfection: On Ethics and Reading in Nineteenth Century British Literature*. Ithaca and London: Cornell University Press, 2007.
Miller, D.A. "*Cage aux folles*: Sensation and Gender in Wilkie Collins's *Woman in White*." *Representations* 14 (Spring 1986): 107–36.
———. *Narrative and Its Discontents: Problems of Closure in the Traditional Novel*. Princeton: Princeton University Press, 1981.
———. *The Novel and the Police*. Berkeley and Los Angeles: University of California Press, 1989.
Miller, J. Hillis. *Speech Acts in Literature*. Stanford, CA: Stanford University Press, 2001.
Miller, William Ian. *Faking It*. Cambridge: Cambridge University Press, 2003.
Mills, Sarah. *Discourses of Difference: An Analysis of Women's Travel Writing and Colonialism*. London: Routledge, 1991.
Minott-Ahl, Nicola. "Dystopia in *Vanity Fair*: The Nightmare of Modern London." *Literary London: Interdisciplinary Studies in the Representation of London* 7.2 (September 2009): electronic journal.
Mitchell, Timothy. "Orientalism and the Exhibitory Order." In Nicholas B. Dirks, ed. *Colonialism and Culture*. Ann Arbor: University of Michigan Press, 1992. 289–318.
Mohanty, Satya P. "Colonial Legacies, Multicultural Futures: Relativism, Objectivity, and the Challenge of Otherness." *PMLA* 110.1 (January 1995): 108–18.
Morgan, Susan. *Place Matters: Gendered Geography in Victorian Women's Travel Books about Southeast Asia*. New Brunswick, NJ: Rutgers University Press, 1996.
Morse, David. *High Victorian Culture*. New York: New York University Press, 1993.

Murphy, Robert F. "Social Distance and the Veil." *American Anthropologist* 66.b (December 1964): 1257–72.
Nagel, Thomas. "Concealment and Exposure." *Philosophy and Public Affairs* 27.1 (January 1998): 3–30.
Nayder, Lillian. "Rebellious Sepoys and Bigamous Wives: The Indian Mutiny and Marriage Law Reform in *Lady Audley's Secret*." In Tromp et al., eds. *Beyond Sensation*. 31–42.
Nemesvari, Richard. "Robert Audley's Secret: Male Homosocial Desire in Lady Audley's Secret." *Studies in the Novel* 27.4 (Winter 1995): 515–16.
Newman, Beth. *Subjects on Display: Psychoanalysis, Social Expectation, and Victorian Femininity*. Athens: Ohio University Press, 2004.
Nietzsche, Friedrich. *The Gay Science* [1882]. Trans. Walter Kaufmann. New York: Vintage Books, 1974.
Nochlin, Linda. "The Imaginary Orient." In *The Politics of Vision: Essays on Nineteenth-Century Art and Society*. New York: Harper and Row, 1989. 33–59.
Nussbaum, Martha C. *Love's Knowledge: Essays on Philosophy and Literature*. New York and Oxford: Oxford University Press, 1990.
O'Farrell, Mary Ann. *Telling Complexions: The Nineteenth-Century English Novel and the Blush*. Durham, NC: Duke University Press, 1997.
Palmer, Donald D. "The Cartesian Conception of Human Nature." In *Visions of Human Nature*. Mountain View, CA, London, and Toronto: Mayfield, 2000. 123–49.
Peel, Katie R. "The 'Thoroughly and Radically Incredible' Lucy Snowe: Performativity in Charlotte Brontë's *Villette*." *Victorians Institute Journal* 36 (2008): 231–44.
Penner, Louise. "'Not Yet Settled': Charlotte Brontë's Anti-materialism." *Nineteenth-Century Gender Studies* 4.1 (Spring 2008): 1–27.
Perera, Suvendrini. *Reaches of Empire: The English Novel from Edgeworth to Dickens*. New York: Columbia University Press, 1991.
Pescador del Hoyo, María del Carmen. "Como fue de verdad la toma de Granada a la luz de un documento inédito" [How the Fall of Granada Really Happened in the Light of an Unpublished Document]. *Al-Andaluz* 20 (1955): 283–344.
Peters, Catherine. *Thackeray's Universe: Shifting Worlds of Imagination and Reality*. New York: Oxford University Press, 1987.
Pierce, Leslie. *The Imperial Harem: Women and Sovereignty in the Ottoman Empire*. New York: Oxford University Press, 1993.
Pietka, Rachel. "Thackeray's *Vanity Fair*." *Explicator* 68.4 (2010): 239–41.
Pionke, Albert D. "Victorian Secrecy: An Introduction." In Albert D. Pionke and Denise Tischler Millstein, eds. *Victorian Secrecy: Economies of Knowledge and Concealment*. Farnham and Burlington, VT: Ashgate, 2010. 1–15.
Plato. *Republic*. In *Great Dialogues of Plato*. Trans. W.H.D. Rouse. New York: New American Library, 1956.
Polhemus, Robert M. *Erotic Faith*. Chicago: University of Chicago Press, 1990.
Poovey, Mary. *Genres of the Credit Economy: Mediating Value in Eighteenth and Nineteenth Century Britain*. Chicago and London: University of Chicago Press, 2008.
Popper, Karl. *The Logic of Scientific Discovery* [1935]. London: Routledge, 2002.
Pratt, Mary Louise. *Imperial Eyes: Travel Writing and Transculturation*. London and New York: Routledge, 1992.
Priestman, Martin. "Sherlock Holmes – The Series." In John A. Hodgson, ed. *Critical Essays in Sherlock Holmes: The Major Stories with Contemporary Critical Essays*. Boston and New York: Bedford Books of St. Martin's Press, 1994. 313–20.

Pykett, Lyn. *The "Improper" Feminine: The Women's Sensation Novel and the New Woman Writing*. London and New York: Routledge, 1992.

Ragussis, Michael. "The Birth of a Nation in Victorian Culture: The Spanish Inquisition, the Converted Daughter, and the 'Secret Race.'" *Critical Inquiry* 20.3 (Spring 1994): 477–508.

Rawls, John. *A Theory of Justice*. Cambridge, MA: Harvard University Press, 1971.

Reynolds, Kimberly and Nicola Humble. *Victorian Heroines: Representations of Femininity in Nineteenth-Century Literature and Art*. New York: New York University Press, 1993.

Ricouer, Paul. *Freud and Philosophy: An Essay on Interpretation*. Trans. Denis Savage. New Haven: Yale University Press, 1970.

Robb, Graham. *Strangers: Homosexual Love in the Nineteenth Century*. New York and London: W. W. Norton, 2003.

Rosenheim, Shawn. "Detective Fiction, Psychoanalysis, and the Analytic Sublime." In Harold Bloom, ed. and intro. *Edgar Allen Poe*. New York: Chelsea House, 2006. 65–88.

Said, Edward. *Culture and Imperialism*. New York: Alfred A. Knopf, 1993.

———. *Orientalism*. New York: Pantheon Books, 1978.

———. *The World, the Text, and the Critic*. Cambridge, MA: Harvard University Press, 1983.

Sale, George. *The Qurán with Preliminary Discourse and Notes on the Authority of Baidháwi, Jaláluddin, Al Zamakhshari, &c.* [1732], republished in 1896 in four volumes by the Rev. E.M. Wherry under Wherry's own name as *A Comprehensive Commentary on the Qurán: Comprising Sale's Translation and Preliminary Discourse*. London: Kegan Paul, Trench, Trübner, 1896.

Sallis, Eva. *Scheherazade through the Looking Glass: The Metamorphosis of the "Thousand and One Nights."* Richmond: Curzon Press, 1999.

Salotto, Eleanor. "*Villette* and the Perversions of Feminine Identity." In Carson et al., eds., 53–75.

Sanders, Andrew. *The Victorian Historical Novel, 1840–1880*. London and Basingstoke: Macmillan Press, 1978.

Sanders, Eli. "Veiled Meanings." *News and Observer*, Raleigh, NC (October 31, 2001): 1e and 14e.

Sansom, William. *The Cautious Heart*. New York: Reynal, 1958.

———. *A Contest of Ladies*. London: Hogarth, 1956.

———. *The Face of Innocence*. London: Reprint Society, 1954.

———. *Something Terrible, Something Lovely*. New York: Harcourt, Brace, 1954.

———. *A Touch of the Sun*. London: Hogarth Press, 1952.

Sartre, Jean-Paul. *Being and Nothingness: A Phenomenological Essay on Ontology* [1943]. Trans. Hazel E. Barnes. New York and London: Washington Square Press, 1992.

———. "Sartre at Seventy: An Interview." Interviewer Michel Conant. Trans. Lydia Davis and Paul Auster. *New York Review of Books* (August 7, 1975): web.

Sattin, Anthony. *Lifting the Veil: British Society in Egypt*. London: J.M. Dent, 1988.

Schegloff, Emanuel A. "Goffman and the Analysis of Conversation." In Drew and Wootton, eds. 89–135.

Scheibe, Karl E. *Mirrors, Masks, Lies and Secrets: The Limits of Human Predictability*. New York: Praeger, 1979.

Schopenhauer, Arthur. *The World as Will and Idea* [1819], 2 Vols. Trans. R.B. Haldane and J. Kemp. London: Routledge and Kegan Paul, 1964.

Scott, James C. *Domination and the Arts of Resistance: Hidden Transcripts*. New Haven: Yale University Press, 1990.

Searle, John. "Reiterating the Differences." *Glyph* 1 (1977): 198–208.
Seboek, Thomas A. and Jean Umiker-Seboek. "'You Know My Method': A Juxtaposition of Charles S. Peirce and Sherlock Holmes." In Eco and Seboek, eds. 11–54.
Sedgwick, Eve. "The Character in the Veil: Imagery of the Surface in the Gothic Novel." In *The Coherence of Gothic Conventions*. New York: Methuen, 1986. 140–75.
Sen, Sambudha. "*Bleak House*, *Vanity Fair*, and the Making of an Urban Aesthetic." *Nineteenth-Century Literature* 54.4 (March 2000): 480–502.
Sharma, U. "Women and Their Affines: The Veil as a Symbol of Separation." *Man* 13 (1978): 218–33.
Sharpe, Jenny. *Allegories of Empire: The Figure of the Woman in the Colonial Text*. Minneapolis: University of Minnesota Press, 1993.
Sherer, S. "Secrecy and Autonomy in Lewis Carroll." *Philosophy and Literature* 20.1 (April 1996): 1–19.
———. "Secrecy in Victorian Fiction." *DAI, University of Virginia* 57.9 (March 1996): 3951A.
Showalter, Elaine. "Desperate Remedies." *Victorian Newsletter* 49 (1976): 1–5.
———. "Family Secrets and Domestic Subversion: Rebellion in the Novels of the 1860s." In Wohl, ed. 101–16.
———, ed. *Speaking of Gender*. New York: Routledge, 1989.
Shuttleworth, Sally. *Charlotte Brontë and Victorian Psychology*. Cambridge: Cambridge University Press, 1996.
———. "'Preaching to the Nerves': Psychological Disorder in Sensation Fiction." In Marina Benjamin, ed. *A Question of Identity: Women, Science, and Literature*. New Brunswick, NJ: Rutgers University Press, 1993. 192–222.
Simmel, Georg. *Conflict and the Web of Group-Affiliations*. Trans. Kurt H. Wolff and Reinhard Bendix. Glencoe, IL: Free Press, 1955.
———. "Group Expansion and the Development of Individuality" [1908]. In Donald N. Levine, ed., and Richard P. Abares, trans. *On Individuality and Social Forms: Selected Writings*. Chicago and London: University of Chicago Press, 1972, 249–93.
———. "The Secret and the Secret Society" [1908]. In Kurt H. Wolff, trans. and ed. *The Sociology of Georg Simmel*. New York: Free Press, 1964. 305–76.
Smith, Greg, ed. *Goffman and Social Organization: Studies in Sociological Legacy*. New York and London: Routledge, 1999.
———. "Introduction: Interpreting Goffman's Sociological Legacy." In Smith, ed. *Goffman and Social Organization: Studies in Sociological Legacy*. 1–18.
Smyth, John Vignaux. *The Habit of Lying: Sacrificial Studies in Literature, Philosophy, and Fashion Theory*. Durham and London: Duke University Press, 2002.
Stern, Rebecca. "'Personation' and 'Good Marking-Ink': Sanity, Performativity, and Biology in Victorian Sensation Fiction." *Nineteenth Century Studies* 14 (2000): 35–62.
Stevenson, Robert Louis. *The Strange Case of Dr Jekyll and Mr Hyde*. Ed. Martin A. Danahay. Peterborough, ON: Broadview, 2005,
Stockton, Kathryn Bond. *God between Their Lips: Desire between Women in Irigaray, Brontë, and Eliot*. Stanford, CA: Stanford University Press, 1994.
Strong, P. M. "Minor Courtesies and Macro Structures." In Drew and Wootton, eds. 228–49.
Surridge, Lisa. "'Are Women Protected?' Sherlock Holmes and the Violent Home." In *Bleak Houses: Marital Violence in Victorian Fiction*. Athens: Ohio University Press, 2005.
Tefft, Stanton K. "Secrecy, Disclosure and Social Theory." In *Secrecy: A Cross-Cultural Perspective*. New York: Human Sciences Press, 1980. 35–74.

Thackeray, William Makepeace. *Vanity Fair: A Novel without a Hero* [1847–48]. Ed. Peter Shillingsburg. New York: Norton, 1994.

Thomas, Ronald R. "Making Darkness Visible: Capturing the Criminal and Observing the Law in Victorian Photography and Detective Fiction." In Carol T. Christ and John O. Jordan, eds. *Victorian Literature and the Victorian Visual Imagination*. Berkeley, Los Angeles, and London: University of California Press, 1995. 134–67.

Thompson, Jon. *Fiction, Crime, and Empire: Clues to Modernity and Postmodernism*. Urbana and Chicago: University of Illinois Press, 1993.

Tillotson, Kathleen. "Vanity Fair." First published in Tillotson, *Novels of the Eighteen-Forties*. London: Oxford University Press, 1954. 224–56. Reprinted in Alexander Welsh, ed. *Thackeray: A Collection of Critical Essays*. Englewood Cliffs, NJ: Prentice-Hall, 1968. 65–86.

Tracy, Jack, ed. *The Encyclopedia Sherlockiana, or Universal Dictionary of the State of Knowledge of Sherlock Holmes and His Biographer, John H. Watson, M.D.* Garden City, NY: Doubleday, 1977.

Trivers, Robert. *The Folly of Fools: The Logic of Deceit and Self-Deception in Human Life*. New York: Basic Books, 2011.

Tromp, Marlene, Pamela K. Gilbert, and Aeron Haynie, eds. *Beyond Sensation: Mary Elizabeth Braddon in Context*. Albany: State University of New York Press, 2000.

Truzzi, Marcello. "Sherlock Holmes: Applied Social Psychologist." In Eco and Seboek, eds. 55–80.

Urquhart, David. *Spirit of the East: Illustrated in a Journal of Travels through Roumeli during an Eventful Period*, 2 Vols. London: H. Colburn, 1838.

Voskuil, Lynn M. "Acts of Madness: Lady Audley and the Meanings of Victorian Femininity." *Feminist Studies* (FSt) 27.3 (Fall 2001): 611–39.

Vrettos, Athena. *Somatic Fictions: Imagining Illness in Victorian Culture*. Stanford, CA: Stanford University Press, 1995.

Watson, Dr. J. *The Sexual Adventures of Sherlock Holmes*. New York: Traveller's Companion, 1971.

Wein, Toni. "Gothic Desire in Charlotte Brontë's *Villette*." *Studies in English Literature 1500–1900* 39.4 (1999): 733–49.

Weinstone, Anne. "The Queerness of Lucy Snowe." *Nineteenth-Century Contexts* 18.4 (1995): 367–84.

Weissman, Judith. *Half Savage and Hardy and Free: Women and Radicalism in the Nineteenth-Century Novel*. Middletown, CT: Wesleyan University Press, 1987.

Welsh, Alexander. *George Eliot and Blackmail*. Cambridge, MA: Harvard University Press, 1985.

Wheeler, Michael. *English Fiction of the Mid-Victorian Period*. New York: Longman, 1985.

White, Luise. "Telling More: Lies, Secrets, and History." *History and Theory* 39.4 (December 2000): 11–22.

Willis, Chris. "The Female Moriarty: The Arch-Villainess in Victorian Popular Fiction." In Stacy Gillis and Philippa Gates, eds. *The Devil Himself: Villainy in Detective Fiction and Film*. Westport, CT and London: Greenwood Press, 2002. 57–68.

Wilson, Margaret D. *The Passions of the Soul, Part I*. In *The Essential Descartes*. New York: New American Library, 1969. 353–368.

Wilt, Judith. "Recent Studies in the Nineteenth Century." *Studies in English Literature (SEL), Nineteenth Century* 35.4 (Autumn 1995): 807–86.

Wisnicki, Adrian S. *Conspiracy, Revolution, and Terrorism from Victorian Fiction to the Modern Novel.* London and New York: Routledge, 2008.
Wittgenstein, Ludwig. *Philosophical Investigations.* Trans. G.E.M. Anscombe. New York: Macmillan, 1964.
Wohl, Anthony S., ed. *The Victorian Family: Structure and Stresses.* London: St. Martin's, 1978.
Wolf, Cynthia Griffin. "Who Is the Narrator of *Vanity Fair* and Where Is He Standing?" *College Literature* 1 (1974): 190–203.
Wood, Allen W. *Kant's Ethical Thought.* Cambridge and New York: Cambridge University Press, 1999.
Wright, Lawrence. "Profiles: The Man behind Bin Laden." *New Yorker* (September 16, 2002): 56–85.
Yeager, Patricia S. "Honey-Mad Women: Charlotte Brontë's Bilingual Heroines." *Browning Institute Studies* 14 (1986): 11–35.
Yeazell, Ruth Bernard. *Harems of the Mind: Passages of Western Art and Literature.* New Haven: Yale University Press, 2000.
Yegenoglu, Meyda. *Colonial Fantasies: Towards a Feminist Reading of Orientalism.* Cambridge: Cambridge University Press, 1998.
York, R. A. *Strangers and Secrets: Communication in the Nineteenth-Century Novel.* London and Toronto: Associated University Presses, 1994.
Zanona, Joyce. "The Sultan and the Slave: Feminist Orientalism and the Structure of *Jane Eyre.*" *Signs* 18.3 (Spring 1993): 592–617.
Zigarovich, Jolene. *Writing Death and Absence in the Victorian Novel: Engraved Narratives.* New York: Palgrave, 2012.
Zipes, Jack, ed. *Arabian Nights: The Marvels and Wonders of the Thousand and One Nights.* Trans. Richard F. Burton. New York: Dutton Signet, 1991.

Index

Abbott, H. Porter 17, 34, 74n46
"Adventure of the Cardboard Box, The" 187–9, 190
"Adventure of the *Gloria Scott*, The," MacGuffin in 182–3
"Adventure of the Noble Bachelor, The," bigamy secret in 183
"Adventure of the Speckled Band, The," plot-driving secret in 183
Adventures of Sherlock Holmes, The (Conan Doyle) 7, 179–205; atavism concerns and 185–6; blackmail secrets and 182, 189–90; class secrets in 184; conservative ideology and 198–201; epistemological theory and 191–7; family secrets in 182; function of secrecy in 181; homosexuality and 186–7; ill-kept secret anxieties motivating 180–8; Indian Mutiny of 1857–58 and 184–5; MacGuffins in 180–1; orientalized secrets in 197–8; overview of 179–80; plot-driving secrets in 182; rationalism and 192–5; secret of Holmes himself 191; structural secrets in 181–2; theory of logical connections and 196–7
Alderson, Brian 146, 147
Alf laila wa laila (One Thousand Nights and One Night) 144
Ali, Muhsin Jassim 145
Alloula, Malek 155
Apter, Emily 155
Arabian Nights: "Ali Baba and the Forty Thieves," secrets in 150; Britain's geographic expansionism and 143–4; children's versions of 145–6; illustrations in 146–7; MacGuffins in 150; narratology of 147–8, 151–3; orientalized secrets in 147, 149–50; plot-driving secrets in 150–1; prologue in 148–9; "Seven Voyages of Sinbad the Sailor, The," secrets in 150–1; sexualized secrets in 148–9; structural secrets in 150, 151; success of, in British Isles 144–5; western readers of 151
Asylums (Goffman) 126
atavism concerns 185–6
Austin, J. L. 11, 59–60, 74n45, 115, 137n17, 174n13, 220

Bad Form: Social Mistakes and the Nineteenth-Century Novel (Cavell and Puckett) 11
Badowska, Eva 65, 70, 113
Barnes, J.A. 35, 67
Batten, J.D. 146
Beardsley, Aubrey 146–7
Behdad, Ali 46
Belsey, Catherine 59, 189–90
Between Women: Friendship, Desire and Marriage in Victorian England (Marcus) 49–50
bigamy, secret of 183; in *Lady Audley's Secret* 111–12, 115–17, in *The Adventures of Sherlock Holmes* 183, 203
blackmail, secrets and 182, 189–90
Bleak House (Dickens) 8
Bok, Sissela 73n34, 114
Bonfantini, Massimo 196
Boone, Joseph 60, 65, 77n62, 219n14
"Boscombe Valley Mystery, The," bigamy secret in 183
Boumelha, Penny 60
Braddon, Mary Elizabeth 7, 13, 36, 58, 59, 109, 113, 118–19, 212–4, 127, 129, 131–5, 179, 183, 201; see also *Lady Audley's Secret*
Briganti, Chiara 125
Brontë, Charlotte 2, 7, 10, 11, 12, 15, 17n21, 18n31, 18n32, 34, 40–2, 44, 49,

51–2, 55–65, 67–70, 109–10, 174n14, 179, 189, 201–2, 210–11, 216; *see also Villette* (Brontë); phrenology and 61–3
Bulwer-Lytton, Edward 7, 14, 36, 158, 166, 167–73, 198; *see also Leila: or, The Siege of Granada* (Bulwer-Lytton)
Burdens of Perfection: On Ethics and Reading in Nineteenth-Century British Literature, The (Miller) 11
Butler, Judith 21, 31–2

Caracciolo, Peter 145, 146, 174n11
Carlisle, Janice 60
Carlyle, Thomas 154
Cavell, Stanley 11
Charlotte Brontë and Victorian Psychology (Shuttleworth) 57, 60–1
Chase, Karen 111
Chattman, Lauren 129
Chesterton, G. K. 5
Christmas Carol, A (Dickens) 8
Clarke, Micael 96
class secrets 4, 7, 8, 13–14, 32–3, 41, 80, 212; in *Adventures of Sherlock Holmes, The* 184, 198–201, 203–4; in *Lady Audley's Secret* 109, 110, 112, 113–15, 127, 130, 134–5, 212; in *Vanity Fair* 80–1, 83, 88, 211
Cohen, Steven, 39n30, 39n33
Cohen, William A. 55–6, 74n36
Collins, Wilkie 8, 59, 125, 129
Comprehensive Commentary on the Qurán: Comprising Sale's Translation and Preliminary Discourse, A (Sale) 168
Conan Doyle, Arthur 202; *see also Adventures of Sherlock Holmes, The* (Conan Doyle); "Adventure of Charles Augustus Milverton, The" 189–90; "Adventure of the Cardboard Box, The" 187–9; "Adventure of the Speckled Band, The" 183; atavism concerns 185–6; conservatism cause and 184; *Daily Telegraph, The* 185; Darwinian theory and 185; detective fiction as inferior and 180–1; end of secrecy and 198–201; epistemological theory and 191–7; homosexuality fears and 186–7; *Hound of the Baskervilles, The* 180, 185, 186; *Memoirs of Sherlock Holmes, The* 188; orientalized secrets and 197–8; plot-driving secrets and 181, 183, 191; satirical writing of 183–4; secrets of cultural repression and 7; sex and 189–90; *Sign of the Four, The* 183, 185; structural secrets and 190; *Study in Scarlet, A* 183–4; Victorian Holmes fictional character 180
conspiracy theories 183
Croutier, Alev Lytle 155
cultural repression, secrets of 7, 8
Cvetkovich, Ann 125, 138n25

da Groot, Joanna 143, 155–6
Dames, Nicolas 10, 44, 65, 69, 71n11, 75n54, 76–77n61
dark secrets 15, 28, 57, 112, 155, 163
Darwin, Charles 22, 88, 183, 185, 186, 199, 212
David Copperfield, selfhood conception in 59
Davidson, Jenny 28
de Certeau, Michel 166
del Hoyo, Pescador 172
de Sade, Marquis 47
Descartes, René 11, 61, 63–4, 75n57, 76n58, 131–3
destabilizing narrative theory 10
Dickens, Charles 8, 17n21, 38n22, 59, 74n40, 77n62, 106n25, 113, 145, 147, 158, 174n14, 210
Discipline and Punish (Foucault) 10–11
Disraeli, Benjamin 160
Doane, Mary Anne 154
Dolan, Tim 57
domestic secret in *Villette* 41–4
Doré, Gustave 146
Dracula (Stoker) 8, 185, 212
duplicity *see* paradox of duplicity

Eco, Umberto 196
egoism theory 8, 83–6, 87–8; *see also Vanity Fair* (Thackeray)
Ekman, Paul 67
empire, secrets of 7
entrusted secrets 29
Erving Goffman: Exploring the Interaction Order (Drew and Wootton) 28

falsifiability, principle of 47
family resemblances (Wittgenstein) 6, 105n8, 213
family secrets 7, 8, 111, 182, 198, 213; in *Adventures of Sherlock Holmes, The* 182; in *Vanity Fair* 80
Flugel, John Carl 154
Ford, H. J. 146
Forster, Edward 146
Foucault, Michel 7, 10, 46–8, 127; repressive hypothesis and 142, 189, 215
Frank, Lawrence 186

Frankfurt, Harry, *On Bullshit* 30, 38n20, 214
Freud, Sigmund 4, 9, 11, 17n26, 20, 46, 64, 129–30, 134, 151, 179, 185, 212

Galland, Antoine 144–4, 148
Gauthier, David 94, 211
Gender Trouble: Feminism and the Subversion of Identity (Butler) 31
Gibson, Andrew 10
Goffman, Erving 1, 4, 8, 11, 12, 13, 20–1, 40, 45, 51, 59, 61, 65, 67–8, 70, 82, 83, 88, 90, 95, 101, 112, 113, 115, 117–8, 122–3, 126, 129, 134, 137n21, 138n29, 139n29, 142, 157, 164, 169, 179, 181–2, 184, 190, 191, 201, 204–5; Butler and 31–2; criticism of 28; fiction and 25–6; gender and 31; misrepresentations and 30–1; performance model weaknesses 25; secrecy/deception need, social interaction and 30; secret types used by 28–9; Shakespeare comparison 27; Simmelian model of society comparison 27; sociology of performance 25–32, 91–2, 142; team performances and 28–9

Habit of Lying, The (Smyth) 154–5
Halperin, John 87
Hardy, Barbara 88
Harvey, Leonard P. 171, 172
Hegel, Georg 173n5
Henry Esmond (Thackeray) 165
Herman, David 18n33
historical novel: Bulwer-Lytton and 167–8, 169–72; critics of 165–6; determinism and 166–7; mistakes in Bulwer's 171–3; Sale and 168–9; secrecy and 165–73
Historical Novel, The (De Groot) 165–6
History of Sexuality, The (Foucault) 11, 46–7
Hitchcock, Alfred 5, 16n15, 34, 180
Hobbes, Thomas 13, 83–4, 88–94, 104
homosexuality 49, 71n20, 186–7
Houghten, A. B. 146
Hound of the Baskervilles, The (Conan Doyle) 180, 185–6
human nature theory 83–4, 89
Humble, Nicola 124
Hume, David 36n2, 123, 132, 207n29
Hunt, Alan 154

implied author 10, 34
inferred author 34

inside secrets 28–9
intentional reading 10, 34
Iser, Wolfgang 93

Jadwin, Lisa 93, 106n20
James, Henry 111
James, William 30–1
Jameson, Fredric 9
Jann, Rosemary 184, 198–9
Jekyll and Hyde (Stevenson) 8
Jenkins, Keith 166
Jitrik, Noé 165, 166, 167
Julius, Anthony 160

Kabbani, Rana 144, 145
Kant, Immanuel 2, 3, 21, 36n2, 165, 194, 207n29
Kernel, narrative 34, 40
Kissane, James 186
Kissane, John 186
Klimt, Gustave 147
Knoepflmacher, U. C. 86–7
Kucich, John 6; power of lies and 21, 32–3; Victorian culture middle-class factions and 32–3; and *Villette* 68

Lady Audley's Secret (Braddon) 7, 58, 109–35; bigamy and 111–12, 115–17; Chattman's propositions concerning 129; class conflict in 113–15; dark secrets in 112; Descartes comparisons to 131–3; divine justice and 119–21; environment of secrecy in 109–10; insanity fears and 125–33; irony in 118–19; overview of 109–10; secrets of performance in 121–5; selfhood in 114–15, 117–18, 131–3; as sensation novel 109, 111–12
Lane, Edward 72n27, 144–6, 148, 149, 151, 173n8, 174n11, 174n23, 175n25
Last Days of Pompeii, The (Bulwer-Lytton) 166
latent secrets 29, 40, 88, 169, 191, 211
La volonté de savoir (Foucault) 46–7
Leibniz, Gottfried 192–3, 195, 201–3, 206n26, 207n27, 207n28
Leila: or, The Siege of Granada (Bulwer-Lytton) 7, 14, 36, 157–73, 198; anti-Semitism in 159–60, 163; historical mistakes in 171–2; as intentionally orientalist novel 143; narrative strategy of 160–1; orientalist stereotypes in 161; orientalized secrets in 161–5; Ragussis on 158–9
Levinson, Michael 111

Lies and lying 2–3, 5, 12, 14, 22, 69, 91, 94, 111, 124, 127, 134, 157, 191, 194, 204, 214; Kucich and 32–3
Lilly, Mark 46, 52, 55
Locke, John 132, 195
Loesberg, Jonathan 114
Lombroso, Cesare 186, 194
Lougy, Robert 89, 97–8, 103–4
Lukács, Georg 165
lying: duplicity and 2; Kant and 2, 3; secrecy and 2–3; Simmel and 3

MacGuffins 5, 8, 34, 40, 180; in *Adventures of Sherlock Holmes, The* 15, 180–1, 184, 186, 187, 188, 191, 197, 202–3; in *Arabian Nights* 150; in *Vanity Fair* 13, 79; in *Villette* 40–1, 69
Machiavellian intelligence 67
madness, secrets of 7, 8, 14, 63, 81, 104n4, 125
Manzoni, Alessandro 165
Marck, Nancy Ann 184
Marcus, Sharon 49–50
Matus, Jill 53
Maynard, John 6, 34, 215
Melman, Billie 145
Memoirs of Sherlock Holmes, The (Conan Doyle) 188–9
Metress, Christopher 188
Michie, Helena 126
Millais, J. E. 146
Miller, Andrew H. 11
Miller, D. A. 9, 10, 35, 40, 59, 74n46, 125, 151–2, 214, 215, 216
Miller, William 146
Mirrors, Masks and Lies (Scheibe) 4–5, 12, 29, 35, 115, 122
Moi, Toril 11
Murphy, Robert F. 35, 156–7

Narrative and its Discontents (Miller) 10, 35, 151
narrative theory 9–12, 21
narratology of secrecy 33–5, 214–18; in *Arabian Nights* 147–8, 151–3; in *Villette* 45–6
Nemesvari, Robert 124, 125
Novel and the Police, The (Miller) 10, 59
Nussbaum, Martha 211, 215

orientalized secrets 7, 8, 213; *Arabian Nights* and 143–53; in *Leila: or, The Siege of Granada* 161–5; in *Vanity Fair* 95–102; veils and, function of 153–7; in *Villette* 50–5
Origin of Species, The (Darwin) 185

PAL (Philosophy, Art, Literature) program, Duke University 11
paradox of duplicity 2; Kant and 3; lying in human interaction and 2; *Vanity Fair* and 3–4
Parks, Robert Ezra 25
performance: in *Adventures of Sherlock Holmes* 205; in *Lady Audley's Secret* 117–8, 121–6, 129, 134; Goffman definition of 25–32, 94–5; in *Vanity Fair* 89–95, 99, 102, 217; in *Villette* 51, 53, 68–9, 157, 191, 201
phrenology, Brontë and 44, 61–4; in *Adventures of Sherlock Holmes* 194
Picture of Dorian Gray, The (Dickens) 8
Pionke, Albert 10–11, 58
plot-driving secrets 180; *see also* MacGuffins; in *Adventures of Sherlock Holmes, The* 182; in *Arabian Nights* 150–1; in "The Adventure of the Speckled Band" 183
Polhemus, Robert 60
political unconscious 9
Poovey, Mary 10
Pope, Alexander 145
Popper, Karl 47
Power of Lies: Transgression in Victorian Fiction, The (Kucich) 32
Presentation of Self in Everyday Life, The (Goffman) 25, 28, 31, 91–2, 117
principle of falsifiability 47
Prioni, Giampaolo 196
privatization of secrecy *see Villette* (Brontë)
Professor, The (Brontë) 55–6
psychological egoism 83–4
Psychopathology of Everyday Life (Freud) 20
Puckett, Kent 11
Pykett, Lyn 111, 114, 124

Ragussis, Michael 158, 173
Repressive Hypothesis 47, 142
Reynolds, Kimberly 124
Robb, Graham 187
Rossetti, Christina 58

Said, Edward 107n35, 108n36, 155
Sale, George 168–9

Sallis, Eva 144, 147–8
Sanders, Andrew 158, 167
Sansom, William 26, 38n15
Sartre, Jean-Paul 1, 16n2, 82, 118, 126, 190
Satellite, narrative 34, 40
Saxon, Jessica 130
Scheherazade *see Arabian Nights*
Scheibe, Karl 4–5, 12, 29, 35, 115, 122
Scott, Walter 72n30, 158, 165, 167, 168, 172, 174n14
Seboek, Thomas A. 196
secrecy: class-based power and 4–5; defined 1–2; end of (*see Adventures of Sherlock Holmes, The* (Conan Doyle)); historical novel and 165–73; historicizing of 142–3; and lying 2–3; motives of 2; narratology 33–5; orientalizing of Victorian (*see* orientalized secrets); privatization of (*see Villette* (Brontë)); selfishness and (*see Vanity Fair* (Thackeray)); silence and 3; sociological theories of (*see* sociological theories of secrecy); study of 1; subjectivity and 4; Victorian 4, 5, 6–7
Secret and the Secret Society, The (Simmel) 21
secrets: of class membership 7, 8; of cultural repression 7, 8; dark 28; defined 1; domestic, in *Villette* 41–4; dominating Victorian fiction 8; of empire 7; entrusted 29; of family 7, 8, 111, 182, 198, 213; inside 28–9; latent 29; of lovers 82; of madness 7, 8; orientalized 7, 8, 50–5; of self 7, 8, 58–60; of sex 7, 46–50; of soul, in *Villette* 55–7; strategic 2, 28, 30; structural 40–1; veiled 153–7; word usage 2
Sedgwick, Eve 154
self, secrets of 7, 8; in *David Copperfield* 59; in *Lady Audley's Secret* 114–15, 117–18, 131–3; in *Vanity Fair* 91–5; in *Villette* 58–60
selfishness in *Vanity Fair* 83–90
sex, secrets of 7; in *Arabian Nights* 148–9; in *Villette* 46–50
Showalter, Elaine 111, 123
Shuttleworth, Sally 10, 57, 69, 126, 131, 216; materialistic psychology of *Villette* and 60–5
Sign of Three: Dupin, Holmes, Peirce, The (Eco and Seboek) 196

silence, secrecy and 3, 22, 33, 46, 47, 49, 81, 214
Simmel, Georg 1, 3, 4, 5, 10–13, 15, 20–5, 27, 29, 32, 35, 51, 57, 58–9, 61, 65, 67–70, 79–83, 91, 92, 103, 109, 111–2, 114, 127, 134–5, 142–3, 147, 153, 156–7, 164–5, 179, 181–2, 191, 198, 199, 201, 202–3, 204–5, 211–2, 216, 218; betrayal and 23; constitutional role of secrecy and 21–5; deception and 21–2; discretion and 23–4; historicity of secrecy 142–3; secret second world of 182; social relationships/interactions, concealment in 22, 91; sociological conclusions of 22–3, 111
Smyth, John Vignaux 154
"Social Distance and the Veil" (Murphy) 156–7
sociological theories of secrecy 20–36, 210–13; Goffman and performance 25–32; Kucich and power of lies 32–3; narratology and 33–5; overview of 20–1; Simmel and constitutional role 21–5
soul, secrets of, in *Villette* 55–7
Stockton, Kathryn Bond 49
Stoker, Bram 184
Strangers and Secrets: Communication in the Nineteenth-Century Novel (York) 58
Strangers: Homosexual Love in the Nineteenth Century (Robb) 187
strategic secrets 28, 134
strategic silences (Foucault) 47, 49, 190; in *Villette* 48–9, 68, 70, 157
structural secrets 40–1, 147, 151, 180, 181, 188, 202
Study in Scarlet, A (Conan Doyle) 183–6, 193
subjectivity, secrecy and 1, 4, 11, 12, 23, 51, 59, 65, 77n61, 143, 182, 211, 215, 216
symptomatic readings 4, 9–11, 34, 184, 190

Tanner, Tony 42, 46, 55,
team performances 28–9, 38n19, 124
Tenniel, John 146
Terry, Ellen 126
Thackeray, William Makepeace 7; *see also Vanity Fair*
Thomas, Ronald R. 194
Towards a Postmodern Theory of Narrative (Gibson) 10
Trivers, Robert 22, 160

Vanity Fair (Thackeray) 3–4, 7, 8, 12–13, 36, 54, 70, 79–104, 165, 167, 173n2, 179, 210, 211, 213, 216–7; *Arabian Nights* references in 96–7; class background secrets in 80–1; egoism theory in 8, 83–6, 87–8; family secrets in 80; as howling wilderness and intolerable dwelling 79–83; human nature theory and 83–4, 89; intelligence gathering as war strategy and 90–1; orientalized secrecy in 95–102; performing self in 91–5; secrets of lovers in 82; selfishness in 83–90

veiled secrets: in British culture 153; in Gothic novels 154; *Habit of Lying, The* and 154–5; men and 156–7; orientalized secrets and 153–7; women and 155–6

Victorian: concept 6; defining 6; fiction, Marxist readings of 9–10; historical novel, secrecy and 165–73; literature, homosexuality and 49–50; period 5–6; secrecy 4, 5, 6–7; sexuality, Foucault and 46–8

Villette (Brontë) 7, 11, 12, 15, 40–78, 79, 110, 121, 131, 134, 179, 189, 201–2, 210, 216; *Arabian Nights* references in 52–3; compromised narratives in 44–5; Dames critique of 44; as domestic novel *manqué* 42–3; domestic secret in 41–4; homosexuality and 49–50; MacGuffins in 40–1; narratological secrecy in 45–6; orientalized secrets in 50–5; secrets of soul in 55–7; self secrets in 58–60; sexual secrets in 46–50; Shuttleworth and materialistic psychology of 60–5; strategic silences about sex in 48–9; structural secrets in 40–1; surveillance/observation/penetration powers noted in 65–8

Virginians, The (Thackeray) 165
Voskuil, Lynn 126

Waverley (Scott) 165, 167
Weissman, Judith 89
Wheeler, Samuel C. 6
White, Hayden 166
White, Luise 33
Wilde, Oscar 79, 186
"Winter: My Secret" (Rossetti) 58
Wisnicki, Adrian 60
Wittgenstein, Ludwig 5–6, 11, 16n17, 18n39, 19n42, 213, 215, 219n9
Woman in White, The (Collins) 8, 125, 129
Wood, Allen 3

Yeazell, Ruth Bernard 153, 156
York, R.A. 58

Zigarovich, Jolene 41–2